Hainan Tourism Customs and Cultures

海南民俗旅游文化

（汉英对照）

朱兵艳　刘士祥　郭汉英　主编

2014年海南省高等学校科学研究项目课题成果（HNKY2014-99）

西南交通大学出版社

图书在版编目（CIP）数据

海南民俗旅游文化=Hainan Tourism Customs and Cultures：汉英对照／朱兵艳等主编. —成都：西南交通大学出版社，2016.11（2020.7 重印）
ISBN 978-7-5643-5134-2

Ⅰ. ①海⋯ Ⅱ. ①朱⋯ Ⅲ. ①民俗学－旅游文化－海南－汉、英 Ⅳ. ①F592.766

中国版本图书馆 CIP 数据核字（2016）第 282606 号

Hainan Tourism Customs and Cultures
海南民俗旅游文化（汉英对照）

朱兵艳　刘士祥　郭汉英　主编

责 任 编 辑	赵玉婷
特 邀 编 辑	任　乐
封 面 设 计	何东琳设计工作室
出 版 发 行	西南交通大学出版社 （四川省成都市二环路北一段 111 号 西南交通大学创新大厦 21 楼）
发 行 部 电 话	028-87600564　028-87600533
邮 政 编 码	610031
网　　　　址	http://www.xnjdcbs.com
印　　　　刷	四川煤田地质制图印刷厂
成 品 尺 寸	185 mm×260 mm
印　　　　张	18.25
字　　　　数	636 千
版　　　　次	2016 年 11 月第 1 版
印　　　　次	2020 年 7 月第 2 次
书　　　　号	ISBN 978-7-5643-5134-2
定　　　　价	48.00 元

图书如有印装质量问题　本社负责退换
版权所有　盗版必究　举报电话：028-87600562

《海南民俗旅游文化》（汉英对照）
Hainan Tourism Customs and Cultures

编委会

主　编　　朱兵艳　　刘士祥　　郭汉英

副主编　　王　燕　　姚立佳　　蒋秀娟

参　编　　吴　丽　　吴婧聆　　林天宇

前言

当今世界,最盛行的莫过于文化旅游,这是一种高层次、高要求、高水平的寓乐于游的美育活动,包括美食、建筑风格、民间艺术、传说故事、文学艺术等各个方面。民俗是一个国家或民族的广大人民在长期的社会生产和生活中创造、使用和传承的习俗。海南地理位置优越,四面环海,独特的生态环境、丰富的旅游资源使得汉族、黎族、苗族和回族在长期的生产劳动和生活中形成了独具魅力的民俗文化。

本书可供学生、教师、中外导游、文化工作者、翻译爱好者、外国游客及民俗研究者使用,有利于向大中学生及普通民众普及海南民俗旅游文化,以便于国外游客了解、体验海南民俗旅游文化,推进海南国际旅游岛的全面建设。

在多方协助和课题组成员的共同努力下,经过两年多时间的资料收集、整理、翻译和校对,本书《海南民俗旅游文化》(汉英对照)顺利完成。在编写本书的过程中,课题组成员参观了海南省博物馆、海南民族博物馆,骑楼、蔡家大院等建筑物,潭门贝雕、根雕及各类海产品,走访了海南各大街小巷、庙宇禅寺,亲身体验了黎族、苗族的传统节日"三月三"、潭门"赶海"活动,观看了在黎族、苗族举行的"竹竿舞""招龙舞""射弩""顶棍""拉乌龟""拔河""割橡胶"等竞技型娱乐活动,以及琼海潭门"祭海仪式",深入了解了海南印尼菜、文昌鸡、加积鸭、烤乳猪,各类美味海鲜及海南各类传统杂粮和小吃,目睹了黎族黎锦、苗族苗绣的制作工艺及各类生产、生活工具的使用等。这些丰富的体验与经历为本书的编写提供了第一手材料和相关精美图片。

课题组成员根据家人、朋友讲述的民间故事、宗教信仰、生活禁忌,以及自身经历的诞生、满月、周岁、结婚、祝寿、丧葬等礼仪,提供了详实的照片和丰富的民俗材料。我们还参考了大量文献资料、国内外网站的相关内容,难以逐一鸣谢,在此谨向相关作者和版权所有者表示诚挚的谢意。

本书共 12 章,包括:概述、人生礼仪民俗、岁时节日民俗、建筑民俗、饮食民俗、服饰民俗、劳动生产民俗、信仰崇拜民俗、海洋民俗、民间艺术民俗、传统竞技民俗、礼仪禁忌民俗,对准确传达跨文化意象、保持民族文化身份、促进海南国际旅游岛的全面建设,具有积极意义。

本书由朱兵艳、刘士祥、郭汉英编著,朱兵艳、刘士祥负责全书的策划、修改与统稿,以及附录和参考文献整理。本书内容的撰写与翻译具体分工如下:朱兵艳负者撰写翻译第 1 章、第 6 章、第 11 章、第 2 章的前两节,第 9 章的前三节;刘士祥撰写翻译第 1 章、第 3 章、第 9 章的 3-7 节;郭汉英撰写翻译第 8 章、第 12 章;王燕撰写翻译第 7 章;姚立佳老师撰写翻译第 10 章;蒋秀娟撰写翻译第 5 章;吴丽老师撰写翻译第 4

章；吴婧聆撰写翻译第 2 章 3-6 节；林天宇撰写了第 9 章前 3 节的部分汉语书稿，在此对以上老师的辛勤付出表示诚挚的感谢。

　　作为项目研究成果，本书获得 2014 年海南省高等学校科学研究项目"海南民俗旅游文化汉英翻译现状与规范化研究"（编号：HNKY2014-99）立项及资助，也获得了海南软件职业技术学院支持及资助；加拿大外籍朋友 Francis Rupert Legge、新西兰外籍朋友 Farr Bassari、我院宾惠老师等同事审读书稿，提出了诸多宝贵的修改意见；苗族朋友李运坚女士提供了许多苗族服饰、竞技活动等精美图片；海南热带海洋学院黄丽华副教授提供附录 3 汉语材料；琼海市图书馆工作人员王太宁和陈美川为查阅相关资料提供了诸多便利；课题组成员家属的协助和鼓励，我们才有时间和精力投入书稿的撰写与校对中；在此，一并表示衷心感谢。

　　由于时间仓促，编者水平有限，书本中难免有疏漏之处，敬请专家、学者、同行及读者批评指正（邮箱：zhubingyan9@163.com），不甚感激。

2016 年 7 月
海南软件职业技术学院

PREFACE

Nowadays, cultural tour or travel, which is extremely popular among people to enjoy life, includes a series of activities, such as having local cuisines, visiting typical buildings, enjoying folk arts, etc. Folk customs, which serve as popular habits and conventions the common people of nation create and practice in their production and life, pass on from one generation to another. With excellent geographical environment and abundant tourism resources, the Han, the Li, the Miao, and the Hui People in Hainan province have formed unique folk customs during their long-term daily production and life.

This book is designed for students, teachers, tour guides, translators, tourists, and folk custom researchers home and abroad. It is conducive to popularizing Hainan tourism cultures to boost the development of Hainan international tourist destination.

With the joint efforts of all the parties concerned, this book has been completed after data gathering, compiling, translating and proof-reading in the past two years. During the process of compiling, the members of this project visited Hainan Museum, Hainan National Museum of Ethnology, Qi Lou (Arcade) in Haikou, the Cai's former residence in Qionghai, etc. We have experienced the March 3rd Festival of the Li and the Miao People, Beachcombing Festival in Tanmen, and enjoyed a lot of recreational activities held in the Li and the Miao minorities, such as Bamboo Rod Dance, Crossbow, Tug-of-war, Rubber Tapping, etc. We have investigated the ways of making fine food such as Indonesian food in Hainan style, Wenchang Chicken, Jiaji Duck, seafood, and the local famous grains, etc. We also viewed the technique of making the Li brocade and the Miao embroidery and production tools. Those wonderful experiences provide us the first-hand materials and exquisite pictures for this book.

The project participants provide a great many pictures and genuine materials according to their experience, and the folk stories, religions and beliefs, taboos from their family members or friends. We also have read a larger number of reference books and searched for scores of materials from the websites. I, therefore, extend millions of cordial thanks to the authors and the copyright owners of the publications and the web resources we have consulted and referred to in writing this book.

Concise and precise, and easy and smooth in both English and Chinese languages, the book gives prominence to knowledge, interest and readability, with lots of pictures inserted in all chapters and sections. Based on the theories of intercultural communication translation, aesthetics of reception, and functionalism, it is foreign tourists-centered, which turns literal introduction to cultural tour or travel in accordance to certain contexts.

This book is written, with Zhu Bingyan, Liu Shixiang and Guo Hanying being chief editors. Zhu Bingyan and Liu Shixiang are responsible for planning, modifying and arranging appendices and references. Zhu Bingyan is in charge of writing and translating Chapter 1, Chapter 6, Chapter 11, section one and two of Chapter 2, and section one to three of Chapter 9. Liu Shixiang writes and translates Chapter 1, Chapter 3 and section three to seven of Chapter 9. Chapter 8 and Chapter 12 are finished by Guo Hanying. Yao Lijia, Jiang Xiujuan, Wu Li, Wu Jingling and Lin Tianyu, respectively complete Chapter 7, Chapter 10, Chapter 5, Chapter 4, section three to six of chapter Two, and section one to three of Chapter 9 (Chinese part), for which I extend my heart-felt thanks to them all.

This book is financially co-supported by the Education Department of Hainan Province (HNKY2014-99) and Hainan College of Software Technology. In addition, I am grateful for Francis Rupert Legge from Canada, Farr Bassari from New Zealand, our colleague Bin Hui who read and provided lots of suggestions. Special thanks to Lady Li Yunjian from the Miao nationality who gave us many pictures for the Miao costumes and sports activities, associate professor Huang Lihua from Hainan Tropical Ocean University who provided the scenic spots about Hainan custom cultures in Appendix 3, and the librarian Wang Taining and Chen Meichuan in the municipal library in Qinghai City who rendered us help while the book was in preparation. A great deal of gratitude is extended to the family members of our participants for their support and courage, so we have enough time to concentrate on writing and translating.

Due to limited professional knowledge, the book may appear more or less with defects or even mistakes which we need to correct on the basis of suggestions and proposals from vast readers (email: zhubingyan9@163.com).

July, 2016
Hainan College of Software Technology

目 录

Table of Contents

01	海南概览	1
	Introduction to Customs and Cultures in Hainan	
1.1	海南名称由来	1
	Origin of Hainan	
1.2	海南地理概况	1
	Geographic Features	
1.3	海南气候	2
	Climate	
1.4	自然资源	2
	Natural Resources	
1.5	宗教信仰	3
	Religions and Beliefs	
1.6	多元文化	4
	Diversified Cultures	
1.7	岁时节庆	4
	Festivals and Holidays	
1.8	特色餐饮	5
	Food and Beverage	
1.9	海南民俗文化旅游	6
	Festivals and Customs-enhanced Tourism	
02	海南人生礼仪民俗	7
	Rites in Hainan Province	
2.1	诞生礼	8
	Birth Rite	
2.2	成人礼	13
	Coming-of-age Ceremony	
2.3	社交礼	15

	Social Etiquette	
2.4	婚姻俗（黎族）	19
	Marriage Customs (the Li Ethnic Group)	
2.5	祝寿礼	24
	Longevity Celebration	
2.6	丧葬俗	25
	Funeral	
03	海南岁时节日民俗	28
	Seasonal and Festival Customs	
3.1	岁时节日民俗概说	28
	Introduction	
3.2	传统节日民俗	36
	Traditional Festivals and Customs	
3.3	农林渔猎等生产性节日民俗	55
	Customs and Production Holidays or Festivals for Farming, Fishing, Hunting, etc.	
3.4	民间信仰与祭祀类节日民俗	58
	Customs during Holidays or Festivals for Religions and Beliefs	
3.5	纪念追忆性节日民俗	65
	Customs during Holidays or Festivals in Memory of Historical Figures	
3.6	其他节日民俗	68
	Other Holidays and Customs	
3.7	海南岁时节日民俗旅游开发思考	76
	Implications on the Tourism Development of Holidays and Customs in Hainan	
04	海南建筑民俗	79
	Architecture in Hainan Province	
4.1	传统民居	79
	Traditional Folk House	
4.2	传统书院建筑	90
	The Traditional Architecture of Academy of Classical Learning	
4.3	传统牌坊建筑	92
	Traditional Memorial Archway Architecture	
05	海南饮食民俗	95
	Hainan Dietary Folk Customs	
5.1	海南多民族融合趋势下的多元饮食民俗	97
	Diversified Dietary Folk Customs	

5.2 黎族饮食民俗 ···101
　　The Dietary Folk Customs of Li People
5.3 南洋饮食民俗 ···110
　　The Southeastern Asian Dietary Folk Customs
5.4 其他少数民族饮食民俗 ···114
　　The Dietary Folk Customs of Other Ethnic Groups

06　海南服饰民俗 ···119
　　Hainan Costumes and Ornaments

6.1 黎族服饰 ···120
　　Costumes and Ornaments of the Li People
6.2 苗族服饰 ···129
　　Costumes and Ornaments of the Miao People
6.3 回族服饰 ···132
　　Costumes and Ornaments of the Hui People
6.4 疍家服饰 ···133
　　Costumes and Ornaments of the Tankas
6.5 海南"岛服" ··135
　　Hainan Island Shirts
6.6 海南服饰民俗旅游开发思考 ···136
　　Implications on the Tourism Development of Costumes and Ornaments in Hainan

07　海南劳动生产民俗 ···139
　　The Production Customs in Hainan

7.1 农业民俗 ···139
　　Agriculture Customs
7.2 渔业民俗 ···146
　　Fishery Customs
7.3 狩猎民俗 ···151
　　Hunting Customs
7.4 采集业民俗 ··154
　　Gathering Customs
7.5 种植业民俗 ··155
　　Planting Customs
7.6 林业民俗 ···157
　　Forestry Customs
7.7 畜牧业民俗 ··160

Animal Husbandry Customs

7.8 手工业民俗 ··· 163
Handicraft Customs

08 海南信仰崇拜民俗 ·· 166
Belief and Worship

8.1 宗教 ··· 167
Religions

8.2 祖先崇拜 ·· 168
Ancestor Worship

8.3 自然崇拜 ·· 169
Nature Worship

8.4 图腾崇拜 ·· 175
Totem Worship

8.5 民间方术 ·· 178
Folk Fang Shu

09 海南海洋民俗 ·· 182
Marine Customs in Hainan

9.1 海洋人生礼仪 ··· 182
Marine Customs in Life

9.2 海洋建筑民俗 ··· 184
Marine-styled Residence

9.3 海洋饮食 ·· 186
Marine-styled Food and Beverage

9.4 海洋节庆 ·· 188
Marine Festivals and Holidays

9.5 海洋神灵崇拜 ··· 193
Marine Worship

9.6 海洋文学艺术 ··· 198
Marine Folk Literature and Arts

10 海南民间艺术民俗 ··· 203
Hainan Folk Arts and Customs

10.1 海南民间工艺美术 ··· 203
Hainan Folk Arts and Crafts

10.2 民间戏曲音乐 ··· 214
Folk Operas and Music

10.3	民间舞蹈	218
	Folk Dance	
10.4	民间乐器	224
	Folk Musical Instruments	
10.5	民间绘画	229
	Folk Painting	

11 海南竞技民俗 ... 231
Hainan Sports Customs

11.1	海南黎族传统竞技项目	232
	Traditional Sports Activities of the Li People	
11.2	苗族传统竞技项目	237
	Traditional Sports Activities of the Miao People	
11.3	回族传统竞技项目	239
	Traditional Sports Activities of the Hui People	
11.4	汉族儿童竞技游戏	241
	Sports Activities for Children of the Han Nationality	
11.5	海南传统竞技项目民俗旅游开发思考	243
	Implication on the Tourism Development of Traditional Sports Activities in Hainan	

12 海南礼仪禁忌民俗 ... 245
Taboo Folk Customs

12.1	海南人生礼仪禁忌	247
	Taboos and Rites	
12.2	海南岁时节日禁忌	249
	Taboos about Festivals	
12.3	海南衣食住行禁忌	252
	Taboos about Food, Clothing, Shelter and Traveling	
12.4	海南劳动生产禁忌	255
	Taboos about Production	
12.5	海南信仰崇拜禁忌	258
	Taboos about Worship	

参考文献 ... 260
Bibliography

附录 1 海南省级非物质文化遗产代表性名录 ... 263
Provincial Intangible Cultural Heritage in Hainan

附录 2 海南省国家级非物质文化遗产项目名录 ... 266

	National Intangible Cultural Heritage in Hainan Province	
附录 3	海南省主要民俗文化旅游景点景区	267
	Customs and Traditions Featured Resorts in Hainan Province	
附录 4	海南民俗节庆简表	269
	Festivals and Holidays in Hainan Province	
附录 5	海南特色乡村田园	272
	Idyllic Villages in Hainan Province	
附录 6	中国历史纪年简表	274
	Timetable of Chinese History	
附录 7	二十四节气	276
	The Twenty-Four Seasonal Division Points	
附录 8	天干地支	277
	Heavenly Stems and Earthly Branches	

01

海南概览

Introduction to Customs and Cultures in Hainan

1.1 海南名称由来
Origin of Hainan

据《新唐书·地理志七》记载:"贞观五年(631年)以崖州之琼山置",建"琼州琼崖郡,下(崖州)都督府",州治改设琼山,自此琼州作为海南的代称。但"海南"二字正式在历史文献中始于南朝梁大同年间(535—545年)。海南简称琼,即"白玉"之意,亦称琼岛、琼州、琼崖。究其原因,海南四面环海,岛上岩石与沙土多为白色,加之盛产优质珍珠,故得此名。千百年来,海南与"琼"字结下了不解之缘,海南当地人喜欢把女孩的名字、山川、学校、商店、刊物、戏剧、政府,甚至军队等冠以"琼"字。

According to *New Tang Book-Geography 7*, Hainan was established as a prefecture named Qiongya in 631 during the Tang Dynasty (618-907), for which Qiongzhou was called for short. But the combined Chinese characters "海南" were first used during Datong Period (535-545) of the Liang Dynasty (502-560). Hainan is also named Qiongdao, Qiongzhou, Qiongya, etc. Located in the south of China and surrounded by the South China Sea, Hainan Island is rich in white sand, white rocks, and white pearls, for which it is called Qiong (white jade) for short. And the local people are used to adding Qiong to the name of their daughters, mountains, rivers, schools, shops, journals, plays, operas, government, and even troops.

1.2 海南地理概况
Geographic Features

海南省位于中华人民共和国领土的最南端,介于东经108°37′~111°05′,北纬18°10′~20°10′之间。海南省北部以琼州海峡与广西、广东划界,西临北部湾与越南民主共和国相对,东濒南海与台湾、香港隔海相望,东南在南海中与菲律宾、文莱和马来西亚等其他东盟国家为邻。海南省是中国陆地面积最小的省份,共3.54万平方公里,但海域面积约200多万平方公里,约占全国海域面积的2/3。海南岛丘陵性低山地形居多,占全岛面积38.7%以上。丘陵主要分布在岛内陆、西北及西南等地区。海南岛地势中部高耸,四周低平,比较大的河流大都发源于中部山区,水资源丰富,独流入海的大小河川154条,其中水域面积超过100平方公里的有38条。南渡江、昌化江、万泉河为海南岛三大河流,其流域面积占全岛面积的47%。

Situated in the southernmost part of the People's Republic of China (abbreviated for PRC), Hainan province lies from 108°37′~111°05′ E. and 18°10′~20°10′ N. Hainan faces Guangxi province and Guangdong province in the north over the Qiongzhou Strait, bordering the Beibu Gulf in the west and Vietnam visible in a distance, near to Taiwan and Hong Kong in the east, and adjoining the Philippines, Brunei, Malaysia, and other ASEAN countries. Hainan province is the smallest province in terms of land area, which totals 35,400 square kilometers. However, Hainan province is the largest province in terms of sea, which roughly amounts to 2,000,000 square kilometers, covering two thirds of the whole sea area of the PRC. Hainan Island is pyramid-shaped, with Mountain Wuzhishan in the middle and broad elevation surrounding it, which results in 154 rivers flowing to the sea directly. And the number of the rivers covering 100 square kilometers adds up to 38 in Hainan province. Nandujiang River, Changhuajiang River, Wanquan River are the longest rivers in Hainan, which cover 47 percent of the whole Hainan Island.

1.3 海南气候
Climate

海南森林覆盖率达62%,热带天然林占全省森林面积的一半左右。海南地处热带北缘,属热带海洋季风气候。海南是中国唯一的热带海洋岛屿省份,占全国热带土地面积的42.5%。海南海岸线总长约1823公里,优质沙滩居多;年光照1750~2650小时,气温最高月份为7~8月份,最冷月份为1~2月份,年平均气温23.8 ℃;每年的5~10月份是多雨季,年均降水量为1639毫米,为热带作物提供了良好的生长条件。

The forest coverage rate of Hainan accounts for 62 percent, and the tropical rain forest takes up half of the whole forest in Hainan. Hainan Island, which lies in the north of the torrid zone, is featured with tropical monsoon climate. Hainan province, the only province bestowed with tropical oceanic climate, covers 42.5 percent of the tropical area in China. The coastline in Hainan stretches for about 1823 kilometers, which is blessed with an overwhelming number of high-quality beaches. The sunshine during the whole year amounts to 1750-2650 hours, and the annual average temperature is 23.8 degrees centigrade with the maximum in the July or August and minimum in January or February. The rainy season lasts six months from May to October, with an annual average precipitation of 1639 millimeters, which is good for tropical crops.

1.4 自然资源
Natural Resources

海南旅游资源丰富,极富特色。热带雨林和红树林为中国少有的森林类型,是开展科研、旅游和教学最理想的选择之地。全省已发现野生维管束植物4622种,占全国植物种类的15%。其中,

491 种为海南特有，48 种被列入国家重点保护野生植物。药用植物 2000~3000 种，有抗癌作用的植物 137 种。果树 142 种，油料植物 89 种，其他经济作物近 200 种，如橡胶、胡椒、椰子、槟榔、咖啡、腰果、茶叶等。陆栖脊椎动物 660 种。其中，23 种为海南特有，123 种被列入国家重点保护野生动物。已探明的矿产 50 多种。海南海岸线长达 1823 公里，热带海滨景观、热带森林、地热温泉、珍禽异兽、文物古迹遍布全省，是我国七大重点旅游区之一。

Hainan is rich in tourism resources, such as unique rainforest and mangroves, which serves as an ideal place to carry out scientific research, tourism and teaching. Hainan boasts 4622 kinds of fascicular plants, accounting for 15% of the plant species in China. 491 plants are endemic to Hainan, and 48 plants are under state protection. The types of medicinal plants in Hainan add up to 2000-3000, taking up approximately 30% of the medicinal plants in the whole nation, of which 137 plants can be used as anticancer medicine. Besides, there are 142 fruit trees, 89 oil plants, and nearly 200 cash crops, such as rubber, pepper, coconut, areca nuts, coffee, cashew, tea, etc. Hainan is also home to 660 vertebrates, of which 23 animal species are endemic and 123 are under state protection. The number of different kinds of verified reserves totals 50 in Hainan province. The coastline stretches for 1823 kilometers, with high-quality beaches, picturesque rainforest, hotspring, rare animals, cultural relics, etc., which makes Hainan one of the top seven destinations for tourists in China.

1.5 宗教信仰
Religions and Beliefs

海南省民族宗教局 2008 年统计资料显示，海南省经登记的宗教活动场所共 127 处，其中基督教 104 处、佛教 15 处、伊斯兰教 7 处、道教 1 处。据记载，道教、佛教在海南出现始于唐朝，伊斯兰教在唐宋时期随着回族迁入而传入海南，天主教在海南的传播始于 1630 年，基督教于 1881 年引入海南。除道教、佛教、基督教、伊斯兰教等四大宗教外，海南还有大量的民间信仰，以及少量外籍的巴哈伊教等（中国民族宗教网，2013）。海南省几乎村村有庙，他们开展形式多样的民俗文化活动，对促进民族融合和民族团结，维护宗教生态平衡，丰富民俗文化资源等意义深远。

Statistics from Ethnic and Religious Affairs Commission of Hainan province in 2008 indicated that the number of registered sites for religious activities totaled 127, of which 104 were established for Christians, 15 for Buddhists, 7 for Islam, and 1 for Taoists. It was recorded that Taoism and Buddhism were introduced to Hainan in the Tang Dynasty (618-907), Islam in the Tang and Song Dynasties (618-1279), Catholicism in 1630, and Christianity in 1881. In addition to Taoism, Buddhism, Christianity, and Islam, there are a great many folk beliefs and few foreign religions from abroad. Temples, big or small, can be seen almost in every village, and villagers carry out folk activities in various forms, which is of significance to promote national integration and unity, safeguard the ecological balance among diversified religions and beliefs, and enrich the folk cultural resources in Hainan.

1.6 多元文化
Diversified Cultures

　　海南岛居住着 30 多个民族，其中汉族、黎族、苗族、回族是世居民族，主要使用的方言达 10 种。黎族是海南岛上最早的居民，也是人口最多的少数民族。世居的黎、苗、回族，大多数聚居在中部、南部的琼中、保亭、白沙、陵水、昌江、五指山、三亚等县市；汉族人口主要聚集在东北部、北部和东部沿海地区。黎族以农耕为主，有自己的语言、文化、习俗；黎锦技艺始于唐宋时期，享誉国内外。苗族是海南第二大少数民族，能歌善舞，保留传统服饰，五色饭是苗族特色美食。回族保留伊斯兰教习俗，古尔邦节是伊斯兰教的传统节日之一。海南也是全国著名侨乡之一，华侨数量仅次于广东、福建。海外琼籍华人华侨有 320 万之多，尤以泰国、马来西亚、新加坡、印度尼西亚、越南、美国、加拿大和澳大利亚居多。如今，琼海彬村山农场印尼村侨民、万宁兴隆的归侨仍保留海外生活习俗。

　　Hainan Island is home to more than 30 ethnic groups, including the Han, the Li, the Miao, and the Hui nationalities, with 10 dialects used by local people. The Li People, the earliest inhabitants on Hainan Island, is the largest minority in Hainan. Most of the Li, the Miao, and the Hui nationalities live in the central and southern parts of Hainan, such as Qiongzhong, Baoting, Baisha, Lingshui, Changjiang, Wuzhishan, Sanya, etc., while overwheming majorities of the Han People live in the northeast. The Li People have their own language, cultures and customs; Li brocade began in the Tang and Song Dynasties (618-1279), which has been renowned home and abroad. The Miao People is the second largest minority in Hainan, with their traditional costumes and five-colored rice preserved. The Hui People in Sanya keep their Islamic customs, and Corban is one of their traditional festivals. Hainan also serves as the third largest hometown of overseas Chinese, with 3,200,000 in Thailand, Malaysia, Singapore, Indonesia, Vietnam, the United States, Canada, Australia, and other countries or regions. Nowadays, returned overseas Chinese in Yinni (Indonesia) village of Qionghai city and Xinglong county of Wanning city still retain their alien customs.

1.7 岁时节庆
Festivals and Holidays

　　岁时节庆民俗包括岁时民俗和节庆民俗两部分，岁时民俗指随着季节、时间变幻，特定区域的人群在生产生活中形成的习俗；节庆民俗是岁时民俗的特定表现形式。海南独特而丰富的民间文化衍生了诸多充满地域特色的岁时节庆民俗，如农林渔猎等生产性节日（潭门赶海文化节、山栏节）、民间信仰祭祀类节日（妈祖信俗、南海传统文化节、二月二龙抬头祭海大典）、纪念追忆性节日（军坡节、伏波将军日）、其他节庆（黎苗族"三月三"、儋州中秋赛歌会、府城换花节、海南保亭七仙温泉嬉水节）。据不完全统计，海南省全年节庆活动达到 109 个，节庆旅游收入约占海南旅游总收入的30%左右（杨春虹，2012）。

Customs are divided into two types, i.e. seasonal customs and festival customs. The former refer to the customs formed during a certain people's social life with the change of seasons, while the latter can be considered to be the typical forms of the former. Diversified cultures and traditions in Hainan sparked different seasonal and festival customs, such as Tanmen Beachcombing Festival, Shan Lan Festival, Matsu Belief and Customs, the South China Sea Traditional Cultural Festival in Tanmen, Sacrifices-offering Ceremony to the sea on the 2nd day of the 2nd lunar month, Junpo Festival, General Fubo's Day, San Yue San Festival (held on the 3rd day of the 3rd lunar month), Songs Contest in antiphonal style during the Mid-Autumn Festival, Flower Exchange Festival in Fucheng, Qixian (7th Fairy) Spring Water Splashing Festival in Baoting, etc. Incomplete statistics showed that the number of festivals and holidays in Hainan province reaches 109, whose revenue approximately accounted for 30 percent of the total tourism income in Hainan province.

1.8 特色餐饮
Food and Beverage

海南饮食独树一帜，不仅有海南四大名菜——文昌鸡、加积鸭、和乐蟹、东山羊，还有临高烤乳猪、万泉鲤、黄流老鸭等地方特色菜肴，誉满全岛。黎族的竹筒饭、苗族的五色饭、回族的酸汤鱼等少数民族的美食别具一格。清补凉、海南粉、抱罗粉、后安粉、咖啡、老爸茶等小吃或饮品进一步充实了地方特色风味。海南是著名侨乡，东南亚国家及其他国家或地区的饮食对海南饮食产生了深刻的影响。琼海印尼村、万宁兴隆归侨把东南亚烹饪技艺与本土相结合，引进或创造了一批具有东南亚风味的美食，如咖喱鸡、咖喱牛腩、椰香九层糕。

Hainan cuisine, featured with distinctive styles in the school of culinary art, includes not only the Four Famous Cuisines, namely Wenchang Chicken, Jiaji Duck, Hele Crab, and Dongshan Mutton, but also a wide variety of local specialties, such as Lin'gao Roast Pigling, Wanquan River Carp, Huangliu Old Duck, etc. Some delicacies by ethnic minorities, such as rice cooked in bamboo tubes by the Li People, five-colored rice in the Miao's style, and fish boiled with tamarinds, pickled vegetables, and tomatoes in the Hui People's Style, are well-known all over Hainan province. Scores of snacks, such as Sam Bo Luong, Hainan rice noodle, Baoluo rice noodles, Hou'an rice noodles, coffee, Hainan Lao Ba Cha, etc., enrich the varieties of local flavors. Hainan is one of the well-known hometowns of returned overseas Chinese, and the cuisine from ASEAN and other countries or regions exerts a far-reaching impact upon Hainanese cooking and drinking. Returned overseas Hainanese, such as people in Yinni (Indonesia) village of Qionghai and Xinglong county of Wanning, have combined the cooking techniques abroad and local fresh ingredients to bring in or create some delicious dishes, such as curry chicken, curry beef brisket, nine-layer steamed coconut cake, etc.

1.9 海南民俗文化旅游
Festivals and Customs-enhanced Tourism

海南民俗文化旅游资源丰富，如特色服饰（黎锦）、饮食（竹筒饭、南撒）、建筑（船型屋、骑楼）、节庆（欢乐节、三月三）、游艺（竹竿舞）、民间艺术（贝雕、椰雕）等；民俗旅游发展态势较好，以实物形态为民俗文化载体开发的旅游产品较多，如槟榔谷黎苗文化旅游区、会山苗族加脑村寨、海南民族博物馆、军坡节、传统体育竞技项目等；开发或经营民俗文化旅游的旅行社或公司 50 余家，海南的民俗文化景区、景点主要集中在海南东部地区，如海口 5 处，三亚 8 处，陵水 4 处，五指山 2 处，保亭 3 处，其他市县 12 处（黄丽华，2014）。然而，海南民俗旅游普遍存在游客参与度低、总体发展规模偏小、内容贫乏、重复开发、粗放管理、宣传力度不足、可观赏性低、民俗文化品牌意识淡薄、民俗文化专业人员缺乏、民族地区交通不畅等诸多问题（赵德钦，1998；黄宇、罗艳菊、毕华，2011；黄丽华，2013）。

Hainan boasts rich tourism resources, such as the Li brocade, rice cooked in bamboo tubes, bamboo rice, Nan Sha (Pickled cabbage in the Li People's style), boat-shaped thatched house, Qi Lou (Arcade in Hainan style), Hainan carnival, San Yue San (March 3rd Festival), bamboo rod dance, shell carving, coconut carving, etc. Folk customs and traditions-enhanced tourism keeps a good momentum of development based on the material folk cultures, such as Hainan Binglanggu Li and Miao Cultural Heritage Park, the Miao's Jianao Village in Huishan of Qionghai, Hainan National Museum of Ethnology, Junpo Festival (Madam Xian Belief and Customs), traditional sports competition, etc. Currently, more than 50 travel agencies or companies are engaged in the customs and traditions-enhanced tourism. Most of the customs and traditions-enhanced resorts are located in southern part of Hainan province, including 5 in Haikou, 8 in Sanya, 4 in Lingshui, 2 in Wuzhishan, 3 in Baoting, and 12 in other places. However, problems still exist in Hainan folk tourism, such as low participation, small scale, poor content, repeated development, extensive management, lack of publicity and folk culture brand awareness, shortage of talents in folk cultures, terrible traffic in ethnic areas, etc.

02
海南人生礼仪民俗
Rites in Hainan Province

  人生礼仪是指人在一生中几个重要阶段上所经历的不同的仪式和礼节，主要包括诞生礼、成年礼、社交礼、结婚礼、祝寿礼和丧葬礼。诞生礼是所有礼仪中第一个最重要的仪式，寓意着人们对新生命的喜爱与期待。同时，新生命也会受到亲朋好友的第一次祝福，感受大家的爱。接下来重要的还有百天仪式、周岁仪式等。伴随着婴儿长大，成人礼是某些少数民族不可少的仪式，例如黎族的"文身"、苗族的"改名"等。

  Life customs refer to different rites and ceremonies that people go through in different periods of life including birth rite, coming-of-age ceremony, marriage customs, longevity celebration and funeral. The birth rite is the first important event which shows people's love and expectation of a new life. On this ceremony, the baby will receive blessings and love from friends and relatives for the first time. After that, the hundredth day and one-year-old birthday are also very important. As the baby grows up, coming-of-age ceremony is indispensable in some ethnic groups, such as the girls putting on tattoos in the Li nationality, and the name change in the Miao ethnic group.

  在日常生活中，人必定和不同的人、不同的事物打交道，从而形成固定的社交礼仪。在海南的交际过程中，槟榔是必不可少的。它不仅是海南居民的日常嗜好品和传统的中药材，还是海南的人际交往、爱情婚姻、祭祀等习俗中的必备用品，蕴藏着传统礼节的内涵，构成了悠久独特的槟榔习俗文化。婚嫁仪式是人一生中最隆重的仪式，也是一对新人最幸福的时刻，而各民族的婚嫁仪式各有千秋，海南黎族婚嫁也是热闹非凡，有着独特的婚嫁民俗。海南岛素有"长寿岛"之称，多地还被评为"世界长寿之乡"。所以寿庆习俗在海南汉族地区比较流行。丧葬则被视为送别仪式，意味着人已经结束了自己的一生。

  The social etiquette is a series of activities in the daily communication. Areca nut is not only a daily snack and a traditional Chinese herbal medicine in Hainan, but also an essential supply in interpersonal relationships, love, marriage, worship and other customs. It bears the connotation of the traditional etiquette and it constitutes a long history of unique custom of areca nut culture. Wedding ceremony, which to some extent is the most important and happiest event in people's life, is held differently by the different ethnic groups. Especially, the wedding ceremony of the Li ethnic group in Hainan is bustling with unique custom. Hainan Island is known as the "longevity island", "world longevity towns". Therefore, longevity celebration custom is quite popular in the Han nationality. Funeral means a person has come to the end of his or her life and is held for people to say goodbye to him or her.

为我们一生中所经历的重要阶段即诞庆、成人、社交、婚嫁、祝寿、丧葬等而举行的相关仪式即为人生礼仪习俗，其有着独特的文化内涵。海南人生礼仪习俗多姿多彩，特别是黎族人生礼仪民俗更是独树一帜，本章将对海南的生育俗、婚姻俗、丧葬俗等进行剖析研究，突显海南丰富的文化内涵。

Therefore, birth rite, coming-of-age ceremony, social etiquette, marriage customs, longevity celebration and funeral are important ceremonies of a person's life with unique inner cultures. The rich and colorful life rites of Hainan people, especially of the Li ethnic group have prompted the author to make some researches in this area in this chapter for the purpose of highlighting the rich custom culture in Hainan.

2.1 诞生礼
Birth Rite

2.1.1 求子 Pray for Pregnancy

在汉族，新婚夫妇或婚后无子女的夫妻通常会采取各种传统的老办法求子。求子方法有三种：一种是求神赐子，去庙里求神拜佛，祈求早日得子；第二种方法是吃涂红的鸡蛋、花生或芋头，因为人们认为这些食物既是好兆头也有助于怀孕。第三种是偷瓜、送瓜或偷灯，夫妇会在吉利的节日如元宵节去地里偷瓜、送瓜或偷灯。在海南汉族人中，有相当一部分人封建思想较为严重，特别重男轻女，而在黎族人不论生男生女都一视同仁（焦勇勤、孙海兰，2008）。

New couples or childless couples of the Han ethnic group often take some measures to seek pregnancy. Generally speaking, there are three ways. The first way is to visit temples and praying for pregnancy. The second way is to eat food which people think would bring good luck and pregnancy, such as red-dyed eggs, peanuts and taros. The third way is stealing or sending melons or lanterns, for example couples who want to have a baby would go out to the field to steal or send out a melon or a lantern on Lantern's Day. Traditionally, people of the Han ethnic group in Hainan province favor baby boys because they believe the son will inherit family property, whereas people of the Li ethnic group treat son and daughter alike without discrimination, for they believe daughters can earn money, give birth and instruct children.

2.1.2 分娩和坐月子 Labor and Confinement (Zuo Yue Zi)

孕妇生育叫"生子"。按照传统的习俗，汉族女子一般不能在娘家分娩。临产时，一般会采用一些吉祥的活动帮助孕妇顺利生产，如把门窗、柜子打开，寓意"宫口"大开。为了不让外人惊动刚出生的婴儿，主人会把一个菠萝用红布或红纸包着悬挂于门外（焦勇勤、孙海兰，2008）。婴儿出生后，父母常用黄连（有去火的功效）抹口后再喂奶，象征着"先苦后甜"。为了宣布孩子出生的喜讯，父母通常要给亲朋好友送去红鸡蛋或水果，女孩送偶数，男孩送奇数。与此同时，新妈妈开始坐月子。在这段时间内，产妇只需待在房间内照看小孩，不必做任何家务。而且，产妇一般不轻易出门，不能洗头发或洗澡，这是为自身的健康着想。在黎族，妇女分娩后，丈夫要煮干饭给妻子吃，用一些中草药给她补身子。产期满后，丈夫杀鸡并用艾叶和黄姜煮汤给妻子喝。

According to the traditional custom of the Han ethnic group, woman can't give birth in her own parents' house. Some auspicious activities which people think would help the woman in labor should be taken, such as opening the door or the cupboard, which means opening uterus. People also hang a pineapple wrapped with a red cloth or paper outside the house to tell others not to disturb the new baby. After the baby was born, parents usually wiped the baby's mouth with coptis (with the function of reducing internal heat) first and then feed milk, which symbolizes happiness coming after suffering. In order to announce the baby's birth, parents will send red-dyed eggs and fruits to relatives and friends with even number for a girl and odd number for a boy. At the same time, the woman will enter a period of confinement or "Zuo Yuezi". During this period, she will be confined to her room to look after her new baby without doing any housework. What's more, going outside, washing hair and taking bath are prohibited within one month after the labor for the sake of her health. Husband of the Li ethnic group has to cook rice and Chinese herbs for his wife after delivering. At the end of the period of confinement, the husband must slaughter a chicken and cook it with Aiye (Folium Artemisiae Argyi) and gingers for his wife.

在黎族，小孩出生时有一种习俗为插物示事，比如家门口挂龙眼树枝表示家中生男孩，请外人勿进，这种记事传信方式在日常生活中广为应用，它为广大黎族人民所认同并遵守，并成为黎族的一种符号语言。

The Li People have the practice of inserting plant branches in the door to tell people what is happening in the house, for example, inserting a branch of longan to tell people a boy is born and not to disturb. This kind of method is widely practiced in the Li ethnic group to record events and deliver messages. It has been so widely recognized and followed by the Li ethnic group and that it has become their language for communication.

海南苗族的生诞习俗与黎族大体相同，此外，还忌在孕妇住的房间内及周围打桩，以免影响孕妇。

The Miao ethnic group has similar birth rite with the Li ethnic group except that pile driving in or around the pregnant woman's house is prohibited, which they think would result in the pregnant suffering from lumbago or the baby dying before birth.

在回族，婴儿不论男女，出生12天，家长都举行"餐会"，当日宴请本寺阿訇和有威望的乡老，给婴儿取"教名"，俗称"做十二日"（海南省志·民俗志，2012）。

For the Hui People, on the twelfth day after the baby was born, the host would invite respectable elders to name the baby, which is called "The Twelfth Day" in the Hui dialect.

2.1.3 满月 Manyue (The Thirtieth Day)

汉族婴儿满月时，主人家里一般要摆满月酒，酒席上必须有炒粉或粉汤，寓意孩子长命百岁。婴儿要剃满月头，剃发时接生婆边剃边唱口彩，然后将头发放起来或挂在婴儿身上。剃发完毕后由父母抱着婴儿与宾客见面，并给宾客分送红蛋。亲友则回赠红包或婴儿衣服、布料等礼物，祖父母送银足圈、项圈等。

When it comes to the baby's thirtieth day or full month (Manyue) in the Han ethnic group, parents of the baby usually will invite relatives and friends to come over to celebrate. On this occasion of celebration, rice noodles are one of the indispensable dishes, which symbolize health and longevity. Head-shaving ceremony is also held on this day by the midwife who will say or sing lucky words while shaving for the baby and then put the fetal hair away or hung it beside the baby. After that, the parents will hold the baby to meet guests and give out red dyed eggs. In return, they will receive red envelopes containing money inside and baby clothes from relatives and friends. It is a tradition for grandparents of the baby to give silver foot rings or necklaces to the baby as gifts.

满月祭祀祖先（吴婧聆 摄）　　　　　　满月酒（吴婧聆 摄）
Offer Sacrifices to Ancestors in Manyue　　The Feast of Manyue (courtesy of Jingling Wu)

2.1.4　起名和称呼 Naming the Child and Addressing

孩子，黎语叫"蒂力"或"织力"。黎族孩子要经历两次取名。出生满月时取名，俗称"乳名"。婴儿的父母和家里的长辈根据孩子出生的特征和出生日子，以及孩子出生期间家里或村里发生具有象征性的事件取名。

Generally speaking, children of the Li ethnic group would be named twice. The first name also called infant name when the baby is one month old. Parents and the elders of the family would discuss to name the child according to his or her birth date, appearance and characteristics for the first time.

黎族孩子的第二个名字通常在小孩满周岁时命名，以直系亲属辈序名次取名，而且要同长辈的名形成韵律。孩子命名要举行仪式，宰鸡杀猪祭先祖，宴请亲朋好友恭贺孩子命名。家长会给孩子设专门的席位，席上摆放一碗干饭、一个鸡腿、一把尖刀、一块银元或纸币等物品。在"奥雅"（令人尊敬的老人）的主持下，父母带孩子向祖先灵位跪拜，并报告新成员的命名。"奥雅"给命名的孩子戴上串着铜钱的项圈，手脚上系着蓝红青三色的"平安线"。然后，父母亲带小孩到专设的席位就坐，当众呼喊孩子的名字。

The second name is given when the child reaches one year old according to his or her position in the family hierarchy. Children of the same hierarchy in the family will have the same word in their names. A ceremony is held for naming the child and relatives and friends are invited to celebrate. Chickens and a pig are slaughtered as sacrifice to their ancestors. Parents will give their child a special seat with a bowl of cooked rice, a chicken ham, a knife, and a silver coin or money and so on in front of him or her. Under the presence of an Ao Ya (a respectable elder), parents help the child pay worship to their ancestors and tell them the new name of the child on bended knees. Then the elder puts a string of coin necklace on the child, and ties "lucky strings" with three colors of blue, red and green around his or her hands and feet. Then Parents take their child to sit down in the special seat announcing the baby's name in guests' presence.

海南苗族人通常有三次取名。首先，父母给出生后的婴儿起乳名，乳名一般在15岁以前使用，15岁后只能在祭祀祖先等仪式上使用该乳名。其次，15岁以后由外人起外号，为父母和亲戚朋友使用。第三个名是汉名，正规的称呼，通常在学校学习、外出打工和各种证件上使用。

Usually, there are three times to name the child in the Miao nationality. Firstly, the infant name which is called named before 15 for offering sacrifices to ancestors is given by his or her parents. Then, the nickname is named by others and used by parents or relatives. The last name is the regular one called in Han style. This name is often used in school, work and different certificates.

海南苗族对曾祖父、祖父、外曾祖父、外祖父一律称为"康图"，曾祖母、祖母、外曾祖母及外祖母一律称为"克"，其他的与汉族没什么区别。对父母同辈的亲属的称呼也用同一个音，如姨妈、舅妈、婶婶、伯母都称为"泰"。堂表兄妹之间的称谓按年龄大小来区分。哥哥称为"克"、姐姐"密"、弟弟"东"、妹妹"莫"（焦勇勤、孙海兰，2008）。

"Kang Tu" and "Ke" are respectively used to call grand-grandfather and grandfather and grand-grandmother and grandmother in the Miao ethnic group. As for their parents' sisters, "Te" is used for aunts. The appellations of cousin and nephew are called according to their age, such as the elder brother is called "Ke", the elder sister is called "Mi", the young brother is named "Dong" and the young sister is named "Mo".

海南汉族称谓与广东、福建等地的汉族称谓大致相同。在海南，汉族一般称祖父为阿公、亚公，称祖母为阿婆、亚婆；父亲为爸、阿爹、阿爸、亚爸、亚爹，称母亲为妈、娘、阿妈、亚妈、亚娘；称父亲的哥哥为伯爹，其妻伯姆，称父亲的姐姐为姆，称父亲的弟弟为叔爹，其妻为婶婶，称父亲的妹妹为姑等。同辈之间，哥哥一般称为阿哥、亚哥，弟弟为阿弟、小弟或老弟。在海南，女孩通常称为"小妹"，男孩被称为"小弟"。

There are no big differences in form of address between the Han People in Hainan and those in Fujian and Guangdong. In the Han nationality, grandfather, grandmother, father, mother, brother and sister are named differently.

2.1.5 周岁 One Year Old

在黎族，小孩满周岁取第二个名字时，父母会准备物品让孩子从席上拿，如果拿饭碗，意为孩子将来有吃且长寿；拿尖刀，就是未来的英雄；拿银元，是发财……这在汉族叫"抓周"，很多地方都有这样的习俗，是为了预测幼儿未来的性情、志向及前途而举行的仪式。

As it is mentioned above, the second name is given when the Li child reaches one year old, and he is told to grab items around him or her. If the baby chooses noodles, it means he or she will be rich and healthy. If the baby picks the knife, it means he or she will be a hero or heroine in the future. If the baby picks silver, it means wealth. This is called "Zhua Zhou" (foretelling the future vacation of an infant) in the Han ethnic group for the purpose of predicting the child's temperament, inclination and prospects.

在汉族，小孩满一周岁时，通常会举行较隆重的仪式。在这天，孩子要穿新衣、戴新帽、祭祀祖先。有些地方还有"抓周"的习俗，然后父母会把准备好的书、笔、墨、算盘、剪刀、水果、针线等端放在孩子面前，任由其自行挑选。传说周岁抓周能预测孩子的性格、事业及抱负。如果孩子抓的是书、笔和墨，预示将来是读书的料。如果抓的是剪刀或针线，则可能会是裁缝。抓周仪式完毕，主人会设宴款待来访的亲朋好友，长寿面是必不可少的一道菜，意味着长寿、健康。

In the Han nationality, when it comes to baby's one year old, a grand ceremony is held. On the day, the baby usually puts on new clothes, wears new hats and parents offer sacrifices to ancestors. Grabbing test is held in some places. Parents put some articles around the baby, including a book, a pen, ink, cactus, and scissors, fruits and needlework. If the baby picks up a book, a pen or ink, it's likely that he or she will be good at studying. If the scissors needle and thread are chosen, the baby will be predicted to be a tailor or costume designer. It is said that the article the baby takes forecasts the baby's future. Usually, the grabbing test is followed by a feast. The noodle is an indispensable dish, which indicates health and longevity.

汉族抓周物品（许宇宁 摄）
Zhua Zhou in the Han People (Courtesy of Yuling Xu)

在回族，婴儿满周岁，俗称"隆随"，经济宽裕的家庭，要举行丰盛的餐会宴请亲朋好友。

In the Hui ethnic group, the baby's one-year-old birthday is called "Long Sui" in the local dialect. Just like the Han and the Li, some rich families often invite relatives and friends to celebrate together.

2.1.6 生儿育女传统观念 The Traditional ideas

黎族人认为生儿育女是祖先安排的，在过去坠胎和虐杀婴儿被视为"茂赖"（即天地不容的行为）。因此，婚外生的孩子也受到保护。婚外生育通常有两种情况：第一种，已结婚的女子，因夫妻感情不和，女方长期居住在娘家私通怀孕。按俗规，女子出嫁私通怀孕，必须回夫家分娩，不允许在娘家分娩。而夫家和其他人则视为正常的事情，生下来的婴儿，是夫家的成员，孩子的命名和抚养都由夫家负责。第二种，由于黎族男女青年多自由择偶，喜欢玩"隆闺"的婚恋方式。如果未婚男女在发生关系，而在"隆闺"私生孩子，也受到舅家的保护。非婚生子女的母亲出嫁时，男家也许诺，抚养非婚生的子女，并确立正式的父子关系，列入养父的直亲血缘，享受平等权益，在社会上不受歧视（中国民俗网，2009）。

It's women's fate to bear children in the Li People's mind. Abortion is unforgivable in the past. Therefore, the extra-marital pregnancy is protected, including two cases. First, a married woman who has separated with her husband and lived with her parents becomes pregnant with another man. However, she must give birth in her husband's house instead of in her parents' according to the practices in the Li ethnic group. Meanwhile, her husband and his families should accept and bring up the baby even though she or he is not the husband's own child. Second, young people of the Li ethnic group have freedom in choosing their love and they like to play a game called "Long Gui". If unmarried men and women fall in love and give birth to a baby in the "Long Gui", the child is protected by the mother's brother. When the unmarried mother (of the baby) gets married, the groom will also promise to bring up the child and establishes a formal relationship between father and son. Thus, the babies enjoy their equal rights in the community without discrimination.

2.2 成人礼
Coming-of-age Ceremony

成年礼，亦称成丁礼或冠礼，是为庆祝家庭中小孩长大成人而举行的礼俗仪式。成年礼在人的一生当中具有重要的意义，但在汉族没有特别的仪式，一般满 18 岁，就可视为成年人。而黎族、苗族、回族则有比较固定的成人礼仪。

Coming-of-age ceremony refers to a rite is held for celebrating one of family members to be an adult, which is very important in one's life. There is no special ritual to celebrate in the Han ethnic group, being 18 is regarded as an adult. However, there are some traditional ways to tell people someone is an adult in the Li, Miao and Hui ethnic groups.

2.2.1 文身 Tattoos

黎族人民为追念黎母繁衍黎人的伟绩，告诫后人：女子绣面、文身是祖先定下的规矩，女人如不绣面、文身，死后祖先不相认。黎族女孩文身是已成年的标志。

Women of the Li ethnic group have the tradition of putting on tattoos on their bodies for the purpose of memorizing the great breeding achievements of the Mother of the Li ethnic group. It is admonished that girls who aren't willing to put on a tattoo will not be recognized by their dead ancestors. It is also a sign of entering into adulthood for girls to put on tattoos.

文身，黎语叫"打登"，亦叫"模欧"。海南汉语叫"绣面"或"书面"。西文则叫"打都"，是黎家人的一种传统习俗。这些文身伴随着她们的一生。尽管在很多人看来，皮肤上刺文身是一件痛苦的事情，但是刺方言文身在黎族传统中却是神圣而纯洁的。

Tattoo, also called Dadeng or Mo'ou in Li dialect, is spoken as Xiumian or Shumian by the Han ethnic group. Tattoo is a traditional custom for the Li People. Although it is painful to put on tattoos, it is believed to be holy and pure by Li ethnic group.

女子从 12 岁左右开始接受刺文手术。仪式需要选择秋天中的一个吉日才能举行。村中的主文婆在女孩的娘家主持仪式，在祭席祖先前报告即将文身者的名字，供奉祭品，祈求平安。然后，在女孩的房间中，主文婆用鸡毛蘸着干香草加炭灰沤制成的蓝黑色文水，在女孩的脸、颈、身体和四肢上绘出代表本支黎族图案符号的文图，用竹刺作文针，按所画文图一针一针地刺，文水渗入女孩的皮肤中，刺上的文身就会终生保留下来。黎族有不同方言，因此文样也不太一样。通常文在脸上的多为对称的三角流线图案，从两颊到下颚，一直与颈部胸部相连，胸前图案为八条直线。黎族妇女身上的文样表达了黎族人的精神世界，揭示了黎族人的信仰和黎族的文化内涵（海南省人民政府新闻办公室，2005）。

In the past, girls of the Li ethnic group were obliged to tattoo their bodies and faces around the age of 12. On the ceremony, a senior woman who would be doing the tattooing would read the girl's name, place offerings and burn incense in front of an ancestral altar to seek for ancestors' blessings. Then she would dip a chicken feather into blue and black paint made by dry sweet grass and carbon soot to draw pictures on the girl's body and face. The pictures were then pricked accordingly with a bamboo needle. The paint was pierced into flesh and would last for a whole life time. The tattoo patterns vary from different dialect groups. Usually people would put on two strings of flowing lines twisting into triangles on the face. The women of Li ethnic group use tattoos to express their spirits, beliefs and culture.

黎族少女成人礼：文身 （朱兵艳 摄于海南博物馆）
The Coming-of-age Ceremony of the Li Girl: Tattoo (Courtesy of Bingyan Zhu)

黎族女子文身图案 （朱兵艳 摄于海南博物馆）
The Patterns of Tattoos of the Li Women (Courtesy of Bingyan Zhu)

中华人民共和国成立后，黎族的文身现象逐步消失。今天，黎族少女成年不再必须绣面文身，但是有关文身的习俗仍然被保留下来。比如，对未文身而去世的妇女，黎家还要在亡者的身上用炭黑划上文身图案才能入殓。

After the founding of the PRC, tattooing in the Li group gradually disappeared, but some customs have been maintained. For example, the dead women without tattoo on their bodies could only be encoffined after their families drew some tattoo patterns on their bodies.

2.2.2 苗族、回族成年礼 Coming-of-age Custom in the Li and Miao Ethnic Groups

苗族的成年礼以改名为标志。在前面也提到过，海南苗族人通常有三次命名。女子和男子改名后，即视为成年人。女子都有自己的本民族名字，长大后可以用原来的名字，也可以改另外一个名字。男子小时父母为他命名，长大或结婚后，可以继续使用原来的名字，也可以再任意选择一个自己喜欢的名字。因此，苗族每人都有两个以上的名字。

Name changing is the symbol of being adult in the Miao ethnic group. As it is mentioned above, the Miao People are named three times. Girls and boys are regarded as the adult when their names are changed in the third time.

回族女孩3岁开始穿耳环，9岁始皈依宗教，接受宗教教育，男孩12岁起请师为之剪发齐眉，白布缠头，围以缦，开始皈依宗教并接受伊斯兰教教育，此时可视为成年人（海南省志·民俗志，2012）。

The Hui girls wear earrings at 3, and accept religion education at 9. The boys will have their hairs cut, tie the white cloth around the heads, and accept Islam education at 12. At that moment, the boys are regarded as adults.

2.3 社交礼
Social Etiquette

2.3.1 吃槟榔 Eating Areca Nuts

槟榔是我国名贵的"四大南药"之一，有"杀虫消积，行气利水"等诸多功效。不仅如此，槟榔还有治青光眼、血压增高等症的效果。据历史记载，海南进贡槟榔始于宋代，海南岛最初的槟榔种植集中五指山附近，种植规模比较大，黎族居民获利良多。到明代，海南岛的槟榔种植范围已从五指山向四周扩展，集中在琼山、澄迈、临高、定安和文昌5县。到了清代，几乎全岛都种上了槟榔。现在海南岛是我国槟榔的主要产区。在琼海、万宁、陵水、定安等市县，槟榔都是其主要的农业经济支柱产业。从1980年至今，海南槟榔迎来了发展的"第二春"。短短的30几年，在市场的带动下，海南槟榔种植面积从1.7万亩增加到136万亩，一跃成为仅次于橡胶的海南第二大热带经济作物。

Areca nut is one of the rare "Four Southern Medicines" in China. It has many functions, such as killing parasite, relieving malnutrition, promoting breath flow and diuresis. Not only that, there is also treatment of glaucoma and high blood pressure. According to historical records, areca nuts as articles of tribute began in the Song Dynasty(960-1279 AD) in Hainan. The cultivation of areca in Hainan was concentrated near Wuzhishan at large-scale and the Li People benefited greatly. To the Ming Dynasty(1368-1644 AD), the range of Hainan areca's planting expanded from Wuzhishan to the surrounding areas, mainly in Qiongshan, Chengmai, Lingao, Ding'an and Wenchang. To the Qing Dynasty(1644-1911 AD), areca had been planted throughout the island. Hainan is now the main area of areca planting in China. Areca is the main economic pillar of their agricultural industries in Qionghai, Wanning, Lingshui, Ding'an and other cities and counties. Since 1980, Hainan areca has experienced the second development. Driven by the market, the area of areca planting has increased from 1.7 acres to 136 acres in Hainan just in 30 years, and areca has become the second largest Hainan tropical cash crops after the rubber.

槟榔是海南人日常生活中的一道必不可少的"零嘴"，嚼食槟榔不分男女老少，在琼海、万宁和陵水地区一般以男性居多，在三亚和乐东地区则一般以女性居多。近年来年轻人偏好食用熏烤槟榔。海南人吃槟榔很讲究，一般挑选青色的比较嫩的槟榔果子（所以在万宁、琼海一带也常称呼嚼食的槟榔果子为青果），先把一个槟榔切成三块或四块，在蒌叶上刷上槟榔灰（槟榔灰为用蚌壳、红螺壳、砗磲等贝壳经过高温烧制后加入水调制而成的膏状物），并把一片片的蒌叶折成三角状，一般为一块槟榔配一个蒌叶放进口里慢嚼，初时味涩，并有绿水，待吐完了绿水，又生丹津，吃后面红耳赤目眩，如醉酒一样。所以在海南甚至还有"以槟榔为命"的说法。若果子熟透成黄色后其果芯就坚硬而不宜嚼食，可将老的果子培育为槟榔苗。正如当年苏东坡即兴写的"两颊红潮增妩媚，谁知侬是醉槟榔"（文京、文明英，2012）。

Areca nut is an essential "snack" in Hainan. People chew areca nut at all ages. In Qionghai, Wanning and Lingshui generally males who chew areca nut are in the majority, while in Sanya and Ledong females are in the majority. In recent years, young people have a preference for eating smoked areca nut. Hainanese who eat areca nut are particular about the areca fruits. They generally choose the cyan and tender areca fruits, which are called cyan fruits in Wanning, Qionghai. First, cut an areca nut into three or four pieces, and brush areca nut ash on each piece.(Areca nut ash is a kind of paste which is made by adding water into the shells mixture after the high-temperature firing of mussel shells, red shells and giant clam shells, etc.) And then told a piece of betel to a triangular-shaped betel horn. People usually put one piece of areca nut with a betel horn into their mouths, chewing slowly. At first it tastes astringent with green water, until you spit out the green water, red water produces. After eating you will get flushed and feel dizzy, like drunkenness. Therefore there is a saying "areca nut is life" in Hainan. If areca nuts ripen into yellow, the fruit cores get hard and should not be chewed. The old areca nuts can be cultivated to areca seedlings. Just as Su Dongpo impromptu wrote that "You have charming flushed cheeks while nobody knows you are drunk because of areanut."

槟榔不仅是海南居民的日常嗜好品和传统的中药材，而且还是海南人际交往、爱情婚姻、祭祀等习俗中的必备用品，蕴藏着传统礼节的内涵，构成了悠久独特的槟榔习俗文化。

Areca nut is not only a daily snack and traditional Chinese herbal medicine in Hainan, but also an essential supply in interpersonal relationships, love, marriage, worship and other customs. It bears the connotation of the traditional etiquette and it constitutes a long history of unique custom of areca nut culture.

如"客至不设茶，唯以槟榔为礼"，（邢植朝、王静，2004）说出了海南人在交往中有用槟榔待客的风俗。逢年过节、婚嫁宴请、邻里串门之时，海南许多地方如乐东、陵水等地的居民便会给客人递上槟榔，作为热情待客的佳果。在黎族少数民族中，有着"一口槟榔大过天"的说法。即如果双方有矛盾交恶，想要和好的一方给对方呈上一口槟榔，对方若双手接下，就表明同意接受和解，双方冰释前嫌。凡探亲访友、劳作闲谈间，海南人都会习惯性地从衣袋里掏出槟榔，互相吃请，犹如请人吸烟一样，槟榔成了促使人际关系和谐的桥梁。也有将槟榔用于祖先和神灵祭祀的习俗。（单憬岗，2014）

For example, "If there is no tea to serve the guest, only areca nut can stand for the etiquette." It just tells us the custom that the people in Hainan entertain guests with areca nut. Every Chinese New Year, wedding banquets, dropping around among the neighborhood, residents in many parts of Hainan such as Ledong, Lingshui and other places will hand areca nuts to the guests as good fruits of hospitality. In the Li nationality, there is a saying that "an areca nut is greater than any other things". That is, if two people are contradictory against each other, the one who wants to make it up should give the other one an areca nut. As long as the other one agrees to take over the areca nut with two hands, it means they have accepted the settlement and bury the hatchet. Areca nut has become a bridge which promotes harmonious interpersonal relationships. When people visit relatives or friends, and chat between working break, they are accustomed to pulling out an areca nut from their pockets to treat each other to chew, as if people treat a smoke. There are also other customs that areca nuts are used in rituals for ancestors and gods.

陵水、三亚、乐东等地还有春节敬槟榔的年俗，在过年的前几天，家家户户都会准备好足量的槟榔和蒌叶，把一个槟榔切成四瓣，再把蒌叶涂上特制的蚝灰后叠成小三角状，称为"蒌角"。串门拜年时手持一瓣槟榔和一个"蒌角"敬给长者，说些吉利话语，这是三亚、乐东等地的民间传统习俗。

Areca nut is also a tribute during spring festival in Lingshui, Sanya, Ledong, etc. A few days before spring festival, every household will prepare a sufficient amount of areca nuts and betel. When pay New Year calls to the elders, the young should offer respectfully a section of areca nut and a betel horn to the elders with two hands, saying some auspicious words. This is a traditional folk custom in Sanya and Ledong.

此外，海南人恋爱婚姻中槟榔是重要的信物和礼品。男女的恋爱、定婚、纳聘、结婚等全程都离不开槟榔。如果一对黎家情人恩爱，需缔结秦晋之好时，他们便把婚事告诉自己的父母。然后男方家的父母兄弟就要选定吉日，带上聘礼，精心采摘槟榔，到女方家去提亲。女方收到槟榔后要挨家挨户地分发给村民。意为将嫁女的喜讯告知大家，黎族称之为"放槟榔"。"放槟榔"，是希望大家给予美好的祝愿，因为槟榔象征婚姻常绿常新，预示男女双方相亲相爱，和睦美满，同时也含有祝福新人多子多孙之意。

In addition, areca nut is the important keepsake and gift in Hainan people's love and marriage. Areca nuts are inseparable in the whole course of love, engagement, betrothal presents and marriage, etc. If one pair of the Li People's lovers devoted to each other and want to get married, they will tell their parents about the marriage. Then the man's parents and siblings will select an auspicious date, bring dowry, which must have carefully picked areca nuts, to propose marriage to the woman. After receiving the areca nuts, the woman's family will distribute them to villagers door to door. That means to tell everyone the good news of their daughter's marriage, which is called "sending areca nut" in the Li nationality. Sending areca nut is expected to be given best wishes by everyone, because areca nut is a symbol of evergreen marriage, indicating that both man and woman love each other and live a happy life.

至今，在三亚、乐东一带的汉族区域，在迎娶结婚期间也同样有类似的习俗，男方家挑着装有聘礼的担子前去提亲时必须带有槟榔，俗称"挑槟榔"。并分发槟榔给前来道贺的亲友嚼食，以表谢意和敬意。该传统习俗在乐东县黄流镇保存得尤为完整。

So far, the Han nationality areas in Sanya, Ledong there are still similar customs during marriage. The man's family must have areca nut in their dowry when they go to propose marriage, commonly known as "carrying areca nut". And they will distribute areca nuts to the coming relatives to chew, in order to express their appreciation and respect. This traditional custom is preserved completely in Huangliu Town, Ledong County in particular.

槟榔虽好，但不宜多吃。据世界卫生组织癌症研究中心指出，加入烟草的槟榔会导致口腔癌、咽癌和食道癌，而不加入烟草的槟榔也会导致口腔癌。各种槟榔制品中含有的槟榔子会导致一种口腔癌前病变（口腔黏膜下纤维化），随时可能会转化成癌症。所以嚼食槟榔要适可而止，不可超量。

Although areca nut tastes good, it should not be over-consumed. The World Health Organization Cancer Research Center pointed out that the areca nuts added tobacco may cause oral cancer, throat cancer and esophageal cancer, while areca nut without tobacco may cause mouth cancer, too. All kinds of areca nut products may lead to mouth precancerous lesion (Oral Submucous Fibrosis), which may turn into cancer at any time. So areca nut chewing should be moderate and cannot be excessive.

结满果子的槟榔树（吴婧聆 摄）
Areca nut tree grown with fruits
(Courtesy of Jingling Wu)

黎族小伙子正在摘槟榔
Young fellow of the Li nationality is picking areca nuts(Source:http://www.baotingtour.gov.cn)

2.3.2 探望病人 Visiting Patients

海南岛东部的琼海市嘉积镇有这样一种传统习俗，去病房或病人家探望病人时所携带的水果中必须要有香蕉，与病人交谈途中探望者会剥开一个香蕉吃掉，意味着祝福病人的病如同剥掉的香蕉皮一样，早日好转，早日康复，并且还需给病人一个表示吉利的红包。有时也会用花生代替香蕉，剥掉花生壳如同祛除掉了病魔。

There is such a traditional custom that one should bring bananas when he visits a patient in Jiaji town, Qionghai city on the eastern Hainan Island. The visitor will peel a banana and eat it while talking with the patient, which means a blessing and hopes that the patient's disease will go away as soon as possible just like the peeled banana peel. In addition, the visitor also needs to give the patient a lucky red envelope expressing good wishes. Sometimes peanuts will use instead of bananas. Peanut's shell is stripped off as if the disease is gotten rid of.

2.4 婚姻俗（黎族）
Marriage Customs (the Li Ethnic Group)

黎族婚姻与家庭的建立，是黎族社会发展的产物，它具有母系氏族社会和父系氏族社会的综合特征，又有封建社会的色彩，构成了黎族民间独特的婚俗。

The establishment of marriage and family is the outcome of social development of the Li nationality, and it possesses the comprehensive features of matriarchal clan society and patriarchal clan society. Also, it has the color of feudal society, forming the unique marriage custom in folk of the Li nationality.

2.4.1　婚姻形式 Marriage Form

海南省黎族人在漫长的历史发展过程中，大部分传承着人类婚姻史上一夫一妻制的婚姻制度。但是古老的婚姻习俗也存在于黎族某些比较原始的"合亩"地区。

In the long historical development process, most of the people of the Li nationality in Hainan province inherit the marriage system of monogamy. However, ancient marriage custom also exists in some relatively original He Mu (meaning "co-acres") areas of the Li nationality.

一夫一妻制婚姻 Marriage of monogamy

其主要的特点是以男子为中心，妻子跟随丈夫居住，子女随父亲姓氏。

The main feature of it is centering on male. Wives follow their husbands to live and children follow the family names of their fathers.

一夫多妻制婚姻 Marriage of polygamy

其主要的特点是一个丈夫有多个妻子。这种婚姻形式大多存在于某些"合亩制"地区。

The main feature of it is that one husband has more than one wife. This kind of marriage form mainly exists in some He Mu (meaning "co-acres") areas.

2.4.2　恋爱习俗 Love Custom

黎族民间男子和女子，长到十五六岁时就不在父母家居住，男子自己上山备料盖"隆闺"（"隆闺"是黎语 boudoir 的音译，比正屋小，指没有设锅、灶的小茅屋，约8～10平方米），女子由父母帮助盖"隆闺"。"隆闺"大多建在父母住屋附近或村边较偏僻的地方。"隆闺"有男女之分，是男女青年谈情说爱、吹奏乐器和对歌定情的场所。

Boys and girls in folk of the Li nationality will leave their parents when they are 15 or 16 years old. Boys will go to mountains to prepare and build the "Long gui" ("Long gui" is the transliteration of Li language boudoir, smaller than the general houses. It refers to the small hut without pot and stove, and it is almost 8-10 square meters). Girls will build the "Long gui" with the help of their parents. The "Long gui" generally is built around the houses of their parents or some remote places. "Long gui" is different of males and females, and is the place where young men and women talk about love, play musical instruments and pledge love with songs.

隆闺
Long Gui (Source:http://news.hainan.net)

站在隆闺门口的黎族女子
A female of the Li nationality is standing in front of the Long Gui (Source:http://news.hainan.net)

黎族民间男女青年普遍自由婚恋，通过外出劳动、探亲、集市、节日、婚礼和夜游等社交活动，以对歌的方式选择心上人。下为男女情投意合歌谣（意译）：

Young men and women in folk of the Li nationality generally love and marry freely. Through social activities of labor out, visiting relatives, market, festivals, wedding, playing at night and so on, they choose the ones they love with the way of singing. In the following, there are songs of falling in love with each other of young men and women (liberal translation):

男唱：哪家的姑娘呀，远眺胜似星斗；穿白衣配花裙，载着圆圈银项；身材似槟榔树，脖子如鲤鱼身；我的心在跳动，怎样才见她脸？（中国青年网，2009）。

Men sing: Ah, where does the girl come from? She looks like a star in the white shirt with flowered skirt, wearing a silver necklace. Her figure is slim like an areca tree, while her neck is flexible. My heart is beating; how can I see her face?

女唱：妹种丛花叶青鲜，种在隆闺生单枝；哥欲种花妹给种，妹愿浇水哥围篱（中国青年网，2009）。

Women sing: The flowers that I plant in Long Gui are blooming and grow out new buds. If you want to grow flowers, I will give you seeds. I'm willing to water the flowers while you are paling.

"夜游"是黎族传统的婚恋习俗。男女青年相互倾情后，以"隆闺"为相会地点。男子一般以玩"隆闺"方式找情人。于傍晚时步行到女方村子的隆闺，经女方同意后，男子会进去隆闺里与女子相互对歌、吹奏鼻箫、洞箫、定婚约。男女青年玩"隆闺"有如下过程：（1）男子在女隆闺门外唱"请开门歌"，女子若同意则唱"请进歌"；不同意则唱"拒绝歌"，男子只能离去，另寻他人。（2）男子若被请进女隆闺后，不能马上坐下，要站着唱"见面歌"，并在女子唱"请坐歌"后，方能按指定地点坐下。（3）接着男子应主动唱"来意歌"表明找情侣或求婚的来意。女子则用歌声表示自己是否已经有情人。(4) 男子唱"试情歌",然后双方借助对歌、口弓或鼻箫来表达感情。(5) 在找到投情的女子后,男子就唱"结情歌",然后双方借助对歌、口弓或鼻箫来表达感情。(6) 男女若情投意合,男子就向女子赠送礼物,女子如接受了礼物,以后双方便经常来往。(7) 男女双方把婚事告诉父母,男方要托媒人在良辰吉日到女方家"放槟榔",以示订婚。这些过程往往历时几个月,久的甚至几年。婚恋期间,双方会互赠爱情礼物。五指山地区的黎族男子,常会编织精致的小腰篓和草笠,送给女友。女子则以织绣图案鲜艳的花带,送给男友。沿海地区的黎族,男子则会赠送耳环和银圈给女友,女子给男友赠送小挂包,以表钟情。男女婚恋期间,不允许三角恋爱,否则就会发生械斗。

"Night-visiting" is one of the traditional marriage customs of the Li nationality. Long Gui will be the meeting site after young men and women fall in love with each other. Men usually look for a lover in the way of visiting "Long Gui". At nightfall, men walk to the Long Gui near woman's village. After consented by the woman, the man will go into the Long Gui singing antiphonal songs, playing nose flute and bamboo flute with the woman. Then they will decide whether to engage to each other or not. There are some procedures when young men and women play "Long Gui" as follows: (1) Man sings the "door-open" songs outside the door of Woman's Long Gui. If the woman agrees, she will sing the "entering" songs. If she doesn't agree, she will sing "refusing" songs. Then the man will leave and look for others. (2) If the man is invited into the woman's Long Gui, he cannot sit down immediately. He should stand and sing the "meeting" song. After the woman sings the "sitting down" song, the man can take the seat at the specified location. (3) Then the man should sing "intention" song to indicate his intention of finding a lover or proposing to the woman. The woman will sing to indicate whether she has a lover or not. (4) The man sings "feeler" songs first, and then they sing antiphonal songs, play mouth-bow or play nose flute to express feelings. (5) After finding a congenial woman, the man sings "love" songs, then they sing antiphonal songs, play mouth-bow or play nose flute to express feelings. (6) When men and women fall in love with each other, the man will give gifts to the woman. If the woman accepts the gift, it means, they will contact with each other frequently. (7) When the man and woman tell their parents they want to get married, the man should entrust matchmaker to go to the woman's home "sending areca nut" on auspicious day. That is an engagement. These processes often last several months, or even years long. During love and marriage, both of them will give each other the gift of love. Men of the Li nationality in Wuzhishan areas often weave small exquisite waist baskets and straw hat and give them to his girlfriend. Woman will present the belt with exquisite embroidery to her boyfriend. In coastal areas, man will give earrings and silver circle to his girlfriend, while woman will present small bag to her boyfriend to express her deep love.

现今,玩隆闺习俗虽不同程度地存在着。但随着社会的发展和传统观念的改变,受升学、打工等因素影响,许多年轻人更愿选择到城市里生活和居住,愿意待在农村务农的年轻人越来越少,玩隆闺的习俗日渐消失。

Today, the custom of visiting "Long Gui" exists in some degrees. With the development of society and the change of traditional concept, many young people are more willing to choose to live in cities. Fewer and fewer young people are willing to farm in the rural areas under the impact of education, work and other factors. The custom of visiting "Long Gui" is disappearing increasingly.

2.4.3 黎家婚俗 Marriage Customs of the Li nationality

一直以来，海南汉族和黎族相互往来，共同劳动与生活，因此，黎、汉两个民族的传统文化互相影响，黎族婚俗仪式跟汉族一样，一般要经过三个阶段：提亲、定亲、迎亲。

The Han nationality and the Li nationality of Hainan interact with each other, collectively work and live all the time. Hence, the traditional culture of the Li nationality and Han nationality influence each other. The marriage custom ceremony of the Li nationality is the same as the Han's, and generally it will have three stages: proposing marriage, engagement, wedding.

第一阶段：提亲

The first stage: proposing marriage

当黎族的年青男女通过传统的"放寮"形式找寻到意中人之后，男方便会按照习俗，委托媒人（或亲戚）带着烟丝和槟榔（配有篓叶和槟榔灰），去女方家提亲。女方若是同意亲事，则会提出定亲要求的彩礼。彩礼一般含抚养费、衣物、猪、米、糖、烟丝、槟榔等。彩礼中一般有生猪两头：一头给母舅表示孝顺，另一头则是交女方家招待亲戚和朋友。槟榔是黎族人亲事的象征。黎族婚俗里有谚语："一口槟榔大如天，味（要）想变心去问它。"不管提亲成或不成，求婚的媒人都会受到女方家的盛情款待，不醉不归。一旦双方谈好条件，就选择吉日定亲。（黄闻健，2013）

After young men and women of the Li nationality find their lovers through traditional Fang Liao (meaning "dating") form, men party will entrust matchmakers (or their relatives) to propose marriage with tobacco and areca nuts (with betel and areca nut ash) to the houses of the women party. If the women party agree to the marriage, they will put forward the required bride price of proposing marriage. The bride price generally includes the alimony, clothes, pigs, rice, sugar, tobacco, areca nut and so on. In bride price, there are generally two live pigs, one of which is given to uncles to show filial piety, and another is given to the family of women party to treat relatives and friends. Areca nut is the token of marriage of people in Li nationality. There is an old saying in the marriage custom of the Li nationality: "the areca nut is big as the sky, and go to ask it if you want to change your heart". No matter the marriage proposing is successful or not, the matchmakers of proposing marriage will be well treated by the women party, and they can come back until they are drunk. Once the two parties appoint the conditions, they will choose a lucky day to have engagement.

第二阶段：定亲

The second stage: engagement

男方派两个有威望且会处事的男长辈和四个会办事的妇人，再请十几位年轻人扛着预定彩礼，一同前往女方家。女方家收下男方带来的彩礼，设宴招待前来定亲的男方家人，长辈们六人坐一桌，年轻人另坐一桌，长辈们席间商定好婚期。此时，家里一片喜气洋洋，乡里乡亲争吃槟榔，个个吃得嘴红心热，并向熟人朋友传告定亲喜事。

The men party assigns two prestigious and politic male elders and four women who are good at handling affairs, and employ over ten young men to carry the ordered bride price, to collectively go to the house of women party. The women party accepts the bride price brought by the men party, and give banquet to treat the people of men party who come to have engagement. Six elders sit at one table, and young people sit at another table. Elders will discuss and decide the marriage data during the banquet. At this time, it is bursting with happiness in the family, and village people striving to eat betel nut. Everyone is happy and convey the engagement to friends.

第三阶段：迎亲

The third stage: wedding

女方家在嫁女儿的前一天先设宴款待亲朋好友。第二天上午，男方派来的迎亲八音队伍和两男两女歌手来到女方家，他们带着两竹篮烟丝和槟榔。女方家立即设宴招待迎亲队伍，同时也请来四名男女歌手陪坐。席间，双方歌手边喝酒边对歌，你问我答，气氛热烈，一直持续到傍晚时分。此刻，女方的母舅出面急催迎亲队上路，赶在雄鸡报晓前返回到男方家，图个吉利。而男方的迎亲人员则散发槟榔和烟丝表示辞别。

On the day before marrying daughters of women party, they will give banquet to well treat their relatives and friends. In the morning of the next day, the eight sounds team of fetching the bride assigned by the men party and singers of two men and two women will come to the houses of women party, and they will carry two baskets of tobacco and areca nut. The family of women party will immediately give banquet to treat the team of fetching the bride, and at the same time, they will also employ four male and female singers to sit accompanying with them. During the banquet, singers of the two parties will drink and sing, ask and answer. The atmosphere is hot till the dusk. At this time, the uncle of the women party will urge the team of fetching the bride to go, and return to the houses of men party before the crow of the rooster, for good luck. And the members of team of fetching the bride will give out areca nut and tobacco to bid farewell.

迎亲队伍一路行一路歌，一直唱到男方家村口。此刻，女方家的男代表须向村寨土地庙烧香斟茶，敬献槟榔，再由男方接亲代表引路先进入村子，并请新郎官出村口迎接新娘，新郎立即在伴郎陪同下出村迎亲，同时把烟丝和槟榔散给女方送亲人员。

接着喜宴开始，喜宴一般吃到很晚，赴宴的歌手们对唱民歌，直到第二天天亮。鸡啼三遍之后，新人要在堂上拜祖先了。在祖宗神位前，新郎左膝下跪，右手托槟榔盘，新娘站在侧位，左手扶住盘子。八音队奏欢快热烈的婚礼乐曲，双方向神位跪拜三次。来宾中的长者和内亲拿走托盘中的一两片槟榔，同时放下数额不限的彩钱。这就是拜堂仪式，至此，整个婚礼仪式结束。

The team of fetching the bride is singing on the whole road, till the village entrance of the men party. At the time, the male representatives of the women party must incense and pour tea to the land temple of local village, and then the men party representatives of picking up the bride guide the way to the village, and the bridegroom will come to the village entrance to pick up the bride. The bridegroom will immediately fetch the bride with the accompanying of the groomsman, while giving out the tobacco and areca nuts to the members of seeing the bride off.

After greeting the wedding procession, there will be a wedding banquet which will last late into the night. People sing folk songs in the antiphonal style until the next day comes. At dawn, when the roosters crow, the couple pay respect to deceased ancestors. During the ritual the groom kneels on his left knee with a dish of areca nuts in his right hand, while the bride stands besides him and holds the dish with her left hand. The band will be present and start to play happy wedding music, and the couple will kneel down at the shrine three times. Afterwards elderly guests and close relatives will pick up the areca in the dish and give the new couple some lucky money. Once this ritual is complete the wedding ceremony comes to an end.

Then the wedding banquet begins, and generally the wedding banquet will be last very long. Singers of attending the banquet will sing folk songs till the dawn of the next day. After the rooster crows for three times, the bride and bridegroom will worship the ancestors. In front of the the memorial tablet of ancestors, the bridegroom will kneel with his left knee, and lift the plate of areca nut with his right hand. The bride will stand on the side place and life the plate with her left hand. The team of eight sounds plays very bright wedding music, and the two parties kneel to the memorial tablet for three times. Elders of the guests and inner relatives will take away one or two pieces of areca nut of the plate, and put the money of unlimited amount. This is the bride ceremony. At this point, the whole wedding ceremony ends up.

婚礼酒俗
Alcohol Custom

宴席与别的地方有极大的不同，是先吃饭后喝酒。除了一对新人和他们的母亲外，别人都是大碗喝酒的。酒席中央放着一个固定座罐，内盛醇香的糯米甜酒，并插有十支吸酒用的小竹管。罐旁放着两对用兽皮制成的藤凳，一对称"正座"，是新郎新娘的位置；一对称"陪座"，是两位亲家母位置。除坐在土罐两旁的人用小竹管吸酒外，其他人都坐着用碗盛酒来饮。喝酒的同时，两位母亲要讲一些勉励新人白头偕老、相亲相爱的吉利话。

The banquet is greatly different from other places in eating before drinking. Except the bride and bridegroom and their parents, others drink alcohol with big bowls. There is a fixed tank in the center of the banquet, and it is filled with mellow glutinous rice wine with ten bamboo tubes to absorb. There are two pairs of vine stools made from hide, and one of them is called "right seat", which is the place of the bridegroom and bride; another of them is called "accompanying seat", which is the place of two mothers-in-law. Expect the people who sit by the tank to absorb alcohol with small bamboo tubes, others drink alcohol with big bowls. At the same time of drinking alcohol, the two mothers will say some words of good omen to wish the bridegroom and the bride live together all the time and love each other.

2.5 祝寿礼
Longevity Celebration

海南岛素有"长寿岛"之称，多地还被评为"世界长寿之乡"。所以寿庆习俗在海南汉族地区比较流行。老人从60岁开始，每十年为大寿。有读书人作文拟对，写寿联。做寿十分讲究，中堂张灯结彩，寿屏高挂，正中桌上摆置寿面、寿糕等。神龛点燃红烛香火，寿星穿着红色或喜庆的服装，端坐中堂，儿孙侄女们等按辈分先后跪拜，并说"福如东海、寿比南山"等祝福语。仪式完毕后，亲戚朋友入宅贺寿，赠送寿礼；同时主人张罗宴客。寿宴席上一定要有海南粉或者粉丝这道菜，寓意长命百岁；加红色包装的糯米糕点和寿桃也是桌上必备的。鸭蛋也是祝寿的一大良品，壳要染成红色，代表吉利。

Hainan Island is known as the "longevity island". Many places of it are also named the "world longevity towns". Therefore, longevity celebration custom is quite popular in the Han nationality areas. Old men greatly celebrate their birthday every ten years from age of 60. People will invite a scholar to write congratulatory couplet or essay for the occasion. The celebration is very ceremonious. The longevity man or woman sits in the middle of the main hall in red clothes, waiting for their sons, daughters and grandchildren who will bow to them according to the seniority in the family and say the blessing words such as "May your fortune be as boundless as the East Sea!" After the ceremony finishes, the relatives and friends enter into the house and present the gifts to the birthday man or woman. At the same time the host prepares for the banquet. It must have the dish like Hainan rice noodle on the banquet, meaning longevity. The red peach and glutinous rice cakes with red envelope are also indispensable. Red dyed duck eggs are common birthday presents expressing good luck.

寿匾（吴婧聆 摄）
Plaque for longevity celebration (Courtesy of Jingling Wu)

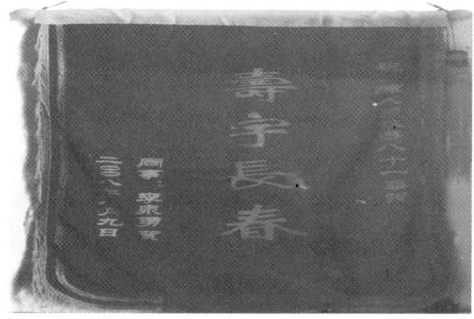

寿旗（吴婧聆 摄）
Banner for longevity celebration (Courtesy of Jingling Wu)

2.6 丧葬俗
Funeral

海南的不同汉族地区的丧葬习俗各有不同，一般说来，琼西、琼南比琼东、琼北更加重视白事，所以琼西和琼南有着"万事不如白事大"的说法。

The funeral customs vary in different Han nationality regions of Hainan. In general, the western and the southern parts of Hainan pay more attention to the funeral affairs than the eastern and northern parts of Hainan. So there is a saying that "funeral affairs are the most important things" in the western and the southern areas.

临终
Deathbed

当亲人或长辈病危的时候，家人便开始着手准备后事。首先将房屋里外打扫干净，然后将房屋内的乐器等娱乐设施撤去，营造出整洁、肃穆的氛围。当亲人或长辈在临终之时，家人要将他的遗体从卧室移到正屋的厅堂，然后给他换上一身新衣。等待的时候，在场的家属要保持绝对的安静，不能大声喧哗甚至发出哭声，以免惊扰到死者，使其安详地寿终正寝。

People begin to prepare for the funeral when their family members or the elders are dying. They first clean up both inside and outside of the house, and remove recreational facilities such as musical instruments in order to create a tidy and solemn atmosphere. They move the body from the bedroom to the hall in the main room immediately after death and then put on new clothes for the dead. While waiting aside, the family members should keep absolute silence so as not to disturb the deceased and to let them pass away peacefully.

报丧
Announcing of Death

一般说来，报丧有口头报丧，也有讣文报丧。在海南民间多以口头报丧和燃放鞭炮向邻里报丧为主。按照传统的规矩，燃放三枚鞭炮就表示报丧，这被称之为"报丧炮"，然后叫人通报亲戚朋友。

Generally speaking, announcing of death can be carried out orally or through obituary. Orally announcing and setting off firecrackers announcing are mainly adopted among Hainan civilians. Traditionally people set off firecrackers for three times to announce the death, which is known as the "announcing firecrackers". Then they send somebody to inform friends and relatives.

奔丧
Hastening for Funeral

在海南民间报丧有许多的规定。接到至亲亡故的噩耗后，首先应号啕痛哭，然后向报丧者询问死因。问完了又要放声大哭，然后起程前往奔丧。亲友们前来吊唁时，孝子们要披头赤足，放声恸哭，而且边走边捶胸膛地去接待客人。吊丧期间，家属亲友的禁忌非常多，通常除了丧事之外，其他的事情一概不谈。妇女尤其忌讳涂脂抹粉。饮食上严禁酒肉，吃素菜淡饭，以表示对死者的哀恸。

There are many rules about hastening for death in Hainan civilians. On receiving the death news of close relatives, one should first wail in mourning, then ask about the cause of death. Having asked that, he should cry again, and then start to hasten for the funeral. When friends and relatives come to mourn, the mourning sons should go and meet them while beating the chest with hair unwrapped and feet bared. During the condolence, there are a lot of taboos for relatives and friends. Usually they do not talk about anything other than the funeral. Woman should avoid making up. Meat and wine are taboo while vegetarian diet is adopted to show mourning for the dead.

入殓
Encoffining

给死者穿上送终的衣服，放进棺材叫做"殓"。殓有大殓和小殓之分。以衣裳包裹尸体被称为小殓。小殓的次日举行大殓。大殓即将尸体放进棺内。大殓就意味着死者与生者的诀别，从此将永无再见之日（董强，2013）。在琼东、琼北地区，在外地的亡者的遗体不得进村，要在村外入棺并在村外送灵柩上山。

Encoffining is to dress the dead in shroud and put into the coffin, which is divided into preliminary encoffining and formal encoffining. Preliminary encoffining is to wrap the corpse with clothes. On the next day of preliminary encoffining, formal encoffining is held. Formal encoffining is to put the corpse into the coffin, which means to bid farewell to the dead. At the same time, the memorial tablet is set up, in front of which an altar is to be put, where offerings of food and drink are placed. Then the memorial ceremony is held. Have all things done, the formal encoffining ends. In the eastern and northern parts of Hainan, the corpse can't enter the village if the dead passes away outside the village.

披麻戴孝

Dressing in Mourning

琼东、琼北一般只有亡者的直系亲属才戴孝；而在琼西、琼南却不同，凡是参加丧事的人都一律头上裹白布、戴斗笠，手上拿一条白布，也叫做"孝布"。

Normally, in the eastern and northern parts of Hainan, only the son of the dead gets dressed in mourning or wears a mourning cap and waistband. While it's different in the western and the southern parts of Hainan, all the friends and relatives hastening for funeral should wrap white cloths on the heads, wear bamboo caps and take white cloths in hands, which are called the "filial cloths".

土葬

Earth Burial

土葬的习俗在海南已经延续了几千年。在实行殡葬改革之前，琼西、琼南地区的坟墓一般都选择在较为偏远的郊外或荒山瘠地，不少有钱的人家还采用钢筋混凝土、花岗岩等石材建造坟墓，墓碑也修建得较为华丽隆重。琼西、琼南的坟头大多为方形，而琼北、琼东的则为圆形。由于传统的习俗根深蒂固，土葬的乱埋乱葬在农村较为严重。近年来实行殡葬改革，海南省各个市县建设了一批公益性公墓并将基本殡葬服务纳入政府公共服务体系后，乱埋乱葬的现象已明显减少。

The burial customs in Hainan have lasted for thousands of years. Before funeral reform, the coffins are generally buried in the remote outskirts or barren hills in the western and southern parts of Hainan. Many rich people even build the tomb with reinforced concrete and granite headstone. And the tombstone is gorgeous and grand. The grave mounds are also different in Hainan. They are usually square in the western and southern areas, while they are round in the east and the north. Due to the entrenched traditional customs, disordered earth burial in the countryside is more serious. After the funeral reform in recent years, a batch of public cemeteries and basic funeral services are incorporated into the government public service system in each county and city in Hainan province, the phenomenon of disordered earth burial has been improved significantly.

03

海南岁时节日民俗
Seasonal and Festival Customs

岁时节日是广大人民群众为适应生产和生活的需要而形成的一种具有纪念意义或民俗意义的社会性活动文化，是中国民俗文化的重要组成部分（方华文，2001）。岁时是中国传统社会特有的时间表述，岁是年度周期，时是年度的季节段落。岁时节日民俗包括岁时民俗和节日民俗两部分。岁时民俗指随着季节、时间变幻，特定区域的人群在生产生活中形成的习俗。节日民俗是岁时民俗的特定表现形式（吴忠军，2007）。区域不同，季节不同，岁时节日名称有别。中国民众的岁时观念来源于他们的谋生活动和生活感受，岁时既有自然属性又有人文属性。岁时节日推崇自然神崇拜，追求自然与人的和谐，敬鬼神而宠万物。

Chinese festivals, in the form of a great many folk activities in order to meet the needs of people's production and daily life, serve as an important part of Chinese folk culture. The phrase "岁时" (suì shí) in Chinese is an expression of time, with "岁" for a circle of a year and "时" for every section of the four seasons during a whole year. And the customs can be divided into two types, i.e. seasonal customs and festival customs. The former refers to the customs formed during a certain people's social life with the change of seasons, while the latter can be considered to be the typical form of the former. Different regions and seasons result in various festival names and activities. The concept of "岁时" in ancient China originates from Chinese people's daily activities and feelings. Worshiping the nature features some Chinese festivals, and people are trying to pursue the harmony between nature and human beings with respect for everything around them.

3.1 岁时节日民俗概说
Introduction

岁时节日，主要是指与天时、物候的周期性转换相适应，在人们的社会生活中约定俗成的，具有某种风俗活动内容的特定时日。岁时节日民俗是指在与天时、物候的周期性转换对应的某个阶段或特定时间而形成的具有纪念意义或民俗意义的社会性活动，并由此所传承下来的民俗事象。

Seasonal customs, which refer to some conventions with specific social activities or customs corresponding to the transformation of a particular period of time during the four seasons, are inherited by a certain people with commemorative or folk significance.

3.1.1 岁时节日民俗的形成 Origins of Festivals

"岁"指时间、年、年龄、一年的收成，"时"指节日在历法中的日期（吴景荣、程镇球，2007）。岁时节日民俗历史悠久、流传范围广，具有普及性、群众性、全民性的特点，与古代天文、历法、科技、农耕经济、家庭组织结构、历史重大事件、民间传说、自然或人为的文化传播等关系密切，是各种复杂文化因素综合作用的结果。一般而言，岁时节日的形成，相对固定的节期、特定的民俗活动两项要素必不可少。

The word "岁" (suì) in Chinese is a certain period of time, a year, a certain age, an annual harvest, while "时" (shí) refers to the specific date in the calendar. Seasonal and festival customs, which enjoy a long history and spread throughout China with great popularity among the whole country, are associated closely with ancient astronomy, calendar, science and technology, agriculture, family structure, major historical events, folklore, and cultural communication. Generally, seasonal and festival customs consist of the two elements: relatively fixed date and specific folk activities.

3.1.2 岁时节日民俗的类型 Types of Seasonal and Festival Customs

一般而言，岁时节日民俗可分为：

Generally speaking, seasonal and festival customs can be broken into the following categories:

3.1.2.1 传统节日
Traditional Festivals

传统节日是一个民族或国家历史文化长期积淀凝聚而形成的，是构成区域文明国家的基本框架，承载着区域特色人文与自然文化内容，如春节、元宵节、寒食节、清明节、端午节、乞巧节（七夕节、中国情人节）、中秋节、重阳节、冬至、除夕等（邢植朝、王静，2004）。

Traditional festivals, which are condensed from a nation's history and culture for a long time, serve as the basic framework of the civilized nations or countries with the regional characteristics, such as the Spring Festival, Lantern Festival, Cold Food Festival, Tomb-sweeping Day, Dragon Boat Festival, the Double Seventh Day (also named Qiqiao Festival, Chinese Valentine's Day), the Mid-Autumn Festival, the Double Ninth Festival, the Winter Solstice, Traditional Chinese New Year's Eve, etc.

3.1.2.2 农林渔猎等生产性节日
Production Holidays or Festivals for Farming, Fishing, Hunting, etc.

生产性节日，一般指在农业、林业、渔业、牧业等生产实践过程中，伴随岁时变换和生产习俗而传承下来的群众性活动，如山栏节、吃棵节、吃新节、新禾节、禾仔斋、牛节、赶海文化节等。

Production holidays or festivals mainly refer to the mass activities in agriculture, forestry, fisheries, animal husbandry, etc., with the change of seasons and production practices, such as the Shan Lan Festival, Ingot-shaped Food Festival, New Rice Festival, He Zai Zhai (the God of Rice) Festival, New Rice-eating Festival, Cattle's Day, Tanmen Beachcombing Festival.

3.1.2.3 民间信仰与祭祀类节日
Holidays or Festivals for Religions and Beliefs

宗教祭祀类节日包括宗教信仰和祭祀两类。前者包括原始宗教信仰或现代宗教信仰，后者主要是敬鬼神、求神和祭拜祖先等祭祀类节日，如中元节（盂兰盆节、鬼节）、圣纪节、开斋节、古尔邦节、妈祖祭典（妈祖信俗、天后圣母节）、灶公节、城隍宫节、公期、行符日、花山节、吃斋节、南海传统文化节、二月二龙抬头祭海大典等。

Holidays or festivals for religious belief are broken into two types: religious beliefs and sacrifices-offering rituals. The former includes primitive and modern religions, while the latter mainly involves worshiping, praying to the Heaven or God, and offering sacrifices to the ancestors, etc., such as Zhong Yuan Festival (Ghost Day, the 15th of the seventh lunar month during which sacrifices are offered to the dead), Mohammed's Birthday, Lesser Bairam (Eid al-Fitr; Festival of the Fast-Breaking), Corban Festival, Matsu Festival (Matsu Belief and Customs), the Festival for God of Kitchen, the Town God's Day, Gong Qi (memorial day for the clan ancestors or goodness or honorable spirits), Xing Fu Day, Hua Shan Festival in the Miao People, Vegetarian Festival in the Miao People, the South China Sea Traditional Cultural Festival in Tanmen, Sacrifices-offering Ceremony to the sea on the 2nd day of the 2nd lunar month, etc.

3.1.2.4 纪念追忆性节日
Holidays or Festivals in Memory of Historical Figures

纪念追忆型节日主要是表达对真实的或传说的人或物的一种留恋、怀念和追忆，如海南军坡节（冼夫人信俗）、伏波将军日、关圣帝生日、西天公节、万宁国际文灯节等。

These holidays or festivals come into being in honor of real or fictional figures, such as Hainan Junpo Festival (Madam Xian Belief and Customs), General Fubo's Day, Guanyu's Birthday, Poet Wang Zuo's Day, Wanning Lantern Festival and so on.

3.1.2.5 其他
Others

其他活动分为三类。一类指为了加强个人和族群或社会团体的交往和友好往来，兼具爱情、友情、娱乐或竞技内容的活动，如海南黎苗族三月三、姊妹节、海口府城换花节、海南欢乐节、保亭七仙温泉嬉水节、团结口、儋州中秋赛歌会、文昌南洋文化节、三亚天涯国际婚庆节、三亚南山太极文化节、海南书香节等。一类为国家为适应现代生活而设定的一些纪念日或社会公共活动日，如元旦节、妇女节、青年节、劳动节、儿童节、教师节、国庆节、中国人民抗日战争胜利纪念日等。一类为受中西文化交流影响而形成的具有浓厚域外风情而为青年群体广泛采纳的节日，如情人节、女生节、愚人节、母亲节、父亲节、光棍节等。

Some festivals or holidays are set to strengthen social relations or facilitate friendly exchanges between individuals and ethnic groups, such as Hainan San Yue San Festival (held on the 3rd day of the 3rd lunar month), Sister Festival, Flower Exchange Festival in Fucheng of Haikou, Hainan Carnival, Qixian (7th Fairy) Spring Water Splashing Festival in Baoting, Solidarity Day among the Miao People, Songs Contest in antiphonal style during the Mid-Autumn Festival, Nanyang Cultural Festival in Wenchang, Tianya International Wedding Festival in Sanya, Nanshan Tai Chi Cultural Festival in Sanya, Hainan Reading Day or Hainan Book and Copyright.

Others refer to anniversaries or particular periods set for some typical activities to adapt to the modern life, such as the New Year, Women's Day, Youth Day, May Day (International Workers' Day), Children's Day, Teachers' Day, National Day, the Commemoration Day of the Victory of the War of Resistance against Japanese Aggression (day commemorating the victory of the War of Resistance against Japanese Aggression) and so on. Some holidays or festivals come into being with the influence of the cultural exchanges between China and the rest of the world or other factors, such as the Valentine's Day, Girls' Day, April Fool's Day, Mother's Day, Father's Day, Singles' Day (Double Eleventh Day).

3.1.3 岁时节日民俗的基本特征 Custom Features

海南省地处热带北缘，是中国国土面积第一大省，其中陆地面积 3.54 万平方公里，热带海洋面积约 200 万平方公里。汉武帝元封元年（即公元前 110 年），在海南岛设置珠崖郡、儋耳郡，属交州刺史管辖，标志着中央政权对海南岛直接统治的开始。长期以来，海南坚持以农业为主，受中原儒家文化影响，海南岁时节日民俗呈现以下特征。

Hainan province, located in the northern part of the tropic, is the largest province in China, with a land area of 35,400 square kilometers and tropical ocean area of 2,000,000 square kilometers approximately. In the first year of Yuanfeng (110 BC) of Emperor Hanwu in the Western Han Dynasty (206 BC-AD 24), Zhuya Prefecture and Dan'er Prefecture were set formally in Hainan, which marked the beginning of the direct rule of Hainan by the central government. Hainan, which was dominated by agriculture for a long time, has been influenced by Confucian culture. Thus, Hainanese folk festivals have some particular characteristics as follows:

3.1.3.1 热带农业文化特色鲜明
Characterized with Tropical Agriculture

海南地处我国最南端，属热带海洋季风气候，光照充足，物种资源十分丰富。农业是海南经济的基础产业、支柱产业和优势产业。在海南，无论是汉族传统节日还是黎族抑或苗族的诸多民俗节日，均是农业文明发展的产物。例如，为了凸显牛在黎族农业生产中的重要作用，在海南黎族合亩制地区，七月秋耕后，人们会聚集在亩头家里杀猪摆宴，通宵达旦敲锣打鼓，举办祭牛神仪式，为牛跳招魂舞蹈（陈立浩、陈兰、陈小蓓，2008）。东方市报板地区美孚方言的村民会在村里设牛神庙。虽然牛节、牛神庙源于原始的牛崇拜，但海南节庆民俗的农业特色可见一斑。

Hainan, situated in southernmost part of China, is particularly rich in the species and resources due to tropical monsoon climate, adequate light and temperature. Thanks to the fact that the agriculture is the basic industry of Hainan, many holidays or festivals in Han, Li and Miao People are associated with agricultural civilization. For example, in order to highlight the important role of cattle in the Li people's agricultural production in Hainan, people would gather, play the drums, dance, and offer sacrifices to the God of Cattle after harvest in July according to Chinese lunar calendar. Some locals of Meifu Li in Baoban in Dongfang city set the temple in the village for the God of Cattle. Although the Cattle's Festival and the Cattle Temple derivred from cattle worship, the general idea of agricultural characteristics in Hainan's festivals and holidays can be understood to some extent.

3.1.3.2 河海情深，海洋特色独特，民间海神信仰文化浓厚
Folk Religions and Beliefs Associated with Sea and Rivers

海南岛孤悬南海，海南各民族均可能为漂洋过海而来，人们的生活与海洋密不可分。海南岛内万泉河、南渡江、昌化江、宁远河、松涛水库、南丽湖等河流湖泊密布，与人们生活息息相关。海南南海传统文化节、二月二龙抬头祭海大典、天后圣母节等民俗节庆河海神灵信仰文化太浓厚，河海神灵雕塑或建筑遍及海南全岛。河海特色不仅在岁时节日民间信仰上独树一帜，在节庆饮食文化上更是别有一番韵味（刘士祥，2016）。例如，海南节庆期间必备的四大名菜嘉积鸭与和乐蟹，即分别选自万泉河润泽的琼海嘉积镇及万宁和乐镇个大膏肥的海蟹；三亚疍家人首创、羊栏镇回族发扬光大的特色美食"酸鱼汤"（酸汤鱼），选用新鲜海鱼，配以酸豆叶和果、酸杨桃、西红柿、酸笋等熬煮而成。现在，充满海洋特色的美食——羊栏酸鱼汤已成为三亚十大名菜之一。

Hainan Island was isolated from mainland of China due to Qiongzhou Strait, and all the ethnic groups came to Hainan across the sea. Therefore, the ocean is inseparable from people' daily life in Hainan. Wanquan River, Nandujiang River, Changhuajiang River, Ningyuan River, Songtao Reservoir, Nanlihu Lake, etc., are closely associated with locals. The religions and beliefs associated with sea and rivers in the sculptures, buildings, or festivals, such as the South China Sea Traditional Cultural Festival, Sacrifices-offering Ceremony to thes sea on the 2nd day of the 2nd lunar month, Matsu Festival (Sacrifice-offering ceremony to Matsu), etc., can be found in Hainan province. Local food features the religions and beliefs related to the sea and rivers. For example, the Jiaji Duck and Hele Crab, as the two of the four famous dishes in Hainan are selected from the Wanquan River coastal town. And the fish boiled with tamarinds, pickled vegetables, and tomatoes in the Hui People's Style has become one of the top ten famous dishes in Sanya.

3.1.3.3 宗祠庙宇，贵人伦而重亲情
Featured with Ancestral Halls and Temples Home and Abroad

我国是一个贵人伦、重亲情的国度，海南特殊的地理环境及自然条件为海南宗族之间、邻里之间、家庭成员之间和谐的关系创造了客观条件。为了维系宗族，海南民间自古就有修纂族谱的习俗，这些谱牒为后人留下了宝贵的文献资料，也丰富了本土历史和乡土文化信息。一般而言，海南李氏宗族、冯氏宗族、王氏宗族、符氏宗族、陈氏宗族、林氏宗族、吴氏宗族、何氏宗族、周氏宗族、张氏宗族等每年都会聚在一起，续修家谱，传承宗族传统，维系与呵护宗族亲情。端午节是中国的传统节日，除了吃粽子、赏龙舟竞技，海南人民赋予了端午节别样的风采。在海南靠近海边的城市，一家人、同村人或同姓氏的族人自中午过后会成群结队赴海边"洗龙水"（即海里游泳），放眼望去，海滩上人山人海，蔚为壮观。清明节，作为中国传统节日之一，是祭祖和扫墓的日子。海南清明祭祖时，时常八音伴奏，吟诵祖训族规。但海南清明祭祖分两种，先祭"己祖"，以一户或几户为单位，在家中祖先牌位前摆放好"三牲"、干饭等祭品，人人跪拜；后祭"众祖"，以几十户或几百户同姓氏的宗族为单位参加，将祭品带到先人的坟墓祭拜，清除杂草，添上新土，以表对先人的思念与感激之情。

China is a typical nation emphasizing human relations and emotional attachment among family and other clan members. In order to maintain the clan, the clan members have a custom of compiling genealogy, which enriches the local history and culture. Generally speaking, the Li clan, the Feng clan, then Wang clan, the Fu clan, the Chen clan. the Lin clan, the Wu clan, the

He clan, the Zhou clan, the Zhang clan, etc., would gather every year to renew their genealogy. The Dragon Boat Festival is a traditional festival among Chinese. In addition to Zong Zi (pyramid-shaped dumplings made of glutinous rice wrapped in bamboo or reed leaves) and Dragon Boat Race, the Dragon Boat Festival in Hainan is endowed with a distinctive feature. Almost all the locals near the sea in Hainan will flock to the beach to swim in the sea or bathe at home (Xi Long Shui in dialect; the locals hold the water on that day is associated with dragon which is the emblem of good fortune). Tomb-sweeping Day, as one of the traditional Chinese festivals, is the day to offer sacrifices to the ancestor and pay respects at the family or clan members' tombs. However, the procedures in Hainan are different from those in other places, with the family ancestor first offered sacrifices by a certain family or a few households as a unit at home and the clan progenitor then worshiped by dozens of families or hundreds of households with the same surname participating in offering sacrifices, removing weeds, adding new soil to the tomb.

3.1.3.4 自然崇拜，敬鬼神而崇万物
Nature Worship

自然崇拜，即对自然神的崇拜，包括天体、自然力和自然物，如日月星辰、山川石木、鸟兽鱼虫、风雨雷电等。海南岛人类历史早期，居民分散，民族众多，自然崇拜的对象不尽一致，与居住的环境密切相关。例如，居住在沿海地区的居民，多崇拜海神；居住在河流两岸的，多崇拜河神；居住在林木山间的，多崇拜山神、树神、土地公、鬼魂。符，本义为信，古代称为符信，是出入关门的凭证，也是朝廷传达命令、调动兵将的凭证。符最早为竹制，一分为二，双方各执一半，合之以验真假，故引申有符合之义，进而形成一种有权力的官职。以符为氏族原始图腾和族徽，最终出现符姓。唐末，有河南宛丘籍符姓南下，始入海南岛，与黎人长期相处，黎人中出现符姓。符姓有"竹子的孩子"一说，竹子早在远古时期就开始深入黎族百姓的生活，如源于祭祀的竹竿舞、黎族民间常用治疗风湿中风的"拔火筒"、被列为国家非物质文化遗产保护对象的"黎族竹木器乐"等。宋代大文豪苏东坡曾说过："宁可食无肉，不可居无竹。"黎族终生与竹为伴的景况可管窥一斑。

Nature worship or the worship of nature, including celestial bodies, natural forces, and natural objects, such as stars, mountains, rivers, stones, woods, birds, animals, fish, worms, wind, rain, thunder and lightning, etc., is related to the environment where people live. For example, the residents who live near the sea worship the Gods of the sea, while those living in the mountain or forest worship the God of the mountain or the God of the earth. The Chinese character "符" (fú), which refers to the letter, is known as the tally by a ruler to a general or envoy as credentials for coming in and going out of a certain city, conveying orders, or mobilizing soldiers in ancient China. At the very beginning, the "符" (fú) was made of two pieces of bamboo, one for each party, and combined to check whether it was true or false. As time goes on, the "符" (fú) was provided with the extended meaning as a symbol of power. In accordance with the totem and emblem, the clan family name "符" (fú) came into being eventually at the end of the Tang Dynasty in current Henan province. And some people with such a family name began to move into Hainan island living with local Li People for a long time when the family name "符" (fú) appeared in the Li People. Some people with the family name "符" (fú) believe they are offsprings of the bamboo for the fact that the bamboo has far-reaching impact upon their daily life both in ancient time and nowadays, just as the poet Su Dongpo from Song Dynasty wrote, "The locals would prefer to have meals without meat rather than live without bamboo".

琼海会山树神祭拜（来源：琼海在线）
Tree Worship in Huishan of Qionghai (Source:http://www.qionghai.ccoo.cn)

3.1.3.5　人情意浓，求真爱而亲友情
More Friendship and Affections for Everyone

我国很多节日是为友情、爱情、亲情而设，海南的很多节日民俗亦为加强人际交往而确定节日形式与内容的，如海南黎族民间最盛大的节日即传统节日"三月三"。"三月三"古称上巳节，是纪念黄帝诞辰的节日，中国自古有"三月三，生轩辕"的说法。魏晋以后，上巳节改为"三月三"，后代沿袭，逐渐演变成郊外游春的节日。黎族"三月三"，又称爱情节、谈爱日，黎语称"孚念孚"，是海南黎族人民悼念勤劳勇敢的祖先、表达对爱情幸福向往之情的传统节日。2006 年 5 月 20 日，该民俗经国务院批准列入第一批国家级非物质文化遗产名录。海口府城换花节据说源于唐末"换香节"。"换香"蕴含互换香火、换吉纳祥、发财旺丁的寓意。基于安全考虑，1984 年，府城民间"换香"习俗改为"换花"，并逐渐成为元宵闹春的主要活动。青年人则把换花节当作交朋结友的大好时机，愿以花为媒，觅到知音，换花节逐渐演变成凝聚友谊、祝福、爱情为一体的节日习俗。

Many of the holidays or festivals in China are established for friendship, love, or affection. Hainanese do the same to strengthen the interpersonal communication in terms of the forms and contents of the holidays or festivals, such as the traditional Hainan San Yue San Festival (held on the 3rd day of the 3rd lunar month). Traditional San Yue San, called Shangsi Festival, is to commemorate the birthday of Xuanyuan Huangdi (Yellow Emperor) on the 3rd day of the 3rd lunar month by the Han People. After Wei and Jin Dynasties (220-420), Shangsi Festival was commonly named San Yue San, followed by the following dynasties, and gradually evolved into the festival for outing in spring. However, the Li People's San Yue San Festival, also known as the Courting Festival or Fu Nian Fu in the Li dialect, is to mourn their industrious and brave ancestors and express their yearning for love and happiness. And the festival was listed in the national intangible cultural heritage by the State Council on May 20th 2006. Fucheng Flower Exchange Festival in Haikou is said to have originated from the Incense Exchange Festival in the late Tang Dynasty (618-907), which had the connotations of good luck, being richer, and giving birth to more babies. Taken the security into consideration, the custom of exchanging incense was replaced by flowers in 1984. And it gradually becomes the main activity of the Lantern Festival in Fucheng. Young people take the festival as an opportunity to make more friends, find a bosom friend or Mr./Ms. Right, which makes it gradually evolve into a festival for friendship, best wishes and courting.

3.1.3.6 内外交融，异域风情文化独特

Exotic Cultures in Hainan

海南是个移民岛，海南岛内外各民族交流频繁，海南民俗特色鲜明。一方面，黎族是海南最早的居民，汉族、苗族、回族、疍民亦是海南的世居民族，还有彝、侗、瑶、壮等少数民族，各民族丰富多彩的民俗文化为海南区域特色民俗的形成奠定了基础。另一方面，海南与东南亚诸国交往频繁，骑楼特色建筑独树一帜。据统计，海外的琼籍华人华侨有320万之多，尤以泰国、马来西亚、新加坡、印度尼西亚、越南、美国、加拿大和澳大利亚较多。随着海南国际旅游岛的建设，海南与世界各民族接触日益频繁，俄罗斯、日本、韩国等大批游客来海南旅游，一年一度的海南欢乐节邀请越来越多海外友人，这都赋予海南节庆民俗更多异域特色。

Hainan is a province of immigrants, whose exchange with other ethnic groups home and abroad is more frequent. And this results in more distinctive folk customs and cultures. On the one hand, the Li people live with the Han People, the Miao People, the Hui People, and other ethnic minorities, which lays a solid foundation for the colorful folk customs and cultures with regional characteristics. On the other hand, Hainanese exchange frequently with people in Southeast Asian countries, and Haikou Qi Lou (the arcade in Hainan style) serves as a typical example. Statistics indicate that overseas Hainanese total 3,200,000 in Thailand, Malaysia, Singapore, Indonesia, Vietnam, the United States, Canada, and Australia, and other countries or regions. With the development of Hainan International Tourist Destination and some well-known festivals like Hainan Carnival, Hainanese have beening contacting an increasing number of foreign visitors more frequently from all over the world, especially from Russia, Japan, Korea, etc., which makes the festivals and holidays more exotic.

3.1.3.7 宗教活动世俗化倾向明显

Secular Tendency for Religious Activities

民间俗众也常把世俗人情寄托于宗教信仰，通过节日活动实现圣俗之间的交往，如浴佛节。浴佛节，为每年的农历四月初八，是中国佛教徒纪念释迦牟尼佛诞辰的一个重要节日，又称佛诞节、佛诞日灌佛会、龙华会、华严会等。2015年5月25日农历四月初八，为恭迎释迦牟尼佛圣诞，三亚南山寺举办浴佛祈福法会，纪念佛教创始人释迦牟尼诞辰2639周年，数百游客信众依次排队浴佛、同沾法喜，共祝国泰民安，社会和谐，世界和平。恰如浴佛节一样，所进行浴佛祈福活动，早期信仰成分重，后世逐渐演变成一种形式传承，神秘性逐渐让位。岁时节日充满了对生活的热爱，对自然和社会和谐状态的追求。

The Buddha's Birthday (8th of the fourth lunar month) is set in honor of Sakyamuni in China. In order to welcome the 2639th birthday of the Buddha Sakyamuni – the founder of Buddhism, the Nanshan Temple in Sanya city held Buddha blessing ceremony on May 25th, 2015, with hundreds of people queuing up to the Buddha in hope of peace, prosperity, and harmony in the world. Some religious activities, just as the Buddha's Birthday in the early stage when the religious belief was overwhelmingly predominant, gradually evolved into a form of inheritance with the mystery gradually replaced by love for life, the pursuit of harmony between the nature and the society.

3.1.3.8 岁时节日民俗的形式、内容及功能由单一向复合演变
Forms, Activities, and Functions Evolving from Single to Complex

节日丰富的缘起，与原始信仰、天文历法、科技水平有关。最早时，敬天、祈福、避邪等观念及活动在节俗中占主导地位。魏晋南北朝以后，节日就逐渐从神秘气氛中解脱，成为人神共欢的日子。隋唐以后，随着经济发展、文化昌盛、科技繁荣、各民族交往频繁，虽然保留了一些传统习俗，但节庆民俗逐渐发展为集信仰、经济、社交、教育、娱乐、情谊等多重功能于一体，成为节庆生活不可或缺的一部分。

Holidays and festivals originate from primitive beliefs, astronomy, traditional lunar calendar, and the limited technology. The earliest activities during holidays and festivals, such as worshiping the Heaven, praying for good luck and warding off evil spirits dominated the whole process. After Wei, Jin, and Southern and Northern Dynasties (220-589), holidays and festivals gradually faded from the mysterious atmosphere and became common time enjoyed by human beings and gods. With the development of economy, science, technology, culture, and frequent exchanges between various ethnic groups, the holidays and festivals were gradually combined with beliefs, economy, society, education, entertainment, friendship, etc., which has become an indispensable part of holidays or festival celebrations while retaining many of the traditions and customs since the Sui and Tang Dynasties (581-907).

3.2 传统节日民俗
Traditional Festivals and Customs

传统节日蕴含中华民族的群体价值观，对中华儿女情感产生一种积极的向心力，是中华民族认同的重要元素之一，也是中华民族文化身份的区别性特征之一，主要包括春节、元宵节、寒食节、清明节、端午节、乞巧节、中秋节、重阳节、冬至、除夕等。

Traditional festivals which contain Chinese collective value exert a positive impact upon Chinese people. And they are not only one of the most important elements of the Chinese identity, but also one of the distinctive features of the Chinese culture, including the Spring Festival, the Lantern Festival, the Cold Food Festival, the Qingming Festival (Tomb-Sweeping Day), the Dragon Boat Festival, the Double-Seventh Day (Qi Qiao Festival), the Mid-Autumn Festival, the Double Ninth Festival, the Winter Solstice, Chinese Lunar New Year's Eve.

3.2.1 除夕与春节 Chinese Lunar New Year's Eve and the Spring Festival

"除夕"最早出现在西晋周处撰著的《风土记》等史籍。除夕，家人欢聚一堂，贴春联、挂灯笼、祭祖、共享团圆饭等。与全国其他地方相比，海南春节民俗大同小异。海南汉族亦俗称春节为"过年"，海南方言称之为"做年"。中秋过后，海南乡村就筹备"做年"：阉公鸡、填肥鸭、圈家猪、

备做年钱。进入农历十二月下旬，"做年"逐渐拉开帷幕。

The Chinese phrase "除夕" (Chinese Lunar New year's Eve) was firstly used in historical record by Zhou Chu (238-299) in Western Jin Dynasty (266-316). On New Year's Eve, the family gather to paste up couplets, put up lanterns, offer sacrifices to ancestors, share the reunion dinner, etc. Compared with customs during the Spring Festival in other places, those in Hainan are more or less the same. However, the Spring Festival is named "做年" (zuò nián) in Hainanese dialect. And Hainanese in villages begin to make preparations after the Mid-Autumn Festival. When it comes to the late December of the lunar calendar, the traditions and customs gradually show up.

送"灶公"
Offer Sacrifices to the God of Kitchen

传说中，"灶公"是玉帝派来人间监督善恶之神，每年十二月二十四日（有些地方为十二月二十三）都要上天向玉帝汇报。家家户户都用竹把或竹枝将屋前屋后打扫干净，香炉也要打扫干净并换上新炉灰，夜间则备酒、果设祭，为"灶公"送行。

According to the legend, the God of Kitchen is sent by the Jade Emperor to supervise the good and evil deeds of human beings, and will report to the Jade Emperor on December 24th of the lunar calendar (or December 23th in some places). Every household should clean the house and the incense burner, replace with some new ashes, and prepare some wine and fruit to see off the God of Kitchen.

扫尘掸土
Do the Cleaning and Washing

民间有"腊月二十五，扫放掸尘土""腊月二十七，里外洗一洗""腊月二十八，家什擦一擦""腊月二十九，脏物都搬走"的说法，家家户户都会将房里屋外打扫干净以示辞旧迎新。但在海南琼海，除清洗蚊帐、被褥、箩筐家具，也有人会把破旧的东西拿到村口放火烧掉，称为"送穷"，祛除晦气，喜迎好运。

Chinese will do the cleaning and washing from December 24th according to the lunar calendar to usher in the new year. In addition to washing mosquito net, bedclothes, bamboo basket, etc., some people may set fire on something old with the connotation of getting rid of poverty or bad luck.

贴春联
Paste up Couplets

一般而言，除丧事不满三年家庭，家家户户都会张贴春联、门神及其他年画。据记载，中国古代春联题写在桃木板上，桃木的颜色是红的，红色有吉祥、避邪之意；随着造纸、印刷技术发展，红纸普及，所以春联大都用红纸黑笔书写。在海南琼海，除贴好门联年画，有些门楣上还贴有一种叫"篱岂钱"的纸符。至今，海南儋州乡村有些家庭会在家门口插上"桃符"（番石榴叶）驱邪。

Generally speaking, every household will paste up the couplets, the God of Door, and others except the families with funerals within three years. According to records, ancient Chinese couplets were inscribed in peach wood board whose color is red, which is auspicious in Chinese. With the invention of paper and printing technology, most of the couplets are written or printed in two strips of red paper on which black or golden Chinese characters are written. In

Qionghai city of Hainan province, some family will stick a magic sign called "篱屺钱" (lí qǐ qián) onto the door lintel, and some rural areas in Danzhou also keep similar custom of hanging up guava leaves to ward off bad luck or evil spirits.

篱屺钱（李俊贤 摄）
Magic sign called Li Qi Qian (Courtesy of Junxian Li)

发灯

Fa Deng (Keep the Lights on all through the Night)

从年三十开始到初四或初五，夜幕降临，家家户户张灯结彩，通宵达旦，海南称之为"发灯"，有"发财添丁"之意。

From the Lunar New Year's Eve to the 4th or the 5th day of the new year, every household will keep the lights on all through the night when it is getting dark, named Fa Deng by Hainanese, which has the connotation of being richer and having more babies born into the family.

祭祖

Offer Sacrifices to Ancestors

海南很多地方祭祖仪式至今承袭。在澄迈，年三十当天就开始用猪肉、内脏、饭团等祭拜"公祖"，祈求"公祖"保佑家人身体健康，五谷丰登，六畜兴旺。在儋州，年三十下午就要开始杀鸡、搓汤圆、蒸红鱼，以上供桌祭祀祖先。供桌上一般有：清水、白酒、小米各一杯，一碟汤圆，一只熟鸡，一盘猪肉，一盘红鱼，一盘年糕，米饭五碗，筷子五双，这些供品取意为"有鱼有肉"，寄托了年丰岁富之意。

Traditional ritual of offering sacrifices to ancestors in Hainan has been inherited in many places. Some people in Chengmai county will offer pork, offal, rice balls, etc. to their ancestors on the last day of the lunar year for health and a bumper harvest, while people in Danzhou will offer chicken, glutinous dumplings, steamed snapper to their ancestors on the afternoon of the lunar new year's eve in the hope of a more prosperous year.

年夜饭

Have Family Reunion Dinner

海南民族众多，年夜饭不尽相同。年三十祭祖完毕，举家欢聚一起吃团圆饭，俗称"围炉"。除了典型的白切鸡、肉、鱼虾海鲜外，海南各族对斋菜情有独钟，斋菜寓意丰富，海南斋菜煲、全家福菜必不可少。在海南许多市县都有做年糕的风俗，三亚的红糖年糕则是众多年糕中的一绝，因为年糕的"糕"与"高"谐音，与粉丝一样，寄意家人高寿。芹菜之"芹"与"勤"同音，勤劳致富；慈菇乃海南方言"除旧"的谐音，蕴含辞旧迎新之意；有些海南人称黄花菜为金针，与黄豆干一样，寓意有财，家底殷实；茄子，海南话寓意一年比一年好。

The family reunion dinners vary from one to another due to the different ethnic groups in Hainan. After offering sacrifices to their ancestors on the lunar new year's eve, family members gather to have family reunion dinner, commonly known as "围炉" (wéi lú, sitting around the stove) is popular. In addition to the typical dishes, such as the sliced boiled chicken, meat, seafood, etc., almost all the ethnic groups in Hainan are fond of vegetarian food. The custom of making lunar New Year Cake (made of glutinous rice) is popular in many cities and counties, with those cakes made of brown sugar and rice in Sanya being one of the best kinds. The Chinese character "糕" (gāo, higher and higher, better and better, or longer and longer) of New Year Cake is homophonic with "high", which means longevity of family members as vermicelli does in Chinese. Similarly, "芹" (celery) is similar with "勤" (hard-working) and "慈菇" (arrowhead) with "除旧" (to say goodbye to the past) in pronunciation respectively. In addition, the vegetables with typical connotations, such as day lily, eggplant, edible black fungus, peanut, are quite popular among Hainanese.

守岁

Stay up all Night on New Year's Eve

守岁，或称除夕守岁，俗名"熬年"，即熬夜迎接新年到来。华夏大地，除夕之夜，灯火通明，无论男女老少都会聚在一起守岁。在海南，除夕之夜，全家大小会围坐一堂，或饮茶叙话或欣赏春节联欢晚会节目，房内灯火通明，家人彻夜不眠，一起守岁；农历正月初一子时起，燃放烟花爆竹，海南称之为"迎年"，意为"迎春纳福"。在澄迈，子时起，村民会在摆祖先香炉灵位的正厅里，摆上两小堆刮去表皮的小块甘蔗、一个柚子、三个桔子及猪内脏等，点上香烛，燃放烟花鞭炮，喜迎新年。

Hainanese, like most Chinese people, would stay up all night on New Year's Eve to welcome the new lunar year. When the very moment of the first day of the lunar year comes, people would let off the fireworks and firecrackers, called "welcome the new year" by the locals with the connotation of "welcoming the new year and ushering in happiness". Some villagers in Chengmai will put two piles of peeled sugarcane, a grapefruit, three oranges, offal, etc. in the temporary memorial tablet of their ancestors, burn the incense, light candles, and set off the fireworks and firecrackers to celebrate the arrival of the new year.

拜年

Send New Year Greetings to Each Other

海南各地拜年的习俗不尽一致，有些地方是初一、二拜年，有的地方却是初一不能去别人家拜年。正月初一开始，亲朋好友相互拜年，见面互道"恭喜发财"等吉利话。晚辈见长辈要拜礼贺年，长辈要给小孩"利市"（压岁钱）。从初二到十五前后，凡拜年的人都要带去鞭炮礼品，听到鞭炮响，就知道那家一定有人来拜年了。琼海福田、上埇、潭门等地，流行一种"做新娘酒"的习惯。年内有女儿出嫁新婚，初一回娘家来拜年，得把叔伯兄弟各户拜遍；家主还得给女儿女婿送红包。女儿女婿只送上爆竹，一般是个"炮车"，一进门就放，告诉大家，儿女回门拜年来了。岳父岳母得准备丰盛的筵席宴之，下午女儿女婿离开时，还得将用红纸包的糖果、年糕等给女儿做"迎路"。三亚流行这样的习俗，姑爷大年初二随同妻子回娘家拜年必须购买鞭炮。每年陪妻子回外家拜年都必须准备鞭炮，来到岳父母家门口后，将鞭炮交给其他亲属，鞭炮放完以后才能进门向老人和其他亲属拜年。带鞭炮到岳父、岳母家拜年，不仅是一种礼节性的需要，同样也是对长辈和其他亲属的祝福。拜年的礼品，一般有柑桔或礼品中夹桔子叶，以表示"今年将大吉大利"的祝福。在拜年的酒桌上，食材也颇有讲究。例如，临高话叫墨鱼为"hong"，发音有点像"通"，新年吃了"通"，一年到头事事顺心如意。

The customs of sending new year greetings in person vary from one place to another in Hainan, and some of which allow no visit on the first day of the lunar new year. Generally speaking, most people will say some auspicious words, such as "Happy New Year", "May you be prosperous", "Wish you all the best", etc., on the first day of the first lunar month when meeting each other. The young should send new year greetings to the aged in person, who may give some money as a gift. From the second day to the fifteenth day of the first lunar month, the people who send new year greetings in person should bring fireworks and firecrackers. In some places of Qionghai, the newly married women should return home with some fireworks and firecrackers and send new year greetings in person to every household of kinship. Similar custom also occurs to Sanya where the newly married women must bring fireworks and firecrackers when returning home to send new year greetings in person. When the fireworks and firecrackers are set off, the newly married couple could send new year greetings. On some occasions, people would bring some oranges or orange leaves to wish good luck all over the year. And people will prepare some particular food for the guests, such as cuttlefish whose pronunciation sounds like "tong" in Lingao dialect with the connotation of all the best during the whole year.

初三是大年的最后一天。是日，海南很多地方人吃甜食，希望甜水长流；也有一些地方叫"炒考"，即将大年三十特地多煮的干饭、吃的鸡鸭头脚用油爆锅炒一炒再吃，以表示去年有东西余到今年，也表示年已过去。

The 3rd day of the first lunar month is considered the last day of the year, when some local people would eat sweet things with the hope that happy days like these can go on forever, while some people in other places would cook more food on lunar new year's eve and eat what has been left in the following two days with the similar wish to be better and better year by year.

初五"接财神"。农历正月初五，民间传说是财神的生日，人们有迎财神的传统习俗。每年，三亚南山文化旅游区龙五爷财神庙会"迎财神"民俗文化活动内容丰富，有舞狮表演、琼剧乐队演奏、琼戏展演、点亮"金元宝灯"、派送财神年画等。海口人从初六开始"行袍"，即把本村庙宇里的菩萨或神灵请下神案，抬着到村里的各家各户去放灯、驱邪。这是海南方言的说法，相当于北方的庙会。

The 5th day of the first lunar month, which is regarded as the birthday of the God of Wealth, is time to welcome the God of wealth. Many folk cultural activities will be held every year in Nanshan scenic spot to welcome the God of Wealth, such as lion dance, Qiong Opera, lighting gold ingot-shaped lamp, sending the pictures of God of wealth and so on. Some people in Haikou would parade with Bodhisattva or other deities of their own villages from the sixth day of the first lunar month to ward off evil spirits and pray for good luck.

初七人日（人胜节）。李商隐《人日即事》诗谓："镂金作胜传荆风，剪彩为人起晋风。"认为"剪彩为人"即晋之"人胜"，镂金箔为人也是"作胜"，看来虽然两种"胜"材料不同，但都是"人胜"。唐人重视"人胜"，将正月七日称为"人胜节"。根据晋人董勋《问礼俗》："正月一日为鸡，二日为狗，三日为猪，四日为羊，五日为牛，六日为马，七日为人。正旦画鸡于门，七日贴人于帐"（《荆楚岁时记》注引），正月初七为鸡人创世神话的日子。中华人民共和国成立后，海南人日习俗渐趋冷淡，但海口、文昌、三亚、乐东、东方部分地区"人日"习俗尚存。是日，乐东县黄流等地杀鸡拜祖，海口一些地方上午以"三牲"祭祖，希望阴间先辈保佑子孙平安；吃粉丝、面条，寓意人生"福寿绵长"。这一习俗虽所用的果菜食材不同，象征取意亦有差别，但与东南、华中、华南地区初七民俗饮食"七宝羹"有异曲同工之妙。

The 7th day of the first lunar month is taken as the Human Day in Tang dynasty (618-907), which was considered as the time for world creation by Chicken according to the book named *Understanding Etiquette and Custom* by Dong Xun in Jin dynasty (266-420). Afer the founding of the People's Republic of China, the custom of the Human Day in Hainan gradually fades out, but it still exists in some parts of Haikou, Wenchang, Sanya, Ledong, Dongfang, etc. On that day, some people in Huangliu of Ledong county and Haikou will offer sacrifices to their ancestors, and they will have vermicelli or noodles during meals with the connotation of living happier with longevity, which is something like the custom of having Seven Vegetables Custard in southern part of China on the same day.

初九天生日，即玉皇大帝的诞辰，海口俗称"老爸生日"。是日，凌晨一点左右，以清茶、素果祭奉；家人用餐皆素，以示敬仰。

The 9th day of the first lunar month is deemed to be the Jade Emperor's birthday in Haikou, commonly known as the Father's Birthday. People would offer tea and fruit at 1:00 o'clock A.M., and family members would have vegetables during meals to show their respect.

海南黎族称春节为"仗""江"或"葛姆"，是为"年"。春节来临，黎族同胞清扫房屋、置备年货、祭拜祖先等，与汉族春节民俗有很多相似之处。然而，海南黎族春节亦有其地域特色。初一，除最基本的日常活动，几乎家家户户闭门守家，生怕好运溜走。初二到初四，走亲访友，相互拜年，但杞方言黎初三不能拜年。黎家把春节从井、河里挑的水视为"福水（圣水）"，挑水时，会放一个铜钱、槟榔或小块年糕，从示"福水"乃从神灵手里购买，寄望家人幸福安康。美孚黎有"量水"民俗。年初一早上，妇女挑一担水回家，与去年存下的水比量；若同，则示近年生活与去年相同；若多，则示较之去年更好；反之，今年生活不如去年。初五，将家里春节期间的生活垃圾倒进竹筐，用竹条扎架，放置稻草人，点燃香烛，两人抬神架及堆过年遗物的箩筐，举行"送神"出寨仪式，男女老少随神出村，以示送走"旧魂"，春节基本结束。神架及生活垃圾至元宵节烧掉，春节至此结束。

The Li People in Hainan name the Spring Festival *zhàng, jiāng* or *gě mǔ* in their dialect. When the Spring Festival is around the corner, the Li people would do something similar to the Han People. However, the Spring Festival of the Li People also has its regional characteristics. Almost every family member would stay at home except for some daily routines on the first day of the first lunar month in case good luck would go away. From the second to the fourth day of the first lunar month, people would send greetings to each other in person or by phone except for people of Qi Li who would not do this on the third day of the first lunar month. Some people would fetch some water traditionally from wells or rivers during the Spring Festival, which is considered holy water. People would put a coin, an areca nut, or a piece of cake beside the well or the river to make it like a purchase from the hands of the God, and they think this would keep the family happy and healthy. People of Meifu Li has the custom of measuring the water. After fetching a load of water as people of Qi Li in the morning of the new year, they will compare it with that of the previous year. The more, the better; the less, the worse; the same suggests the living standard would be the same as last year. On the fifth day of the first lunar month, people would pour the garbage into the bamboo basket, put a scarecrow in, light candles and incenses, and send them out of the village to bid farewell to the past. What has been piled out of the village will be burned on the Lantern Festival, which brings an end to the Spring Festival.

海南苗族春节民俗颇有地方特色。除夕前，苗族女婿要给岳父岳母买礼物，与妻子一起回娘家过年。除夕晚上，杀鸡宰羊，用糯米拌糖和猪肉包粽子，拜祭祖宗后，全家聚集享用年夜饭菜；五更过后至初一夜晚忌荤食，初一夕阳西下，准备饭菜，祭拜祖宗、家神，燃放鞭炮后，恢复荤食。初二早晨，亲朋好友，互相拜年。正月初三"拜坟"，给祖先"拜年"。家人将坟墓清扫干净，燃三炷香，焚化钱纸，将酒、肉、饭和糍粑等祭品供到墓前，跪在墓前磕三个头，燃放鞭炮，仪式完成。回娘家期间，女婿几乎要承担一切日常家务。有些地方，女婿要住到初七才回家。

The customs of the Miao People in Haian during the Spring Festival are typical of local characteristics. Before the lunar New Year's Eve, sons-in-law of the Miao People should buy gifts for their fathers-in-law and mothers-in-law, and celebrate the New Year together with them. On the lunar New Year's Eve, they would have family reunion dinner, including mutton, chicken, Zongzi (a pyramid-shaped dumpling made of glutinous rice wrapped in bamboo or reed leaves), etc., after offering sacrifices to their ancestors. Meat dish is forbidden from dawn (3:00-5:00 a.m.) to dusk (5:00-7:00 p.m.) on the first day of the lunar month after offering sacrifices to their ancestors. New year greetings would be sent to each other on the second day. They would send greetings to their ancestors on the third day of the first lunar month, and prepare some food, burn sticks of incense and paper money, kneel down and kowtow 3 times, and set off fireworks and firecrackers in the graveyard. The son-in-law would be in charge of almost all the housework when his wife visits her parental home during the Spring Festival somewhere.

春节作为一切开端的象征，华夏儿女春节期间的一切行为均具有象征性、仪式性。春节时住的房子要清扫干净，装饰一新；穿的衣服要是新的，期待新的开始；年夜饭要有鸡有鱼，吃饭要有剩余，以求"大吉大利、年年有余"；孩子打碎了碗，要说"碎碎（岁岁）平安"……春节被赋予了不同的文化意义。

The Spring Festival marks the beginning of everything. Therefore, all the activities during the period are symbolic and ritual, such as cleaning the house, having on new clothes, taking chicken and fish and so on. And the Spring Festival is endowed with different cultural significance.

3.2.2 元宵节 The Lantern Festival

正月十五日是一年中第一个月圆之夜，古代称夜为宵，故称"元宵"。根据《岁时杂记》记载，唐初受道教的影响，把正月十五日、七月十五日、十月十五日分别称为上元、中元、下元，即"三元"。因正月十五日为上元，元宵节又称"上元节"，唐末才偶称元宵。宋代以后称元宵为灯夕，清代称之为灯节，所以元宵节英文 The Lantern Festival 为外国所知。海南元宵节主要习俗有吃元宵、游灯、"装军"、舞狮舞龙、"换香/换花"、放风灯、赛肥鸡、人偶同台演出等。

The 15th day of the first lunar month witnesses the first full moon of the new lunar year. According to the records, the 15th day of the first, the 7th, and the 10th lunar month are respectively called Shang Yuan, Zhong Yuan, and Xia Yuan due to Taoism in the early Tang Dynasty (618-907). Therefore, the Lantern Festival is also known as Shang Yuan Festival until the end of Tang Dynasty (618-907). And it was named Lantern Festival since Song Dynasty (960-1279), for which Yuan Xiao Festival is also known as the Lantern Festival. The customs or traditional activities during the Lantern Festival in Hainan can be summarized as follows: taking rice dumplings, parading with lanterns, imitating army expedition, lion dance, dragon dance, incense or flower exchange, wind lantern (Kongming Lantern in Hainan style), fat chicken competition, puppet show, etc.

游灯
Parade with Lanterns

元宵之夜，海南竞相推出各色灯展，工艺精美，造型各异。家家户户高挂灯笼，喜气洋洋。琼海沿海渔乡"鲤鱼灯闹春"是展现海洋文化的一道风景线，庆祝过去一年的丰收，展望来年的美好，其历史渊源可追溯到明朝，历经几百年至今仍常盛不衰。嘉积溪仔古街的石板路形成于明初，至今已有 700 年的历史。夜晚，溪仔街小巷挂满各式灯笼：传统型的冬瓜灯、祈福灯、吉祥灯，万泉鲤鱼灯"游"上了墙面，山羊灯躲进了草丛，灯笼异彩纷呈，游灯热闹非凡。乐东黄流花灯已有百年历史，与其他地方最大的区别在于灯车和灯游。元宵这天，人们会用轿子抬着木制的关公像、驾牛灯车、手持灯笼，风风火火，锣鼓声、鞭炮声此起彼伏，男女老少夹道相迎，场面蔚为壮观。陵水元宵游灯是传统习惯。民国时期，每年农历正月的十三日至十六日是元宵节的"游公日"；建国后，游"公"活动停止；到 20 世纪 80 年代初期恢复，但游"公"被游"灯"取代。万宁"元宵灯会"可以观赏到各式各样的花灯，如十八罗汉、雄鸡起舞、观音座莲、孔雀开屏等。游客可参与或欣赏规模较大的海口游灯活动，热闹非凡。

During the Lantern Festival in Hainan, a great variety of exquisite lanterns in different shapes would be displayed. Featured with marine culture, the custom of Carp-shaped Lanterns reveling in the spring in coastal villages of Qionghai to celebrate the harvest in the previous year and the coming years can date back to Ming Dynasty (1368-1644). Lanterns of various shapes would be hung on both sides of Xizai stone road which was formed in the early Ming Dynasty (1368-1644). People in Huangliu of Ledong will carry a wooden statue of Guan Yu with a sedan to parade with lanterns, which will be welcomed warmly by men and women, old and young on both sides of the road. Parading with lanterns in Lingshui is a traditional custom. During the period of the Republic of China, the time from 13th to 16th of the first lunar month was Gong Parading Festival, which was suspended after the founding of the people's Republic of China. The custom of parading with lanterns was restored in the early 1980s. And people can also appreciate the different kinds of well-deigned lanterns in Wanning or participate in the parade with lanterns on a larger scale in Haikou.

装军
Imitate Army Expedition

海南"装军"民俗是为纪念冼夫人在海南领兵出征的场景，规模较大，内容丰富，一般白天举行。该项活动随着海南"冼夫人信俗"申报国家非物质文化遗产，规模越来越大。

The custom of imitating army expedition is held in memory of Mrs. Xian in the daytime with thousands of people acting as soldiers in battle field. Nowadays, the tradition is even grander as Beliefs and Customs in Mrs. Xian has been listed as a national intangible cultural heritage.

舞狮舞龙
Lion Dance and Dragon Dance

元宵佳节，海南多地均有舞狮舞龙的习俗，万宁万城镇宾王村被誉为"海南龙乡"，舞龙文化颇负盛名。万城镇西门社区的西门青龙和宾王村的宾王红龙经常受邀出行；青龙比红龙体形稍大，相传西门青龙为龙母，宾王红龙为龙公，深受人们欢迎。

Lion dance and dragon dance can be seen in Hainan during the Lantern Festival, and Binwang village in Wancheng town of Wanning is honored as the Hometown of Dragons, whose dragon culture is quite prestigious home and abroad. Green dragon from Ximen community and golden dragon from Binwang village have been invited for their excellent performance more often. The green dragon is slightly larger than the golden one, because the legend describes that the green dragon is the mother, and the latter one is father, both of whom are quite popular with the young and the old.

换香/换花
Incense or Flower Exchange

海口府城最具特色的民俗当属换花节。"换花节"源于"换香节"，唐末已存在元宵换香习俗。"换香"蕴含着互换香火、换吉纳祥、发财旺丁之寓意。由于换香人数过多，出于安全考虑，1984年，府城民间"换香"习俗改为"换花"。"换花节"逐渐成为人们元宵闹春的主要活动之一，演变成年轻人增进友谊、寻觅佳音、互相祝福、共享幸福美好的元宵新习俗。2015年元宵，海口28万市民游客参与闹元宵，欢度换花节。

Flower exchange is typical of Fucheng in Haikou city. Flower Exchange Festival in Haikou is said to have originated from the Incense Exchange Festival in the late Tang Dynasty (618-907), which had the connotation of good luck, being richer, and giving birth to more babies. Taken the security into account, the custom of exchanging incense was replaced by flowers in 1984, which has been one of the main activities for the young to take it an opportunity to make more friends, find a bosom friend or Mr./Ms. Right. During the Lantern Festival in 2015, the number of citizens and tourists participating in this event amounts to 280,000.

放风灯
Wind Lantern (Cone-shaped Lantern, Kongming Lantern in Hainan Style)

海南原属古崖州的沿海地区和万泉河畔的汉族地区有元宵放风灯的习俗。风灯一般高两米左右，直径一米左右，呈圆锥形，中空，圆底，用竹扎成支架，糊上心爱的彩约即成。它依靠多烟燃烧物燃烧积聚的气体冲力，升上夜空，因升空后顺风飘移，故名风灯。"灯"与"丁"谐音，最初是人们为祈求人丁兴旺而制做的。随着社会发展，放风灯蕴含之意愈来愈广：生意商贾希望发财，农民希望风调雨顺，学生希望美好前程……放风灯逐渐成为人们庆祝丰年的娱乐活动。风灯升到一定高度，响起阵阵鞭炮，表明风灯已经离开"地界"到达"上天"，故当地人称之为"过地炮"。高空的风灯越来越多，随风飘摇，组成品字形，人们称其为"三星灯"；排成一排，则为"七星灯"。

Some regions near the coastal ancient Yazhou and Wanquan River have the custom of launching the wind lantern (Kongming lantern in Hainan style). In general, a cone-shaped wind lantern, two meters high, one meter or so in diameter, would be made of bamboo scaffold and beloved color as its cover. It relies on depends on the accumulated gas to rise in the sky drifting with the wind after launching, due to which it is named wind lantern. The Chinese characters "灯" (dēng, lantern) and "丁" (dīng, baby) are homophonic in pronunciation, which contain people's hopes of bearing more babies. With the development of society, the connotations of wind lanterns have been extended: merchants for more fortune, farmers for good harvest, the students for a better future…Launching wind lanterns has gradually become an entertainment for people to celebrate harvest. As wind lanterns rise to a certain height, frequent bursts of firecrackers can be heard, which indicates the lantern has crossed the boundary between the earth and sky. More and more lanterns flying in the sky form a shape of "品" or in a row, which would be named three-star lanterns or seven-star lanterns respectively by the local.

赛肥鸡
The Fattest Chicken Competition

或许鸡与"吉"谐音，琼海乐城有元宵节赛肥鸡的习俗。元宵佳节，在青石砖铺就的老街两旁，各家门口都摆出一张八仙桌，桌上摆着一只泛着油光、让人垂涎欲滴的水煮鸡，由村里乡贤组成的评委会评选夺魁肥鸡。肥鸡嘴里叼着鲜花，脖子挂着项链，象征美好生活。谁家的鸡最肥，说明谁家会养鸡、最勤劳。

Possibly as the Chinese characters "鸡" (jī, chicken) and "吉" (jí, being auspicious) are homophonic in pronunciation, people in Lecheng of Qionghai have the custom of competing for the fattest chicken during the Lantern Festival. Boiled chickens are laid on the tables on both sides of the ancient street. And the judges from the village will award prize for the fattest ones. In the mouth of the fat chicken are flowers, with necklace hanging in the neck, which is a symbol of a better life. Those whose chicken is the fattest are considered the most hardworking people.

人偶同台演出
Puppet Show

临高元宵节有演人偶戏的习俗。临高木偶戏，据说源于当地村民祈求平安而演出的一种戏，海南称其为"公仔戏"，以琼剧唱腔与表演为基调，在人物上也有生、旦、杂、丑等角色之分，已有四百年历史。临高"人偶同台表演"，舞台不设布幛，演员擎仗头木偶化装登台，人偶合演，互为一体，自成一派，成为我国木偶稀有剧种。

People in Lingao have the custom of performing the puppet show during the Lantern Festival. The puppet show in Lingao, which is said to originate from praying for peace and safety, is based on singing and performing of Qiong Opera. It is divided into male role, female role, painted-face role, comic role, etc., with a history of four hundred years. Since the stage is set without a large cloth sheet, the actors and the puppet in their hands are integrated with each other on the stage, which has become one of the rare operas in China.

海南黎族俗称元宵节为"小年""年仔"。是日，不作生产，家家户户杀鸡买肉放爆竹，家宴丰盛，全家齐集，祭祀祖先。保亭加茂地区元宵节分为汉人年仔节和黎人年仔节两种。汉人年仔节即元宵节，黎人年仔节要举行两次。黎族以12天为一周期，每天以一种动物命名，顺序依次为：鸡日、狗日、猪日、鼠日、牛日、虫日、兔日、龙日、蛇日、马日、羊日、猴日，周而复始（高泽强、文珍，2008）。按照生肖属日计算，即除夕为牛、马、鸡等日时，离除夕后12天第一次过元宵节，白天，男子上山行猎，女子下河捕鱼，停止农活；夜晚，灯火通宵达旦。第二次年仔与第一次相隔12天，包裹糯米粽，可以从事农业生产，男女不再打猎或捕鱼。

The Lantern Festival is commonly known as Xiao Nian (minor year) by the Li People in Hainan, when the whole family gather and offer sacrifices to their ancestors. The Lantern festival in Jiamao of Baoting area is divided into two kinds: the Han style and the Li style. The former is the Lantern Festival, while the latter will be held twice. The Li People make 12 days a cycle, with each day named after a certain animal following each other in an unending cycle: Chicken Day, Dog Day, Pig Day, Mouse Day, Cattle Day, Worm Day, Rabbit Day, Dragon Day, Snake Day, Horse Day, Goat Day, Monkey Day. According to the Chinese zodiac, if the new year's eve is the date of cattle, horse, chicken and so on, the festival will be held in 12 days, during which men go hunting, women go fishing in the river, and the lights will be on all through the night. The second one will be set 12 days later, and people can be engaged in agricultural production, have glutinous rice dumplings without hunting or fishing.

海南苗族称元宵节为"过年仔"。农历十四晚，家家户户杀鸡宰鹅，置备菜肴；用糯米拌糖包粽子。元宵节当天，家人祭拜祖宗家神后，围坐一起用餐。是日，停止一切农活，晚上灯火通宵达旦。

The Miao People in Hainan name the Lantern Festival "Guo Nian Zai". On the 14th night of the first lunar month, every household will kill chickens and geese and make glutinous rice dumplings mixed with black sugar. In the following day, the family members can have meals after offering sacrifices to their ancestors and Gods. During the Lantern Festival, the farm work is forbidden and lights are on all through the night.

随着国际旅游岛建设，海南有些地方少数民族同胞与汉族同胞一样，也开始吃汤圆、闹元宵。

With the development of international tourist destination, different Peoples have some customs in common during the Lantern Festival.

3.2.3 寒食节与清明节 Hanshi Day (Cold Food Day) and Tomb-Sweeping Day (Qingming Festival)

寒食节，亦称"禁烟节""冷节""百五节"。寒食节，清明节前一或二日，历时两千余年，曾被称为民间第一大祭日。是日，有祭扫、踏青、秋千等风俗，只吃冷食，故称"寒食节"。唐代诗人卢象的《寒食》诗，"之推言避世，山火遂焚身。四海同寒食，千古为一人。深冤何用道，峻迹古无邻。魂魄山河气，风雷御宇神。光烟榆柳火，怨曲龙蛇新。可叹文公霸，平生负此臣。"即描述寒食节"之推绵山焚身"的来历。相传，此俗源于纪念春秋时晋介子推(姓介名推，子为敬称)。当时介子推与晋文公重耳流亡列国，割股肉供文公充饥。文公复国后，子推不求高官厚禄，与母归隐绵山。文公焚山以求之，子推坚决不出山，抱树而死。文公葬其尸于绵山，修祠立庙，并下令于子推焚死之日禁火寒食，是为寒食节。次年寒食节次日，晋文公素服登绵山至子推被焚的那棵柳树下置祭，发现此柳竟复活了。睹物思人，念及子推一生追求政治清明的远大抱负，晋文公封此柳为"清明柳"，将此日定为清明节。后因两节相邻，渐合二为一。

Hanshi Day (or Cold Food Day), one or two days ahead of Tomb-Sweeping Day, bears a history of more than 2000 years. People would not eat hot food on that day due to a legend about Jie Zitui and Duke of Jin State (1033 BC-376 BC). During the Spring and Autumn Period, Duke of Jin State was sent in exile, and he fainted for starvation. Jie Zitui, one of the few loyal followers, cut his flesh and cooked for the Duke. When the Duke became the King, Jie Zitui was eager for neither high official titles nor high salary, hid in the Mountain Mianshan with his mother, and refused to see him. The Duke ordered troops to search the mountain for him, in vain. And the Duke set fire on three sides of the mountain to force him out from the rest side. But he remained in the mountain and died, with their arms holding tightly a scorched willow. The Duke buried him in the mountain with a memorial temple, and ordered no fire or smoke was allowed on that day, which is the reason why it is named Cold Food Day. One day after Cold Food Day of the next year, the Duke climbed the mountain to Jie Zitui's tomb for condolence, only to find the burned willow alive, which was named Qingming Willow and the day was set as Tomb-Sweeping Day (Qingming Festival) by the Duke. Tomb-Sweeping Day and Cold Food Day are so adjacent that they are integrated into one.

海南临高，农历三月三日为寒食节。是日，人们将鸡屎藤叶与使君子叶混合春稞吃，以驱除人体内寄生虫。海南很多地方，即便人们春节不便回家，但清明节无论多远一定会回家祭祖扫墓。清明节在海南的地位，恰如当地百姓描述："清明节跟春节一样，不过春节是活人过的，而清明节是祖先过的。"海南乐东县黄流镇当地的居民祖先大多数来自福建，清明风俗至今保留闽南遗风。一般而言，从农历二月下旬开始，这里的群众就陆陆续续过清明节。按照当地的传说，如果家里有人过世还没满三年，那么他/她在那个地方依然是属于"新贵（新鬼，未过三年的坟墓）"，要提前给他/她过节，给很多祭品，让他/她领取到祭品后可以送给附近的"老贵"，希望"老贵（过世已过三年的坟墓）"可以照顾，也让他/她过得体面一点，故当地百姓也称之为"新清明"。"老贵"的清明节一般以一个镇或一个村一起过，一般都在国家法定清明节之前，不能在之后过，那样怠慢先人，是为不敬。除了买冥钱，当地人有的把红纸剪成同样大小的长方形纸块，这是往先人坟墓上贴的"纸钱"，所以一定剪得"规矩"。祭品除了纸钱、鸡、菜，也要鞭炮、蜡烛、槟榔、香，以及烟和酒。先人安葬的地方是村里固定下来的，称之为"公坟场"，一般清明节才来，所以荒草丛生。首先，把先人的"房子"清理干净，若发现坟墓有损坏，那必须立即找工具修葺。其次，将一张张剪成长方形形状的纸钱贴在坟墓前，有石碑的则贴在石碑上。再次，摆放祭品，好菜要摆放在前面，像鸡、鱼一定摆放在主要位置。然后，点燃香烛，家人在坟墓前跪拜，燃放鞭炮。最后，回到家里把祭拜品摆放在大堂的祭桌上，再点燃香烛，敬酒三次，主人再跪拜一次，再鸣放一挂鞭炮，整个祭拜仪式结束（孙令正，2012）。

The 3rd day of the 3rd lunar month is the Cold Food Festival in Lin'gao of Hainan, when some local people will mix leaves of rangooncreeper (Chinese honeysuckle) and paederia scandens with food to get rid of parasites in human beings. In general, Hainanese would go back home on the Tomb-sweeping Day no matter how far it is, as the Tomb-sweeping Day serves as the Spring Festival for their ancestors. The ancestors of the people in Huangliu of Ledong county mostly came from Fujian province, and customs of their ancestors during the Tomb-Sweeping

Day have retained till now. Generally speaking, the people here will make preparations from the last ten-day period of the second lunar month. According to locals, if someone has been dead for less than three years, he/she belongs to the new ghost. And people should offer more sacrifices ahead of the Tomb-Sweeping Day so that he/she can offer some to the elder ones who have been dead for more than 3 years. People should offer sacrifices to the elder ones before Tomb-sweeping Day to show their respect. A kind of red paper money cut by locals would be pasted on the tombs. In addition to paper money, chicken, vegetables, firecrackers, incenses, candles, areca nuts, cigarettes, and alcohol would also be offered to their ancestors. The graveyard may be full of weeds, so people should clean, repair it if damaged, paste the paper money, place the offerings with chicken and fish in the primary position, burn the candles and incenses, kowtow to their ancestors, set off firecrackers, go back home, place the offerings on the table, burn the candles and incenses again, propose a toast to their ancestors three times, kowtow once again by the owner, and set off firecrackers again. That is considered the complete offering ceremony.

海南有宗族祭祖的习俗，俗称"上祖"。按照规模大小，祭祖分两种：以一户或几户为单位，在家中祖先"神位"前祭"己祖"；以几十户或几百户为单位，同姓氏宗族参加祭"众祖"。海南清明节填土上坟、红漆填写墓碑、野外踏青、放风筝等传统习俗依旧延续，海南清明节有食糟公（即饭团，象征圆满富足，合家团圆；文昌人自称为"饭珍"，万宁人称为"饭贡"）、五花肉蘸盐巴、烤乳猪、薏粑等习俗。烤乳猪历史悠久，早在1400多年前南北朝时期，农学家贾思勰在其著作《齐民要术》中记载："色同琥珀，又类真金，入口则消，壮若凌雪，含浆膏润，特异凡常也。"

Hainanese have the custom of offering sacrifices to their ancestors with all the members of the same clan, which could be divided into two kinds in terms of the number of participants: a certain family ancestor' sacrifices would be offered by a certain family or a few households as a unit at home, while those of the clan progenitor's would be offered by dozens of or hundreds of families with the same surname. Hainanese also have the custom of adding new soil to the tomb, painting the inscriptions of the tombstone in red, eating rice balls and roast piglings and so on.

海南黎族通常在新坟祭祀3年后不再扫墓，称为"封山"。随着通婚、经济、文化交流日益频繁，每逢清明有些黎族在家祭祀祖先神灵后，也开始携酒、饭、菜祭祀祖坟，除草填土，用红白纸压坟顶。

In general, the Li People in Hainan would not offer sacrifices to the dead within 3 years after burial, which is called "closing the mountain" by locals. With the development of economy, cultural exchanges, and frequent contact with other ethnic groups, some people also offer sacrifices to their ancestor, clear the weeds, and put a piece of red or white paper on the top of the tomb, as other Peoples do during the Tomb-Sweeping Day.

3.2.4　端午节 Dragon Boat Festival

农历五月初五端午节，俗称端阳节，已被列入世界非物质文化遗产名录，是纪念伟大的爱国诗人——屈原的节日。海南东方市等地称其为"五月节"。海南端午节约始于宋代，有"洗龙水"、包粽子、赛龙舟等传统习俗。

The 5th day of the 5th lunar month is the Dragon Boat Festival in commemoration of the patriotic poet named Qu Yuan who committed suicide as a form of protest against corruption in 278 BC, which has been listed in the world intangible cultural heritage. People in Dongfang of Hainan province call it May Festival. The Dragon Boat Festival in Hainan dates back to the Song Dynasty (960 AD-1279 AD), with the traditions of Xi Long Shui (swimming in the sea or bathing in the water), making and eating Zongzi (pyramid-shaped dumplings made of glutinous rice wrapped in bamboo or reed leaves), and dragon boat race, etc.

海南"洗龙水"一般在中午12点左右,是最具地方特色的端午节习俗。一般认为,端午节这一天用海水、河水、井水甚至是自来水洗澡,就算"洗龙水"。《崖州志》记载,五月端午"又采芦花、香草、菖艾,浸水供神,浴体,或折艾悬门,以避疫"。海南传统的"洗龙水"程序较为复杂:端午节前一天晚上,一定准备好富含寓意的5种花草:槟榔花、海棠花、野菠萝花、艾草、一种芦苇的芯。端午节大清早到水井先将5种花草用龙水洗净,然后用龙水泡着端回家放在祖屋门口。中午时分祭祖,龙水让祖先们先行享用洗漱。傍晚时分,人们再用泡了一天花草的芳香扑鼻的龙水来沐浴。如今,靠近海边的一般选择去海里"洗龙水"。"洗龙水"寄托了海南人们祈求健康平安的心愿,希望可以洗去身上的病魔和晦气,健健康康、平平安安。至于"洗龙水"的起源,有人认为,海南四面环海,百姓认为屈原投江后变成了龙神,在端午节这一天会出来活动,这天所有的水也就变成"龙水"。人们认为"洗龙水"可以得到龙神的保护,身体健康不长热疮热痱,一年健健康康、平平安安。也有人认为,端午节这一天,天上的龙会下到凡间,从地上所有的水中经过,龙经过后,水沾染了龙气也就成为"龙水",用来洗最直接的效果就是不长痱子,不得皮肤病。端午节"洗龙水"后,有些地方老人会掏出一包红黄的粉末,和水,涂在孩子的眉心、肚脐、手掌和脚掌,即"点红泥"(雄黄、二硫化二砷)习俗。

Xi Long Shui (swimming in the sea or bathing in the holy water) is generally at 12:00 or so. Generally speaking, bathing in the sea, river or at home on this day would be considered bathing in holy water. The traditional custom of *Xi Long Shui* is more complex. On the day before the Dragon Boat Festival, areca flowers, malus spectabilis, wild pineapple, mugwort, and core of reed would be prepared in advance. Early in the morning of the Dragon Boat Festival, the flowers and grass should be washed, immersed in the holy water, and taken back home. At noon, their ancestors should bathe in the holy water first after being offered sacrifices. In the evening, people bathe in the holy water. Nowadays, the people near the coast would flock to bathe in the sea. The custom of *Xi Long Shui* indicates people in Hainan pray for health and peace. As for its origin, some people think that Hainan is surrounded by the sea, and people think that Qu Yuan has become a dragon after passing away. The dragon will be in the water all day on the fifth day of the fifth lunar month, and all the water becomes holy, which can keep people healthy. Having had Xi Long Shui, some Hainanese would dab some reddish yellow powder mixed with water on one's forehead, naval, hand and foot.

海南儋州百姓会在门楣上插艾叶、菖蒲,门槛上撒雄黄酒,儋州一带的客家人,称端午节这一天的洗浴为"洗勒草"。除了"洗龙水",海南文昌部分地区,端午节早上父母会煮鸡蛋,连壳在小孩肚脐周围滚几圈,等孩子醒后再把鸡蛋吃掉,据说这样可防止孩子闹肚子。

People in Danzhou would place mugwort and calamus on the lintel of the door, and sprinkle realgar wine over the threshold. In addition to *Xi Long Shui*, some parents in

Wenchang will boil some eggs in the morning of the Dragon Boat Festival, and roll a few laps around the navels of their children who will eat the eggs after waking up, which is said to prevent children from diarrhoea.

粽子古称"角黍",传说是为祭祀屈原而发明的,已有 2000 余年悠久历史,文化积淀厚重。海南粽子种类繁多,有正三角、正四角、长方形、方形等形状,有裹蒸粽、咸肉粽、八宝粽等,以定安黑猪肉粽、儋州洛基粽子、澄迈瑞溪粽子最为驰名。海南定安粽子已注册为中国地理标志证明商标,"定安粽子"是产于定安的糯米、黑猪肉、红泥咸鸭蛋黄、食用熟花生油和食用调料,用柊叶作为包裹物,经包馅、成形、煮制等工艺加工而成,主要在端午节食用,具有口感甘、香、糯、韧,可谓香浓淡兼备,味荤素俱佳。

Zongzi is said to have been invented in honor of the great poet and statesman Qu Yuan (340 BC-278 BC) with a history of more than 2000 years. There are various kinds in the shape of triangle, square, rectangle, etc. with different stuffing, with those in Ding'an, Danzhou, and Chengmai most famous. Ding'an Zongzi, which is rewarded Chinese geographical indications trademark, is made up of Ding'an glutinous rice, black pig pork, yolk of the salted duck's egg, peanut oil, etc., popular with both the young and the old.

海南端午节赛龙舟锣鼓喧天,看得人血脉贲张。侨乡万宁"龙舟小镇"和乐镇小海周边,澄迈县金江镇南渡江沿岸,琼海博鳌三江入海口的龙舟赛等……船头发号,船尾擂鼓,两排男子齐心齐力划桨击水,一时间,岸上水里锣鼓声、呐喊声、号子声、助威声,声声入耳,蔚为壮观。

Dragon Boat Race during the Dragon Boat Festival is stirring, especially in Hele town of Wanning, Jinjiang town of Chengmai County, estuary near Jade Belt Beach in Bo'ao of Qionghai, etc. Two rows of racers in a dragon boat make a concerted campaign towards the destination hurriedly with the sound of drums, cheers, and screams, etc. What a spectacular festival it is!

黎族过端午节,家家包粽子,有三色粽和椰叶粽。部分黎族、苗族群众还举行一些形式活泼的娱乐活动。

The Li People would celebrate the Dragon Boat Festival with tricolored Zongzi and those wrapped in coconut leaves. In addition, some of the Li and Miao People also have some other activities during the festival.

3.2.5 乞巧节 Double-Seventh Day (Qi Qiao Festival)

农历七月初七是乞巧节,又名七夕节、七巧节或七姐诞,源于汉代。东晋葛洪《西京杂记》有"汉彩女常以七月七日,穿七孔针于开襟楼"的记载。魏晋南北朝时,乞巧习俗已极为普遍。唐代祖咏作诗《七夕》:"闺女求天女,更阑意未阑。玉庭开粉席,罗袖捧金盘。向月穿针易,临风整线难。不知谁得巧,明旦试相看。"完整地叙述了七夕乞巧风俗中祭拜织女、对月穿针、养喜蛛比结网疏密、网形周正等习俗。显然,乞巧节属于闺中待嫁女儿的节日,她们在自家院子里,乞求心灵手巧,祈望幸福姻缘。2006 年 5 月,国务院将乞巧节列入首批国家级非物质文化遗产名录。因受外来文化影响,部分商家和媒体将乞巧节视为"中国情人节"。

The 7th day of the 7th lunar month is Double-Seventh Day, also known as Qi Qiao Festival or Qi Xi Festival, which dates back to the Han Dynasty (206 BC-AD 220). The custom of pleading for needlework skills was quite popular in Wei (220-265), Jin (265-420), and the Southern and Northern Dynasties (420-589). Girls during the Double-Seventh Day used to have customs of offering sacrifices to the Weaver Girl, threading through a special needle with seven holes, and keeping a spider to see whose spider has woven the thickest or the best-looking web, etc., which indicates the festival is sent for would-be-married girls who are longing for perfect needlework and happy marriage. In May of 2006, the Double-Seventh Day was listed in national intangible cultural heritage by the State Council. Due to the influence of foreign cultures, it is also regarded as the Chinese Valentine's Day by some people, businessmen and media .

是日，会在保亭七仙广场主会场及其他分会场举办中国海南七仙温泉嬉水节，游客可以欣赏"取圣水""敬七仙""祈愿"等精彩环节，还可以参与嬉水狂欢，闹隆闺、攀藤摘花、拉乌龟、爬槟榔、黎族竹木器乐表演、黎锦织绣展示、劈椰子等欢快喜庆的黎族民俗互动项目。海南文昌有"七月初七夜，牛郎织女相嫁娶"的民谣。

On the 7th day of the 7th lunar month, the Qixian (7th Fairy) Spring Water Splashing Festival will be held in Baoting. And tourists can enjoy the performance or participate in water splashing, girl-courting game around the Li People's traditional boat-shaped house (commonly known as *Fang Liao*), La Wu Gui (pulling the turtle, tug-of-war in the Li People's style), climbing the areca trees, playing bamboo musical instrument in the Li People's style, weaving Li brocade, etc. And there is a folk song of "the Cowherd marries the Weaver Girl on the seventh night of the seventh lunar month" in Wenchang city.

3.2.6 中秋节 Mid-Autumn Festival

因其恰值三秋之半，故名中秋节，又名仲秋节、月夕、八月节、追月节、玩月节、拜月节、团圆节等。中秋节，始于唐初，盛行于宋朝，至明清时，已成为与春节齐名的中国主要传统节日之一。2006年5月，中秋节被国务院列入首批国家级非物质文化遗产名录。

The Mid-Autumn Festival, which started in the early Tang Dynasty (618-907), became as important as the Spring Festival in the Ming and Qing Dynasties (1368-1912). It was listed in national intangible cultural heritage by the State Council in the May of 2006.

在海南过中秋，除了赏月、吃月饼以外，尤以"拜月娘、会嫦娥"的风俗最为盛行。中秋之夜，端起装满水的盆子，透过水面光影斑驳的月痕，等待折射出"嫦娥"，以拜会"月娘"。海南的渔民们会在中秋月圆之夜，点燃香烛，拜月祭神，祈求出入平安。东方市，中秋有吟诵赏月名篇的习俗。澄迈县是农业大县，中秋节当地人吃桂花，祈求健康。海南东部的几个市县是海南省拥有海外华侨和现有归侨最多的地区，"放天灯"最具有侨乡特色。海南东部许多村落的天灯，与内地孔明灯不同，中秋"放天灯"是某一村落或某一宗族迎月、贺月的重要仪式。据说，天灯是用竹篾和纸事先糊出一个水桶般大小的、外形酷似灯笼的一个小型天灯，然后再将这些天灯用绳子垂直连接成一条"火龙"，将其挂于高处。中秋之夜，月上枝头，天灯升起，村庄里的人们走出家门观赏天灯。

In addition to traditional celebrations during the Mid-Autumn Festival in Hainan, some customs are even more attractive. Some fishermen in Hainan would offer sacrifices to a goddess named Chang E for safety in ship or on land. The people in Dongfang have the custom of chanting famous moon-related poems or articles, while people in Chengmai county are used to eating osmanthus flowers in the hope of good health. Some cities and counties with more returned overseas in the eastern part of Hainan province prefer to launch Tian Deng (hang up a string of lanterns high), which serves as an important ceremony for a certain village or patriarchal clan to welcome the Mid-Autumn Festival. Tian Deng is a string of bucket-sized lanterns which are said to be made of bamboo and paper, and should be hang high vertically. During the night of the Mid-Autumn Festival, the people in the village go out to enjoy a bright full moon and strings of lanterns hung high in the yard or on the street.

黎族称中秋节为"八月会"或"调声节"。中秋佳节，以村寨或乡镇为单位举办歌舞聚会，由"调声头"（即领队）率领参加，互赠月饼、香糕、甜粑、彩扇、织锦等礼物。是夜，青年男女聚集在篝火旁，赏月、吃月饼、烤食野味、饮酒唱歌，未婚青年则借此良机挑选佳偶、互赠信物。正如一首民歌所言："儋州自古称歌海，山歌催得百花开；家家都有民歌手，山山水水是歌台"。海南儋州中秋节，中和镇北门江畔成千上万人参加唱山歌、"调声"对歌赛，一般为下午三点到六点，以"唱倒"对方为止；到了晚上，男女歌手一起对唱情歌，抒发男女之间的永恒爱情，美丽的服装和悠扬的歌声充斥着节日的儋州，场面热闹非凡（纪俊超，2009）。

The Li People called the Mid-Autumn Festival the August Get-together or Diao Sheng Festival (singing songs in antiphonal style in local dialect). On the day of the Mid-Autumn Festival, the people organize dance-and-song party in terms of villages or towns, during which moon cakes, fragrant cakes, color fans, brocades and other gifts will be given to each other. When the night falls, young men and women gather around the campfire, enjoy the bright full moon, eat moon cakes, barbecue, drink wine or juice, and sing songs. And they take this opportunity to choose Mr./Ms. Right, giving each other something pledging their love. Tens of thousands of people in Zhonghe Town of Danzhou during the Mid-Autumn Festival will hold a grand Diao Sheng Folk Song Contest on the bank of Beimen River, which lasts from 3:00 p.m. to 6:00 p.m to defeat the counterpart. In the evening, male and female singers sing love songs in antiphonal style to express their eternal love between a man and a woman. The Mid-Autumn Festival in Danzhou is full of beautiful costumes and melodious songs.

逗月，是临高中秋特有的风俗。祭祖结束，长辈刚把月饼摆上席，孙子、外孙们就争着要香去逗月。是夜，男孩会点起香插在月饼上，唱着儿歌比谁的饼大，谁的饼香，跑到祠堂前去请"月老"，赶"天狗"。女孩将月饼放在一边，玩起跳绳，比谁的绳跳得高。人们还会相邀亲朋好友去临高角赏月。

The tradition of tantalizing the moon during the Mid-Autumn Festival is typical of Lingao in Hainan province. After offering sacrifices to their ancestors, boys are eager for incense to tease the moon the moment the elder put moon cakes on the table. Boys would burn the incense and insert them in the moon cake, sing songs to check whose cake is bigger and whose is more fragrant. And they run to the ancestral hall to invite the matchmaker and drive away the beast like a raccoon dog in legend. Girls may put the cakes aside, competing in rope skipping. In addition, some people may invite their friends and family members to enjoy the bright full moon at the Cape of Lin'gao.

3.2.7 重阳节 Double Ninth Festival

重阳节，又称登高节、重九节、九月九、茱萸节、菊花节等，与除夕、清明节、中元节构成中国传统四大祭祖节日。《易经》中把"六"定为阴数,把"九"定为阳数,九月九日,两九相重,故曰重阳。重阳节在战国时期形成,魏晋气氛日渐浓郁,唐代正式定为民间节日,沿袭至今,有出游、登高、赏菊、遍插茱萸、吃"重阳糕"、饮菊花酒等习俗。2006年5月,重阳节被国务院列入首批国家级非物质文化遗产名录。海南过重阳节有登高望远、插茱萸、送"重阳糕"、"赶山猫"的习俗。

The Double Ninth Festival, the Lunar New Year's Eve, the Tomb-Sweeping Festival, and Zhong Yuan Festival serve as the four festivals to offer sacrifices to one's ancestors in China. *The Book of Changes* makes the number six Yin and nine Yang. The ninth day of the ninth lunar month contains two ninths, so it is named the Double Ninth Festival. The Double Ninth Festival, which came into being in the Warring States period (475 BC-221 BC), was officially set as a folk festival in the Tang Dynasty (618-907). People have the customs of traveling, climbing up to enjoy a distant view, enjoying chrysanthemum, wearing cornels, eating Chongyang rice cakes, drinking chrysanthemum wine, etc. It was listed in national intangible cultural heritage by the State Council in the May of 2006. People in Hainan have the customs of climbing up to enjoy a distant view, wearing cornels, presenting Chongyan Cake, and driving away the wild cat, etc.

登高
Climb up to Enjoy a Distant View

在《重阳节登铜鼓岭歌》的土歌中,民间语言描述把自然景观与游人的情感紧密结合。据史载,明代礼部尚书、定安人王弘诲在游览铜鼓岭后,倡议海南文人、学子每逢"九九重阳"之际,在此吟诗作画,缅怀先人。海南文昌,中秋佳节天不亮就有些人赶到文昌的铜鼓岭山脚下一同爬山,趁日出之前登临山顶,观日出,听涛声,为美好的生活祈福迎祥。

The folk song named *Climbing the Tongguling Ridge during the Double Ninth Festival* combines the description of the natural landscape and the emotion of visitors. It is recorded that Minister of Rites named Wang Honghui (1541-1617) in the Ming Dynasty (1368-1644) suggested scholars and students in Hainan take the initiative in reciting or composing poetry and doing brush-work, cherishing the memory of the ancestors after having a sightseeing in Tongguling Ridge. Many people in Wenchang would climb the Tongguling Ridge in the early morning and reach the top before sunrise to enjoy the view of the sunrise, listen to the sound of waves, and pray for a better life during the Double Ninth Festival.

送"重阳糕"
Present Chongyan Cake to the Elder

因为"高"和"糕"同音,海南民间有登高吃糕的意思,有步步升高的吉祥意味。在海南万宁、琼海一带,乡邻之间,给年纪较大的长者赠送"重阳糕",表达尊老敬老的习俗,沿袭至今。

The Character "高" (gāo, high) is pronounced the same as "糕" (gāo, cake) in Chinese, so many people in Hainan have the customs of climbing up and eating cakes with the connotation of being better step by step. People in Wanning and Qionghai nowadays have followed the customs of presenting Chongyan Cake to the elder between neighbors or relatives to show their respect.

"赶山猫"
Drive away the Wild Cat

临高、儋州等地，重阳节当天，人们早起，点燃火把，大家齐声高喊"赶山猫哎，赶山猫嘞……"，唱着一些歌曲，将视为象征邪恶的、专门残杀老人的"山猫"赶走，祈祷老人长寿百岁，福寿安康。

People in Lingao and Danzhou may get up early, light torches, shout "catch the wild cat, drive away the wild cat" in chorus, and sing songs to drive away the evil wild cat and pray for longevity and health for the elder.

洗艾叶水
Bathe with Mugwort

在琼海、文昌、万宁等地，重阳节还有用艾叶水洗头、沐浴的习俗。

People in Qionghai, Wenchang, and Wanning, etc., also have the customs of bathing and washing their hair with mugwort.

3.2.8 冬至 Winter Solstice

冬至，是中国农历中一个重要的节气，也是中华民族的一个传统节日，俗称"冬节""长至节""亚岁"等。北方有冬至吃水饺的风俗，南方有吃汤圆（甜丸）、糯糕、麻糍等习俗。

Winter Solstice, which serves as one of the 24 divisions of the solar year in traditional Chinese lunar calendar, is a traditional festival for Chinese. People in the northern part of China have the custom of eating dumplings, while those in the south eat Tangyuan (dumplings made of glutinous rice flour served in soup), glutinous rice cake, and fried glutinous rice puddings during winter solstice.

海南冬至又被成为"冬节""小清明"，有深厚的文化底蕴，彰显了海南独特的热带风情。除了吃汤圆，海南冬至更是一个扫墓的日子。冬至这天，很多地方店铺关门落锁回家过冬至、吃汤圆，清明节未扫墓的人家上坟祭祖，一座座坟山香烟缭绕，一处处墓地都花团锦簇。海口冬至祭祖供品一般有汤圆（甜丸）、糕点。临高一般有拜祭祖坟、新坟填土扫墓、糯米煮饭或做粿（糕点）等习俗。万宁地区有"饲牛小子节"，不犁田，让耕牛休息。一些百姓用蒌叶装米做粿（糕点），配以咸蛋食之。海南有些苗族也有冬至"扫墓"的习俗。海南部分黎族地区冬至当天会将米粉、毛薯、红糖、水拌匀蒸熟食用，俗称"吃锞节"。

The Winter Solstice in Hainan is also a day for tomb-sweeping in addition to eating Tangyuan (dumplings made of glutinous rice served in soup). Those who don't respect for their ancestor's tomb and offers sacrifices during the Tomb-Sweeping Day can make it up. Sacrificial offerings should include Tangyuan and cakes in Haikou during the Winter Solstice. Some people in Lin'gao have the same customs as they do during the Tomb-Sweeping Day. The Wanning Cattle's Day occurs on the same day, during which the cattle can not be asked to do anything but rest. Some people used to make rice cakes wrapped in betel, and eat them with salted eggs. Some of the Miao People in Hainan have the custom of tomb-sweeping during the Winter Solstice, while some of the Li People used to steam and blend rice noodles, Hainan winged yam, brown sugar, and water together for a better flavor, commonly known as the Ingot-Shaped Food Festival.

3.3 农林渔猎等生产性节日民俗
Customs and Production Holidays or Festivals for Farming, Fishing, Hunting, etc.

3.3.1 禾仙节 He Xian (the God of Rice) Festival

在琼海等地,农历四月早稻或九月晚稻即将成熟的季节,农户会到自家田地挑选少量早熟稻谷收割回来,舂米做饭,盛若干碗置于米缸,翌日着装整齐,取而食之,称之为"祭禾仙",祈求"禾仙"保佑五谷丰登。随着人们生活水平、文化水平的提高,琼海等地"禾仙节"逐渐淡出人们视野。

In the early fourth lunar month or the late ninth month, some peasants in Qionghai used to pick some mature rice in their rice paddles. After husking the rice, they steam, put some in the bowls, place in a pot, and eat them the next day while dressed neatly, which is called offering sacrifices to the God of Rice, praying for blessing to have a better harvest. With the development of society, the festival gradually fades out.

3.3.2 苗族禾斋节 He Zhai (the God of Rice) Festival in the Miao People

苗族禾斋节在农历六月六日举行。是日,苗族杀鸡买肉,糯米包粽,并带到田间祭祀"禾斋公"。祭祀完毕,家人才可以食用粽子,但不分给外人。如今,苗族基本不过此节。

He Zhai Festival is held on the 6th day of the 6th lunar month, when people will bring sacrifices, such as chicken, meat, and Zongzi to the field to offer to the God of Rice. Having completed the ritual, only the family members can eat Zongzi. Nowadays, few people celebrate the holiday.

3.3.3 苗族禾仔斋 He Zai Zhai (the God of Rice) Festival among the Miao People

禾仔斋是苗族古老而隆重的节日,于农历六月七日举行。节日前,民主选举斋主、道公。该节日的目的为召回"禾神",确保五谷丰登。如今,苗族基本不过此节。

He Zai Zhai, a festival by the Li People held on the 7th day of the 6th lunar month, is to recall the God of Rice to ensure a bumper harvest. Nowadays, fewer people celebrate the holiday.

3.3.4 黎族禾节 Rice Festival among the Li People

黎族认为稻米有灵魂,分为"稻公""稻母",丰收靠稻魂。收割前,必须先收回稻公、稻母,才能确保来年庄稼丰收。在合亩制地区,每年晚稻秋收后的"龙日"举行招"禾魂"的仪式,黎语称"外林"(直译为"洗镰刀")。亩头在家摆酒席,人们载歌载舞,通宵达旦敲锣打鼓,欢跳招魂舞蹈,祝愿来年大丰收。如今,黎族基本不过此节,但影响尚存。

The Li People used to think the rice has soul, who was in charge of the bumper harvest. The male and female rice must be brought back before the harvest to make sure a bumper harvest. In the areas of He Mu System (paternal families of blood relationship with the land, cattle, and others shared by all the members), the rite of calling back the spirit of the rice used to be held on the Dragon Day after harvesting the late rice. The leader used to give a feast, and the people sung songs, beat drums and gongs, danced all through the night to pray for a bumper harvest in the coming year. Nowadays, few people celebrate the holiday, although its influence still exists.

3.3.5 黎族牛节 Cattle's Day in the Li People

在生产条件相对落后的年代，牛能犁地耙田、运输，在人们生产生活中起着举足轻重的作用，人们由此产生爱牛、惜牛、敬牛传统。

Cattle, used to play a prominent role in ploughing the land and transporting produce, makes the people love, cherish and respect them.

黎族认为牛是财富和吉祥的象征，有些村中设立牛神庙，家中设"牛魂宝盆"，用彩色的小石头（当地人称之为宝石）代表牛，盆里石头的多少就代表牛的多少。每年秋耕后七月或十月的牛日，"亩头"主持举行祭牛神、招牛魂仪式；"亩头"夫妇要用盆洗宝石（黎族人视宝石是牛魂的象征和发展牛群的福气），给牛喝一种"牛魂石"浸过的米酒补身；人们通宵达旦敲锣打鼓，欢跳招牛魂舞蹈。民间牛日禁止杀牛。

The Li People think cattle symbolize great fortune and good luck, for which some people set up Cattle Temples in their villages and Treasure Bowls at home, with the color stones (commonly named gems by locals) representing their cattle. Mu Tou (the leader, the man in charge of the He Mu System in the Li People) will preside over a rite of offering sacrifices to the God of Cattle and calling back his spirit on the Cattle Day of the seventh and tenth lunar month after ploughing. Mu Tou (the leader, the man in charge of the He Mu System in the Li People) and his wife will wash the gems and serve the cattle with rice wine. People beat drums and gongs, and dance all through the night to call back the spirit of cattle. It is prohibited to slaughter the cattle on Cattle Day according to the Li People's calendar.

3.3.6 吃新节 New Rice-Eating Festival

海南黎族、苗族均有过"吃新节"的习俗。吃新节，是中国南方少数民族地区为了庆贺丰收并祈福来年丰收而举行的传统农事节日。但黎族吃新节忌外人参加，认为外人吃了会歉收。农历七月十三日是海南苗族吃新节。人们参加斗牛、赛马、射箭、跳芦笙舞、"游方"（青年男女谈情说爱）、对歌等活动。

Both the Li and the Miao People have tradition of celebrating the New Rice-Eating Festival, which is held by the minorities in the southern part of China to celebrate the harvest and pray for a more bumper harvest in the coming year. Only the Li People are allowed to participate in their New Rice-Eating Festival, or they would have a poor harvest if people from other nationalities share new rice with them as they hold. The 13th day of the 7th lunar month witnesses the New Rice-Eating Festival of the Miao People in Hainan. During the holiday, they hold many activities, such as bullfighting, horse racing, archery, Lusheng (a reed-pipe wind instrument used by the Miao, Yao and Dong nationalities) dance, You Fang (social gathering of boys and girls of the Miao People during the festivals or the slack season, where they sing songs, exchange gifts, and make advances to each other), and singing in antiphonal style, etc.

3.3.7 苗族新禾节 New Rice Festival in the Miao People

海南苗族有举办"新禾节"的习俗。该节日没有固定日期，一般在农历八月山栏稻穗扬花时节选择黄道吉日，买香烛、杀鸡、采摘 3~5 片稻叶放在饭里蒸，祈求禾神保佑，预祝稻谷丰收。进食时，这些饭仅供家人使用，外人忌食。

The Miao People in Hainan used to have the tradition of celebrating the New Rice Festival. There's no fixed date, generally in the 8th lunar month when Shanlan rice is flowering. Having set an auspicious date, people used to buy incense, candles, chickens, cook rice with 3 to 5 pieces of rice leaves, pray for the blessing from the God of Rice, and wish themselves a bumper harvest. All those cooked can only be eaten by family members.

3.3.8 供新节 Gong Xin Festival (Harvest Festival)

农历九月七日为汉族地区供新节，亦称为收获节。此时，晚稻初熟，农民提前几日到田里捻几穗成熟稻谷。除留下一穗备用，其余晒干舂成米，于供新日煮成干饭，将备用的稻穗、煮熟的猪肉一起放于祖先灵位前祭祀，以谢恩赐，并祈求祖先保佑风调雨顺，稻谷满仓。祭祀完毕，家人食用祭品。随着农业技术进步、生产力水平提高，此俗已少见。

The 7th day of the 9th lunar month is named Gong Xin Festival, also known as Harvest Festival. As the rice grows mature, the peasants pick ears of rice, only one of which would be kept in stock, with the rest cooked after being husked. And they would place the remaining ear of rice and cooked pork in front of their ancestors' memorial tablet to thank them, and hope they can be blessed with a bumper harvest. Having completed the rite, the family members share the offerings. With the development of agricultural technology, the custom is rare to be seen.

3.3.9 黎族山栏节 Shan Lan Festival in the Li People

"山栏节"是东方市江边乡一年一度的黎族传统节日，具有浓厚的民族传统色彩。山栏节源于一个古老的传说：一位老人有 8 个儿子分居 8 个峒，其中，老八的山稻长势最好，收获最多。老人经过了解悟出道理：要想收获更多，就要像鸡那样早起忙碌。于是老人在十一月第一个"鸡日"杀猪，召集 8 个儿子一起饮酒唱歌，并将悟出的道理分享给 8 个儿子。儿子们听从教诲，果然山栏丰收。后人为了纪念先祖的教诲、感谢鸡对黎族百姓的启示、预祝风调雨顺，便把农历十一月的第一个"鸡日"定为"山栏节"。"山栏节"前夕，黎族同胞集体狩猎，用盐腌渍兽肉，以备节日期间享用。是日清晨，人们杀猪宰牛，忌杀鸡，制作糯米糍粑；太阳升起，家家户户摆上肉、酒、糍粑等供品，请祭师诵经祭祖，鸣放粉枪，祈求先祖保佑家人安康、五谷丰登。至第二个"鸡日"举行"栈忾"（美孚方言，"栈"指停止鸡鸣，"忾"指鸡），"山栏节"仪式结束。是日，忌杀生，用糍粑和粽子喂鸡，希望大家像鸡一样勤劳。黎族"山栏节"体现了对鸡的图腾崇拜，大概与黎族最初的母系氏族社会存在某种关系。

Shan Lan Festival is an annual tradition for the Li People in Dongfang city. The festival originates from an ancient legend. An old man had 8 sons living in 8 separate caves, with the 8th son's rice growing best. The old man realized that people could gain more if they could get up and start working as early as chickens. The old man, therefore, slaughtered a pig on the Chicken Day of the eleventh lunar month, gathered his sons drinking and singing, and shared what he realized with his sons. They took the advice, and obtained a bumper harvest. This is why Shan Lan Festival is set on the Chicken Day of the 11th lunar month. In general, on the eve of Shanlan Festival, the Li People hunt together and put salt on or in the meat to prepare for the festival.

When the sun rises in the morning, the family members offer sacrifices, such as the meat, wine, glutinous rice cakes, etc., to their ancestors in hope of good health and bumper harvest. The festival comes to an end on the next Chicken Day, when the chickens are fed glutinous rice cakes and Zongzi. People are expected to be as industrious as chickens. The Shan Lan Festival reflects the Li People's totem worship, which probably is related to their original matriarchal society.

随着国际旅游岛建设，黎族"山栏节"形式和内容已发生一些改变。最近几年"山栏节"期间，当地艺术团和黎族民间艺人表演歌舞、器乐、黎族传统体育竞技等丰富多彩的节目，现场还举行手工织锦、纺线和对歌比赛以及黎族美食与传统用品展。当地黎族同胞们连续狂欢 3~5 天，并走家串户，访亲会友，共庆丰收，互送祝福。

With the development of Hainan International Tourist Destination, some changes have taken place in Shan Lan Festival. In the past few years, local art troupe and the folk artists dance, sing pop songs, play traditional musical instrument, hold the Li People's traditional sports, weave Li brocade by hand, spin by hand, take part in folk songs contest in antiphonal style, enjoy the Li People's food, and show around traditional necessities exhibition. The festival lasts for 3 to 5 days, when the Li People can visit relatives and friends, celebrate the harvest, and sent their best wishes to each other.

3.4 民间信仰与祭祀类节日民俗
Customs during Holidays or Festivals for Religions and Beliefs

3.4.1 苗族花山节 Hua Shan Festival in the Miao People

海南苗族同全国各地的苗族一样过自己的传统节日，其中的"花山节"最为隆重、颇具特色。苗族花山节的起源，已无从考究，但其依旧保持围着高树吹芦笙、载歌载舞的习俗。据史籍记载，花山节已有 2000 多年的历史，历代沿袭，逐渐演变成苗家人缅怀祖先、欢聚一堂、祈求丰年的节日。海南苗族主要分布在海南中、东、南部，花山节日期不定。农历正月初二至初九，海南苗族群众在空旷、洁净、布置得十分庄重的山场设立"花山场"，举行隆重的"采花山"（亦称"踩花山"）。场内竖起几十米高的两根花杆，一根蓝色、一根红色，花山顶端装饰着绚丽的花束彩旗，吸引着远近数十里的群众。

The Miao People in Hainan have their own traditional festival, known as Hua Shan Festival. The origin is still not known, but some typical customs are still maintained. According to historical records, Hua Shan Festival has been gradually evolving into a combination of traditions to cherish the memory of their ancestors, hold a joyous gathering and pray for a bumper harvest, with a history of more than 2000 years. Most Miao People live in the central, eastern, and southern parts of Hainan, for which the date to hold the festival varies from one place to another. From the second to the ninth day of the first lunar month, Hua Shan Square will be set on the spacious clean land to hold a grand event named Cai Hua Shan (climbing up the pole). In the center are two erected poles topped with colorful flags to attract people from near and far.

苗家人，无论男女老幼，欢天喜地聚集在空气清新的广场上，参加或观看各种饶有兴趣的活动，如爬花杆、斗牛、跳芦笙舞、"踢脚"等，还可以逛逛贸易集市，到处是欢歌笑语，令人流连忘返。

The Miao People, young and old, will gather in the square to enjoy a variety of interesting activities, such as climbing up the pole, bullfighting, Lusheng dance, the game of kicking your opponent, and taking a stroll in the fair trade, which may be unwilling for you to tear away yourself from it.

3.4.2 苗族吃斋节 Vegetarian Festival in the Miao People

农历正月初三开始、持续半月的苗族吃斋节期间，乡村苗族群众男女老少上山祭拜神灵，不吃猪肉。

The period from the 3rd to the 18th day of the first lunar month is Vegetarian Festival, during which the Miao People used to climb the mountain to offer sacrifices to the deities. However, pork is forbidden during the holiday.

3.4.3 海神娘娘 Goddess of the Sea

相传海神娘娘是龙王的女儿，在狂怒的大海救下石福、石秀渔家父子，并以莲花灯指引他们来到海南宝岛，父子便定居于此，过着富裕的生活。每年正月十三是海神娘娘的生日，夜幕降临，全家人将亲手制作的渔船、渔灯放归大海，燃放鞭炮，祭拜海神，祈求家人平安归来，鱼虾满仓。

As the legend goes, Goddess of the sea is the daughter of the Dragon King, who saved two fishermen in the furious sea: the father Shi Fu and the son Shi Xiu. She led the way to the Hainan Island by lotus lamp, and they settled on the island and lived a rich life. The 13th day of the 1st lunar month is her birthday, when people go to the beach to offer sacrifices to her. They release the handmade boats and lamps, set off firecrackers, and pray for health, safety and harvest when the night falls.

3.4.4 行符日 Xing Fu Day

农历正月初七到三十日，海口很多村（坊）陆续抬神公游村"行符"祈福、辟邪。海口的"行符"大概始于汉孝文帝期间，最早可能始于白沙村一带的先民，即如今的新安、福安、吉安、过港、园尾、白沙坊、板桥、山旺等村庄。

From the 7th to the 30th day of the 1st lunar month, many villagers in Haikou will carry the statues of historical or beloved figures parading through the village to ward off evil spirits and pray for good luck. The tradition named Xing Fu probably began during the Emperor XiaoWen (202 BC-157 BC) in Western Han Dynasty (202 BC-8 AD), while the custom in Hainan may originate from the ancestors near the Baisha Village, such as Xin'an village, Fu'an village, Ji'an village, Guogang village, Yuanwei village, Baishafang village, Banqiao village, and Shanwang village.

通常"行符"的前一天，庙里的义工会向坊间各家各户发送"灯鸟"（用纸包住如圆铜钱大的旧瓦片，经浸泡松香或腊或桐油制作而成），傍晚时分放在门的两旁，由庙里的义工到各家各户点燃，或由各户人家到庙里接火点燃。"灯鸟"与"丁鸟" 谐音，意为添丁添福，多子多孙，人丁旺盛之寓意。

One day before Xing Fu, the volunteers will send "Deng Niao" (ancient coin-sized tiles wrapped in paper, and soaked in resin, wax or oil) to every family, put on both sides of the door as the night approaches, light them or light by family members themselves with the fire taken from the temple. Chinese phrase "Deng Niao" is homophonic with "Ding Niao" in local dialect, which means more babies and happiness.

正月十九日,是海口得胜沙地区的行符日。上午,得胜沙街冼夫人纪念馆的公婆神像装扮一新;午时过后,人们抬出神像,挨家挨户地去祈福。大多村民都在门口备好香案,香炉压住神符挂在案前。旧时,案台上必摆好五供,即香烛、花、灯、果、水;如今,大多只备香烛、果蔬。

The 19th day of the 1st lunar month is Xing Fu Day in Deshengsha area of Haikou city. In the morning, the statues in Madame Xian's Memorial Hall in Deshengsha Street will be dressed new. After the noon, people carried the statues to pray for good luck door to door. Most of the villagers prepare sacrifices on the long desk with an incense burner, with a piece of rune (magic figure or sign drawn by Taoist priest to invoke or expel spirits and bring good or ill fortune) pressed under the incense burner and hung up in front of the incense burner. There used to be incense, candles, flower, lamp, fruit, and water on the long desk. However, only incense, candles, fruits, and vegetables are placed on the table now.

按照海口的习惯,行符日吃斋,案台上供奉的食物均为素食(焦勇勤、孙海兰,2008)。"行符"完毕,在庙前路口举行祭送瘟神仪式。"公祖"在锣鼓、喝喊声中,紧跑急走将瘟神、妖邪、精怪祭送出坊间。靠近海边、河边的村庄还要扎一纸船,让它们远离乡里街坊,俗称"走公"也叫"遣瘟"。晚上,各家各户必备丰盛晚餐招待应邀前来的亲戚朋友,称为"吃行符";宴后,各家各户及亲戚朋友互相招呼结伴前往庙前临时搭建的戏台看"斋"(祭祀仪式性戏曲,斋戏源自于海南民间的道教祭祀仪式;古有"北有傩戏,南有斋戏"之说)。

The custom in Haikou suggests only fruits and vegetables are allowed during Xing Fu Day. Having completed the rite, the ceremony will be held in front of the temple to expel the evil spirits. The people near the sea or river should make a paper boat, put it in the water, and let it flow away with the evil spirits. In the evening, a dinner will be prepared to entertain relatives and friends, and a kind of opera which is derived from sacrifice-offering rite by Taoist priest will be put on.

3.4.5 二月二 Er Yue Er Festival (February 2nd Festival on the 2nd day of the 2nd Lunar Month)

农历二月初二,又被称为"春耕节""农事节""春龙节",民间有"二月二,龙抬头"的说法,庆祝该节,以示敬龙祈雨,保佑丰收之意。海南民间称之为"土地公诞辰日",亦称"土地公节",主要分布在儋州、临高、澄迈、定安、琼海等地。是日,群众将煮熟的母鸡、猪肉供于土地庙前,跪拜土地神,祈求丰收、人畜平安。有些地区农民用糯米制作软粿塞鼠洞,使老鼠无法出洞破坏庄稼,民间有"二月初二日,做粿塞鼠穴"的民谣。儋州的海头镇百姓奉祀钟太祖(传言为九天圣帝),建太祖庙,将2月2日定为太祖诞辰日。是日,人们拜神祭祖,抽签占卜。及至现在,该节日已演变为民间文娱活动,周围白沙、昌江民众也会来此观看舞龙舞狮、装台角、对歌、调声等。

The 2nd day of the 2nd lunar month is also known as the Farming Festival, which is celebrated to respect the Dragon King for the blessing of a bumper harvest. The festival is commonly known as the Birthday of the God of Land, mainly celebrated by people in Danzhou, Lin'gao, Chengmai, Ding'an, Qionghai, etc. On the second day of the second lunar month, the villagers will put the cooked hens and pork in front of the tiny temple housing the God of Land, kowtow to the God of Land, and pray for safety and good harvest. Some local farmers used to stuff the hole with steamed glutinous rice in case the mice go out to destroy crops. Villagers in Haitou town of Danzhou used to offer sacrifices to a god named Zhong Tai Zu. Nowadays, folk cultural activities would be held during the festival, such as dragon dance, lion dance, folk songs contest, etc., with some people from Baisha and Changjiang involved in.

3.4.6 天后圣母节（妈祖文化节、妈祖信俗）Matsu' Day (Matsu Cultural Festival, Matsu Belief and Customs)

农历三月二十三日为海神天后圣母节。天后圣母，即"天妃"，俗称"妈祖"。相传妈祖为福建莆田林姓人家女儿，生于宋太祖建隆元年（960年），从小吃斋茹素，后来羽化升天，经常在海上抢险救难，被皇帝敕封为"天后""圣母"（蒋明智，2013）。据记载，宋元时期"天后娘娘"落籍海南。据《琼州府志》记载，海南天后庙达12处之多（王贵章，2011）。海口仍保存白沙门、中山路两座天后庙：一是海甸岛白沙津250年前的天后宫，占地面积1000多平米，内有5座石碑，详细记载了天后宫的来历；二是中山路水巷口的天后宫，为市级文物保护单位。2009年9月30日，妈祖信俗被联合国教科文组织正式列入人类非物质文化遗产，成为中国首个信俗类世界遗产。2011年1月5日，海口举行海南省妈祖文化交流协会成立大会。"天后祀奉"作为妈祖信俗的一项民间活动，构成了地域色彩鲜明的民间文化体系，经过了700多年的反复积淀，已发展为有海外华人参与的一项具有深远意义的民间活动。

The 23rd day of the 3rd lunar month is Matsu' Day. It is said Matsu whose surname was Lin was born in 960 in Putian of Fujian province. She was a vegetarian, and turn into a goddess after passing away. She often saved the people in the sea, and was conferred the Queen of the Heaven by the emperor. It is reported Matsu was introduced into Hainan between Song and Yuan Dynasties (960-1368), and 12 temples were recorded, two of which have been remained till now. One is in Baishajin in Haidian Island of Haikou city, covering an area of 1000 square meters; the other is on Zhongshan Road, being the key historical site under municipal protection. The Matsu Belief and Customs was officially included in the intangible cultural heritage by UNESCO in 2009. Matsu Cultural Exchange Association was established in 2011 in Haikou. The Matsu Belief and Customs has been a grand festival for the Chinese home and abroad with a history of more than 700 years.

3.4.7 城隍公节 Town God's Day

城隍公是防御城池、保卫治安的神灵。海口人信奉的城隍公，既有"府城隍公"又有"县城隍公"。每逢农历五月二十七日诞期，人们在城隍庙前组织舞龙、舞狮、故事人物装扮、彩灯游街等活动，非常热闹。

Cheng Huang Gong (the Town God) is responsible for the city defense and security. As for the people in Haikou, Cheng Huang Gong refers to both Fucheng Town God and County God. On the 27th day of the 5th lunar month, people hold activities, such as dragon dance, lion dance, roles play, parading with colorful lamps, etc, in front of Town God's Temple.

3.4.8 灶公节 Festival for God of Kitchen

琼海、定安、屯昌等地区农历六月六日举办"灶公节"。是日，人们将做好的饭菜置于厨房灶头祭灶神，同时于厅堂摆设酒饭菜肴祭祀祖先。随着城镇化进程、人们生活方式的变化，该节日逐渐淡化。

Some people in Qionghai, Ding'an, Tunchang, etc. will celebrate the Festival for God of Kitchen on the 6th day of the 6th lunar month. People will offer sacrifices to the God of Kitchen in the kitchen, and their ancestors in the hall. With the process of urbanization, the festival also fades out.

3.4.9 安村节 Harmonious Day for the village

农历六月六日是海南苗族的安村节。是日，苗族同胞家家包赤糖粽，三天不吃油肉，只吃素菜，以示遵守村规。

The 6th day of the 6th lunar month is Harmonious Day for the Miao villages in Hainan, when some of the Miao People make Zongzi with brown sugar, with only vegetables eaten within three days to demonstrate their compliance to the village rules and regulations.

3.4.10 送鬼节 Ghost-sending Day

农历7月1日为"送鬼节"，主要流行于定安、屯昌、澄迈及琼中北部一些农村。传说，阎罗王七月一日打开"鬼门关"，饿鬼出了"鬼门关"四处觅食，七月十五日才将鬼魂收回。村民采摘鸡屎藤，取一部分摘其叶和糯米磨成粉，另一部分留作它用。"送鬼节"当天，家家户户做鸡屎藤粿吃，俗称"吃七一粑"。同时，将另一部分留下的鸡屎藤做成脚环、手镯给孩子带上或挂于门窗，以避鬼驱邪，保家人平安。

The 1st day of the 7th lunar month is named Ghost-Sending Day, which is quite popular in some villages in Ding'an, Tunchang, Chengmai, and Qiongzhong. It used to be widely rumored that the Gate of Hell would be opened by the King of Hell (Yama) on the first day of the seventh lunar month. The hungry ghosts would look for food here and there, and return on the fifteenth day of the same month. The villagers will pick paederia scandens, take some leaves, grind them, and blend with glutinous rice, with the remaining reserved for others purposes. On the Ghost-Sending Day, glutinous rice cake with paederia scandens will be made by every household. And other Paederia scandens will be made into a foot ring and bracelet for children or hung on doors and windows to ward off evil spirits and keep their family members safe.

3.4.11 三江晶信夫人 Madame Jingxin of the Three Rivers

三江晶信夫人是海南部分地区信奉的海上神祇，主要在琼海地区。据记载，宋代天圣元年(1023)，疍家人集资在博鳌建起三江庙。南宋赵汝适在《诸蕃志》"海南"中提到："琼州……属邑五：琼山、澄迈、临高、文昌、乐会，皆有市舶，于舶舟之中分三等，上等为舶，中等为包头，下等名蜑舶。""蜑"同"疍"，蜑舶即疍民打渔连带居住的船舶。据推测，宋代疍民便在乐会（今博鳌、潭门一带）活动。《正德琼台志》载，三江庙"在县（乐会）东十里博鳌浦，宋天圣元年，乡人建祠三江显信夫人，七月二日持牲致祭"（唐胄，2006）。

Madame Jingxin of the Three Rivers (San Jiang, namely Wanquan River, Jiuqu River and Longgun River) is believed to be a god of the Sea in Qionghai. It is recorded that San Jiang Temple was completed in 1023 by Tankas (fishermen living in boat or ship in coastal areas). And people used to offer sacrifices to her on the second day of the seventh lunar month.

3.4.12 中元节 Zhong Yuan Festival (Ghost Day)

中国古代一、七、十月之十五日分称上元、中元、下元：上元是天官，赐福；中元为地官，赦罪；下元为水官，解厄。农历 7 月 15 日，是道教的中元节，佛教在这天要做盂兰盆会，海口、琼海、乐东等民间将该日称为"七月半""鬼节"，有祭祖等活动。

The 15th day of the 1st, 7th, and 10th lunar month is named Shang Yuan, Zhong Yuan, and Xia Yuan respectively in ancient China. Therefore, the fifteenth day of the seventh lunar month is called Zhong Yuan Festival by Taoist, Obon by Buddhist, commonly known as Ghost Day. The people in Haikou, Qionghai, Ledong will offer sacrifices to the deceased during the Ghost Day.

3.4.13 108 兄弟公信俗 108 Bothers Belief and Customs

"108 兄弟公"为海南岛土生土长的海神。琼海渔民祭祀"108 兄弟公"活动可分为三种模式：远航启程前的祭祀通俗叫"做福"，即"琼海渔民祭兄弟公出海仪式"；远航归来后的祭祀通俗叫"洗咸"，即感恩"兄弟公"保佑船只和船员平安且丰收归来的一种谢恩仪式；逢年过节和航船到达某新海域时的一般拜祭通称"做兄弟公"。祭祀流程大同小异，均以肉、饭、酒贡祭"108 兄弟公"，然后焚纸钱、燃放炮竹等。每年孟冬，当东北季风即将或刚刚来临，琼海各远航渔船的主人在备汛充分之后，便请"半仙"挑选一个黄道吉日来举行"祭兄弟公出海仪式"。该仪式唯有琼海渔民才沿袭至今。现在，潭门每一个村子都有兄弟庙，文教村的尤为出名。潭门人每年正月十五、五月初五和七月十五要祭拜三次"兄弟公"，祈求保佑出海的人平安归来。

108 Bothers are the specific gods of the Sea for Hainanese. The sacrifices- offering tradition can be classified into three modes: the custom of Zuo Fu or setting sail ceremony is arranged before leaving for the South China Sea; Xi Xian or thanksgiving ceremony is set after safe return from the Sea; Zuo Xiong Di Gong or the regular sacrifice offering ceremony occurs during the holidays or when the ship gets to new areas in the Sea. The procedure of sacrifice offering rite is more or less the same, including meat, rice, wine, paper money, firecrackers and so on. When the northeast monsoon is imminent or has just arrived in the tenth lunar month, the captain of every ship will choose an auspicious day to hold the ceremony of offering sacrifices to the 108 Bothers, which has been followed till now. The villages in Tanmen town of Qionghai city are featured with temples for 108 Bothers, with the 108 Bothers' Temple in Wenjiao village being the most well-known. The people in Tanmen will pay respect to the 108 Bothers three times every year, namely the 15th day of the 1st lunar month, the 5th day of the 5th lunar month, and the 15th day of the 7th of lunar month, to pray for the fishermen' safe return.

3.4.14 古尔邦节 Corban Festival

古尔邦节是穆斯林的盛大节日。"古尔邦"在阿拉伯语中称为尔德·古尔邦，或称为尔德·阿祖哈。"尔德"是节日之意。"古尔邦"和"阿祖哈"都含有"牺牲""献身"的意思，所以一般把这个节日叫"牺牲节"或"宰牲节"（洪梅香，2012）。2015年中国古尔邦节为公历9月24日。节日前一天，三亚羊栏镇回民男子"游坟"（俗称"走坟"，即扫墓），以便"给亡人祈祷"；回家后，开始宰牲（牛、羊），炸油香，迎接佳节到来。是日，三亚凤凰区回新、回辉两村回民穿着节日盛装，举行集体会礼，听伊玛目（穆斯林集体礼主持礼拜者）宣讲《古兰经》，并举办多项体育比赛。

Corban Festival is a grand holiday for Muslim. The word Corban means sacrifice or dedication. September 24th in 2015 witnessed the Corban Festival. One day before the event, the Hui People in Yanglan town of Sanya would pay respect at the deceased family members' tombs to pray for themselves. And they will slaughter the cattle or goat, fry You Xiang (cakes made of mixed flour, water, and salt) after returning home to welcome the approaching festival. During the festival, the villagers of the Hui People from Huixin village and Huihui village are dressed neatly, stage the gathering ceremony, listen to the Koran preaching, and hold a number of traditional sports competitions.

3.4.15 水尾圣娘庙会日 Goddess Shuiwei Temple Fair

水尾圣娘，也称为南天夫人，又称"水尾云感圣旨莫氏夫人""南天闪电感应火雷水尾圣娘"。莫氏族人认为，水尾圣娘为定安县水尾莫家祖公莫瑚之妹，族人尊其为"圣旨婆祖"，建有庙宇供奉。水尾圣娘庙除定安县岭口镇水尾村外，还有三座，一座在四川，一座在定安，还有一座在文昌，其中以文昌水尾圣娘庙最为典型。据记载，文昌东郊西南1公里处的水尾圣娘庙是因为"明正德年间，有石炉飞至此，因建庙焉"。清光绪元年（公元1875年）曾重修，其上有大书法家张岳崧"慈云圣母"手笔。传说"圣娘"这一封号为嘉庆皇帝敕赐。张岳崧高中探花，归琼亲临圣庙，印证京城梦遇，随即挥毫慈云镜海牌匾奉献，返京后，将访集圣娘显圣事迹向主皇上奏，嘉庆皇准奏，并勅赐封号为"南天闪电感应火雷水尾圣娘"。文昌人俗称水尾圣娘为"婆祖"，农历十月十五日至十七日则为文昌东郊圣娘庙会日，举行很多民俗活动，在海内外信众颇多。

Goddess Shuiwei was deemed a daughter whose surname was Mo in Ding'an county, and a temple was built for her. Besides, there are another 3 temples in Sichuan, Ding'an, and Wenchang, with the last one being most well-known home and abroad. It is recorded the temple was built during the reign of Emperor Wuzong (1506-1521) in Ming Dynasty (1368-1644), and was renovated in 1875, with the great calligrapher Zhang Yuesong's handwriting on it. It was rumored that the title Holy Mother was conferred on her by the Emperor Jiaqing (1795-1820). The people in Wenchang commonly call the Goddess Shuiwei Po Zu (the beloved mother), and the period from the 15th to 17th day of the 10th lunar month is Goddess Shuiwei Temple Fair, with various folk activities and a great many believers and followers home and abroad.

3.5 纪念追忆性节日民俗
Customs during Holidays or Festivals in Memory of Historical Figures

3.5.1 公期 Gong Qi (Memorial Day for the Clan Ancestor or the Gods or Spirits)

公期是海南各乡村宗族公祖或神灵的纪念日。琼山羊山地区的"公期"时间各村有别，大致从正月四日至二十二日。拜公宴席期间，各村亲朋好友互相串吃，不认识的也可入席，谁家客多谁体面，还给客人送"红封"，以示吉利、富有。

Gong Qi is the memorial day for the clan ancestor or the gods or spirits in rural areas of Hainan. The time of the anniversary varies from village to village in Qiongshan District, roughly from the 4th to 22nd day of the 1st lunar month. During the festival, villagers invite each other to enjoy the dishes, even those they don't know, and send Hong Bao (red envelope containing money) to the guests.

3.5.2 冼夫人文化节（军坡节、冼夫人信俗）Mrs. Xian' Cultural Festival (Junpo Festival, Mrs. Xian Belief and Customs)

冼夫人（522—602），南北朝时高凉郡（今阳江、电白、高州一带）人，梁高凉太守冯宝妻，是位杰出的政治家、军事家，文韬武略。冼夫人奏请梁武帝在海南设立崖州，恢复对海南岛的实际统治。虽身逢乱世，历梁、陈、隋三代，但从冼夫人建议设立崖州到她的孙子冯盎总管海南 3 州 12 县，将近 110 年时间，为维护民族团结、政局稳定、经济繁荣、国家统一做出卓越贡献，深受两广地区和海南人民爱戴景仰（菲利普·吉威尼尔、韩斌，2010）。周恩来总理称她为"中国巾帼英雄第一人"，江泽民总书记赞誉冼夫人是"我辈后人永远学习的楷模"。

Mrs. Xian (522-602) was an outstanding stateswoman and military strategist in Gaoliang prefecture (current area in Yangjiang, Dianbai, Gaozhou) during Northern and Southern Dynasties(420-589). Madame Xian presented a memorial to the Emperor Liangwudi (464-549) to set up Yazhou prefecture in Hainan to restore the rule of the Island. Living in troubled times through the Liang Dynasty (502-557), Chen Dynasty (557-589), and Sui Dynasty (581-618), Mrs. Xian and her grandson spent 110 years suggesting establishing the prefecture and exercising control over the whole Hainan Island, contributing greatly to national unity, political stability, and economic prosperity, for which they have been respected and loved by the people in Guangdong province, Guangxi province, and Hainan province. She was deemed the No.1 Heroine of China by the late premier Zhou Enlai, and the role model by Jiang Zemin, the General Secretary of the Communist Party of China.

冼夫人文化节，又称军坡节、冼夫人信俗，是海南东北部市县规模最大的民间祭祀节日，相传已有 1300 多年的历史。海南许多地方都"闹军坡"，琼山市新坡镇的"梁沙婆期"颇为隆重。每年农历二月九日至十二日，当地群众表演冼太夫人出征及阅兵仪式，人山人海，场面壮阔，是海南地域特色节庆活动。2015 年第十四届冼夫人文化节在海口举行，除了保留民间祭祀和庙会纪念活动等传统项目外，还举办了文艺演出、公仔戏、琼剧等特色的文化活动。2014 年 11 月，冼夫人信俗已被列入第四批国家级非物质文化遗产代表性项目名录。除海口外，澄迈、屯昌、定安、琼海、万宁等地举办军坡节。海南琼海白石岭旅游区有军坡表演，尤其是"穿杖"表演令人瞠目结舌。

Mrs. Xian's Cultural Festival, also known as Junpo Festival, is the grandest folk festival in the northeast of Hainan province with a history of more than 1300 years. The festival is celebrated all through the northeastern areas, with that of Xinpo town of Qiongshan district the most well-known. From the 2nd to the 12th day of the second lunar month, imitating Mrs. Xian's army expedition with a sea of local people features the festival. The 14th Mrs. Xian's Cultural Festival was staged in Haikou in 2015, holding sacrifices offering ceremony, temple fair, puppet show, and Qiong Opera show, etc. Mrs. Xian Belief and Customs was listed in the national intangible cultural heritage in November 2014. Besides Haikou, other cities, such as Chengmai, Tunchang, Qionghai, Ding'an, Wanning, will also celebrate the festival. There is minimized Junpo show in Baishiling Ridge Scenic Spot, with a stainless steel rod or silver wand piercing their cheek(s) being the most impressive.

3.5.3 两伏波将军日 General Fu Bo's Day

伏波将军是古代对将军个人能力的一种封号，伏波意为降伏波涛，历朝历代中曾出现多位被授予伏波将军封号的人物。第一位出任伏波将军的即汉武帝时候的路博德，最著名的伏波将军是东汉光武帝时候的马援。传说农历五月三日是西汉伏波将军路博德渡海开琼之日，民间便以此作为两位伏波将军纪念日。伏波庙遍布海南，但史料记载修建时间最早、规模最大的是龙岐村的伏波庙。是日，民众前来拜祭，香烟缭绕，场面壮大。

General Fu Bo is an ancient title for a general's personal competence, and Fu Bo means overpowering the rolling waves. There are many generals awarded the tile Fu Bo, and General Lu Bode was the first to be awarded the title during the reign of the Emperor Hanwudi (156 BC-87 BC) in Western Han Dynasty(202 BC-8 AD), but General Ma Yuan was the best-known one during the reign of the Emperor Guangwudi (5 BC-AD 57) in Eastern Han Dynasty(25-220). Rumor has it that General Lu Bode arrived in Hainan on the 3rd day of the 5th lunar month, which was set by local people to commemorate the two generals. Many General Fu Bo's temples can be seen in Hainan, but the General Fu Bo's temple in Longqi village of Haikou is believed to be the first one and the largest one according to historical record. Local people come to offer sacrifices to them during the General Fu Bo's Day.

3.5.4 关圣帝生日 Guan Yu's Birthday

农历五月十三日是关公生辰，关公是海南民间信仰得最多的神。关羽，本字长生，后改字云长，东汉末年名将。建安二十四年（219年），关羽围襄樊，东吴吕蒙又偷袭荆州，关羽腹背受敌，兵败被杀。关羽去世后，逐渐被神化，被民间尊为"关公"，又称美髯公。历代朝廷多有褒封，清代奉为"忠义神武灵佑仁勇威显关圣大帝"，崇为"武圣"，与"文圣"孔子齐名。是日，从零时开始，海口新民西路关帝庙附近的民众陆续地前来祭拜，还会抬着关公像巡游。

The 13th day of the 5th lunar month is Guan Yu's birthday, who is considered to be a god with the largest number of believers in Hainan. Guan Yu was a general at the end of the Eastern Han Dynasty(25-220). Guan Yu was trapped and killed during the war in Xiangfan city of Hubei province in 219 AD. Guan Yu, commonly called Guan Gong by people, was deified after his death, and conferred on a great many titles by the following dynasties. People living near Guan Yu's temple in Xinmin West Road of Haihou city will offer sacrifices from the very early morning on the thirteenth day of the fifth lunar month, and they will parade with the statue of Guan Yu.

3.5.5 西天公节 Wang Zuo's Commemoration Day

农历五月十五是西天公——明代海南著名诗人王佐纪念日。王佐被誉为明清时期海南四大才子（邱濬、海瑞、王佐、张岳崧）之一，尤以诗文见长，世称"吟绝"。王佐爱国惠民，深得琼州人民爱戴。明代隆庆年间（1567—1572），琼州府海一带商民在海口市义兴街关门坊修建西天庙，奉祀王佐。因王佐是临高县透滩村人，透滩村在海口的西边，王佐公亦仙游西天，故尊称为"西天公""西天大爷""西天大士"，雅称"阿爸"。自建立以来，香客不断，香火甚盛。是日，祭祀活动较多，充分体现了老百姓对王佐先贤的崇敬之情。

The 15th day of the 5th lunar month is the commemoration day for the poet Wang Zuo in Ming Dynasty (1368-1644), who was recognized as one of the Four Talents (Qiu Rui, Hai Rui, Zhang Yuesong) in Hainan. He loved the country and the people, and was respected and loved by Hainanese. Xitian Temple was completed on Yixing Street in Haikou during the period from 1567 to 1572 to commemorate him. Due to the fact that Wang Zuo was born in Toutan village of Lin'gao county which lies to the west of Haikou, he was named Xi Tian Gong after passing away. A great many pilgrims have paid a visit to Xitian Temple since it was built. During Wang Zuo's Commemoration Day, sacrifices will be offered to him with scores of sacrificial activities, which fully reflects the people's reverence for him.

3.5.6 东坡文化节 Su Dongpo Cultural Festival

2010年11月18日，来自海南儋州、广东惠州和湖北黄冈的政府代表在北京出席"东坡节新闻发布会"，惠州市与儋州市、黄冈市、眉山市三个城市缔结为友邦城市，轮流举办东坡文化节，以传承中国渊源流传的优秀传统文化。2010年12月18-19日，首届东坡文化节在海南省儋州市举行。公元1097年，宋代大文豪苏东坡被贬儋州，居儋三年，大力传播中原文化，关心百姓疾苦，与当地群众结下深厚情谊。2015年第六届东坡文化节于12月1日至3日在惠州举行，第七届东坡文化节在湖北省黄冈市举行。

On November 18th 2010, government representatives from Danzhou in Hainan province, Huizhou in Guangdong province, and Huanggang in Hubei province attended the press conference about Su Dongpo Cultural Festival in Beijing. Huizhou city, Danzhou city, Huanggang city, and Meishan city will take turns to organize the Su Dongpo Cultural Festival to inherit the excellent traditional cultures. The first festival was firstly held on December 18th 2010 in Danzhou city of Hainan province. The great poet Su Dongpo (1037-1101) was banished to Danzhou in 1097, and stayed in Danzhou for three years, during which he widely disseminated the cultures of the Central Plains. He was deeply concerned about the sufferings of the people, and forged unbreakable friendship with local people. The 6th Su Dongpo Cultural Festival was held in Huizhou on December 18th 2015, and the 7th Festival was held in Huanggang city of Hubei province.

3.5.7 圣纪节 Mohammed's Birthday

圣纪节是伊斯兰教三大宗教节日之一。圣纪节，亦称圣忌节，阿拉伯语称"冒路德"节。相传，穆罕默德（约570—632年）的诞辰和逝世都在伊斯兰历三月十二日。为了纪念这位伟人的丰功伟绩，铭记穆罕默德圣训、教诲，穆斯林在该日举行宗教集会。节日活动在清真寺举行，通常由当地清真寺伊玛目主持。

Mohammed's Birthday is one of the three most important religious holidays among Muslims. Legend has it that Muhammad (about 570-632) was born on March 12th and passed away on March 12th according to the Islamic calendar. Religious gathering, therefore, is held every year on March 12th in memory of him for his great achievements. In general, the Imam will be in charge of activities held in the local mosque.

3.6 其他节日民俗
Other Holidays and Customs

3.6.1 海口府城换花节 Fucheng Flower Exchange Festival

随着夜幕降临，农历正月十五海口琼山区的府城换花节拉开帷幕。府城"换花节"源于"换香节"，唐末已有换香活动。"换香"寓意互换香火，有换吉纳祥、发财旺丁之意。最初，府城作为琼州府驻地，每年元宵举行灯会，花灯竞放，成千上万民众出门赏灯。由于当时没有路灯，为了夜行方便，人们会拿一把点燃的香烛用以照明，路遇没有香的人便送几枝，有时偶遇亲朋好友，互换香烛，说些祝福的话语，逐渐演变成海南岛上人们表达情感的一种特殊方式（赛门·卡尔巴赫、鲁道夫·兰诗保尔、蔡彧岚，2007）。出于节庆安全考虑，1984年，府城民间"换香"习俗改为"换花"逐渐形成了凝聚友谊、寻找爱情的新节庆形式。正所谓"年年岁岁花相似，岁岁年年人不同"。海南的换花节被赋予更多新意。多数人换花意在新春伊始，互相祝福；青年人则把换花节当作结交新朋友的好时机，愿以花为媒，觅到知音或人生伴侣。

Fucheng Flower Exchange Festival, held on the fifteenth day of the first lunar month in Fucheng of Haikou city, is said to have originated from the Incense Exchange Festival in the late Tang Dynasty (618-907), with the connotations of better luck, being richer, and giving birth to more babies. There used to be no street lamps, and people would take lit incenses to enjoy the lanterns show on foot in the evening. When encountering someone with no incense, they would share with him or her and say a few words of blessing, which gradually evolved into a special way to express their emotions during the Lantern Festival in Hainan. Taken the security into consideration, the custom of exchanging incense was replaced by flowers in 1984. And it gradually becomes the main activity of the Lantern Festival in Fucheng. Young people take the festival as an opportunity to make more friends, find a bosom friend or Mr./Ms. Right, which makes it gradually a festival combined with friendship, best wishes and courting gradually.

3.6.2 团结日 Solidarity Day among the Miao People

农历二月初二日为苗族团结节日。是日，村中男女老幼聚在一起，由一位德高望重的长者主持，告诫后代要诚实、守纪、守信。

The 2nd day of the 2nd lunar month is considered as the Solidarity Day among the Miao People, when all the people would gather and be admonished to be honest, obey the rules, and keep true to one's word.

3.6.3 春分 Vernal Equinox

春分，二十四节气之一，是春季九十天的中分点。《月令七十二候集解》："二月中，分者半也，此当九十日之半，故谓之分。"春分也是节日和祭祀庆典，古代帝王有春天祭日，秋天祭月的礼制。万宁一些乡镇有春分扫墓、祭祖的习俗。村民除了扫墓，还轮流当事，购置祭品，集中在祠堂祭祀祖先，举办"开丁"活动，即一年来谁家生了男孩，于春分之日可领得一份花丁肉，以示添丁添福。此节现已废止。

Vernal Equinox is not only a day marking one of the 24 divisions of the solar year in the traditional Chinese calendar but also a day for offering sacrifices. It used to be common for the emperors to offer sacrifices to the Sun in spring and to the Moon in autumn. Some people in Wanning have the custom of paying respects at the tombs of the deceased and offering sacrifices to them during the Vernal Equinox. In addition, some people in Wanning used to take turns to buy sacrifices, offer them to their ancestors in the ancestral hall, and stage the ceremony named Kai Ding, namely the family who has gotten a baby boy in the past year can be given a piece of pork. The custom ceased existing.

3.6.4 海南黎族"三月三" San Yue San Festival in the Li People (Held on the 3rd day of the 3rd Lunar Month)

黎族"三月三"（又称爱情节、谈爱日，黎语称"孚念孚"）是海南黎族人民悼念勤劳勇敢的祖先、赞美美好的生活、表达对爱情幸福向往之情的传统节日，每年农历三月初三举行（符和积、朱寒松、范晓军，2013）。黎族"三月三"有个美丽的爱情传说：远古时代，人类遭受灭顶洪灾，一对男女躲进葫芦漂到荒无人烟的海南岛。为了繁衍人类，二人在三月三日结为夫妻，繁衍了黎族后代。东方、昌江的美孚方言区，"三月三"纪念活动甚为隆重。海南南部地区的黎族，三月三日备齐猪头、米酒、饭团等祭品，前往三亚落笔洞、甘石岭山洞拜祭祖先、祈求家人平安。1984年起，保亭县黎族苗族人民过"三月三"节，未婚男女都穿上鲜艳的民族服装，在鼓笛齐鸣之中起舞同欢、对歌传情。同年，根据黎族人民的意愿和要求，广东省人大和广东省人民政府决定将"三月三"确定为黎族的传统节日。2006年5月20日，黎族"三月三"经国务院批准列入第一批国家级非物质文化遗产名录。

San Yue San or March 3rd Festival, which is held on the 3rd day of the 3rd lunar month, is a tradition for the Li People to commemorate their diligent ancestors, eulogize their happy life, and pray for true love. It originated from a myth among the Li People. A deluge killed almost all the people but a man and a woman, who hid in a huge gourd and drifted to the lonely Hainan Island. They got married for more descendants, for which the festival is set in memory of them.

People of Meifu Li in Dongfang and Changjiang will hold grand ceremony, while the Li People in the south will go to Luobi Cave and Ganshiling Cave in Sanya to offer sacrifices to their ancestors and pray for health and safety. The neatly dressed Li and Miao People has celebrated the festival by dancing and singing in antiphonal style since 1984, when the festival was considered as the traditional festival for the Li People. And it was listed in the first national intangible cultural heritage on May 20th 2006.

黎族"三月三"历史悠久，宋代史籍中就有记载。宋范成大《桂海虞衡志》云："春则秋千会，邻峒男女装束来游，携手并肩，互歌互答，名曰作剧。"每年农历三月初三，东方、昌江、乐东、琼中等县黎族人民都会身着节日盛装，挑着山栏米酒，带上竹筒香饭，从四面八方汇集一起，或祭拜始祖，或相会、对歌、跳舞、摔跤、拔河、射击、荡秋千、吹奏乐器来欢庆佳节，青年男女更是借节狂欢，直到天将破晓。如今，海南黎族各聚居区每年都要举行规模盛大、内容丰富的庆祝活动，有赛歌会、篝火晚会、彩车比赛、花灯展览、民族传统体育比赛、男女青年对歌、民族歌舞表演及经贸活动等，吸引数万国内外游客。

San Yue San Festival has been recorded in the Song Dynasty (960-1279). The well dressed Li People from Dongfang, Changjiang, Ledong, and Qiongzhong would gather to offer sacrifices with Shanlan Rice Wine and rice cooked in bamboo tube. They used to participate in many activities, such as singing in antiphonal style, dancing, wrestling, shooting, swing, playing traditional musical instrument, etc. Nowadays, more activities have been held, such as singing songs contest, campfire party, float parade, lanterns exhibition, traditional sports games, folk songs and dance, and other economic activities, which has attracted a sea of people home and abroad.

3.6.5 琼海（会山）苗族传统文化节 The Miao People's Traditional Cultural Festival in Huishan Qionghai

为更好地保护和传承琼海苗族传统文化精髓，充分展示会山苗族风情与自然生态的独特魅力，首届琼海（会山）苗族传统文化节于2013年农历三月三日开幕，至今已成功举办三届。2016年，第四届琼海（会山）苗族传统文化节于农历三月一日至三日在会山镇墟举行一系列庆祝活动，包括"黎苗风彩·小调会山"苗族传统文化节启动仪式、苗族特色文化展、文艺汇演、民族传统体育竞技、篮球比赛、琼剧专场等活动，全方位展现苗族人民民俗民风和团结奋进的精神风貌。

The 1st Miao People's Traditional Cultural Festival was held in Huishan town of Qionghai city on the 3rd day of the 3rd lunar month in 2013 to inherit the Miao People's traditional culture and fully display the peculiar charm of the Miao People and natural landscape. Various activities were held from the first to the 3rd day of the 3rd lunar month during the fourth Miao People's Traditional Cultural Festival, including the opening ceremony, the Miao People's traditional culture exhibition, art show, traditional sports games, basketball match, Qiong Opera and so on, which exhibits their folk customs and high spirits in all-round way.

3.6.6 姐妹节 Sisters' Day

农历三月十五到十八日，是我国苗族女性的"姊妹节"。是日，苗家姑娘们都要吃一种"姊妹饭"，由山上采摘的野生植物的花和叶将糯米染成五颜六色后蒸制而成。有些苗家姑娘还互赠礼物，以示吉祥。吃罢姐妹饭，苗族村寨姑娘们与小伙身着节日盛装和民族服装，观赏或参加斗牛、唱苗歌、跳芦笙舞、银饰服装走秀和"游方"（青年男女谈情说爱）等活动（黄友贤、黄仁昌，2008）。

The 15th to the 18th day of the third lunar month is set for the Sisters' Day among the Miao women. The Miao girls will eat dyed colorful rice which is made by picking wild plant flowers and leaves in the mountain. Some Miao girls exchange gifts for good luck. After having dyed colorful rice, the traditionally dressed Miao girls and boys gather to watch or participate in bullfighting, singing the Miao songs, indulging in Lusheng dance, the Miao's traditional costumes and accessories show, You Fang (social gathering of boys and girls of the Miao People during the festivals or the slack season, where they sing songs, exchange gifts, and make advances to each other), and other activities.

3.6.7 中国海南保亭七仙温泉嬉水节 Qixian (7th Fairy) Hot Spring Water Splashing Festival

农历七月七日（即七夕节，又名乞巧节、七巧节或七姐诞），是七仙女与董永鹊桥相会的好日子，是中国的情人节。在海南少数民族聚居地保亭县，人们以温泉"圣水"泼洒对方，形成一系列乐趣无穷的嬉水活动。最初的保亭嬉水节源于七仙女用七仙岭脚下的温泉水救治失明老妈妈的传说。是日，男女老幼到温泉沐浴嬉戏，用桔叶互相泼洒温泉"圣水"，祈求祥和幸福、身体健康、福寿绵长。

The Qixian (7th Fairy) Hot Spring Water Splashing Festival is celebrated on the 7th day of the 7th lunar month, which is named Chinese Valentin's Day for the reunion of the 7th Fairy and Dong Yong. The Li and Miao People in Baoting county splash water from the hot spring, and interesting water-splashing activities come into being. The Baoting Water Splashing Festival originates from the local tale that an old mother's eyes were cured by rinsing with the water from the hot spring on the Mountain Qixian. A sea of people will splash water to each other with orange leaves and pray for happiness, health, and longevity at this event.

2000年，举办首届温泉嬉水节。2002年，保亭县政府将农历七月七日定为中国海南保亭七仙温泉嬉水节。中国海南七仙温泉嬉水节是保亭黎族苗族一年一度盛大的民间传统节庆，由黎苗民间祭水习俗演变而来。至今，嬉水节已成功举办16届，品牌影响力逐渐增强，规模逐年增大。2010年荣获"2010中国十大著名节庆品牌"称号，2011年被联合国教科文民间艺术组织等评为"中国最具人气的民间节会"。2015年第十五届保亭七仙温泉嬉水节在保亭黎族苗族自治县七仙广场举行，突出本土黎族苗族文化特色，上万名中外游客嬉水狂欢，感受嬉水节的热情和魅力。

The first Hot Spring Water Splashing Festival was held in 2000. Baoting County government formally set the seventh day of the seventh month in the lunar calendar for the Qixian (7th Fairy) Hot Spring Water Splashing Festival. The annual festival by the Li and Miao People in Baoting is a grand folk festival, evolving from the folk custom of offering sacrifices to the water. The festival has been successfully held 16 times, which was considered one of the Chinese top ten famous festivals in 2010 and Chinese most popular folk festival by UNESCO in 2011. The 15th Qixian (7th Fairy) Hot Spring Water Splashing Festival was held in Qixian Square in the Li and Miao Autonomous County-Baoting, with thousands of tourists home and abroad participating in the water splashing.

3.6.8 万宁国际文灯节 Wanning Lanterns Festival

文灯又称孔明灯、天灯，相传是由三国时代的孔明（诸葛亮）发明的。传到海南，每逢喜庆日子或盛大的节日，海南各地民众喜欢点起文灯表达美好心愿，已成为当地的一种很有特色的民间风俗。在万宁，放文灯已成为盛行已久的民间习俗。中秋节前后，当地民众会放飞各种文灯，祈求身体健康、学业有成、事业辉煌、生活幸福。

Wanning Lantern, also known as Kongming Lantern, is said to have been invented by Zhuge Liang during the Three Kingdoms (220-280). People like to fly the lanterns during the festive days or grand festivals to express their good wishes when it is introduced to Hainan, which has become a local unique folk custom. It has become a popular folk custom for a long time. During the Mid-Autumn Festival, the local people will fly various lanterns to pray for good health, academic success, brilliant career, and a happy life.

3.6.9 儋州中秋调声节 Danzhou Diao Sheng Folk Songs Contest

中秋对歌是儋州北部地区群众在中秋佳节举行的民间娱乐活动。当地民众利用中秋节集市会面的机会，在附近山坡田野自发组织"调声"对歌比赛。儋州调声发源于西汉年间的儋州北部地区，自儋州民歌活动中演变而来，不断吸收古曲、现代歌曲及外国歌曲旋律，已成为海南儋州广为流传的一种民间歌舞艺术，被誉为"南国乐坛的奇葩"，曾斩获国家级金奖、银奖等奖项。2006年5月20日，儋州调声经国务院批准列入第一批国家级非物质文化遗产名录。

Singing in antiphonal style during the Mid-Autumn Festival is a folk entertainment activity held in northern area of Danzhou. Local people spontaneously organize Diao Sheng Folk Songs Contest (singing folk songs in antiphonal style in local dialect) in the open air when they meet each other in the bazaar. The Diao Sheng originates from the northern part of Danzhou during the Western Han Dynasty (202 BC-AD 8), evolving from ancient folk songs. Constantly absorbing melodies from the classical, modern and foreign music, it has been a most popular folk song-and-dance art, which has won many national gold and silver awards. And the festival was listed in the national intangible cultural heritage by the State Council on May 20th 2006.

为了进一步弘扬儋州调声艺术，2001年，经儋州市人大常委会通过，正式确立每年农历八月十五为儋州调声艺术节，并于同年中秋节隆重举办首届儋州调声艺术节。2002年儋州市调声山歌协会成立。每年中秋佳节，儋州的中和镇，作为原调声的主会场，人们盛装而来，独唱、对唱、齐唱、合唱，歌声绵延不绝。主要活动内容是儋州山歌、调声对歌比赛和"赏月"等项目。一般由一个村的一组男青年与另一个村的一组女青年各排成一列，每列队员互相勾住尾指，面对面对歌。每队都有"歌头"负责起调、领唱、指挥、选择歌词。对歌时，一般先由男方歌手领唱，后由女方歌手唱答，队形变化多样，歌手手舞足蹈，男唱女答，热闹异常。比赛不受时间限制，以"唱倒"对方为止（即对方不能答歌为准）。赛歌活动一般为下午3至6时。夜晚的中秋调声节以村为主体举办"中秋歌会"，又称"中秋情酒歌会"，男女青年歌手对唱情歌。女子主动敬酒表示"钟情"，男方接过酒一口饮尽，并以歌投情，表示"领情"。儋州中秋调声节，"赏月"对歌，共享月饼，直至凌晨。

In order to further promote the folk art of Diao Sheng in Danzhou, the Standing Committee of Danzhou Municipal People's Congress formally set the 15th day of the 8th lunar month for the

Danzhou Diao Sheng Festival, which was held for the first time during the Mid-Autumn Festival of the same year. And the Danzhou Diao Sheng Folk Songs Association was established in 2002. During the annual Mid-Autumn Festival, Zhonghe town of Danzhou serves as the main site to hold Diao Sheng Festival, including solo, singing in antiphonal style or in chorus. However, the contents are composed of folk songs, Diao Sheng contest in antiphonal style, and full moon enjoying, etc. In general, a row of men from one village sings songs facing the other row of women from other villages, with their pinkies holding each other of the same team. The leading singer of each team is in charge of music and lyrics. Generally speaking, the team of men will sing first, and the other team of women answer by singing, with various forms in dance and singing. The contest, which generally lasts from 3:00 p.m. to 6:00 p.m, ends with defeating the counterpart, namely the other team can't answer by singing in time. In the evening, the Mid-Autumn Songs Party will be held, with love songs sung by man and woman singers in antiphonal style. The woman may actively propose a toast to a man, who should drink them all and sing songs to appreciate her kindness. Danzhou Diao Sheng Folk Songs Contest in Danzhou may continue till the midnight, with singing in antiphonal style, enjoying the full bright moon, and sharing the moon-cakes.

3.6.10 海南欢乐节 Hainan Carnival

为了发掘和提升海南的旅游文化、树立"热带海岛，度假天堂"的品牌形象，由海南省政府和国家旅游局主办的旅游节庆活动，突出"政府主导、企业运作、百姓参与"三大特点，在全省多个旅游市县同步举行，活动特色鲜明。该盛会于 2000 年开始举办，时间一般在每年 11 月中下旬。第十六届欢乐节于 2015 年 11 月 27 日至 12 月 3 日举行。欢乐节期间，举办各种文艺表演、烹饪美食、花车巡游、旅游产品展销等，展示海南的区域特色、多元文化及得天独厚的热带海岛型旅游资源，吸引更多海内外游客、媒体及参展商，进一步提升海南区域特色节庆的国内外知名度，推介海南国际旅游岛。2016 年 11 月 25 日至 12 月 31 日，第十七届欢乐节在全岛隆重上演，包括首届海口欢乐购物节、三亚西岛海洋节、琼海南海文化节等。

In order to further explore and promote tourism culture, the Hainan Carnival sponsored by the Hainan Provincial Government and China National Tourism Administration was launched in 2000 for the first time, with activities full of distinctive local features to establish the brand image of "Tropical Island, Holiday Paradise". It is generally held in second or the last ten-day period of November, and the 16th Hainan Carnival was staged from November 27th to December 3rd. A variety of performances, culinary delicacies, floats show, tourism products exhibition, etc. was hosted to fully display the regional multicultural characteristics and rich natural tropical tourism resources to attract more tourists, media, and exhibitors home and abroad. The 17th Hainan Carnival was held from November 25th to December 31st in 2016, including the first Haikou Shopping Festival, West Island Marine Festival in Sanya, the South China Sea Cultural Festival in Qionghai, etc.

3.6.11 开斋节 Lesser Bairam (Eid al-Fitr; Festival of the Fast-Breaking)

开斋节已成为信仰伊斯兰教各民族的传统文化节日，有 1400 余年历史。开斋节是阿拉伯语"尔德·费图尔"的意译，尔德这个阿拉伯词语由"阿达"（Aada）演变而来，原意是"返回"，演变为"聚会"，故穆斯林将开斋节的礼拜称为"会礼"。

Lesser Bairam is a Muslims' traditional cultural festival with a history of more than 1400 years. Lesser Bairam is the free translation of Eid al-Fitr in Arabic language, and the word Eid evolves from the Arabic word Aada which means return originally to get-together nowadays, so Muslims' going to the mosque during the week of Lesser Bairam is named gathering.

开斋节是三亚羊栏回族最盛大的传统节日。每年伊斯兰教历九月为斋月，除老幼孕弱病残，成年健康男女都入斋，静心寡欲。斋月二十七日夜称为"盖德尔夜"，为真主颁降《古兰经》之夜。为了欢度"盖德尔夜"、讨取好兆头，前一天晚上人们忙着准备油香、油饼、糯糕等，黎明时分各家互送，以示情谊深厚、生活富足。夜幕降临，人们到清真寺沐浴，然后虔诚礼拜、祈祷、诵经，祈求真主赐恩于父母、亲朋好友。有些人彻夜诵经以示诚心，成为"坐夜"。到月底二十九或三十日，新月的出现预示斋月结束，次日开斋，即为开斋节。是日清晨，穆斯林到清真寺大净（全身沐浴）或小净（洗手、脚、脸）；晚上，全部盛装参加或观看聚礼。会礼后，亲戚朋友串门、拜斋，宾主互道"塞俩目"（祝你平安之意），客人主动入座诵经。开斋节后，当地恢复正常生活。

Lesser Bairam is considered the grandest traditional festival among the Hui People in Yanglan town of Sanya. The 9th month in Islamic calendar is Ramadan. The 27th night of Ramadan is referred to as Al-Gadr, which is said to have revealed Koran to the prophet Muhammad by Allah. To celebrate the Al-Gadr for good luck, traditional food, such as You Xiang (cakes made of mixed flour, water, and salt), deep-fried dough cakes, glutinous rice cakes, etc., will be prepared the night before Ramadan and sent to each other at dawn for the sake of their deep friendship and rich life. When night falls, people go to the mosque to bathe, chant, and pray for the grace of Allah for their parents, relatives and friends. Some people chant in all sincerity during the whole night. On the 29th or 30th day when the crescent of the new moon turns up, the Ramadan comes to an end, and Lesser Bairam starts the nest day. Muslims will bathe in the mosques in the morning and dress themselves to attend the gathering in the evening. The relatives and friends send greetings to each other after gathering, and guests take the initiative in chanting. After the festival, everything returns to normal.

3.6.12 三亚天涯国际婚庆节 Tianya International Wedding Festival in Sanya

1996年至今，三亚天涯国际婚庆节已成功举办十九届，已发展成为集婚庆旅游和蜜月度假于一体的精品旅游节庆活动。2015年12月22日，第十九届中国·三亚天涯海角国际婚庆节以"互联网+"的思维重磅打造了"天涯海角年度婚礼""婚礼产品发布秀"两大主体活动。活动期间，天涯海角游览区通过真人演绎、实景展示方式，为市民游客现场还原俄罗斯、哈萨克斯坦、伊朗、新疆等丝绸之路沿线国家充满异域风情的婚俗。尤为重要的是，市民游客还领略了我国传统汉唐婚礼及黎苗特色婚俗并参与现场互动，让大家尽情领略天涯海角爱情圣地的无穷魅力。

Tianya International Wedding Festival, which has been successfully held for nineteen times since 1996, has developed into a combined celebration for wedding or honeymoon trip. The 19th Tianya International Wedding Festival was held on December 22nd 2015, with two major activities named Tianya Haijiao Annual Wedding and Wedding Products Show. During the event, the exotic wedding customs in Kazakhstan, Russia, Iran, Xinjiang province and other countries or regions along the Silk Road will be displayed by interpretation and show. And the participants can also experience the traditional Chinese wedding customs in the Han Dynasties (202 BC-220 AD) and Tang Dynasty (618-907) and those in the Li and Miao People or participate in the on-site interaction.

3.6.13 海南乡村旅游文化节 Rural Tourism Cultural Festivals

为了向全国展示海南乡村旅游，拉动对海南乡村旅游的消费和投资需求，推出海南特色乡村产品，开发海南乡村旅游新业态和探索海南乡村发展新模式，"2011年首届海南乡村旅游文化节"在海南省文昌市八门湾绿道霞场段开幕，2013年第二届海南乡村旅游文化节暨文昌市南洋文化节在文昌市开幕。2015年5月15日，第三届海南乡村旅游文化节在海南省琼海市开幕，并举办了海南乡村旅游商品展销会。

In order to fully display rural tourism in Hainan, stimulate the consumption and investment demand for rural tourism, launch rural products full of Hainan's characteristics, and probe into new development modes of rural tourism, the 1st Hainan Rural Tourism Cultural Festival was held in Xiachang Section of Bamenwan Greenway in Wenchang City, Hainan province. The 2nd (2013) and 3rd (2015) Rural Tourism Cultural Festival were held in Wenchang city and Qionghai city respectively, with commodities fair also exhibited during the 3rd festival in Qionghai city.

3.6.14 万宁国际冲浪节 Wanning International Surfing Festival

2010年11月6-8日，由国家体育总局水上运动管理中心、海南省旅游发展委员会、海南省文化广电出版体育厅及万宁市人民政府联合主办的首届中国海南万宁国际冲浪节在海南万宁石梅湾、南燕湾、日月湾等海域举行，内容主要包括开幕式、国际冲浪健将冲浪表演、国际冲浪邀请赛、冲浪历史文化暨冲浪用品展、冲浪运动国际研讨会及冲浪主题晚会等。2015海南万宁国际冲浪赛于12月4日—12日在万宁日月湾举行，共有120名世界顶尖冲浪选手参加，比赛由世界冲浪联盟(WSL)首次进行世界直播，上百万名冲浪爱好者可以观看精彩的冲浪比赛。

From November 6th to 8th 2010, the 1st International Surfing Festival was held in Shimei Bay, Nanyan Bay, Sun and Moon Bay of Wanning city, jointly organized by Water Sports Administration under the jurisdiction of General Administration of Sports of China, Hainan Provincial Tourism Development Committee, Department of Culture Radio Television Publication and Sports, and the Wanning Municipal People's Government. 2015 witnessed the International Surf Events with 120 talents participating in. Held in Riyue Bay of Wanning city from December 4th to 12th, it was broadcast live by WSL for the first time, which made it possible for the surf fans all over the world to watch the match at the same time.

限于篇幅，其他节庆，如元旦、情人节、女生节、妇女节、植树节、复活节、愚人节、劳动节、青年节、母亲节、儿童节、父亲节、教师节、国庆节、光棍节、圣诞节、中国人民抗日战争胜利纪念日、文化遗产日、海南盈滨龙水节、海南省艺术节、海南书香节、海南动漫节、海南花梨文化节、海口青少年文化艺术节、临高渔民文化节、临高渔歌节、海鲜美食文化节、韩国美食文化节、龙泉文昌鸡美食节、茶文化节、酒文化节、三亚海洋文化节、三亚南山太极文化节、三亚南山健康长寿文化节、三亚国际玫瑰节、三亚国际沙滩音乐节、三亚龙抬头节、三亚疍家文化节、文昌南洋文化节、旅游地产文化节、旅游摄影文化节、健身康体节、万春会（万绿园新春年会）、荔枝文化节、大路镇大米文化节等，不再赘述。

Duo to the limited space, other festivals will not be described, such as New Year's Day, Valentine's Day, Girl's Day, Tree-Planting Day, Easter, April Fool's day, May Day, Youth Day, Mother's Day, Children's Day, Father's Day, Teachers' Day, National Day, Singles' Day, Christmas, the Commemoration Day of the Victory of the War Resistance against Japanese Aggression (day for commemorating the victory of the War of Resistance against Japanese Aggression), China Cultural Heritage Day, Yingbin Dragon Water Festival, Hainan Atrs Festival, Hainan Reading Day or Hainan Book and Copyright Day, Hainan Animation Festival, Hainan Huang Hua Li Rosewood Cultural Festival, Haikou Youth Arts and Cultures Festival, Lin'gao Fishermen Cultural Festival, Lin'gao Fishing Songs Festival, Seafood Gourmet Festival, Food Cultural Festival of Korea, Wenchang Chicken Festival, Hainan Tea Cultural Festival, Hainan Wine Cultural Festival, Sanya Marine Cultural Festival, Nanshan Tai Chi Cultural Festival in Sanya, Nanshan Longevity Festival in Sanya, Sanya International Roses Festival, Sanya International Beach Concert Festival, Dragon's Head-raising Festival in Sanya, the Tankas' Cultural Festival in Sanya, Nanyang Cultural Festival in Wenchang, Cultural Festival of Tourism-induced Real Estate, Tourism Photography Festival, Fitness and Health Festival, Lunar New Year Party in Evergreen Park, Litchi Cultural Festival, Dalu Rice Festival in Qionghai, etc.

3.7 海南岁时节日民俗旅游开发思考
Implications on the Tourism Development of Holidays and Customs in Hainan

海南省"十三五"期间，海南将重点打造海洋旅游、康养旅游、会展旅游、乡村旅游、文体旅游、婚庆蜜月旅游六类旅游产品。随着国际旅游岛及新型城镇化建设推进，适度保护性地开发海南岁时节日民俗旅游，意义深远。

The following six types of tourist products, such as tourism related to tropical marine, health care, MICE (meeting, incentives, conference or convention, and exhibition), rural sightseeing, arts and sports, wedding and honeymoon, will be focused on during the period of the 13th 5-year Plan of Hainan province. With the development of the International Tourist Destination and new urbanization, it is of far-reaching significance to make the best of festival and holiday customs-based tourism in a protective way.

3.7.1 挖掘多元节庆民俗文化，进一步彰显地域特色节庆民俗文化 To probe further into the multiple folk cultures during the festivals and holidays with typical regional characteristics

海南岛内外各民族交流频繁，岛内外多民族丰富多彩的民俗文化为海南特色民俗奠定了坚实的基础。例如，海南欢乐节、儋州中秋调声节、冼夫人信俗（军坡节）、府城换花节、七仙温泉嬉水节、黎族"三月三"、会山苗族传统文化节、苗族花山节等民俗文化应该进一步深入挖掘，凸显海南地域特色民俗文化的独特魅力。

Hainanese exchange with other ethnic groups home and abroad more frequently, which contributes more to their distinctive folk customs. For instance, the folk cultures in Hainan Carnival, Danzhou Diao Sheng Folk Songs Contest during the Autumn Festival in Danzhou city, Mrs. Xian Belief and Custom (Junpo Festival), Fucheng Flower Exchange Festival, Qixian (7th Fairy) Hot Spring Water Splashing Festival in Baoting, San Yue San Festival, the Miao People's Traditional Cultural Festival in Huishan Qionghai, Hua Shan Festival in the Miao People, etc. should be further explored to highlight the unique folk cultures in the charming land.

3.7.2 充分展示农耕民俗文化，适度推介健康节庆饮食民俗，进一步完善以农产品为主要内容的康养及乡村采摘旅游 To fully display folk cultures and customs in farming and appropriately popularize diet customs to improve the agriculture produce-enhanced tourism for picking and health

光照充足，资源丰富，农业是海南的优势产业，无论是汉族的传统节日还是黎族抑或苗族的民俗节日，大多均为农业文明发展的产物。海南乡村旅游开发过程中，一方面要保护黎族山栏节、吃新节、黎族牛节、元宵赛肥鸡等传统节日，另一方面更要重视乡村节庆民俗的参与性及趣味性，适度开发，稳步推进。

Agriculture is an advantageous industry in Hainan with adequate light and rich resources. Whether they are traditional festivals of the Han People or folk festivals of the Li or the Miao People, most of them result from the development of agricultural civilization. While developing the rural tourism in Hainan, more attention should be paid to the traditional festivals, such as Shan Lan Festival, New Rice-Eating Festival, Cattle's Day in the Li People, Fat Chicken Competition during the Lantern Festival. On the other hand, the participation and interest of the folk festivals in rural tourism should be developed steadily and moderately.

3.7.3 重点推介耕海民俗文化，进一步充实海洋节庆旅游 To concentrate on the farming customs and cultures in the sea to enrich the marine festivals-related tourism

海南四面环海，耕海文化独特，海洋神灵信仰文化浓厚，适当借鉴妈祖信俗（天后圣母节）、水尾圣娘庙会日、三江晶信夫人信俗、108兄弟公信俗、潭门南海传统文化节、潭门赶海文化节、海南盈滨龙水节、临高渔民文化节、临高渔歌节、海鲜美食文化节、三亚海洋文化节、三亚龙抬头节、三亚疍家文化节、文昌南洋文化节等，充实海洋节庆旅游文化内涵。

Hainan Island, which is surrounded by the South China Sea, is bestowed with unique belief and customs in god or goddess of the sea. Therefore, it is urgent to enrich the marine festival-enhanced tourism customs and cultures in Matsu Belief and Customs, Goddess Shuiwei Temple Fair, Belief and Customs in Mrs. San Jiang Jing Xin, 108 Brothers Belief and Customs, the South China Sea Traditional Cultural Festival in Tanmen, Tanmen Beachcombing Festival, Yingbin Dragon Water Festival, Lin'gao Fishing Cultural Festival, Lin'gao Fishing Songs Festival, Seafood Gourmet Festival, Sanya Marine Cultural Festival, Dragon's Head-Raising Festival in

Sanya, Tankas' Cultural Festival in Sanya, Nanyang Cultural Festival in Wenchang, etc.

3.7.4 凸显地域特色，进一步升级以传统节日为依托的节庆旅游 To highlight the local characteristics and further upgrade the traditional festivals-based tourism

传统节日形式多样，内容丰富，是文明进步的产物，是中华民族悠久的历史文化的重要组成，是中华民族身份认同的最直接方式之一。以传统节日端午节"洗龙水"习俗为例，基于龙水文化，海南可以开发更多旅游产品，突出热带海洋特色，加强民俗文化品牌意识，促进传统节庆旅游升级。

Traditional festivals with various forms and rich contents, which evolve with a long history of civilization, serve as an important composition of the Chinese long history and one of the most direct ways of the Chinese identity. Taking the custom of Xi Long Shui (swimming or bathing in dragon water) during the traditional Dragon Boat Festival for example, more tourism products can be developed based on the dragon water culture to strengthen folk culture brand awareness and upgrade traditional festival-based tourism.

04

海南建筑民俗
Architecture in Hainan Province

中国是一个地域辽阔的国家，许多独特的地方习俗造就了丰富多彩的民间建筑风格。海南的传统建筑记录了海南的历史，见证了海南的发展，在海南的发展史上具有非凡的意义。

China is a country of vast territory with many distinctive local customs, which diversifies the folk architectural styles. The traditional architecture means a lot to the development of Hainan Island which records the history and witnessed the development of Hainan.

4.1 传统民居
Traditional Folk House

中国的民居文化体现了人类对定居生活的需要。海南民居是海南文化的一种象征。在海南方言中，"屋"字包含了"家""室""房"三个字的意思。所以在海南说一个人"有屋有头"就是指这个人有房屋、有产业、有根基。由于海南岛四面环海，常受台风侵害。独特的地理及气候条件要求海南人民在建房时必须考虑建房材料、房屋结构等因素，因而房屋的造价相对较高，盖一座房子往往得耗费一家人多年的血汗。因此，海南人把建房作为人生中的头等大事。

Chinese residential culture is derived from the human's needs to settle down. Hainan dwelling houses are the carriers of the culture of Hainan. Hainan Island is surrounded by the sea, and often affected by typhoon. Therefore Hainanese should take the building materials, structure, firmness into consideration when they build a house because of the unique geographical and climate conditions. That's the reason why the Hainan people pay more attention to housing and building. House is the external manifestation of the value of a person's life, and it means "family" and "home" as well in Hainan dialect. Based on status of "house" in the heart of Hainanese, building a new house is a very important event in a family. A whole family has to spend many years and even the rest of their lives on building a new house.

自古以来海南人对于房子的选址、走向、择日进屋的仪式等十分重视，并形成习俗世代流传。人们比较喜欢选择"前水后山"的位置建房，水寓意有龙庇佑，山表示有靠山，可保佑家庭人丁兴旺、财源广进。座向以坐北朝南居多。海南人喜欢在房子周边种植树木，如椰子树、槟榔树、龙眼树、荔枝树、竹子等，不但有经济价值，又可起到美化、绿化的作用。

When Hainanese builds a new house, they attach great importance to the location, the orientation of the "house", the date to build and the ceremony to move in since ancient times, and the building customs have passed from generation to generation. The ideal place to build a new house should be near water or behind hill, and the house should be faced toward the south. Besides, people are inclined to plant trees around their houses. Fruit trees are the best choices, such as coconut trees, litchi, betel nut trees, bamboos, Longan trees and so on. These trees with great value freshen the air and beautify the surroundings as well.

建房之前，屋主要先请来风水先生看屋场风水，确定房子朝向，然后选择建房的良辰吉日。建房时的升梁是作为祭典来庆祝的，各地各家风俗不同、做法不一，但无论是谁都应在升梁前用红纸写梁斗，贴在梁上；同时用红布缝袋，装进钱米，挂在梁中央，然后将梁放置于宅基的前面，吉时到了就升梁，然后燃放鞭炮。接着祭拜祖先后，要摆酒席宴请前来祝贺的亲戚及建房工人。建房这一天，在外地工作的儿子能回来的都得回来，出嫁的女儿也得和女婿拖儿带女，挑着用米做的"粑果"回来庆贺。当父母的则是高高兴兴地将"粑果"一一分送给邻居，一起分享建新房的喜悦，这个习俗作为海南的特有的文化一直保留至今。

Before building a house, the owner will invite a geomancer to check the terrain and choose an auspicious day for building. And then there will be a ceremony to celebrate "ridge purlin lifting". The ceremony is different in varies places. However, one thing should be done is to write down some Chinese characters in a red piece of paper and stick it on the ridge purlin, meanwhile, the owner puts some money and rice into a red bag and hangs them on the ridge purlin. After that, the family offers sacrifices to ancestor, holds the worship and feasts the builders. The family members who work in other places will come back home to celebrate with "BaGuo" — a kind of cake made from rice. The owner will distribute the "BaGuo" to the neighbors to share the happiness and joy of building new house. The custom has been remained until now as the unique culture in Hainan.

海南省的典型特色民居可分为四个区域十种类型，分别是：琼北民居——多进合院、火山石民居、南洋风格民居、南洋风格骑楼；琼南民居——疍家渔排、崖州合院；琼西南民居——儋州客家围屋、军屯民居；琼中南黎族民居——船型屋和金字屋（海口旅游网，2013）。

The typical characteristic dwelling houses in Hainan Province can be divided into ten types in 4 districts as follows. Northern Hainan: houses with multi-entrance courtyard, dwelling houses in Nan yang style, Arcade building in Nan yang style, Volcanic rock houses; Southern Hainan: the Tankas fishing rows, Yazhou courtyard; Southwest of Hainan: Hakka quadrangle in Dan Zhou Style, Garrison houses; Central section of Hainan: boat-shaped houses and pyramid houses.

4.1.1 琼北民居之多进合院 Houses with Multi-entrance Courtyard

多进合院延续了大陆传统民居中常见的合院式空间布局的基本格局。多进合院主要分布在琼北地区的海口、文昌、琼海、定安、澄迈等市县境内村庄。多进合院式传统民居一般由头门、正屋、檐廊、横屋、厨房、庭院、翘头、雕刻、彩绘等组成，其中正屋为主体建筑，包括厅堂和厢房两部分（政协琼海市委员会，2009）。这种房屋模式千百年来世代传承，成为海南居家文化的一大特色，反映了海南民间的风俗风情。

Houses with multi-entrance courtyard still have been remained the common courtyard structure of the traditional dwelling houses in mainland. The houses mainly exist in the natural villages in Northern Hainan, such as Haikou, Wenchang, Qionghai, Ding'an, Chengmai and so on. The structure of houses with multi-entrance courtyard includes main entrance, main room, eaves gallery, transverse room, kitchen, courtyard, everted flanges, carving, color painting, and laneway and so on. And the main building of a house is the main room, including hall and bedroom. A house model like this has been inherited for thousands of years, and it has become a major feature of Hainan house culture.

头门

Main Entrance

头门，也被称为"门脸""门面"，是民居院落界定内外的标志，代表屋主的身份、地位以及文化品位。头门一般设在偏向前墙的一侧，两边有门框，目的是为了保护生活的私隐性。家道殷实的人家会把头门建成小楼阁，称之为门楼。门前留着台阶，用石板或砖头垒成，一般为三级，有步步升高或连升三级的意思。

The main entrance is a symbol to define residential compounds, and often represents the householder's identity, status, and cultural taste. Therefore, it is often called "Men Lian" and "Men Mian" in Chinese. In order to protect the privacy of the family, main entrance generally locates in the side of the front wall, with the doorframe on both sides. The well-to-do people always build the main entrance like a small pavilion, called gate building. Meanwhile, there are three stairs built of stones or bricks in front of the main entrance, meaning promotion step by step.

正屋

Main Room

正屋是位于宅院正中央的房屋，通常高于横屋和厨房。正屋一般设有6个门，前门后门，两侧厢房各有上下两个房门，共四个房门。正屋的中间部分是厅堂，厅堂里常摆设神龛和各种木制家具；正厅的左右两侧是厢房。正屋是祭祀祖先、办理婚庆等大事的地方，因此海南人都想方设法把正屋建得有气派、有威严。有些家境殷实的人家将正屋屋顶上的四个角建成在东南亚一带建筑中盛行的"龙翅""云公"，有避邪和对神灵的崇拜的寓意。这种柱头的大小、规模也是一个家庭社会地位与经济地位的象征。富贵人家的柱头有飞龙走凤，气势威严壮观。一般正屋的前面或后面带有走廊，海南方言俗称"飘"，可挡风遮雨。正屋的厅堂、卧室两面都开有窗户以保持四面通风，屋顶开有透明的天窗以确保光线对流。

The main part of the house locating in the middle is called main room, generally higher than transverse room and kitchen. The middle part of the main room is the hall, where various wooden furniture and shrine are generally placed. The rest are the bedrooms. Since the main room is used for ancestor worship, wedding and other important events, Hainan people are trying to build the main room in dignified style. The rich decorates the roof corner of the main room like "Dragon Wings" and "Cloud" which can be seen in Southeast Asian buildings, meaning to ward off evil spirits and worship the gods. At the same time, the size of the "Dragon Wing" is also a symbol of a family's social status and economic conditions. In front of or behind the main room there are corridors commonly known as "piao" in Hainan dialect, and they can prevent the rain and wind. There are some windows in both the hall and bedrooms; even the roof is provided with transparent windows.

厅堂
Hall

厅堂的大门是对扇结构，为木制门框，门槛也多为木制，但在山区房子的门槛多用石条。因门槛镇宅，海南人忌讳用脚踏在上面。自古以来，有钱人家会在大院内盖三至四个厅堂以显示其身份和社会地位。厅堂主要用于节期祭祀祖先、接待宾客以及商谈家庭大事，因而厅堂的设置十分讲究。一般用木板隔成屏风（俗称"堋桨"）将厅堂的后堂和前堂隔开。1949年前，屏风的作用是方便女眷进出厅堂与厢房。在"男女授受不亲"的旧礼教下，每当在厅堂招待来访的男客时，家中的女眷只能从后门，在屏风的保护下，遮遮掩掩地从上房门口走进自己的房间。屏风的顶部设置神堂，用于供奉祖先的灵位（即俗称"香炉"）及香火福龛。屏风前放置一张八仙桌用于祭祀时放置供奉的食物。

The door of the hall usually is two-leafed with a wooden doorframe and a wooden threshold, some of which are made of stone slabs in the mountainous areas. It is a taboo to step on the threshold. The hall is a place to celebrate or discuss all kinds of important events and receive visiting guests. There is a screen made of wood planks near the back of the hall; thus passersby outside cannot witness the activities inside. Moreover, the screen prevents the wind from directly blowing through when the gate is opened. On the top of the screen there is a shrine for their ancestors, and there is a square table near the screen. Before 1949, the screen was used for the girls to avoid visiting man guests who were sitting in the hall when they entered into bedroom from the back door because of the old ethical concepts of "no contact between man and woman".

厢房
Bedroom

厢房即卧室，通常用木板隔开，分为上厢房和下厢房。儿子结婚时，父母会在下厢房给儿子放置一张围床，在上厢房给媳妇安放架子床和梳妆台，上下厢房即是儿子和媳妇的寝室。

The bedrooms are for the owners' and their married eldest son and his wife. It is usually separated into two parts by the wood plank, a dressing table and a sofa bed are placed in the first part, and canopy bed is placed in the back part.

神龛
Shrine

神龛设置在厅堂的屏风顶端，可置放香炉，祭拜祖先。从古至今，海南人乐于选用纹理细腻、色泽金黄的菠萝蜜木制作神龛。神龛的左右两边设有窗棂，刻上或贴上有寓意的对联以祈求祖先保佑家人平安健康、人丁兴旺、出人头地。神龛下面摆放着八仙桌或翘头桌，两边放置太师椅、官帽椅、罗汉床，彰显家族的尊贵。

On the top of the screen there is a shrine for their ancestors with an incense burner in it. Since ancient times, Hainan people love to choose Jackfruit tree, which is of golden color and delicate texture, to make a shrine. There are window lattices on both sides of the shrine. An antithetical couplet are even carved or pasted on the lattices. An alter table or a square table stands beneath the shrine, and there are arhat bed, fauteuil, Mandarin chair around the table, which show the family's dignity and grace.

横屋
Transverse Room

横屋指的是正屋的两侧相对低矮的屋子，有些地方叫横屋或屋仔，也叫厨房。横屋是存放五谷杂粮、杂物或是给已长大的子女居住。

The transverse rooms are on the side of the main room using as cook room, utility room and even bedroom for the mature sons and daughters.

檐廊
Eaves Gallery

檐廊指的是屋檐下的通道，正屋门外常用砖柱或石柱承托檐檩，檐檩下构筑砖拱，仰视有弧形美感。檐廊具有遮阳挡雨的功能，也可用来放蓑衣、斗笠、水桶等生活用具，还可以晾晒衣服。

Eaves gallery built by bricks or stones is an aisle under the eaves to keep the room in shadow and provide a shelter from rain, where people always place home appliances, like straw rain cape, bamboo hat, and bucket etc. Clothes can be hung on the porch as well.

庭院
Courtyard

房屋中间被建筑物环卫的场地称为庭院。在海南民居中，庭院是不可或缺的一部分，一般面积都不大，多数是以青砖铺地，可用作晒谷场，像结婚、庆生等喜庆活动一般也都在庭院里进行。大户有钱人家的多进院落中，庭院又可分为前院、中院和后院，伴有小型花池等美化生活环境，庭与院之间通常有小门或者廊道连通。宽敞的后院一般种植果树，既可遮荫又能美化环境。除此之外，后院还用于喂养家畜家禽。这种外封内敞的庭院空间对家庭生活的私隐性起到了很大的保护作用。

The site surrounded by buildings is called a courtyard. Courtyard is an integral part of the local house in Hainan. It is generally not large, and mostly paved with brick. Festive activities or events can be held there like wedding, birthday party etc. Also courtyard can be used as drying yard, where the hosts dry the rice in the sun. The rich's courtyard can be divided into the front yard, center yard and backyard. They have landscaped their center yard with a small pond, shrubs and lawn. Fruit trees are planted in the spacious backyard, which can not only provide some shade but also beautify the environment. The backyard is also generally a place for feeding livestock and poultry. The courtyard plays an important role in protecting the privacy of home life.

翘头
Everted Flanges

翘头是民居建筑中颇有特色的部位，指的是屋顶四角正脊两端的部分。海南民居中的翘头造型多样，各有不同的寓意，有用鳌鱼头部表示独占鳌头；有的设置蛟头象征富贵尊严，也有用缠枝花草给屋宅增添灵巧精致的情趣。

The everted flanges are the most distinctive parts of a local house in Hainan. They locate in the top four corners and at the two ends of the ridge of the roof. There are a variety of the everted flanges in Hainan dwelling house. Some are built as a turtlehead with the connotation of getting the first place, some as a dragonhead with the connotation of wealth and dignity, and some as flowers and grass to add the taste of the house.

雕刻

Carving

海南人通过在门窗、神龛与家具上雕刻各种文字或图案来表达美好的祝福。如"寿"字表示长寿；仙鹤也象征长寿；牡丹表示富贵；桂花表示文才等。雕刻主要采用透雕、浮雕、阴刻等手法。

Hainan people are inclined to carve characters or pictures on the doors, windows, shrines and some furniture by using carving techniques like engraving, embossing, and intaglio to show the best wishes. For example, the carving red-crowned crane symbolizes longevity; the peony symbolizes wealth and rank.

彩绘

Color Painting

彩绘是中国传统民居中常用于装饰的一种民间艺术。海南民居的彩绘大多绘在墙体上，图案多种多样，有飞龙走凤、田园景色、山水风光等。彩绘一般色调清雅，线条简洁流畅，具有很高的观赏性，充分表达了海南人民休闲生活的审美情趣和对美好生活的追求。

Color painting is a kind of folk art used to decorate traditional dwelling houses in China. The painting designs are various, including landscapes, pastoral scenery, fruits, flowers, trees and so on. Most of color paintings are usually painted on the wall of Hainan dwelling houses. Lines of the paintings are smooth and brief, and colors are simple and elegant which show leisurely aesthetic taste and the people's pursuit for a better life.

巷道

Laneway

巷道是村庄中各家各户间的通道。巷道虽不宽敞，但给海南人民出门劳作、邻里走门串户提供了很大的方便。

Laneway is the channel between households in the village. It is convenient for people to go out and into the house although it is not spacious.

4.1.2 琼北民居之南洋风格民居 Dwelling Houses in Nanyang style

南洋风格民居的基本结构是在传统琼北民居的基础之上逐渐形成的，但其外观、内部空间设置、构件、规模等方面受外来文化的影响，在筑造过程中发生了变化，因此形成了具有琼北特色的南洋风格传统民居新形式。现在保存完好的南洋风格民居主要在琼北地区的海口、琼海、文昌、定安等市县的部分村庄有分布，存量不多，大多是建于 20 世纪初至 20 世纪 30 年代初。

The dwelling houses in Nan yang style has formed based on the type of traditional houses in northern Hainan, but their appearance, the layout of inner space, component and scale are a little bit different from the traditional northern style; thus a new style has been formed. The well-preserved buildings, which mainly exist in Haikou, Wenchang, Qionghai, were mostly built during the time from the early twentieth Century to 1930s.

建于 1934 年的蔡家大院位于今琼海市博鳌镇留客村，属于典型的南洋风格民居，是全国重点文物保护单位。蔡家大院的建筑群庞大而完整，是一座二层三厅四合楼，外观酷似城堡，属于木、砖、瓦、水泥钢筋混合结构。院墙和柱子均采用坚固的青砖砌成。整栋建筑是用钢筋水泥浇筑成的走廊连成一个环形的结构，宅院内上下连通，紧密相连，就算正屋、横屋以及前后庭院之间也是有走廊相互连接的。这样的四通八达的环廊具有挡风遮光避雨的功能，大宅内一年四季清爽宜人。

The Cai's former residence built in 1934 is the typical Nan yang styled dwelling house, which locats in Liuke village, Boao town. And it is also a national key cultural relic protection unit. The whole building was built with brick, tile, wood, steel and concrete. It is a large and integrated quadrangle structure with two floors, which looks exactly like a castle, including three halls. A major feature of the Cai's former residence is the use of the corridors, which are made of reinforced concrete, linking all the buildings, giving shelter to the residents who can walk every corner all over the courtyard without an umbrella on rainy or sunny days, and therefore making the house clean, pleasant and warm like spring all year round.

4.1.3 琼北民居之南洋风格骑楼 Arcade Building in Nan Yang Style

海南是著名的南洋侨乡，南洋建筑文化在一定程度上影响着海南的建筑史，它是近代海南民居建筑的代表。海南各地的骑楼建筑风格迥异，各有特色。这些骑楼建筑是主人根据自己在外辛苦闯荡时的所见所闻加上自己喜好，融入风水文化，重新加工而成的。

Hainan belongs to the cultural circle of Southeast Asia and also leaves a mark on the history of Southeast Asia culture. There is no doubt that the arcade in Nan yang style is representative of modern architecture in Hainan. The style of arcade is various in different cities. The hard working overseas Chinese build them by copying and reworking the Nan yang buildings according to their own preferences based on what they have seen and heard.

骑楼指的是建筑物底层沿街铺面前留出的公共人行空间，用立柱支撑，内部形成的人行道，供行人行走时避风雨、防日晒的街道，是一种集商贸和居住为一体的建筑，反映出海南商业文化与社会文化的地域特色。保存相对完好的骑楼建筑主要分布在琼北地区归侨比较集中的琼海、海口、文昌、万宁等市县。

Arcade is a kind of commercial and residential buildings, whose feature is that the front part of the first floor of the building is for pedestrians to avoid wind, rain and strong sunshine. The intact arcade buildings are mainly distributed in northern Hainan areas like Haikou, Wenchang, Qionghai, Wanning city, where the returned Overseas Chinese and their relatives inhabit.

海口骑楼（吴丽 摄）
Arcade buildings in Haikou (Courtesy of Li Wu)

4.1.4 琼北民居之海南火山石民居 Volcanic Rock Dwelling Houses

由于海南琼北传统民居和多风雨的气候等多种因素影响，海南火山石传统民居的建筑风格是以火山石为主体建材的热带风情建筑，多建于明清时代，属于木石结构。房屋之间有巷道相连，排列整齐的村巷路面铺设着青石板，既干净又便于排水。村巷狭长而幽深，给邻里往来互帮带来了便利。民居的前厅后院是整齐排列的横向通道，层层布局，风流和水流畅通，是典型的梳式布局结构，极富特色。院落沿用竹筒屋短面宽、长进深的布局特征，两户之间形成巷道，多排并列形成村落。建筑工艺主要采用传统的海南"十柱屋"的特点，但石柱及木质梁少有雕刻。传统的火山石民居的中间木结构与瓦结构使用一段时间后都要进行翻新，但火山石墙体可以一直保留。现存完好的火山石民居的木结构与瓦结构都经过多次翻新，而火山石墙体一直沿用至今。

  The traditional volcanic rock dwelling houses built of wood and volcanic rock began to be built in the era of the Ming and Qing Dynasties. Houses are connected by village lane built of green slab-stones, which are narrow, deep and neatly arranged. The lanes are convenient for neighbors' visiting; besides, they are easy to keep clean and drain. The hall and backyard of a house are well laid-out arranged, whose layout is the typical comb structure to keep the air, the wind and water flowing smoothly. The traditional construction technology mainly adopts the characteristic of Hainan "Decastyle house". The wood and tile of existing volcanic rock houses have been renovated many times, but the volcanic rock wall has been used until now.

海口遵潭镇火山石民居（蔡云 摄）
Traditional volcanic rock houses (Courtesy of Yun Cai)

4.1.5 琼南民居之疍家渔排 The Tanka Fishing Rows

  海南疍家人为了适应水上养殖，在延续传统水居船屋、临水吊脚屋功能的基础上，结合新时期生产和生活的需要，建造了集养殖、捕鱼和居住为一体的渔排，是疍家民居的典型样式之一，现在的疍家渔排还发展了渔排餐业和观光等商业活动。海南疍家渔排分布在疍家人聚居地的港湾河汊地——陵水新村、三亚红沙等。

  Tanka refers to the fisher family who fish and live in a boat. The Tanka fishing rows refer to the pontoon rows of the fisher houses. It is one of the typical styles of Hainan Tanka's dwellings. On the basis of the function of the traditional water boathouses and stilted houses, modern Tanka family build the pontoon row houses to meet needs of production and living, which own the function of breeding, fishing and living in order to adapt to the aquaculture. Tanka fishing rows are mainly distributed in harbor and branch of a river, such as Lingshui and Sanya, where Hainan Tanka families inhabit.

疍家渔排（代国夫 摄）
Tanka fishing rows (Source: http://hd.hinews.cn/2/CM_dg_2013.php?xuh=63769)

4.1.6 琼南民居之崖州合院 Yazhou Courtyard

琼南地区常年干热，雨季有暴风雨，受这样的气候特点的影响，形成了独具琼南特色的典型传统接檐式民居——崖州合院民居。建筑形式在一定程度上受广府民居和闽南民居的影响。崖州合院主要分布在乐东至三亚等市县沿海汉族村落。

Yazhou courtyard is a typical traditional local house in southern Hainan areas. To a certain extent, the dwelling houses of Fujianese and Cantonese influence the layout of the building. Considering the climate characteristics of perennial dry, hot and rainstorm in rainy season, Sanya and Ledong residents build such unique southern Hainan special eaves-linked houses. The Yazhou courtyard is mainly distributed in coastal villages in Sanya, Ledong and other cities.

崖州合院（陈延鹏 摄）
Yazhou courtyard
(Source: http://www.hkwb.net/news/content/2014-11/30/content_2437545_4.htm)

4.1.7 琼西南民居之儋州客家围屋 Hakka Quadrangle in Dan Zhou Style

儋州客家围屋是具有开拓进取精神的客家人到海南岛后建造居住，并在当地发展了客家文化。儋州客家围屋沿袭了内陆客家围屋的建筑特点，以南北子午线为中轴，东西两边对称，坐落有序，主次分明，前低后高，布局整齐。儋州客家围屋主要分布于儋州东南部地区，以和庆镇、南丰镇范围为主。

Hakka quadrangle in Dan Zhou Style is also called Wei dragon house, turn roundhouse, Hakka enclose dragon house, which was built by the Hakka people when they came to Hainan Island and settled down. Danzhou Hakka build their houses following the architectural features of the Hakka in main land, which are well laid-out arranged based on North and South meridian. Danzhou Hakka quadrangles are mainly distributed in the southeastern region of Danzhou.

儋州客家围屋（李幸璜 摄）
Hakka quadrangle in Dan Zhou Style
(Source: http://hnrb.hinews.cn/html/2008-11/03/content_78477.htm)

4.1.8　琼西南民居之军屯民居 Garrison Houses

军屯民居是军屯文化特征明显的民居类型，是儋州市西北部地区独有的民居形式。院落布局沿袭了典型的中原四合院布局，并与儋州西北部地区的环境相结合，经过时代变迁，形成了如今特有的军屯民居形式，主要分布于儋州西北部地区。

Garrison houses are typical dwelling houses with garrison culture features in the northwestern regions of Danzhou City, whose courtyard layout follow that of quadrangle in central plain of China. After the evolution of the era, the garrison residential construction has formed a new style of dwelling houses fitting for the local environment. Garrison houses are mainly distributed in the northwestern region of Danzhou City.

4.1.9　中南黎族民居之船型屋 Boat-shaped Houses

船型屋，又称船型茅草屋，是黎族人民的传统住宅建筑，也是海南岛富有浓郁民族风情和地域特色的建筑文化。相传黎族人是为了纪念乘船渡海而来的祖先，模仿船的样子而建造的房屋。这种屋子的屋檐像船蓬一样贴到地面，形状如倒扣的船只，故起名为船型屋。可见船型屋与海洋有着密切联系。

Boathouse, also known as boat-shaped huts, is also the oldest and traditional residence of the Li People, which shows the architectural culture with rich ethnic customs and strong local characteristics. According to the legend, the Li People built houses by imitating the shape of a ship in order to commemorate their ancestors.

船型屋通常由前厅、居室和后部的杂用房三部分组成。建筑材料取自于大自然，主要以竹木为框架，用竹片和藤条捆扎，屋顶捆扎成拱形，覆上茅草。船型屋外观如倒扣船状或龟壳状，房檐向外伸出，可用于舂米，也可用于存放衣具或柴草等。船型屋一般不设窗户，内部不隔间，地板铺设竹片或木板，内设火坑，白天煮饭，晚上烤火取暖。

The boat-shaped house consists of three parts: the front hall, bedroom and the back utility room. The frame mainly uses bamboo as a support and is tied by rattan and bamboo. The roof is covered with the thatch. The eave wall is built with branches of bamboo and then wiped mud and straw. The boat-shaped houses do not have windows and compartments inside, and the floor is paved with pieces of bamboo or wood. The hall is equipped with a fireplace used for cooking and heating.

船型屋是黎族精神文化和物质文化的重要组成部分，经过历史的沉淀，它已经不是纯粹的建筑形式，而是蕴藏着一个民族的灵魂和精神，富含着深厚的民族价值观。

Boat-shaped house is one of the important carriers of history and culture of the Li People. For thousands of years of historical accumulation, the Li traditional architecture is not only a kind of typical building, but also an embodiment of a culture, which contains profound ethical values.

船型屋（关景迪 摄）
Boat-shaped house (Source: http://news.hainan.net/hainan/2009/10/26/645064.shtml)

4.1.10 琼中南黎族民居之金字屋 Pyramid-shaped House

金字屋可以说是船型屋的改良版。随着与汉族人民接触的增多，黎族人民逐步吸收了汉人的房屋建造技术，船型屋建造也发生了改变，房形结构和搭建材料都与过去有了很大的不同，随之出现了以木字金字架支撑屋顶的仿汉式金字形屋。但金字屋仍保留原有的矮小的竹编泥糊的檐墙，内部布置还与船型屋相似。解放后，黎村便已普遍采用汉族的金字，从屋檐下的墙体开门，设有小窗，墙体修高，采光通风条件得到改善，建造材料改为泥涂墙或泥砖墙和瓦盖顶了。金字屋的布局规模有大有小，类型多样，有单间、双间、三间、四合院式等。受汉文化的影响，金字屋的建筑结构由前廊、起居室、卧室、厨房组成，在后墙正中还设有祖先神台。卧室内有木制或竹制睡床和其他一些物品等，厨房购置有炉灶、炊具、水缸、烘物架等。金字屋的室内布局有了现代房屋的雏形。金字屋主要分布在海南的黎族自治县（沈志成、沈艳，2008）。

With increasing contact of Li and Han people, the Li People gradually absorbed the Han Chinese housing construction technology, and they changed the shape of the boat-shaped house and chose different building materials. Experiencing a series of evolution, the boat-shaped house has gradually been replaced with the pyramid-shaped house whose structure and building materials are different. After liberation, boat-shaped house has totally been replaced. The ventilation and lighting conditions were improved with windows. Moreover, the building materials were changed from only plants to mud or clay brick and tile roof. The roof was replaced with a pyramid-shaped roof and walls were built much higher. There are single, double or three rooms, and even a quadrangle. It consists of the front porch, living room, bedroom and kitchen in a pyramidal house. There is a bed and other wooden or bamboo articles in the bedroom and stove, water tank, cooker, drying rack etc. in the kitchen. The interior layout in pyramid-shaped house is the rudiment of modern housing. Pyramid-houses are mainly distributed in the Li People Autonomous County.

金字屋 （贺立樊 摄）
Pyramid-shaped house
(Source: http://news.163.com/14/1203/11/ACHOL5OA00014Q4P.html)

4.2 传统书院建筑
The Traditional Architecture of Academy of Classical Learning

唐贞观二十年（646年），王义芳被贬到今昌化旧县村任县丞期间，开设讲堂，开海南教育之先河。晚唐以后，许多被贬到海南的朝廷命官，设堂讲学，传播中原文化，尤其是大文豪苏东坡对海南文化教育的影响巨大，儒学开始在海南得到发展。各种官办、私立学堂相继出现，书院逐步发展，教育得到了发展，为海南文化历史的提高与发展奠定了坚实的基础（沈志成、沈艳，2008）。

Since the late Tang Dynasty, many officers who were demoted to Hainan Island disseminated the culture of Confucianism; especially the literary giant Su Dongpo had a huge impact on Hainan education. Confucianism began to develop in Hainan from then on. Various official and private schools have gradually been set up and developed. The education has been developed, which laid a solid foundation for the improvement and development of culture of Hainan.

4.2.1 东坡书院 Dongpo Academy

东坡书院是北宋大文豪苏东坡的讲学场所，位于海南省儋州市中和镇东郊，是全国重点文物保护单位。东坡书院原名载酒堂，始建于1097年。整个书院占地面积达2500平方米，设有前门、大殿、东西厢房（现为书画廊）、东坡祠、载酒堂、载酒亭、钦帅堂、尊贤堂、迎宾堂、望京阁、陈列馆等主要建筑物以及东坡讲学彩雕像、春牛石雕、东坡铜像、钦帅井和碑刻等。自1982年以来书院进行了数次大规模的扩建和维修，成为海南重要的人文景观之一（沈志成、沈艳，2008）。

Dongpo Academy is a national key cultural relics protection unit, which lies in the eastern outskirts of the Zhonghe town, Danzhou City, where the literal giant Su Dongpo gave lectures in Song Dynasty. Dongpo Academy was built in 1097, covering an area of 31,200 square meters, and consisting of front door, hall, Zaijiu pavilion, Zaijiu Hall, Dongpo Hall, East and West Rooms, Zunxian Hall, Chinshuai Hall, Wangjing Pavilion, Yingbin Hall, Exhibition Hall and other major buildings and so on. Since 1982, the academy has been maintained and expanded several times, and become one of the most important cultural landscapes in Hainan.

东坡书院 载酒亭 （谢振安 摄）
Zaijiu pavilion
(Source: http://news.hainan.net/gundong/2015/02/04/2243484.shtml)

4.2.2 溪北书院 Xibei Academy

溪北书院位于海南省文昌铺前镇文北中学内，是海南目前保留得规模最大、最完好的清代建筑群。由清末著名书法家潘存筹建于 1893 年，清朝光绪十九年，当时是海南著名书院之一。书院占地面积大约 13333 平方米，是一所三进四合院的砖瓦结构古建筑群，坐北朝南。由大门、讲堂、经正楼、经堂和斋舍五部分组成，东西走廊相连建筑群，四周有围墙环绕。三进正堂为"经正楼"，是书院的主体建筑，1921 年改建成中西合璧的二层楼建筑（沈志成、沈艳，2008）。

经正堂 （朱含霓 摄）
Jingzheng Building (Courtesy of Hanni Zhu)

Xibei Academy is located in Wenbei Middle School in Wenchang. It is one of the famous academies and well-preserved and large-scale building group of the Qing Dynasty in Hainan. The academy was built by a famous calligrapher Pancun in 1893, and covers an area of about 13,333 square meters. It includes five parts: the entrance building, lecture hall, Jingzheng Building, Sutra Hall and book room. Jingzheng Building is the main building, and it was rebuilt to a two-floor building with a combination of Chinese and Western styles in 1921. It is a historical and cultural heritage in Wenchang.

琼台书院大门（吴其润 摄）
Entrance building of Qiongtai Academy (Courtesy of Qirun Wu)

4.2.3 琼台书院 Qiongtai Academy

琼台书院建于 1705 年，位于海口市府城中山北路和文庄路的交叉路口南侧。相传是为纪念海南第一才子丘濬而建，因其号"琼台"的缘故而得名"琼台书院"。琼台书院是清代海南唯一的府立书院，被誉为琼州最高学府。书院创建之初，仅有一亭二院，设备简陋，书籍匮乏。经几次扩建后才成为藏书量多、斋舍齐全的大型书院。建于乾隆十八年（1753 年）的奎星楼是琼台书院主体建筑，是一座具有民族风情的绿瓦、白墙、红廊的二层砖木结构楼阁，至今保存完好。书院至今还保存有古老书卷、书橱、书桌等文物，楼前还设有香炉，每逢重大考试前香火仍然旺盛（沈志成、沈艳，2008）。

Qiongtai Academy, a top institution with higher learning, was built in 1705. There was only a pavilion and two courtyards in the academy at first. After several expansions, it became a large-scale academy. Kuixing Building is the main building, which was founded in the-Eighteenth-year of Qianlong Qing dynasty. The two-floor building with red porch, green tile, sand white wall was built of brick and wood, and has been well preserved.

4.3 传统牌坊建筑
Traditional Memorial Archway Architecture

牌坊乃中华民族的瑰宝，是中国独有的标志性建筑物，由门演化而来。牌坊在海南民间俗称"梁派""风牌"，一般是四根间柱形成三个空间，由额枋相连，中间称明间，两边称次间。间柱前后有支撑台座的夹杆石（木牌坊另加戗杆）固定以稳固抗风雨。牌坊品种多样，造型各异。然而由于地震和台风等地质灾害与人为因素的影响，海南的古牌坊群所剩无几，不是在地震与台风中倾倒，就是在战乱和"文化大革命"动乱中被扫荡拆毁，只有少数深藏在茂密荆棘野岭中的牌坊躲过劫难而存留下来。

The memorial archway, a unique and typical Chinese architecture, was evolved from "door", which was known as "Liang Pai", "Feng Pai" in Hainan. Generally speaking, the frame consists of four pillars, which are connected by architraves. In order to stabilize the pillars in the wind, there are supporting pedestals and clamping rod rocks before and after the rib pillars to fix the memorial archway. The forms and styles of memorial archway are various and different. However, they died out because of earthquakes and typhoons, and were destroyed by the war and the unrest of "Cultural Revolution".

4.3.1 海南牌坊的种类 Types of memorial archway

海南，曾被称为"牌坊之岛"。牌坊的种类之多、分布之集中，丝毫不亚于牌坊的故乡徽州，在中国历史上占有一席之地。牌坊在海南民间俗称"梁派""风牌"，一般是四根间柱形成三个空间，由额枋相连，中间称明间，两边称次间。间柱前后有支撑台座的夹杆石（木牌坊另加戗杆）固定以稳固抗风雨。有的牌坊还在额枋上设有隔扇斗拱相叠，斗拱上覆以有檐有脊的楼顶构件，坊额上书写、凿刻坊名。牌坊品种多样，造型各异（沈志成、沈艳，2008）。

Hainan Island has ever been called "Memorial Archway Island" because of various types of memorial archway and their concentrated distribution, which is no inferior to those in the hometown of memorial archway, Huizhou. The memorial archway was known as "Liang Pai", "Feng Pai" in Hainan. Generally speaking, the frame consists of four pillars, which are connected by architraves. In order to stabilize the pillars in the wind, there are supporting pedestals and clamping rod rocks before and after the rib pillars to fix the memorial archway. The forms and styles of memorial archway are various and different.

一般来说，海南的牌坊主要有四种分类：

There are four kinds of classifications on memorial archway:

从形制上分：屋宇式；冲天式；仿阙式。

Classified from the shape：

The shape is like a house. On this type of memorial archway, there are overhanging eaves and bucket arch on the architrave and with a roof on the top;

The shape is like a Cupola evolved from Huabiao Pillar – a traditional architecture way of the Han nationality, without bucket arch and roof. The rib pillar is higher than the architrave and points to the sky;

The shape is like an imperial palace, which building small towers on the top to show the high and noble, with imposing extraordinary charming.

从结构上分：两柱一间；四柱三间。

Classified from the structure: A structure with two pillars and one space; A structure with four pillars and three spaces.

从材质上分：有木制的；有竹制的；有火山石砌；有仿琉璃坊；石制。

Classified from the building material: Built by wood; Built by bamboo; Built by volcanic bricks; Built by imitating glass; More built by stones.

从内容上分：标志坊；功德坊；过街坊；山门坊；墓道坊；节操坊。

Classified from the function: Built for a sign; Built to show merits and virtues; Street-crossing archway; Gate archway; Tomb archway; Moral integrity archway.

4.3.2 海南牌坊的现状 Present Situation of Memorial Archway in Hainan

牌坊（蔡云 摄）
Memorial Archway (Courtesy of Yun Cai)

立牌坊在封建社会象征着崇高荣誉，可流芳百世，是人们一生的追求。把历代名人名事凿刻在石坊上，世代流传，以昭示后人。由于地震和台风等地质灾害与人为因素的影响，海南的古牌坊群所剩无几，不是在地震与台风中倾倒，就是在战乱和"文化大革命"中被扫荡拆毁，只有少数深藏在茂密荆棘野岭中的牌坊躲过劫难而存留下来（沈志成、沈艳，2008）。

To set up a memorial archway was a way to show the highest honor, virtue, and imperial favor in the feudal society. However, the memorial archways throughout Hainan nearly died out because of earthquakes and typhoons or were destroyed by wars and the unrest of "Cultural Revolution" under the replacement of dynasties. Only those hidden deep in the thick thorns and deserted mountains survived but there are not much left.

05

海南饮食民俗
Hainan Dietary Folk Customs

海南岛，南中国海的天堂岛，也是中国第二大岛屿，面积仅次于台湾岛。海南岛人文历史悠久，文化灿烂，在博大精深的华夏文明中独树一帜，从远古到现代，她都是中华文明的重要分支。

Hainan Island, China's island Paradise, is the second largest island in China (next in area to Taiwan island). Hainan Island is an island with long history and splendid culture, which is unique with profound Chinese civilization. From ancient to modern times, she has always been an important branch in Chinese civilization.

饮食是一种文化，更是一门艺术。海南的饮食和烹饪是海南文化的体现，是灿烂的海南文化中浓墨重彩的一笔。

Cuisine is an art rather than culture. Hainan cuisine and cooking is the reflection of its culture, which holds an important position in the brilliant Hainan culture.

海南饮食既有独特的岛屿文化特征又受到了内陆饮食的影响，同时印尼、马来西亚、泰国、越南等东南亚国家的饮食也对其产生了深刻影响，这使海南饮食民俗具有多元化、多民族融合、国际化趋势明显等特征。

Hainan cuisine characterizes with the unique island culture and mainland cuisine, and at the same time, the cuisine of some southeastern countries, such as Indonesia, Malaysia, Thailand, Vietnam, etc., exerting profound influences on it, which makes Hainan cuisine diversified, multi-ethnic and internationalized.

海南具有独特的岛屿文化，本土饮食文化特色鲜明，充满着原生态，追求自然的生活、饮食习惯和烹饪方法，对菜肴的烹制更加注重环保和生态（黄闻健，2013）。

Hainan's unique island culture has imbued its cuisine with the tastes of its original residents. Hainan aboriginal cuisine culture is marked with distinctive features: pursuing natural life, dietary habits and culinary skills, focusing on environmental protection and conservation when cooking.

南宋末年，因逃避战乱，汉族人继续南迁，几十万闽南的莆田人移民到海南岛。后来，苗族、回族等民族相继移居海南，逐步形成海南今天多民族聚居社会。移民浪潮将内陆的文化传统、生活习俗、饮食习惯、烹饪技艺引入了海南，促进了海南饮食文化和烹饪文化的发展。

Late in the Southern Song Dynasty (1127-1279), in order to escape from wars and riots, the Han people continued to move to the South. Hundreds of thousands of Putian People in Hokkien immigrated to Hainan Island. Later, some ethnic groups such as the Miao ethnic group and the

Hui ethnic group moved to Hainan, which formed today's multi-ethnic groups society in Hainan. The immigration wave brought mainland's cultural tradition, living customs, dietary habits and culinary skills to Hainan, which promoted the development of Hainan cuisine and cooking culture.

东南亚饮食给海南饮食风俗带来了巨大影响，确切地说，这种影响是相互渗透的（黄闻健，2013）。自20世纪50年代起，印尼、新加坡、马来西亚、泰国、越南等东南亚国家的海南华侨们纷纷返乡。归侨们不仅带来了东南亚各国的民风民俗，更带来了充满神秘色彩的东南亚美食和烹饪技艺。海南人把东南亚归侨的烹饪技艺与本土菜式相结合，创制了一批具有东南亚风味元素的海南菜，而海南本土的一些经典菜式也由华侨传播到了东南亚一些国家。在某种程度上，海南美食已经成为海南文化的绝佳代言。

The cuisine from Southeast Asian countries exerted considerable influence on Hainan dietary customs, to be exact, the influence is interactive. Since 1950s, the overseas Chinese have moved back to Hainan from some Southeast Asian countries such as Indonesia, Singapore, Malaysia, Thailand, Vietnam, etc. The returned overseas Chinese have brought along the folk customs from Southeast Asia as well as their exotic dishes and culinary skills. Hainanese combined the culinary skills brought by the returned overseas Chinese from Southeast Asian countries with local dishes, developing a lot of local dishes with Southeastern Asian elements, while some typical local dishes have been introduced to some Southeastern Asian countries by overseas Chinese. To some extent, Hainan cuisine has become the perfect representative of Hainan Culture.

海南的民间菜式异常丰富，不仅有文昌鸡、加积鸭、和乐蟹、东山羊四大名菜名扬海内外，也有临高烤乳猪、万泉鲤、定安黑猪骨头汤、姜盐琵琶虾、黄流老鸭等地方特色浓郁的名菜誉满全岛。一些少数民族的美食也为海南的饮食文化增添了一道亮丽的风景，如黎族的竹筒饭、苗族的五色饭等。除了这些美味佳肴之外，街头巷尾的海南风味小吃和饮品也是海南饮食版图中必不可少的点缀，如清补凉、海南粉、抱罗粉、咖啡、老爸茶等。

Hainan is abundant in local dishes. Hainan Four Famous dishes–Wenchang Chicken, Jiaji Duck, Hele Crab and Dongshan Mutton are well known at home and abroad, and some other local specialities, such as Lin'gao Roast Pigling, Wanquan River Carp, Ding'an Black Pig Bone soup, Deep-fried Squilla with ginger and salt, Huangliu Old Duck, etc., are famous in Hainan. Some delicacies of ethnic minorities also made their own contributions to the brilliant Hainan cuisine culture, say, Rice cooked in bamboo tubes of the Li people and Five Colored Rice in Miao's style. In addition to the above-mentioned delicacies, some local snacks and drinks on the streets and lanes are also the inevitable elements on Hainan food map, such as Sam Bo Luong, Hainan rice noodle, Baoluo rice noodles, coffee and Hainan Lao Ba Cha, etc.

1992年版的《中国烹饪百科全书》这样描述海南菜："取材立足于海南特产，鲜活为主，味以清鲜居首，重原汁原味，甜酸辣咸兼蓄，讲究清淡，菜式多样，适应性较强。"这些特征与海南岛的地理位置、地形、气候特征等息息相关，形成了独特的烹饪方法。这在一定程度上决定了海南饮食文化的特色。

According to *The Chinese Cuisine Encyclopedia* (1992 version), Hainan cuisine is depending on local animals and plants, mainly fresh and alive, whose flavor is various and light, with diversified but mild seasonings. Altogether its offerings span a wide range of dishes with both local and exotic flavors. The characteristics of Hainan cuisine are closely connected with the geography, landscape and climate of Hainan Island. Therefore, the culinary skills of Hainan cuisine are unique, which decides the Hainan dietary culture to a certain extent.

民以食为天。饮食在海南人的日常生活中占有十分重要的位置。海南的风俗是逢节必吃，逢喜必吃，祭天祭地祭神祭祖，全部都以食品当贡品，"吃"紧扣着海南人生活的每一个环节（郑庆杨，2007）。海南民族众多，各地区、各民族的饮食习俗五花八门，各具特色。现择其有代表性的部分，从日常食俗、节日食俗、待客食俗和特殊食俗等方面进行介绍和分析。

When it comes to food, the Chinese have a common saying, "The masses regard food as their heaven". Food plays a very important part in the daily life of Hainanese. In Hainan folk customs, "eating" is inevitable in every festival and every joyous occasion, and food is served as sacrificial offering when offering sacrifices to Heaven, Earth, gods and ancestors. "Eating" is closely connected with every sector of Hainanese life. There are many ethnic minorities in Hainan, the dietary folk customs of different regions and ethnic minorities are varied and have different features. Some representative parts are chosen in this book, which are introduced and analyzed from daily dietary customs, festival customs, hospitality customs and special dietary customs.

5.1 海南多民族融合趋势下的多元饮食民俗
Diversified Dietary Folk Customs

海南是一个完整意义上的移民省份。我们今天所说的"移民"通常是指在黎族之后来到海南的其他族群。其中，汉族是人数最多的族群，在今天的810万海南人口中汉族占到了80%以上（海南省人民政府新闻办公室，2005）。

Hainan is an immigration province. Nowadays, "immigrants" are usually referred to the other tribes immigrated to Hainan after the Li ethnic group. Among these tribes, the Han has the largest population, which accounts for over 80% of Hainan's 8.10 million people.

海南岛的汉族主要从事农业，主食以小麦、玉米、稻米等为主，副食主要有蔬菜、豆制品和鸡、鱼、猪、牛、羊肉等，传统饮料有茶和酒。汉族人习惯将大米做成米饭、粥、米粉、米糕、汤圆、粽子、年糕等各种不同的食品，麦面则做成馒头、面条、花卷、包子、饺子、馄饨、油条、春卷、炸糕、煎饼等。不同地区的汉族人民以炒、烧、煎、煮、蒸、烤和凉拌等烹饪方式，经过长期的实践，形成了不同的地方风味。

The Han people in Hainan Island are mainly engaged in agriculture. Their staple food are wheat, corn and grains of rice, etc., supplemented by vegetables, bean products, chicken, fish, pork, beef, lamb and other non-staple food. Tea and alcoholic drinks are their traditional drinks. The grains of rice are used to make steamed rice, congee, rice noodles, rice cake, sticky rice balls, Zongzi, sticky rice cakes, etc. Wheat is usually made into steamed bread, noodles, steamed buns, dumplings, wonton, fried dough sticks, spring rolls, fried cake, pancake, etc. The Han people in different regions practice frying, roasting, boiling, steaming, baking, salad and other culinary skills, through long-term practice, developing different local flavor.

黎族的饮食文化多姿多彩。黎族人习惯一日三餐，大米为主食，有时也吃一些杂粮。做米饭的方法主要有两种：一是用陶锅或铁锅煮，另一种是颇具特色的野炊方法。做米饭的野炊方法独具特色：在竹筒里装进适量的米和水，然后放在火堆里烤熟，用餐时剖开竹筒取出米饭，这便是有名的"竹筒饭"。若把猎获的野味、瘦肉混以香糯米和少量盐，放进竹筒烧成香糯饭，更是异香扑鼻，是黎族人招待宾客的美味佳肴。

The dietary culture of the Li people is colorful. The Li people are accustomed to three meals a day, and their staple food is grains of rice and coarse cereals are eaten occasionally. Ceramic pots or iron pots are usually used to cook grains of rice and the stewing way is much the same with the Han people. Another cooking way is picnic, which is to put a right amount of rice and water into a section of bamboo and then grill it on the fire. When the rice is ready, cut the bamboo and get the rice, this is the famous Rice cooked in bamboo tubes. If the bamboo tubes are filled with the hunting game, pork, fragrant glutinous rice and a small amount of salt and then baked on the fire, the fragrant smell will spread afar. This delicacy is usually served when entertaining guests.

苗族是海南的第二大少数民族。今天的苗族主要生活在海南岛的五指山、黎母岭、雅加大岭三大山脉构成的湿润、半湿润地区。苗族人民继承和发展着本民族原有的传统和文化，而且与海南岛独特的地理环境融合，约定俗成地形成了具有地域特色的苗家风情。

The Miao ethnic group is the second largest ethnic group in Hainan. Today the Miao people live in the humid and sub-humid areas in the Wuzhishan, Limuling and Yajiadaling mountains. The Miao people have carried on their traditions and customs, and integrated with the unique local geographical environment, forming a special Miao culture with local style.

三色饭是苗族最具特色的食品，用山栏糯米等制成。一般是在农历三月三节庆之时，苗寨家家户户都制作。万花茶是苗家人敬客的上乘饮料，苗家青年男女还用它来表达爱慕之情。

Three-colored rice in Miao style is unique in the Miao ethnic group, which is made of Shanlan glutinous rice. At the San Yue San Festival, every Miao family will prepare three-colored rice. Wanhua (literally meaning "ten thousand flowers") tea is the preferred Miao drink for guests, and the young Miao people usually use it to express their love.

宋朝时期，为数众多的回族先民从大陆迁入海南。今天的海南回族主要聚居在三亚市羊栏区的回辉和回新两乡。海南回族在饮食方面与汉族有明显的不同，他们喜食米饭，常吃鱼类，忌食猫、狗、猪肉，也忌食一切动物的血和一切自死动物，这些风俗都源出于伊斯兰教。由于海南盛产椰子，又地处海边，所以羊栏回族的食具常以椰壳为碗、碟，独具地方色彩。

During Song Dynasty (960-1279), a large number of the Huis (Muslims) immigrated to Hainan from the mainland. Today, the largest Hui communities are at the Huihui and Huixin townships in Yanglan District of Sanya city. Hainan Huis and the Han people are apparently different in eating. The Huis love rice and fish, and their dietary taboo is cat, dog, pork, the blood of all animals and all dead animals. All these traditions originated from Islam. Hainan is located beside the sea and abundant in coconuts, so the Huis of Yanglan communities usually make coconut shells into bowls and plates, which is unique with local color.

海南人是受西方文化影响较早的中国人,这主要源于与世界各国频繁的人员和物资往来,使得他们在生产和生活方面不断受到国外各个方面的影响。例如,从海外回流的海南人从100多年以前就开始饮用咖啡和奶茶,海南也成为中国最早种植咖啡的地区之一(海南省人民政府新闻办公室,2005)。

Owing to frequent personnel and economic exchanges with other countries, the Hainanese were among the first in China to experience Western influences in their lives and production. For example, the returned overseas in Hainan started to drink coffee and milk tea more than a century ago and China's first coffee plantations were set up in Hainan.

海南华侨有着很深的"故土情结",年轻时出海闯南洋,积累了一定资金后就会考虑回乡建屋定居。海南归国华侨在海口得胜沙一带修建的"外廊式建筑"—骑楼,与海南的自然条件有机结合,形成了独具特色的商业街。一些老华侨还在得胜沙开起了西式茶店,供应红茶、咖啡、牛奶、西式糕点等,规模大些的茶店,还向茶客提供汤面、粥粉以及海南最地道的小吃番薯汤、绿豆汤、木薯汤、煎粽、猪杂等,海南人把这样的茶店称为"老爸茶店"。如今,"老爸茶店"遍布海南大街小巷,已经成为海南人特有的生活方式。

The overseas Hainanese have a strong love for their hometown. When they were young they sought their fortune in Southeastern Asia. After saving some money, many returned to their hometown to build their residential houses. Some returned overseas Hainanese built some Arcade – a kind of veranda-style buildings, along some streets in Deshengsha, Haikou city, which grew into a unique commercial district. Some returned overseas Hainanese opened western cafes on Deshengsha Srteet, serving black tea, coffee, milk and western pastries. Some big teahouses offer noodles, congee and local snacks, such as sweet potato soup, mung bean soup, cassava soup, etc. The local people call them "old Daddy's teahouses", which have become the unique lifestyle of Hainanese.

来海南旅游度假不必为不习惯海南的饮食而担忧。得天独厚的自然资源优势,风情浓郁的少数民族,开放的地域文化使得海南的饮食呈现出新鲜、天然、奇特、丰富的特点(海南省人民政府新闻办公室,2005)。在海口和三亚的很多大酒店,都聘有外籍厨师,能够用新鲜的原料做出正宗的欧式大餐。除了酒店之外,海口、三亚、琼海等地的一些餐厅也非常具有异国风情,主营韩国料理、日本料理、泰国菜、印尼菜等的餐厅也在海南日渐盛行。

When travelling in Hainan, don't worry about if the Hainan diet will satisfy your appetite. The advantages of natural resources, unique ethnic minorities and open regional culture make Hainan's diet fresh, natural, special and colorful. Many hotels in Haikou and Sanya have foreign chefs, who can use fresh ingredients to make authentic European dinner. In addition to the hotels, some restaurants in Haikou, Sanya and Qionghai also have exotic features, offering cuisines from foreign countries, such as Korea, Japan, Thailand, Indonesia, and so on. These restaurants are becoming prevalent in Hainan

在海南最负盛名的莫过于海南的四大名菜:文昌鸡、加积鸭、和乐蟹、东山羊。

The most famous dishes in Hainan are the Wenchang Chicken, Jiaji Duck, Hele Crab and Dongshan Mutton.

海南素有"无鸡不成席"的说法。"四大名菜"之首的文昌鸡因产于文昌市而得名。传统的吃法是白斩，也叫"白切"，是最能体现文昌鸡鲜美嫩滑的做法。同时配以鸡油、鸡汤精煮的米饭，俗称"鸡饭"。吃文昌鸡的佐料很讲究，蒜泥、酱油和桔子汁是必备的。海南人没有吃醋的习惯，桔子汁也就成了天然醋。在海南不论是筵席、便餐或家庭菜都少不了白斩文昌鸡。这道菜在香港、东南亚一带也备受推崇，名气颇盛。

There is a saying in Hainan "Chicken is indispensable in a Hainan banquet". Wenchang Chicken, top of the "the four most famous dishes" in Hainan, receives its name from its place of origin. The traditional way of cooking Wenchang chicken is boiling, which sustains its tender and smooth texture. This dish is eaten with rice cooked in chicken oil and soup. The seasoning of Wenchang Chicken is unique—mashed garlic, soy sauce and lime juice. Hainanese are not accustomed to vinegar, so lime juice is used as the natural vinegar. Sliced boiled Wenchang Chicken is found in banquets, refection or family dinner, which is well received in Hongkong and Southeastern Asia.

加积鸭以产于琼海市加积镇而得名，是琼籍华侨早年从国外引进的良种鸭，俗称"番鸭"。其特点是鸭肉肥厚，皮白滑脆，皮肉之间夹一薄层脂肪，特别甘美。加积鸭的烹制方法有多种，但以"白斩"最能体现原汁原味，因此最为有名。

Jiaji Duck is named after Jiaji Township in Qionghai, where it is produced. It is a good species introduced from abroad by overseas Chinese. Jiaji Duck is characterized with fleshy meat, white, smooth and crisp skin, sandwiched with a thin layer of fat, which is especially tasty. There are many ways to cook Jiaji Duck, but the best and most famous is boiling, which can sustain its tender, smooth texture.

文昌鸡（蒋秀娟 摄）
Wenchang Chicken（Courtesy of Xiujuan Jiang）

加积鸭（蒋秀娟 摄）
Jiaji Duck（Courtesy of Xiujuan Jiang）

和乐蟹产于万宁县和乐镇，以甲壳坚硬、肉肥膏满著称。特别是其脂膏，金黄油亮，犹如咸鸭蛋黄，香味扑鼻。烹调方法多种多样，蒸、煮、炒、烤均具特色，尤以清蒸为最佳，既保持原味之鲜，又兼原色形之美。

Hele Crab, produced in Hele Township of Wanning County, is well known for its hard shell, full meat and tasty roe, especially its golden roe, which looks like the yolk of salted duck egg and smells good. Different ways of cooking, such as steaming, boiling, stir-frying and roasting, give it different tastes. However, steaming is the best, which can sustain its natural flavor and original shape.

05 海南饮食民俗
Hainan Dietary Folk Customs

东山羊产于万宁东山岭，毛色乌黑，肉肥汤浓，鲜而不腻。其美味据传是因羊食东山岭上稀有草木所致。其用特产东山羊肉，配以各种香料、味料，经过滚、炸、纹、蒸等多种烹调法精制而成。

Dongshan Goats are raised on the Dongshan Ridge in the east of Wanning city, which characterize with black fur, fleshy meat and fresh flavor. It is said that the mutton from these goats is tasty because they eat the rare grass and leaves on the ridge. The mutton is cooked with various spices in many special ways, such as boiling, deep-frying, stewing, steaming.

和乐蟹（蒋秀娟 摄）
Hele Crab（Courtesy of Xiujuan Jiang）

东山羊（蒋秀娟 摄）
Dongshan Mutton （Courtesy of Xiujuan Jiang）

海南名菜还有临高烤乳猪、清蒸万泉河鲤、五指山山牛肉、大洲燕窝、后安鲭鱼、曲口海鲜等。

Other famous dishes in Hainan include Lingao Roast Pigling, Steamed Wanquan River Carp, Wuzhishan Mountain Beef, Dazhou Edible Bird's Nest Soup, mullet from Hou'an and seafood from Qukou.

海南温暖的气候、优越的自然条件以及宽容、善良的原著民使得不同民族、不同宗教信仰和文化的族群在这里繁衍生息、和谐相处并形成了多元文化共融的局面。各国、各民族饮食习惯在不断融合的过程中相互影响、相互渗透，形成了海南独具特色的多元饮食民俗。

With mild climate, superior natural conditions, tolerant and kind aboriginal tribes, different tribes, religion beliefs and culture thrive in Hainan. They live harmoniously here and form a multi-cultural melting situation. In the process of continuous integration, the dietary habits of different countries and ethnic groups influence and penetrate mutually, which form unique Hainan diverse dietary folk customs.

5.2 黎族饮食民俗
The Dietary Folk Customs of Li People

海南黎族主要居住在海南省三亚市、五指山市、东方市、琼中黎族苗族自治县、保亭黎族苗族自治县、陵水黎族自治县、乐东黎族自治县、昌江黎族自治县、白沙黎族自治县等9个市县。在热带地理、环境的影响下，黎族传统饮食习俗，从形式到内容都十分丰富，并形成了特有的饮食文化，其显著特点是善于利用自然条件，因地制宜，就地取材，体现人与自然和谐共存（中国网，2009）。

The Li people are mainly living in Sanya City, Wuzhishan City, Dongfang City, Qiongzhong Li and Miao Autonomous County, Baoting Li and Miao Autonomous County, Lingshui Li Autonomous County, Ledong Li Autonomous County, Changjiang Li Autonomous County and Baisha Li Autonomous County. Under the tropical geographical and environmental influence, the traditional dietary customs of the Li ethnic group are unique with rich forms and contents, whose remarkable characteristics are applying natural conditions, adjusting measures to local surroundings and using local materials, which have manifested the closeness of human and nature.

5.2.1 主食的类别、制作和特点 The Categories, Making and Characteristics of the Li people's Staple Food

海南黎族一日三餐以稀饭为主。在日常生活中，主食主要有大米饭、山栏米饭、竹筒饭、南瓜饭、红薯饭、玉米饭等。

The Li people in Hainan mainly have congee for their daily meals and steamed rice, Shanlan rice, rice cooked in bamboo tubes, sweet potato rice, pumpkin rice and corn rice are their staple food.

大米饭

Rice

大米饭是海南黎族人的主粮。黎族人十分重视对粮食的保护：在山区，村边有一座座小粮仓，在沿海平原地区，家家户户都备有大竹篓，用于存放谷物。稻米有白米、红米和糯米3种，主要保存在木桶或陶缸里。白米、红米是制作米饭的原料，糯米是制作饭团、包粽子和酿酒的原料。黎族同胞制作米饭的过程也比较独特：在三角石灶生火置锅，把锅内的水煮沸后，按水下米，用勺子搅均匀，火候一定要适中。米饭煮半熟时盖上锅盖，将灶里柴火取出，用火炭的余热将米焖成香喷喷的米饭。

Rice is the Li people's staple food in Hainan. The Li people attach great importance to the protection of food: in the mountain areas, there are small barns around the villages. In the coastal plain areas, every family has large bamboo baskets for storing grains of rice. There are three kinds of rice: white rice, red rice and glutinous rice, which are usually stored in wooden barrels or ceramic vats. White rice and red rice are the ingredients for making steamed rice and glutinous rice is the raw material for making rice balls, Zongzi and rice wine. The process of steaming rice is unique: make a fire and then put a pot on the triangle stone stove, when the water is boiling, put a right amount of rice into the pot and stir the rice evenly, the heat should be moderate. Cover the pot when the rice is parboiled and then take out the burning firewood and the remaining heat will make the rice fragrant and tasty.

山栏米饭

Shanlan Rice

山栏米是一种旱稻米，盛产于海南五指山地区。黎族在山上以刀耕火种的生产方式开发山栏园，种植山栏稻，每年四月播种，秋天收割。山栏米质好，营养丰富，煮成米饭，清香扑鼻，是黎家迎宾待客的上品。

Shanlan rice is a kind of dryland rice, which is widely farmed in the Wuzhishanshan area.

The Li people develop Shanlan rice garden by slash-and-burn cultivation. Shanlan rice is sowed in April and harvested in autumn. With high quality, Shanlan rice is nutritious. When it is made into steamed rice, its fragrance will spread afar, which is served by the Li people to treat distinguished guests.

竹筒饭

Rice Cooked in Bamboo Tubes

来海南的游客最感兴趣的是黎族竹筒饭。在黎族居住区旅游，游客可以亲自烧制竹筒饭。先砍一节较粗的嫩竹，装入适量的香糯米和水，还可以拌入猎获物的瘦肉块及盐，架于火堆上熏烤。水沸后，以树叶或木塞封口，随时转动竹筒，使其受热均匀，待饭香溢出，取下稍候，打开便可食用。竹筒饭不易变质，可保存一周，因此黎族人出门远行多带竹筒饭用餐，每逢喜庆佳节时也会制作竹筒饭。现在，竹筒饭已成为酒店宴席上人们品尝黎家风味的佳品。

Visitors to Hainan are interested in Rice Cooked in Bamboo Tubes of the Li people. When travelling in residential areas of the Li people, tourists can make Rice Cooked in Bamboo Tubes by themselves. Firstly, prepare a section of bamboo and put the right amount of glutinous rice and water into the bamboo or mix with prey meat and salt and then roast the bamboo on fire. When the water is boiling, block the ends of the bamboo with leaves or corks, rotate the bamboo, the rice inside will be evenly heated, when the aroma is smelt, take the bamboo off the fire. After a while, cut the bamboo and enjoy the rice. The Rice Cooked in Bamboo Tubes can be kept for a week, which is a must for the Li travellers. During festivals, the Li people will prepare Rice Cooked in Bamboo Tubes. Nowadays, Rice Cooked in Bamboo Tubes has become a delicacy in the hotel banquets, where people can taste the Li people's special cuisine.

红薯饭

Sweet Potato Rice

黎族家家户户都种红薯。红薯饭的制作方法有二：一种是把生红薯洗净切成小块，待米煮半熟时放入红薯，以三成米二成红薯混合煮成稀饭或干饭；另一种是把红薯切成小片晒干，掺米煮成稀饭。红薯稀饭清甜可口，凉爽解热，是夏季食用佳品。

Sweet potatoes are planted in every Li family. There are two ways for making sweet potato rice: one way is to cut the sweet potatoes into small pieces, when the rice is parboiled, put the sweet potato pieces into the parboiled rice, mix three fifths rice and two fifths sweet potatoes together, you can make congee or rice. Another method is to cut the sweet potatoes into small pieces and then dry them in the sun. You can make congee by mixing dried sweet potatoes pieces and rice. Sweet potato congee is sweet and it can remit heat and quench thirst as well, which is the best food for summer.

南瓜饭

Pumpkin Rice

五指山地区，人们常煮南瓜饭。制作南瓜饭时，先削去瓜皮，清除瓜瓤，把瓜肉切成小块掺米下锅，煮成稀饭或干饭。或是糯米掺南瓜肉，用蒸锅蒸成米饭后，用木白舂烂，制成南瓜饭团，也有一种独特的风味。

In Wuzhishan area, people often cook pumpkin rice. Before making pumpkin rice, pare the rind and remove the pulp, then cut the pumpkin flesh into small pieces, mix these pieces with rice, you can make pumpkin congee or rice. You also can mix glutinous rice with the pumpkin flesh, steam them with a steamer, then pestle the pumpkin rice with a wooden mortar and make them into pumpkin rice balls, which also have a unique flavor.

黄姜饭
Turmeric Rice

黄姜生长在五指山地区，属草本植物，根块似姜，黄色，无辣味。把生黄姜舂烂，取其黄色姜水煮米饭。饭质黄色，有独特的香味，具有清热解毒的功效，可用来为产妇补身子。

Turmeric grows in Wuzhishan area and it is a kind of herbaceous plant. Its root looks like ginger, yellow and not spicy. Pestle the turmeric root and boil rice with its juice. The turmeric rice is yellow with unique flavor, which has the effect of preventing fever and detoxification and can be used to build up the lying-in women's health.

竹筒饭 （蒋秀娟 摄）　　　　　　　　　黄姜饭（蒋秀娟 摄）
Rice Cooked in Bamboo Tubes（Courtesy of Xiujuan Jiang）　Turmeric Rice（Courtesy of Xiujuan Jiang）

5.2.2 饮料的类别、制作和特点 Categories, Making and Characteristics of the Li People'S Beverage

黎族人热爱生活，酒是日常生活中不可缺少的饮料。节日、婚娶、丧葬、入新屋、生育、社交和举行宗教仪式等活动，都要摆席设宴饮酒。黎族人热情好客，他们以酒为礼，敬酒时对歌，形成了别具一格的酒文化。黎族日常生活中饮料有如下几类：

The Li people love life. Alcohol is an indispensable beverage in their daily life. During events like festival, wedding, funeral, house warming, baby shower, social communication and religious ritual, etc., banquets and alcohol will be prepared. The Li people are hospitable. Treating guests with alcohol is a common courtesy, and making toast and singing at the same time is their own unique alcohol culture. In the daily life of the Li people, their beverage is as follows.

山栏酒（俗称糯米酒）
Shanlan Rice Wine（Commonly Known as Glutinous Rice Wine）

山栏酒是黎族采用山栏稻酿制而得名。山栏酒是真正的绿色酒类，黎民采用当地山中特有的植物并运用传统自然发酵的办法酿制而成。对于黎族来说，山栏酒就像国外的香槟一样，一般逢贵客来临或重大节庆才拿出来痛饮。山栏酒制作方法有二：一是将山栏米蒸熟揉散成粒，掺入黎山特定植物和米粉制成的"球饼"粉状，装进坛内一日后，取少量冷水沁入并封口，埋到芭蕉树下一年后呈黄褐色，数载则显红色甚至黑色；另一种方法是将蒸熟的山栏米和碾碎的"球饼"混合放置在垫满芭蕉叶的锥形竹筐中，上面也用芭蕉叶封盖。三天后，朝下的竹筐尖部开始往筐下的陶罐里滴出浆水，这就是山栏纯液，呈乳白色。山栏酒根据存放的时间长短味道而不同，刚酿好的酒存放十天左右时是甜的，这也是黎族人通常叫"BIANG"的酒。这种"BIANG"甜而微辣、辣而不燥。据说黎家妇女生孩子之后，都要喝此酒用以滋补养身，去湿防病。随着时间的推移，"BIANG"的甜味慢慢消失，酒的香味渐浓，埋入地下一年后酒呈黄褐色，数载则显红色甚至黑色，此时便是真正的山栏酒。

The name of Shanlan rice wine comes from its main ingredient-Shanlan rice. Shanlan rice wine is real green liquor. The unique plants grown in the local mountains and the traditional natural fermentation method are used to make Shanlan rice wine. For the Li people, Shanlan rice wine is like champagne in some foreign countries, which is generally drunk during festivals or to entertain distinguished guests. There are two methods for making Shanlan rice wine: the first method is to crumble the steamed Shanlan rice and mix them with the distiller's yeast powder made by unique plant and rice flour, then put the mixture into a jar. Put a small amount of water into the jar the next day, seal the jar and bury it under the banana tree. A year later, the color of the Shanlan wine will turn brown and red even black several years later. Another way of making Shanlan rice is as follows: put the mixture of steamed Shanlan rice and crushed distiller's yeast into a awl-shaped bamboo basket with banana leaves on the bottom, then cover the basket with banana leaves. Three days later, milky white liquid will drip down from the pointed part of the bamboo basket into the ceramic pot below, which is the pure Shanlan rice wine. The taste of Shanlan wine varies according to the stored time. Shanlan rice wine is sweet and a little spicy but not dry after storing for ten days, which is usually called "BIANG" by the Li people. It is said that, after giving birth to a child, the Li women will drink "BIANG" for building up health and preventing wet and diseases. As time goes by, the sweetness of "BIANG" disappears gradually and the fragrance of wine gets stronger and stronger. Buried underground for a year, it will become brown, several years later red or black, which is the real Shanlan rice wine.

玉米酒
Corn Wine

玉米淀粉多，酒度高。黎族人把玉米舂碎，煮成玉米干饭，与酒饼混合后盛入陶盆并盖封。酒料发酵15天后，酒汁可饮。封存一个月后，便可用蒸酒锅蒸馏出高浓度的玉米酒。

Corn contains a lot of starch, so the corn wine is high in alcohol. The Li people cook crushed corn into corn rice, put the mixture of corn rice and distiller's yeast into the ceramic pot and then seal the pot. After 15 days' fermentation, the wine can be drunk. Sealed for one month, the high-alcohol corn wine can be distilled by using a vaporizer.

番薯酒、木薯酒
Sweet Potato Wine and Cassava Wine

将切成小块的生番薯用锅煮熟晾干，加入酒饼拌匀，盛入大坛密封一个月，发酵成酒料，再将酒料倒入蒸酒锅蒸馏成甜醇的番薯酒。此酒有浓厚番薯味道，酒浓度不高，适合盛夏季节畅饮。木薯酒蒸制方法与番薯酒一样，但木薯酒浓度高，适合酒量大者饮用。

Boil the small pieces of sweet potatoes and dry them in the air. Mix the dried sweet potatoes with distillers' yeast, put them into a big jar and then seal the jar for a month. Put the fermented materials into a vaporizer and then pure and rich sweet potato wine is ready after distillation. This wine has strong flavor of sweet potato, alcohol is not high and is suitable for drinking in summer. The method of making cassava wine is the same with that of making sweet potato wine, however the alcohol of cassava wine is high, which is suitable for good drinkers.

芭蕉酒、南瓜酒
Banana Wine and Pumpkin Wine

芭蕉果实淀粉含量多,是制酒的好原料。制作芭蕉酒时,把未成熟的芭蕉果实斩成小块,煮熟晾干后投入酒饼调匀,放入坛子发酵一个月,便可获得芳香的酒料。把酒料和清水调稀后盛入蒸酒锅熬煮,制出酒质清香的芭蕉酒。南瓜淀粉多,也是酿酒的好原料。黎族同胞把加工后的南瓜掺入糯米蒸成酒料,再把发酵后的酒料酿成南瓜酒。另一种酿制方法是从南瓜蒂上开一个小洞,将酒饼放进瓜内,密封洞口一个月,经酒曲的发酵,南瓜内便盛满酒汁了。

Banana contains a lot of starch, which is a good ingredient for making wine. When making banana wine, chop the unripe banana fruit into small pieces, mix the cooked and dried banana pieces with the distillers' yeast thoroughly and then put them into a jar, after fermentation in a sealed jar for a month, fragrant material for making banana wine will be ready. Boil the mixture of the fermented material and fresh water in a vaporizer, fragrant banana wine will be done. The starch content of pumpkin is high, which is also a good material for making wine. Steam the mixture of processed pumpkin and glutinous rice, and you will get pumpkin wine from the fermented mixture. Another brewing method is to open a small hole on the pumpkin pedicle and then put the distillers' yeast into the pumpkin through the hole and then seal the pumpkin for a month, you will get pumpkin wine after fermentation.

水满茶
Shuiman Tea

五指山南麓的水满地区,常年云雾缭绕,夜间多露水,树木葱翠碧绿,盛产优质的五指山水满茶。当地黎族采集自然生长的茶叶和根杆,煮泡味道浓醇的茶水。常喝水满茶,有保健效果。冲泡浓茶水,3次饮用,可消除重感冒。

The Shuiman area in the south ridge of Wuzhishan mountain is misty all the year round, nocturnel dew is abundant and the trees are lush, which is rich in high-quality Shuiman tea. The local Li people collect wild tea leaves and stems to make strong Shuiman tea. Drinking Shuiman tea frequently will make one healthy. A bad cold can be driven away by drinking strong Shuiman tea three times.

苦丁茶
Kuding Tea

保亭七仙岭周边地区雨量充沛,气候适宜,土地肥沃,盛产苦丁茶,农民采摘加工,制作味道醇香的饮用茶。苦丁茶被誉为"长寿茶""美容茶",内含熊果酸、香树脂醇、槲皮素、天然硒化合物、氨基酸等250多种物质以及人体所必需的多种有机质和微量矿物质元素,是一种纯天然多功能保健珍品。

With plenty of rainfall, suitable climate and fertile soil, the surrounding areas in Qixianling Mountain, Baoting are abundant in Kuding tea. Farmers collect and process the Kuding tea and produce drinkable tea with pure and fragrant taste. Kuding tea is known as "longevity tea" and "beauty tea", for it contains more than 250 kinds of materials and a variety of organic matters and trace mineral elements essential to the human body. It is a natural multifunctional health-care product.

5.2.3 菜肴、佐料和零食 Dishes, Condiment and Snacks

在黎族饮食结构中，菜肴品类丰富。有家种的南瓜、葫芦瓜、冬瓜、木瓜、黄瓜、豆角、西红柿、韭菜、萝卜、莲藕、小白菜、空心菜等蔬菜，野菜主要有木耳、山菇、山芋、山竹笋、莉嫩、子温、雷公根等，家禽有鸡、鸭、鹅，家畜有牛、羊、猪等。

On the Li diet, the food category is very diverse. Their home-grown vegetables are pumpkins, bottle gourds, wax gourds, papayas, cucumbers, beans, tomatoes, leeks, turnips, lotus roots, cabbages, spinaches, etc. Edible wild herbs are edible fungus, mountain mushrooms, yams, bamboo shoots, Lineng(in the Li dialect), Ziwen (in the Li dialect), centella, and so on. On poultry, they have chickens, ducks, geese, and on livestock, they have cattle, sheep, pigs, and so on.

黎族男女善捕捞。男子平时爱好上山安装各种捕猎器具，捕捉鼠类、鸟类、蛇类和野猪，以及五指山草龟、金钱龟等野物，还善于下河捕捞水鳖、鱼、虾、蟹等。在农闲、节日时，全村集众上山放狗围捕山猪、黄猄、野鹿等，并把兽肉熏干保存日后食用。黎族日常下田劳动，男子带刀篓，女子带小腰篓，捕捉田蛙、田蟹、稻虾等动物，回家杂烩煮后食用,菜味新鲜，营养丰富。

The Li people are good at hunting and fishing. Usually, men set hunting traps in mountains, aiming to capture mountain rats, birds, snakes, boars, and tortoises. They are also good at fishing soft-shelled turtles, fish, shrimps and crabs etc. In the off season or holiday times, the villagers will set dogs to hunt boars, barking deer, wild deer etc., and then smoke the meat for the future consumption. When working in the field, the male Li people will have knife bamboo baskets, while the female Li people will have small waist bamboo baskets with them for catching frogs, crabs and shrimps, etc. All these captures will be cooked together, which are fresh and rich in nutrient.

黎族菜肴习惯把肉菜一起煮，或者把几种菜混合煮。食盐是菜肴的主要调料，小辣椒是平时餐桌上的佐料。黎族居住地带热带地区，喜好清淡，少食炒炸食物。现在黎族饮食方式有所改变，普遍学习汉人菜肴制作技术。

The Li people are accustomed to cooking all kinds of meat together, or to cooking several dishes together. Salt is the main condiment in a dish and small chili pepper is usually served on the table as seasoning. The Li people live in tropical areas and they like light food but not stir-fried or fried food. Nowadays, the dietary habits of the Li people have changed and they usually learn the culinary skills of the Han people.

黎族传统饮食中，除上述菜肴外，有独特风味的还有以下几种：

Except for the above-mentioned dishes, there are some other unique dishes in the traditional Li diet:

"南杀"

Nan Sha – the Li Nationality Pickles

居住山区的黎族，采集野菜，洗干净后盛入陶罐，倒入凉米汤后密封3个月或更长时间，让其发酵，腌制出具有独特味道的酸菜。"南杀"是黎家餐桌上的独特菜肴，常吃"南杀"可以清除体内毒素和身体内的杂质。特别是黎族砍山栏，收拾焚烬余杂的劳动时，灰尘冲天，吃了"南杀"可排除被吸进肺部的尘埃。

The Li people who live in mountain areas collect wild herbs and put them into jars after washing, pour cold rice soup into jars and then seal the jars. Fermented in jars for three months or longer, unique-flavored pickles will be done. Nan Sha is the unique dish on the Li people's daily meals. People who have Nan Sha frequently can get rid of toxins and impurities in the body. Especially when the Li people are harvesting Shanlan rice, burning embers or doing some other miscellaneous work, dust is everywhere, and eating Nansha can clean the dust in lungs.

肉茶、鱼茶
Rou Cha and Yu Cha (Literally Meaning Meat Tea and Fish Tea)

鱼茶和肉茶是黎族招待客人的主要菜肴，也是黎族人的风味食品。把生肉或生鱼，混炒米粉，加入少许的食盐，用陶罐封存，发酵一个月后打开即食。

Yu Cha and Rou Cha are the main dishes for the Li people to treat their guests, which are also their unique food. Mix the raw meat or raw fish with stir-fried rice flour, adding a little salt, then ferment the mixture in a sealed jar for a month. It can be eaten upon opening the jar.

糯米粽、糯米团
Glutinous Rice Dumpling and Sticky Rice Ball

黎族每逢喜庆佳节，探亲访友都要制作糯米粽、糯米团等食品。合亩制地区的黎族，制作米粽时，先把糯米浸泡，淘干净后掺进芝麻或黄姜水，用粽叶包成圆长形的米粽。其他黎区则包三角形的米粽，粽内夹着猪肉片。制作糯米团时，把糯米浸泡后蒸成干饭，用木臼舂烂，揉捏成圆形的糯米团，沾上芝麻，大人小孩都爱吃。把糯米团晒干，可以保存一个月食用。吃时，用水浸泡后放进火烘，热软即吃。

The Li people make glutinous rice dumpling, sticky rice ball and some other food for visiting relatives and friends during festivals. The Li people in Hemu System areas make glutinous rice dumplings like this: firstly, soak glutinous rice, then mix them with sesame or turmeric water, lastly, wrap the mixture into round elongated bag of rice dumplings by using bamboo leaves. The Li people in other areas will wrap the rice dumpling in triangular shape, sandwiched with pork pieces. When making sticky rice balls, steam the soaked glutinous rice and then pound the glutinous rice with a wooden mortar, knead the sticky rice into round shape, coated with sesame, which are favored by adults and children. The dried sticky rice ball can be preserved for a month. When eating, soak them in the water and then bake them on the fire, they can be eaten when heated soft.

水果及零食
Fruit and Snacks

日常生活中，黎家食用的种植水果有荔枝、龙眼、芒果、菠萝、杨桃、黄皮、波罗蜜、香蕉、甘蔗、酸豆等；野生水果也是黎家经常食用的水果。爆玉米花、焗煮番薯和木薯是黎家的零食。

In the Li people's daily life, they have home-grown fruits like litchi, longan, mango, pineapple, star fruit, wampee, jackfruit, banana, sugar cane, tamarindus and so on. They also have wild fruits frequently. Popcorn, baked sweet potatoes and boiled cassava are snacks for the Li people.

吸烟
Smoking

黎族喜好吸水烟。自种的烟草晒干后切成烟丝，以竹制烟筒吸烟。烟丝、烟筒是黎族社交必备的礼品。

The Li people are fond of smoking tobacco by using water pipe. Cut the dried home-grown tobacco into shreds and smoke them by using bamboo pipes. Tobacco and bamboo pipes are gifts in the Li community.

5.2.4 饮食禁忌 Dietary Taboo

食肉类方面
On Meat

海南黎族大致可以分为五大方言区：位于乐东的哈方言区、位于五指山的杞方言、位于白沙的润方言、位于保亭的赛方言以及位于东方的美孚方言。五指山市合亩制杞方言和东方市美孚方言视牛为崇拜物，禁止牛日杀牛。合亩制的亩头和妻子，不吃狗、猫、蛇、鹧哥鸟和乌鸦的肉，并禁止在家里煮此类食品。黎族民间，怀孕妇女不吃蛇和猴子肉。五指山地区黎族妇女生小孩"坐月子"期间，禁止吃鱼肉和鸡蛋等。唯有乐东哈方言对吃肉没什么禁忌，无论家禽家畜，还是飞禽走兽均可食用。

The Li ethnic group in Hainan can be divided into five major dialect areas: Ha dialect in Ledong, Qi dialect in Wuzhishan, Run dialect in Baisha, Sai dialect in Baoting and Meifu dialect in Dongfang. Cow slaughter is banned in Wuzhishan Hemu System (a kind of patriarchal production and social organization, which is unique in the Li people living in Wuzhishan area) Qi dialect area and Dongfang Meifu dialect area, for cows are worshipped by the Li people in the above-mentioned two dialect areas. The head and his wife in Hemu System don't eat dogs, cats, snakes, mynas and crows, and cooking of these animals at home is banned. The Li pregnant women do not eat snakes and monkeys. During the confinement in childbirth, the Li women in Wuzhishan area are banned to eat fish and eggs. Only the Li people in Ledong Ha dialect area have no taboo on meat eating and poultry, livestock, birds and animals can be eaten.

用餐方面
On Dining

黎族人在吃饭时忌用筷子敲打饭碗或吹口哨；在家里吃饭不得戴草笠，不得狼吞虎咽。请客人吃饭，不得把饭碗倒扣。如果客人吃完饭后，把筷子交叉地放在饭碗上，意为对主人有意见。通什合亩制地区黎族请客人吃饭时，主人不得在餐席上看客人盛饭吃菜。白沙南开地区部分润方言习俗，入新屋或年节，全家吃饭不用碗，只用手抓饭或以勺子舀饭菜进食，以此方式感念先祖的恩赐。

It is inauspicious for the Li people to whistle or tap on the bowl with chopsticks when dining. It is not allowed to wear straw hat and gobble the food up when eating at home. When entertaining guests, it is inauspicious to put the bowls upside down. After dinner, if the guests cross the chopsticks on the bowl, it means they have complaints about the host. In the Li Hemu System area, Tongshi district, when treating guests to dinner, the hosts should not view the guests eating at the table. According to customs in some Run dialect areas in Nankai, Baisha district, the family members should eat with hands or spoons but not bowls, which is the way the Li people show their gratitude to their ancestors.

饮酒方面

On Drinking

黎族男女喜爱饮酒，各地饮酒方式和禁忌都不相同。杞方言把碗斟满酒，以双手举酒碗敬客人；哈方言和美孚方言对客人敬酒时要夹肉送到客人口中，并把客人灌醉，表示热情好客。合亩制地区敬酒要对歌，歌对不上者则被罚喝大碗酒。平时喝酒席间，要点过世者的名字，同时把碗里的酒倒在地下，表示吉利。

The Li people love drinking and drinking ways and taboos are not the same in different areas. The Li people in Qi dialect areas fill their bowls with wine and make toast to their guests with both hands holding the bowls. In Ha dialect and Meifu dialect areas, it is a hospitable way to put meat into their guests' mouths while making a toast and make them drunk. In Hemu System area, antiphonal singing is indispensable when making a toast, and those who can't sing will be punished for drinking a bowl of wine. During drinking in a feast, the name of the dead must be mentioned and at the same time the wine should be poured on the ground, which means auspiciousness.

5.3 南洋饮食民俗
The Southeastern Asian Dietary Folk Customs

自 20 世纪 50 年代起，印尼、马来西亚、泰国、越南等东南亚国家的海南华侨们纷纷返乡。归侨们不仅带来了东南亚各国的民风民俗，更带来了充满神秘色彩的东南亚美食。东南亚美食选料注重天然，以特有的植物调味，并以丰富的海陆物产为主要食材，讲求营养成分的最佳搭配，自成一格，与中、法、意美食并称"世界四大美食"（新华网海南频道，2014）。

Since 1950s, the overseas Chinese have moved back to Hainan from some Southeastern Asian countries such as Indonesia, Singapore, Malaysia, Thailand, Vietnam, etc. The returned overseas Chinese brought along the folk customs from these countries as well as their exotic dishes and culinary skills. Southeastern Asian cuisine focuses on natural choice of materials, applies special plants as seasoning and chooses the land and sea plants and animals as the main ingredients, seeking the perfect match of nutrients and uniqueness, which has been recognized as one of "the world's four gourmets" with cuisine from China, France and Italy.

东南亚与海南岛在物产上有极多相似，所以在海南制作东南亚菜，在原材料上就占了极大的便利。在东南亚菜系中，椰浆和咖喱的使用最为广泛。

On products, there are many similarities between Southeast Asia and Hainan, so there are many advantages in raw materials for making Southeastern Asian cuisine in Hainan. In Southeastern Asian cuisine, coconut milk and curry are most widely used.

东南亚号称世界香料王国，丰富的香料成就了东南亚美食。种类繁多的香料、丰富的天然物产，以及后来由西方殖民者带来的西式餐饮精华，使得东南亚美食成为世界美食的精华。

Southeast Asia is known as the kingdom of spice, and abundant spice makes the Southeastern Asian cuisine unique. A variety of spices and rich natural products and the western-style food essence brought by western colonists make Southeastern Asian food the essence food in the world.

东南亚菜非常讲究酱料的调配和运用，又称为"酱料菜"，使得东南亚菜色味浓郁，而在口味上又多以酸、辣、甜、鲜等为特色。虽然同属热带气候，但海南菜更多受粤菜影响，讲究清淡、甜鲜，在烹饪上讲究原汁原味，所以大多采用白切、白灼、清蒸等。

Southeastern Asian cuisine is very particular about the use of sauces, which is known as "sauced dish", making the Southeastern Asian dishes rich in color and flavor, with sour, spicy, sweet and fresh as its features. Although Hainan and Southeast Asia both belong to the tropical climate, the Hainan dishes are more influenced by Cantonese dishes. Thus, light, fresh and sweet is Hainan cuisine's feature. In cooking, authentic flavor is highly stressed, so the cooking methods of most Hainan dishes are boiling, scalding, steaming, etc.

被称为椰岛的海南岛，椰子也被广泛运用在海南菜中，如被宋子文念念不忘的椰奶鸡就是其中最著名的。而海南菜也因为对椰子的完美应用在粤菜中独树一帜。再说到咖喱，虽然海南本地人很少食用，但制作的配料当地都有出产。

Hainan Island is named Coconut Island and coconut is widely used in Hainan dishes, such as chicken stewed with coconut milk-one of the most famous, which is borne in mind constantly by Tse-ven Soong. Hainan cuisine is also unique in Cantonese cuisine because of its perfect application of coconut. Speaking of curry, although Hainan local people rarely eat it, yet the ingredients of curry are available in Hainan.

咖喱是由多种香料调配而成的酱料，常见于印度菜、泰国菜和日本菜中，是亚太地区的主流酱料之一，又有"十国咖喱，风味也不尽相同"之说，其中，新加坡和泰国的咖喱风味以酸辣为主，而马来西亚咖喱则重椰汁，可以说，咖喱是除了茶之外的少数真正泛亚的菜肴或饮料。

Curry is a kind of sauce mixed by a variety of spices, which is common in Indian, Thai and Japanese dishes and is one of the mainstream sauces in Asia-Pacific region. There is a saying "The curries from ten countries have ten flavors". The curry from Singapore and Thailand is mainly hot and sour, while the curry from Malaysia has thick coconut milk flavor. It is said that, in addition to tea, curry is truly pan-Asian dish or drink.

咖喱的组成香料非常多，如丁香、肉桂、茴香、小茴香子、豆蔻、胡荽子、芥末子、黑胡椒、辣椒以及用来上色的姜黄粉。这些香料均各自拥有独特袭人的香气与味道，有的辛辣有的芳香，交揉在一起，不管是搭配肉类、海鲜或蔬菜，将其融合而绽放出似是冲突又彼此协调的多层次口感，是咖喱最令人为之迷醉倾倒之处。

The spice composition of curry is very large, such as clove, cinnamon, fennel, cumin, cardamom, coriander, mustard, black pepper, chili powder and turmeric for coloring. Each of these spices has unique aroma and flavor. The spicy flavor and aromatic smell mix, whether matched with meat, seafood or vegetables, which seems to conflict and coordinate with each other, bursting out multi-level taste, which is most fascinating.

下南洋的海南人以及后来的归侨们，陆续把一些香料种子带回海南岛，加之海南的气候与东南亚相似，不少香料也就在海南落地生根。在海南兴隆，大厨们几乎都是用产于海南本地的材料来调制咖喱的，如香茅、辣椒干、花生酱、黄姜以及椰浆。为了适应海南当地口味清淡的特点，海南咖喱的口味会相对平和，不会太过辛辣、浓厚。咖喱鸡、巴厘岛焗蟹等都是兴隆最有特色的东南亚美食。

The returned overseas Hainanese brought some spice seeds back to Hainan Island. Since the climate in Hainan is similar to Southeast Asia, many spices took root in Hainan. In Xinglong, Hainan, chefs make curry by applying local raw materials to make curry, such as lemongrass, dried chilli, peanut butter, coconut milk and turmeric. Hainan curry is relatively mild and gentle, not too spicy and strong, which is suitable to the light taste of the local people. Curry chicken, Bali baked crab and some other dishes are the distinctive Southeastern Asian dishes.

咖喱鸡（蒋秀娟 摄）
Curry Chicken（Courtesy of Xiujuan Jiang）

巴厘岛焗蟹（蒋秀娟 摄）
Bali Baked Crab（Courtesy of Xiujuan Jiang）

虽然咖喱是舶来品，但海南毕竟是侨乡，对东南亚的习俗或是美食都更易吸收，加之海南菜的兼容并蓄，现在的海南菜谱中也有不少咖喱美食，如海南椰奶咖喱蚝、红咖喱金瓜加积鸭等都是兼具咖喱风味的海南菜。

Curry is imported. However, as the hometown of overseas Chinese, Hainan absorbs Southeastern Asian customs or cuisine. In addition, Hainan cuisine is inclusive. Right now there are curry delicacies in Hainan recipes, such as Hainan Oyster with Coconut Milk and Curry, Jiaji Duck with Red Curry and Pumpkin, which are Hainan dishes with curry flavor.

20世纪50年代起，兴隆成为印尼、马来西亚、泰国、越南等21个国家归侨的新家。归侨们不仅带来了东南亚各国的民风民俗，还带来了充满神秘色彩的东南亚美食。至今，归侨们仍以东南亚风味的餐饮为主：七层糕、千孔糕、椰香脆饼、咖喱鸡、沙爹肉片、加多加多等（美丽三亚网，2010）。

Since the 1950s, Xinglong has become the new home of returned overseas Chinese from Indonesia, Malaysia, Thailand, Vietnam and other 21 countries. The returned overseas Chinese have not only brought back folk customs of Southeast Asia, but also a mysterious Southeast Asian cuisine. So far, the returned overseas Chinese are still keeping the Southeast Asian dietary habits：seven-layer steamed cake, thousand－hole cake, coconut crackers, curry chicken, satay meat，Indonesian Vegetable Salad with Peanut are still on their tables.

七层糕（蒋秀娟 摄）
Seven-Layer Cake（Courtesy of Xiujuan Jiang）

千孔糕（蒋秀娟 摄）
Thousand-Hole Cake（Courtesy of Xiujuan Jiang）

椰香脆饼（蒋秀娟 摄）
Coconut Crackers（Courtesy of Xiujuan Jiang）

加多加多（蒋秀娟 摄）
Indonesian Vegetable Salad with Peanut
（Courtesy of Xiujuan Jiang）

近年来，琼海市提出打造田园城市发展战略，充满异域风情的印尼村备受热捧（董武，中国侨网，2015）。印尼归侨独特的印尼文化以及独具特色的印尼美食让很多游客慕名而来。如今印尼村里的伊娜偌印尼餐厅已正式营业，独具特色的印尼菜色香味浓、十分爽口。沙爹烤肉串、咖喱鸡、咖喱牛肉、烤鱼……种类繁多的菜肴配上金灿灿的黄姜饭，让人胃口大开，回味无穷。

In recent years, Qionghai City has proposed the development strategy to create a garden city, and the exotic Indonesian village in Qionghai has been highly valued. The Returned Indonesian Chinese's unique Indonesian culture and cuisine are attracting many tourists. Now the Indonesian-style restaurant Ninanoi has been officially opened in the Indonesian village. With fragrant smell and thick flavor, Indonesian dishes are refreshing. The eaters' appetite will be built up when a variety of dishes-Satay Kabob, Curry Chicken, Curry Beef, Grilled Fish and golden turmeric rice are before them, and the eating experience will be memorable.

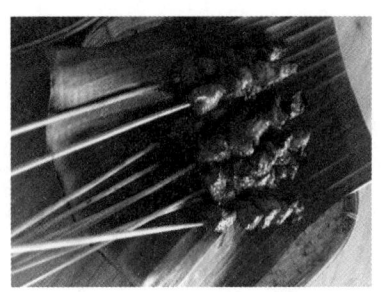
沙爹肉串（蒋秀娟 摄）
Satay Kabob （Courtesy of Xiujuan Jiang）

咖喱牛肉（蒋秀娟 摄）
Curry Beef （Courtesy of Xiujuan Jiang）

琼海彬村山华侨经济区的万隆印尼风味美食店在当地已小有名气，在主题"品琼海味道·享幸福生活"的首届"琼海味道"嘉年华活动中获得"十佳农家好味""十佳美食名菜"和"十佳美食小吃"三个荣誉称号（中新网海南频道，2015）。美食店以东南亚和广东饮食习惯为基础，根据当地口味不断地改良菜品，最终推出大众喜欢的"琼海味道"。椰香咖喱蟹、椰香九层糕备受食客喜爱。

Bandung Indonesian Gourmet Restaurant in Qionghai Bincunshan Overseas Chinese Economic Zone has been prevalent in the local. The first "Qionghai flavor" Carnival themed "Taste Qionghai Flavor. Enjoy Happy Life", Bandung Indonesian Gourmet Restaurant got three honorary titles: Top Ten Farmers' Gourmet Food, Top ten Famous Gourmet Food and Top Ten Gourmet Snacks. Based on Southeast Asian and the Cantonese dietary habits and the local flavor, Bandung Indonesian Gourmet Restaurant improves its dishes constantly and introduces "Qionghai Flavor" loved by all. Curry Crab with Coconut Flavor and Nine-layer Steamed Coconut Cake are favored by eaters.

琼海印尼归侨有午后喝咖啡的习惯，而各种自制糕点也是咖啡的绝配。在印尼归侨的日常饮食中，糕点是必不可少的，逢年过节制作的品种更有30多种，蒸的、炸的、烤的一应俱全，有象征日子越过越红火的九层糕、有香脆爽口的太阳糕，还有蛋香、椰香浓郁的各种动物、植物模型饼干。

The returned Indonesian Chinese in Qionghai have the habit of drinking coffee in the afternoon and they will prepare all kinds of home-made snacks to match coffee. Snacks are indispensable at homes, and during New Year and festivals, the home-made snacks will be more than 30 kinds. The making methods includes steaming, deep-frying, roasting etc. There is Nine-layer Steamed Coconut Cake symbolizing the booming life, the fragrant, crispy Sun Cake and all kinds of animal or plant-shape cookies with thick egg and coconut fragrance.

5.4 其他少数民族饮食民俗
The Dietary Folk Customs of Other Ethnic Groups

5.4.1 苗族的饮食民俗 Dietary Folk Customs of the Miao Ethnic Group

海南大部分地区的苗族一日三餐均以大米为主食。油炸食品以油炸粑粑最为常见。苗家的食用油除动物油外，多是茶油和菜油。以辣椒为主要调味品，有的地区甚至有"无辣不成菜"之说。苗族的菜肴种类繁多，常见的蔬菜有豆类、瓜类和青菜，大部分苗族都善做豆制品。

The Miao people have three meals a day in most parts of Hainan and their staple food is rice. Deep-fried glutinous rice ball is very common for the Miao people. Besides animal oil, the Miao people usually use camellia oil and vegetable oil as their cooking oil. Pepper is their main seasoning. There is a saying in some areas "a dish is not a dish without pepper". The Miao people have a wide variety of dishes. Beans, melons and vegetables are very common. Most Miao people are good at making bean products.

海南苗族特别爱吃酸食。由于他们世居深山峻岭之中，山高路遥、交通不便，很难吃上鱼肉类和蔬菜，为适应日常生活的需要，家家户户都设置酸坛，制作酸鱼、酸肉、酸菜及其他酸食。

The Miao people in Hainan love sour food very much. They have been living for generations in the mountains and the traffic has been inconvenient, so it is difficult for them to have fish and vegetables. To meet the needs of daily life, every household prepares jars for making sour fish, sour meat, pickled vegetables and other sour food.

苗家制作酸鱼多用鲤鱼。酸鱼的做法奇特：先将鲜鱼用清水洗净，剖开去其内脏，置于酸坛里，撒上一些辣椒面、盐，再与生姜、大蒜、香料拌匀，过三四天后，再将坛里的鱼取出，在酸坛底放上一层糯米饭，根据鱼的多少，一层一层装入酸坛内。摊一层鱼、撒一层糯米面或玉米面，每层都得用手压实。装完以后，再压上一层拌好的糯米饭，接着密封、盖紧。这种酸坛坛口有一个盛水凹槽，放进适当的水，与外界空气隔绝，不使坛内的酸鱼氧化变质。这种制作酸鱼的方法，时间愈长，味道愈好。如今，好客的苗家人把它当作上等的好菜，每当家里来了贵客，总要从坛子里取一钵酸鱼做菜。

The Miao people usually make sour fish by carps. The technique of making sour fish is unique: firstly, wash the fish with cool water, cut the fish and get rid of the viscera, mix the fish with some pepper powder, salt, ginger, garlic and spices, then put the fish in the pot, three or four days later, take out the fish, place a layer of glutinous rice on the bottom of the jar, then place the fish into the jar layer by layer, place a layer of glutinous rice flour or corn flour between two layers of fish and press each layer firmly. Place a layer of mixed glutinous rice on the top when the process finishes, lastly, seal the jar. This kind of jar has a water-containing groove on the mouth, in which proper amount of water is put, which can isolate the air between inside and outside, avoiding acid oxidation and deterioration of the fish. This making method makes the sour fish taste better as the time goes by, the longer the better. Nowadays, the hospitable Miao people regard sour fish as their finest dish. Whenever guests come, a bowl of sour fish will be served on the table.

酸肉制作方法与酸鱼大致相同。把猪肉切成不大不小的块，在自家设置的酸坛里，按一层肉一层盐的办法，层层压实，待盐溶化后，再把肉取出，在每块肉上均匀地搓上糯米饭和酒糟后，另加入一些香料和辣椒面，再放进酸坛里盖严。这样做的肉，不但味道鲜美，而且可以保存一到两年。

The making methods of sour meat and sour fish are roughly the same. Cut the pork into proper blocks and then put them into the jar layer by layer, salt is sprinkled between each layer and press each layer firmly. Take out the pork when the salt melts, then rub glutinous rice and distillers' grains evenly on each piece of pork, add some spice and pepper, and then put them into the pot again, seal the pot tightly. Meat made in this way not only tastes well but also can be preserved for one to two years.

酸汤菜是苗家人餐桌上必不可少的一道菜。酸汤菜不但爽口、解渴，而且具有增进食欲、帮助消化的功能。酸汤菜的做法比较简单：把白菜、韭菜、豆芽菜、辣椒、黄瓜、萝卜等放进酸坛内腌制，随时取出食用。还可以把带叶子的菜如芥菜、白菜等洗净，放进锅里煮沸后，加进一些酸醋和香料，接着一起放进酸坛，经过一些时日即成。

Pickled vegetable is an indispensable dish on the Miao people's table. Pickled vegetable is not only refreshing and thirst-quenching but also can increase appetite and help digestion. The making method of pickled vegetable is relatively simple: put pickle cabbages, chives, bean sprouts, red pepper, cucumber, radish, etc. in jars, when they are ready, take them out and have a taste. You can also boil the vegetables with leaves, such as mustard, cabbage, etc., add some vinegar and spices, then put them into the jar. They will be ready in a few days.

苗家五色饭是海南中部山区苗族人民的传统小吃，具有节令性，一般在农历"三月三"节庆之时，苗寨家家户户都制作。五色饭有红、黄、蓝、白、黑五色，皆用独特植物汁液作为天然色素拌在米中，并放进特制的木蒸笼中蒸制而成。如今已经有很多地方的苗族人把苗家五色饭已改为三色饭，分别为红、黄、黑三色，取色于新鲜植物红葵、黄姜和三角枫。但每年"三月三"，在儋州南丰镇五色饭这一传统美食依然随处可见。

The Five-colored rice in Miao's style is a traditional seasonal snack for the Miao people in the central mountain areas of Hainan, which is usually made by every Miao family during San Yue San festival. There are five colors in Five-Colored Rice in Miao's style, namely, red, yellow, blue, white and black. When making this kind of rice, you should mix the rice with unique plant juice, which is used as a natural pigment, and then steam the rice in the specially made wooden steamer. Nowadays, the Miao people in many areas have changed Five-Colored Rice into Three-Colored Rice, which are red, yellow and black, whose colors are from the fresh plants of nightshade, turmeric and maple. However, during San Yue San festival, this traditional delicacy–the Five-colored rice in Miao's style can be seen everywhere in Nanfeng town, Danzhou city, whose fragrance will be unforgettable.

五色饭（蒋秀娟 摄）
Five-Colored Rice in Miao's Style)
（Courtesy of Xiujuan Jiang）

三色饭（蒋秀娟 摄）
Three-Colored Rice in Miao's Style
（Courtesy of Xiujuan Jiang）

苗族的饮食民俗与禁忌
Dietary Folk Customs and Taboo of the Miao People

海南苗族是一个热情好客的民族。客人进屋，主人搬凳挪椅请客人就坐，先敬茶递烟，再请吃饭。主人招呼，客人要自觉就坐，不得辞让。若不能就席，要说明原委，请求主人谅解，否则主人就会认为是客人嫌弃,不愿意交朋友。用餐时,男客是先酒后饭,女客则是先饭后酒。酒是苗族生活中必不可少的东西,但苗族喝酒自制力强,只有逢年过节或招待客人时才痛痛快快地多喝一些,平时饮量较少。苗族男子喝酒一般不劝酒,能喝多少就喝多少。喝的酒多是自家酿造,几乎每家每户都懂得酿酒并有酿酒的工具。如果席上有野味、鸡鸭等,主人会不断把菜夹进客人的菜碟里"劝吃",是为厚待。客人酒足饭饱后,千万不能说吃饱了,不吃了,那主人会误解为是饭菜做得不好,客人厌吃,客人应该说,饭菜很香之类的话,主人听了会很高兴地再次敬酒。苗族忌食狗肉、猫肉,怕污秽祖宗神位而招致疾病。年初一,没有祭祀祖神是不许荤食的,否则视为对祖宗不敬。

The Miao people in Hainan are hospitable. When the guests enter the room, the host will serve stools or chairs, the host will invite the guests to dinner after offering tea or cigarettes. Upon invitation, the guests should not say "no" but sit down. If the guests can't sit down, they should offer reasons and ask for forgiveness; otherwise the host will regard it as dislike and not wanting to make friends. During dinner, male guests drink alcohol first and then have rice, while the female guests will have rice and then drink alcohol. Alcohol is essential in the Miao People's life. However, the Miao people exercise self-control on drinking alcohol. Thus, they drink a small amount of alcohol in their daily life, only on holidays or when entertaining guests, and they will drink to their hearts' content. Usually, the Miao people don't urge their guests to drink. The alcohol served on the Miao people's table is home-made and nearly every household has tools for alcohol-brewing and knows how to do. If game, chicken or duck are served on the table, the host will offer dishes to their guests' plates and urge them to eat, which is regarded as hospitality. Even if the guests are full, they shouldn't tell the truth, otherwise the host will misunderstand it as the guests disliking the food and not wanting to have it. The guest should say the food is tasty and the host will be very pleased and make a toast again. Cats and dogs are tabooed food on the Miao People's table for eating them will insult their ancestors and make them ill. On New Year's Day, the Miao people are not allowed to have meat dishes before offering sacrifices to their ancestors.

5.4.2 回族饮食民俗 The Dietary Folk Customs of the Hui People

海南回族主要居住在三亚羊栏镇的回辉村和回新村,他们多才多艺,尤其经商。回族的主要宗教节日为开斋节、古尔邦节。

Today the Hui (Muslim) communities are mainly at the Huihui and Huixin villages in Yanglan Town of Sanya city. Hui people are versatile, especially good at doing business. The Hui's main religious festivals are Eid al-Fitr and Eid al-Adha.

炸油香
Fried Dough Cakes

炸油香是一种以牛肉伴香料制成的馅饼,是三亚回族款待宾客、赠送亲友的名馔,他们把制作炸油香视为神圣之事,制作炸油香前须沐浴净身,炸制时还要燃香薰室。此俗一直沿袭至今。

Fried Dough Cake is a kind of tart made of beef and spices, which is a preferred food for Sanya Hui people to treat their guests or a gift for their friends and relatives. Since the Hui people regard making Fried Dough Cake as sacred, before making it, they must have showers, and during making it, incensing is a must. This custom has been followed so far.

手抓饭
Hand-Served Rice

三亚回族中不少人，特别是老年人，至今保持因手抓饭的习惯，或用勺子而不用筷子进食。因地处海边，椰林成片，人们便就地取材，以椰壳为碗、碟，海贝壳为勺。

A lot of Hui people in Sanya, especially elderly people, have maintained a habit of having rice with hands or with a spoon instead of chopsticks. Living by the sea and surrounded by coconut palms, the Hui people there use local materials to make their tableware, for example, they will make coconut shell bowls, plates, sea shell spoons.

炸油香 （蒋秀娟 摄）
Fried Dough Cakes (Courtesy of Xiujuan Jiang)

手抓饭（蒋秀娟 摄）
Hand-served Rice (Courtesy of Xiujuan Jiang)

三亚回族谨奉伊斯兰教规，常吃鱼类，忌食猪肉，不养猪。他们也忌食一切动物的血及一切自死动物。三亚回族人视喝茶为生活之必需和礼俗，闲时常聚集一处品茶，过节走亲访友时还常以茶叶为礼品。伊斯兰教规严禁烟酒。

Sanya Hui people live strictly by Islamic terms. Sanya Hui people eat fish frequently and their tabooed food is pork. They don't raise pig. Sanya Hui people regard having tea as a part of their daily life and custom. In their spare time, they often gather to have tea. During festivals or visiting friends or relatives, tea is often served as a gift. Tobacco and alcohol are also strictly forbidden in Islamic law.

06

海南服饰民俗
Hainan Costumes and Ornaments

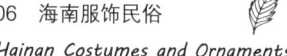

服饰文化特质的形成离不开特定的环境。海南服饰文化鲜明特色的形成与其地理环境因素息息相关。海南属于热带湿热气候,全年暖热、长夏无冬、雨水充沛,花开四季对海南服饰的形制、用料、色彩和图案都产生了很大影响。因此,海南服饰的最大特点是服装的季节变化不分明,且形式简便。这是海南人在长期的生产劳动、生活的历史过程中,对环境适应的产物。

The distinctive features of Hainanese costumes and ornaments are closely related to geographical location. Hainan is featured with tropical humid climate, warm throughout the year, which exerts great influence on designing Hainan costume including shapes, materials, colors and patterns. Therefore, fewer dramatic changes occur during the four seasons, which are formed throughout the long-term production of labor, history and environmental adaptation.

在海南服饰文化中,黎族服饰特色突出,有着独特的民俗风情和工艺,尤其是黎锦、刺绣独具一格。不同方言地区的黎族妇女,服装风格迥异,与之佩戴的饰品更是衬托出黎族妇女的美丽和勤劳。苗族是海南的第二大少数民族。海南苗族刺绣和悠久的民间工艺——蜡染,衬托出苗族服饰鲜明的民族风格和浓厚的乡土气息。海南羊栏回族服饰美观、简朴、舒适和独具特色的头饰"盖头"使整个回族服饰清新、秀丽、明快和悦目。不可忽略的以"水上人"著称的海南疍民服饰别具风格,制作以蓝色为基调,源于蓝天和海洋的图腾,突出了疍民的勤劳和朴实。

The Li People's costumes and ornaments are prominent with the unique ethnic characteristics. Particularly, the Li brocade and embroidery are distinguished with different styles in different branches. Wearing ornaments stands out the beauty of the Li women and their diligence. Besides, the local Miao embroidery and traditional wax printing make their dress distinctive with strong local ethnic flavor. The garments of the Hui ethnic group are simple and comfortable. Especially, their unique headdress makes the Hui ethnic costume more fresh, bright and pleasing to eye. What's necessary to mention, the Tanka' costumes are particular in design, with the major color of blue, which demonstrates the pure and hardworking of the Tanka People.

此外,海洋性热带季风气候使"岛服"成为海南最流行的旅游衫,海南岛服的样式简洁、质朴,色彩艳丽缤纷,也深受内地游客的喜爱。

In addition, Hainan island shirt whose style is simple, colorful and loved by tourists has become one of the most popular souvenirs in Hainan.

总而言之,海南服饰文化多姿多彩,少数民族服饰尤为艳丽夺目,如今少数民族风情旅游也是海南旅游的亮点之一，游客目睹黎族、苗族纺织工艺、体验少数民族服饰风情，感受海南岛服给予的舒适和恬静。

In a word, the costume culture in Hainan is colorful, especially the Li and the Miao's bright-colored costumes which are highlights for touring in Hainan. Tourists can see the procedures of the Li and the Miao techniques of spinning and weaving, and wear ethnic clothes in person. It is comfortable and relaxing to wear Hainan Island shirt waking along the beach as for tourists.

6.1 黎族服饰
Costumes and Ornaments of the Li People

6.1.1 海南黎族树皮布 Bark Clothes

海南树皮布文化可以追溯到3000年以前，黎族祖先用树皮制成树皮布、树皮帽、树皮腰带和树皮被等（海南省人民政府新闻办公室，2005）。在当时，用厚树皮或蒗麻制成是树皮布衣服和裤子主要有遮羞、保暖等用途，是海南黎族祖先最为普遍的一种衣服原料。在明代，居住在五指山腹地的部分黎族人普遍穿这种树皮衣服。树皮衣的制作方法较为简单，具体有两种：一种是纯粹的树皮衣，先将树皮从书上剥下来，然后经过敲打、浸泡、晒干等工序，即可缝制成一块可遮羞的树皮布；另一种是去掉树皮最外面的表皮，取里层的树皮，经过一定的工序后取纤维，纺成线，织成衣服或被子。史图博在《海南岛民族志》中写道"海南岛的布等用树皮经捣击后做成的"，在书中他还用1909年柏林民族学博物馆陈列的海南树皮布来证实。衣服和被子做好后，黎族人会把制好的树皮布、衣服和被子等放入特有的箱子。箱子的外面用红藤或白藤编织，上面用葵叶铺上，再用竹篾编一层，以使葵叶稳实。

The bark was used by the Li People at the very beginning, and it can be dated back to 3000 years ago, when the Li ancestors made the cortex of the castor and lannea trees into textile for garments, hats, belts or quilts for the purpose of keeping warm. During the Ming Dynasty (1368-1644), the bark clothes were very popular among some Li tribes in the hinterland of the Wuzhi Mountain up to the 15th century. In general, there were two basic ways to make this kind of clothes. One was the pure bark clothes. After sewing them into G-strings, the Li People were to hammer, macerate, and sun the plant rinds. The other was to deal with the inner layer of the bark to obtain fibers, and then weaved them into cloth. Stubel mentioned that to the effect Hainan residents pounded bark to make cloth. Meanwhile, he provided an example of the bark cloth from Hainan that was exhibited in the Berlin Ethnological Museum in 1909. After the bark clothes and quilts were made, the Li People had a special method for preserving bark clothes. They usually put a rattan suitcase with Chinese leaves which had the effect of getting rid of insects, compact them with bamboo matting, and place the bark clothes on top of this.

06 海南服饰民俗
Hainan Costumes and Ornaments

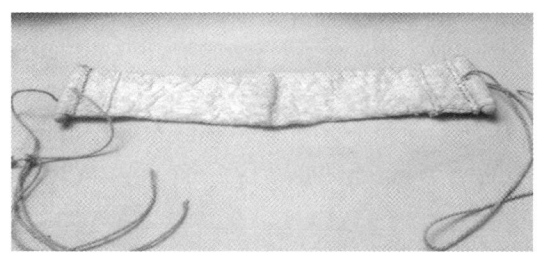

树皮腰带（朱兵艳 摄于海南省博物馆）
Bark Belt (Courtesy of Bingyan Zhu)

树皮帽（朱兵艳 摄于海南省博物馆）
Bark Hat (Courtesy of Bingyan Zhu)

6.1.2 海南黎族扎染 Dyeing in the Li People's style

"扎染"古称"绞缬"，是黎族特有的一种染色法。把理好的纱线两端固定在一个长形的木架上，用来做作经，然后依经线将青色或褐色的棉线扎成各种图案花纹后，取下并放入染缸着色，染后晾干，摘去所结的棉线，就显出色斑花纹的经线，然后在色斑花纹的经线上织上彩色的纬线，织成筒裙布（海南省志·民俗志，2012）。

Zha Dying, called Jiao Xie in ancient time, is a unique method of dyeing of the Li nationality. Both sides of the yarn are fixed on a rectangular wooden shelf as warp, and then follow the warp to embroider many beautiful patterns with black or brown cotton thread. After that, dye and dry it in the sun. When the cotton threads are removed, the warps with patterns are shown, and then embroider the weft with colorful cotton thread, which can be used to make clothing of wrapped skirt.

黎族传统纺染织绣技艺：绊染

黎族传统纺染织绣技艺：染色

（来源：海南非物质文化遗产网）
The Traditional Dyeing of the Li Nationality
(Source: Hainnan Provincial Preservation Center of ICH)

6.1.3 海南黎族织锦 Li Brocade

海南岛属于海洋性热带季风气候，全年都受季风的影响，高温多雨。这样的自然地理条件，是影响黎族纺织技艺的重要因素之一。为了生存和解决日益增加的人口所需要的食物，人们必须每天上山捕猎，从溪河捕捉鱼虾，在这个过程中学会了用绳结网，从而开启了纺织技术。宋代志书更多地记载了黎族妇女在棉纺织工艺方面的卓越成绩。在宋人笔记里，我们可以看到黎族妇女纺织品种繁多、工精艺巧的"黎锦"作品，证明黎族纺织工艺在历史上具有相当高的水平。

Hainan Island is featured with maritime tropical monsoon climate with abundant rainfall in the whole year, which serves as an important factor that affects the textile technique. In order to make a living, people hunt and catch fish every day and learn rope netting. Since then, spinning and weaving techniques were started. The women's outstanding achievements in cotton textile technology were recorded in the Song Dynasty (960-1279 AD). In the notes of Song Dynasty, it can be read that the Li women can weave a variety of brocades, which proved that Li textile technology has reached a very high level in history.

黎锦是中国最早的棉纺织品,古称吉贝布、崖州被、棉布,有精细、轻软、洁白、耐用的特点,是黎族的一种特色花布。黎族人民采用木棉花蒴果内的棉毛、苎麻纤维,及分别来自美洲和印度的海岛棉、巴西木棉、大陆棉和树棉等灌木类棉花,以织锦、织染、织花为主,刺绣较少,用天然色素作颜料,纺织成一种特色花棉布。因木棉又名吉贝,故黎锦也叫吉贝。宋朝以前,黎族人的棉纺织技术领先于中原汉族,后来灌木类棉花逐渐从海南岛传入中国南方。元朝时,黄道婆改进了黎族的纺纱、织布等技术,随之传播到内地,推动了长江下游棉纺织的发展,使棉织品取代纺织品成为生活必需品,掀起了持续数百年的"棉花革命"(海南省人民政府新闻办公室,2005)。黄道婆为我国棉纺织业的发展作出了贡献,推动了中国纺织业技术的革新。

The Li brocade, which is called Ji Bei cloth, Ya Zhou quilt or cotton, is the earliest cotton weaved product in China with the characteristics of being white, soft, smooth and endurable because of the Li People's super craft. The Li People used to spin with the fiber of ramie and various species of cotton, including kapok, dye the yarns with natural pigments, and weave them into cloth of various designs. According to historical document, brocade is described as being "as gorgeous as clouds". Before the Song Dynasty (960-1279 AD), the Li People excelled the Hans of the Central Plains in the cotton weaved industry, but later cotton species were gradually exported into southern China from Hainan. During the Yuan Dynasty (1271-1368), Huang Daopo renovated the spinning and weaving techniques of the Li People and introduced them into the inland, promoting a cotton textile industry in the lower reaches of the Yangtze River. What's more, cotton revolution appeared and went on for centuries in China, and cotton replaced linen as the major textile in people's life. Huang Daopo was a technical innovator of China's textile industry.

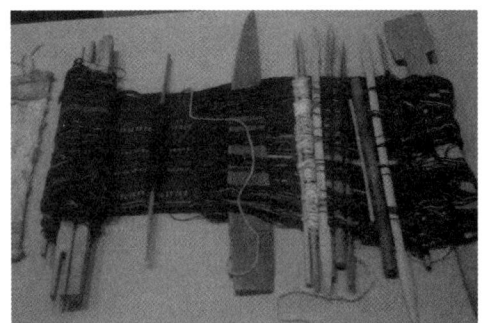

纺织机 (朱兵艳 摄于海南省博物馆)
Spinning and Weaving Tools (Courtesy of Bingyan Zhu)

黎锦图案的工艺制作主要由纺、织、染、绣四大工艺组成。黎锦图案的色彩主要体现在服饰图

06 海南服饰民俗
Hainan Costumes and Ornaments

案上，多以黑色或者深蓝色为基本色调，以红、黄、绿、白相间，紫、棕、粉红、咖啡色为辅助色，有深色也有浅色，有对比色彩也有调和色彩，花纹多以平行线、三角形、直线、菱形组成的几何形，常用人、龙、蛇等图案呈现抽象的人物角色。

The patterns of the Li brocade are finished by four techniques of spinning, weaving, dyeing and embroidery. The use of color is also of vital importance in the Li brocade. The backdrop is traditionally black or blue, matched with red, yellow, green and white, supplemented with purple, brown, pink and coffee. Most of patterns are geometric shapes such as triangle line, square line, diamond line, and abstract figures of people, snakes and dragons, etc.

黎锦图案的工艺精致，反映了黎族人民对生活、劳动和大自然的热爱，也体现了黎族文化的主要内涵。黎织图案可以分为两类：一类主要集中反映在妇女服饰上的各种花纹图案，多以人形纹、动物纹、植物纹、生产工具纹以及利用直线、平行线、三角形、菱形等多种几何形的纹样，内容丰富，色彩美观。另一类是放映在龙被、织锦壁挂、织锦挂包以及各种装饰物品上的图案。图案多以吉祥物体为主，比如，人形纹、龙纹、凤纹、鹿纹、蝴蝶纹、青蛙纹和花卉、树木、青草以及自然界的雷、电、日、月、水、火等。这些图案呈现出云彩缭绕，旭日东升，山水翻腾，龙凤戏珠，图腾动物活灵活现，花草树木鲜艳欲滴的画面，令人叹为观止。黎锦可用来制筒裙、上衣、头帽、花帽、胸挂、围腰、挂包、龙被和壁挂等（海南省人民政府新闻办公室，2005）。古时候，黎锦是"岁贡"珍品，早在汉代黎锦就作为贡品进贡朝廷，也被国内富商珍藏，因而非常名贵。

The Li brocade testifies to the high textile producing skill and ethos of the Li People, including the scenes of the Li's daily life and nature. The patterns of Li brocade can be classified mainly into two types: one can see colorful patterns of women's garments. Most of the designs are in geometric shape, and are abstract figures of people, dragons, horses, snakes, pigeons, frogs, vines and fruits; other patterns can be seen in various costumes and ornaments such as dragon quilt, handbag. Most of patterns highlight auspiciousness with human and animal shapes, flowers, trees and natural phenomenon such as thunder, lightening, sun, moon, fire and so on, which are vivid, colorful, beautiful and pleasing to eyes. In general, the Li brocade is used to make wrap-around skirts, upper clothing, head caps, chest hang, corset, hanging bags, quilts and wall hanging by the Li women, etc. In ancient times, brocade as a tribute was provided to the emperor, which can be traced to the Han Dynasty (25-220), and was treasured by the rich.

龙被是黎族织锦中的一种，也是黎族特色之一。龙被，也被称为崖州被，有着"广幅布"之称。龙被是黎族在纺、织、染、绣四大工艺过程中难度最大，文化品位最高，技术最高超的织锦工艺美术品，是黎族进贡历代封建皇朝的珍品之一。龙被难度最大是在刺绣花纹图案这部分，因为图案繁多，包罗万象，举凡天上、地面、人间诸多事物，以及神话传说中诸多形象，色彩丰富，表现的范围较广。一幅龙被，不论从色彩或者图案上看，都是比较完整的工艺美术作品，具有浓郁地方民族特色。

The dragon quilt, which bears another characteristic of the Li nationality, is one of the Li brocades. The dragon quilt, also known as Yazhou quilt, has a wide range of cloth, which is finished with the most difficult techniques: spinning, weaving, dyeing and embroidery. With its highest cultural taste and brocade crafts, dragon quilt is one of the treasures and tributes of the ancient feudal dynasty. The most difficult part in making dragon quilt is its embroidery patterns because of various patterns including sky, earth as well as the myths and legends of many images. A piece of dragon quilt is a relatively complete work of arts and crafts with strong local ethnic characteristics, in terms of colors or patterns.

黎锦图案（朱兵艳 摄于海南省博物馆）
The Li Brocade (Courtesy of Bingyanzhu)

黎锦图案（刘士祥 摄于海南省博物馆）
The Li Brocade (Courtesy of Shixiang Liu)

6.1.4 海南黎族刺绣 The Embroidery of the Li Nationality

黎族刺绣美轮美奂、技艺精湛、历史悠久。黎族刺绣多是先分片在胚布上刺绣，绣好后再缝缀到服装上。黎族还有织花后再加绣的传统，以突出重点部位。这种绣法分夹牵和织地绣两种。夹牵是在织锦或绣好的绣片上，用拉锁针、珠绣等针法沿花纹边缘加绣，使图案轮廓更清晰，形象更鲜明。织地绣是在织好的条纹或格子布上加绣图案。

The Li embroidery has a very long history with beautiful patterns and great craftsmanship. When making Li embroidery, people usually embroider patterns on the Grey cloth at first, then stitch it to the garment. There is also another tradition to add embroidery to the weaved patterns to highlight the key parts. As usual, there are two ways of stitching techniques. One way is called clip. Clip is needle along the edge of pattern with a zip on the brocade or embroidery to make the outline clearer and more vivid. The other one is woven knit embroidery which is to embroider patterns on good stripe or grid cloth. The Li Embroidery can be completed in different stitches.

黎族刺绣分为单面绣和双面绣两种，其中白沙润方言女子上衣的双面绣最为著名。与黎族单面绣不同的，双面绣是一针同时在一块底料上绣出正反色彩一样的图案。单面的绣法简单，只要正面工致，反面可以不管；而双面绣则要求正反两面都一样整齐匀密。此外，润方言双面绣创造了一种两面加工的彩绣，制作精工极具特色，一般用于妇女服饰上，充分表现了黎族人民的才能和智慧。

The embroidery of the Li nationality is divided into one-faced embroidery and double-faced embroidery, among which the Run women's double-faced embroidery in Baisha is extremely famous. Compared to one-faced embroidery, double-faced embroidery embroiders the same patterns with one needle at both faces on a cloth at the same time. The method of making one-faced embroidery is easy, as long as the front side is exquisite, whereas the double-faced embroidery must be finished evenly on double faces. In addition, the Run People create a colorful both-faced embroidery, which is of fine workmanship with unique characteristics. The double-faced embroidery is often taken to make clothes for the Li women, which reflects their talent and wisdom.

双面绣 （来源：海南非物质文化遗产网）
Double-faced Embroidery of the Li Nationality
(Source: Hainnan Provincial Preservation Center of ICH)

常见的黎族刺绣工艺品有花带、花帽、头帕、头巾、围裙、围巾、腰带、出嫁时用的嫁衣、嫁裙，定情用的荷包、花袋以及节日穿戴的筒裙、花帽等。这些刺绣工艺品均以棕黑色或灰白色的棉布为底，用红、黄、绿、紫等色线和刺花针精心绣出精美的图案来。图案花纹的形状多样，有正方形、三角形、圆柱形、棱形、小纹形、波浪形等，有的还绣上青蛙跳水、双蝶恋花、双龙戏珠和鲤鱼跃水等图案，惟妙惟肖，美观大方。

The handicraft made of embroidery are often seen in Li People's daily life, such as hat kerchief, scarf, belt, the clothes and dresses as dowry when marrying, and pouch, handbag for engagement, wrapped skirt and hat worn in some festivals. The backdrop of these handicrafts is often brown, black or white, taking red, yellow, green and purple treads and needle to embroider beautiful patterns with different shapes such as square, triangle, diamond and so on. Some of handicrafts are used to embroider exquisite and vivid patterns with frogs, flowers, fish, and dragon.

6.1.5 海南黎族服装 The Li Garment

海南黎族服饰主要采用木棉花蒴果内的棉毛、苎麻纤维及海岛棉、巴西木棉、树棉等灌木类棉花织制缝合而成（海南省人民政府新闻办公室，2005）。黎族服饰并非全是根据体型而定，服饰的尺寸由于各个方言的地域语言、崇拜、祭祀、丧葬以及生活环境的差异，因而所喜爱的服饰款样标准自然也不相同。随着时间的推移和各民族交往的频繁，黎族服饰也不断地变化着，且大多数的黎族青年男女早已改穿汉服，这也体现了时代进步的必然趋势。目前，位于五指山市的海南省民族博物馆收藏的各种黎族纺织品中，有黎锦、被服和男女服饰。藏品中包括上衣、下服、花筒（裙）、花巾、花带、花挂等。

The Li People made the clothes with the fiber of ramie and various species of cotton, including kapok, dye the yarns with natural pigments. The Li costumes are made with various dialect regions, different worship, funeral and the living environment, not according to the size and figure. With the passage of time and the communication of different ethnic groups, the Li costume has been constantly changing. Nowadays, most of the youth in the Li ethnic group wear Han garment which reflects the trend of the progress of the times. At present, the Ethnological Museum of Hainan province has a rich collection of the Li textiles, including brocade, quilts and garments.

黎族男人的衣服较简单，大都穿的是无领无袖的对襟衣，一般由粗麻布织成，染成黑色。现在，黎族男子基本上都改穿汉族服装了。

The Li males' garment is relatively simple, including sleeveless and collarless front-buttoned vests, made by coarse linen woven with dyed black. Nowadays, they dress themselves in the Han's style.

黎族妇女服饰，主要有上衣、下裙和头巾三部分，这三部分都织绣着精致的花纹图案。黎族主要有5个支系：哈方言、杞方言、润方言、赛方言和美孚方言。各支系妇女穿着也不一样。哈方言妇女上衣多为对襟无领，饰边简繁不一，下装均为筒裙，服饰款式多样，图案花纹丰富。杞方言妇女服饰折射出海南琼中的服饰习俗。服饰特点是用金属纽扣装饰的对襟开胸上衣并有口袋绣着精美的花草，筒裙上锈有几何形图案。

The Li women's costume mainly includes three parts, coat, skirt and kerchief, on which exquisite patterns are stitched. As the Li People scatter all over the island, different areas have various costumes culture with obvious characteristics. Generally, there are five branches of Li dressing: Ha, Qi, Run, Meifu and Sai. The women of Ha Li wear jackets with buttons down the front without collar and short straight skirts. The clothing styles and patterns are diverse. The Qi branch reflects the costume custom about Qiongzhong. Their open-front long jackets are decorated with metal buttons and the pockets on both sides are embroidered with patterns of flowers and grasses, and their tube skirts are also embroidered with plant or geometric figures.

润方言妇女服饰地域特征十分鲜明，妇女上衣较为独特，为宽大而稍短的古老"贯头衣"，下身穿短而窄的筒裙，根据不同人的身材缝制，一般要求裙子紧贴腰部，它是黎族筒裙中款式最古老的一种，也是所有支系的筒裙中最短的了，以上、中、下三幅布打横连接起来，素有"超短裙"之称。

Women of Run wear poncho-like coats and straight skirts which are made of three strips of cloth sewn together horizontally and are the shortest among all of the Li groups.

赛黎主要分布于保宁、陵水、三亚市，人口约占黎族人数的百分之七。妇女上身穿着圆包胸左侧开襟浅蓝色上衣，下身穿宽大长筒裙。它的中间一般不绣花，下摆花纹很精致、秀气。

The people of Sai Li account for seven percent of Li People in Hainan, and they are mainly distributed in Baoting, Lingshui and Sanya. The women of Sai Li wear upper coat in azure color and buttoned through on the left and baggy long skirt with not embroidering in the middle but exquisite and delicate pattern on the lower hem.

美孚黎主要分布于昌化江下游两岸的东方和昌江两县，人口约占黎族总人数的百分之四。女子头裹黑白相间的头巾，上穿黑蓝色方领上衣，下身穿又长又宽的筒裙——这种筒裙是所有支系中最长的。

The people of Meifu Li mainly spread at Dongfang and Changjiang, which account for four percent of the Li People. Women wear long black and white head kerchiefs with lattice patterns.

They are traditionally clad in blue square neck coats and straight skirts that extend down to the calf, which is the longest skirt among all the Li branches.

黎族五大方言服饰
The garments of the four branches (Sources:lizu.baike.com)

据上所述，哈方言、杞方言、润方言、赛方言和美孚方言 5 支系的服饰特点用以表 6.1 呈列更简单明了。

表 6.1 黎族 5 个支系服饰特点
Characteristics of the Li' Garments of Five Branches

黎族各支系 Five Branches of the Li People	服饰特点 Characteristics of Costumes	
	上衣 Upper Coat	裙装 Skirt
哈方言 The Ha Li	上衣多为对襟无领 wear jackets with buttons down the front without collar	下装均为筒裙 short straight skirts
杞方言 The Qi Li	用金属纽扣装饰的对襟开胸上衣并有口袋 open-front long jackets are decorated with metal buttons and the pockets on both sides	筒裙上锈有几何形图案 The tube skirts are also embroidered with plant or geometric figures.
润方言 The Run Li	为宽大而稍短的古老"贯头衣" poncho-like coats.	下身穿短而窄的筒裙，黎族支系中裙子最短 The shortest skirts among all of the Li groups
赛方言 The Sai Li	圆包胸左侧开襟浅蓝色上衣 buttoned through on the left	下身穿宽大长筒裙 baggy long skirt
美孚方言 The Meifu Li	黑蓝色方领上衣 blue square neck coats	下身穿又长又宽的筒裙 the longest straight skirts that extend down to the calf

实践证明黎族服饰不论在审美和实用方面都有自己独特的个性。它对中华民族服饰的丰富和发展有着不可替代的作用。随着时代的发展，国际旅游岛的建设，我省各大酒店、商店和旅游景点，

为了体现其旅游点的地域和风情的特色，不少服务人员穿戴黎族服饰。中外游客都以能目睹或穿戴绚丽的黎锦、黎服为幸，并以盛装留影纪念。黎族服饰文化是黎族人民智慧的结晶，是人类共同的文化遗产。

Practice has proved that the Li costume has its own unique characteristics. Its enrichment and development play an irreplaceable role in Chinese costumes. With time going by, nowadays most local workers wear the Li costumes in the hotel, scenic spots, shop, etc., which reflect the characteristics of Li ethnic cultures during the process of the development of Hainan International Tourism Destination. Therefore, tourists at home and abroad have the chance to wear gorgeous Li costumes and take pictures. The Li costume culture reflects the wisdom of the Li People.

6.1.6 海南黎族饰品 The Li Ornaments

黎族服饰的精美必定少不了琳琅满目的装饰品。饰品有银、铜、玉、珍珠和动物骨头等，但最受欢迎的是银饰品。黎语把银叫"赶"，头饰、项链、手镯、纽扣都用银，认为银能驱邪。姑娘出嫁时，身上非戴上银饰品不可，其次是玉和珍珠，黎语叫"亲雅"（意思是宝石）（焦勇勤、孙海兰，2008）。黎族各地妇女的装饰品各有特色，通什、琼中、保亭一带的黎族妇女喜欢佩戴多重项圈和月牙形项圈。

The Li ornaments are the indispensable decorations in the Li exquisite costume. Ornaments consist of silver, copper, jade, pearl and animal bones, etc., yet silver jewelry is the most popular among them. Silver is called "Gan" in the Li dialect. Most of their jewelries such as necklaces, bracelets and buttons are made by silver, because silver is regarded as sacred thing to drive out evil spirits. When a girl gets married, she must wear silver ornaments followed by jade and pearl. The ornaments women from different branches have their own characteristics. For example, the women in the vicinity of Tongshi, Qiongzhong, Baoting like wearing multiple necklaces and crescent shaped necklaces.

沿海地区的黎族妇女则喜欢佩戴多个圆形耳环。白沙润方言妇女喜欢佩戴人形骨簪，骨簪用牛腿骨雕刻而成，有单头和双头两种，雕刻非常精细。骨簪的人像是古代黎族人崇拜的部落头领，头部有很高的头冠，是权力的象征。陵水、保亭一带黎族妇女装饰品最为齐全，全套的装饰品分为首饰、颈饰、胸饰、腰饰、肢饰等5种。

The women in coastal area are fond of wearing round earrings. The Run Li in Baisha like bone hairpin with the shape like human body with exquisite carvings. Bone hairpin portraits the tribal leaders with a high crown on the head as the symbol of power worshiped by the ancient people. The women in the areas such as Lingshui, Baoting obsess a full set of accessories for neck, pectoral waist and feet etc.

首饰有银针、银钗、银铃、耳环、骨簪等；颈饰有银项圈、玉珠串、玻璃珠串等；腰饰有银链和小银铃等；肢饰有金（银）戒指，手脚银（铜）圈和玉镯。在过去黎族妇女佩戴的装饰品越多越重，是富贵的象征。

Ornaments include silver hairpin, silver bells, earrings and bone hairpin, etc. Necklaces consist of silver necklaces, jade bead strings, and glass beads and so on. Waist ornaments include silver chains and small bells, limb ornaments are gold (silver) ring, hands and feet silver (copper) rings and bracelets. The Li women use full set of ornaments, which are a symbol of wealth.

6.2 苗族服饰
Costumes and Ornaments of the Miao People

苗族人民继承和发展着本民族固有的传统和文化,并与海南岛独特的地理环境相融合,形成了具有地域特色的苗家风情。苗族服饰至今仍保留着浓厚的民族特色。

The Miao ethnic group is the second largest ethnic group in Hainan. The local Miao People have passed on their traditions and cultures, and formed their unique Miao customs under the effect of geographic environment of Hainan. The costumes of the Miao have still maintained their own national features.

6.2.1 苗族服装 The Miao Garment

由于苗族地处于热带山地气候,夏无酷暑,冬无严寒,四季湿润,又受到黎族服饰的影响,苗族的服装没有明显的季节之分。苗族男子的服饰与汉族男子的唐装有点相似。男子服装上衣有两种:一种是对胸开襟短衣,质地为棉布,有领。另一种是,襟向右开,有圆球铜钮扣或布钮扣 3 枚,无领。男子服饰工艺简单,结实耐穿,适合苗族群众的生产生活需求。

Due to the fact that the Miao People live in the tropical climate, there is no obvious difference between the Li and the Miao in costume during the whole year. The Miao male' dress is similar to the Han garment. There are two kinds of male's garments: one is in cardigan jacket in cotton with collar. The other is short shirt, lapel to the right with three spherical copper buttons or cloth button without collar. The Miao' clothe which is simple, strong and durable is suitable for their living.

苗族女子服饰十分讲究和精致。上衣都穿蓝黑棉衣。苗族妇女上身穿无领、开右襟、长及膝的长衣,肩脖内有一层蓝布垫衣,领口用五色彩线绣有简单的花纹,最外层有一白布边,胸襟和袖口用红线饶边。下穿长过膝的蓝黑色棉布短裙,裙的两头上部均有小绳用来绑扎,短裙的身前有处短小的开襟为的是便于上下山行走。苗族人民的服装仍保留打裹腿的习惯。脚上一般不穿袜子,赤足,腿部缚布带,布带一般长 2 米,宽 8 厘米,绑腿布时先将布缠绕在小腿上,然后各用两条长 1 米的红色彩带结成菱形将绑腿绑紧。彩带两头是蓬松的彩丝,彩丝团垂飘于小腿之上,给人以飘然轻盈的感觉,极具美感(海南省人民政府新闻办公室,2005)。

The costumes of the Miao women are flowery and elaborate in design with several obvious features. Their black or blue collarless frocks are long and loose, tied by red ribbons at the belly. There is simple embroidery of various colors and white pipe along the neckline, and the cuffs and fronts parts are frilled with red thread. The Miao women wear dark skirt with a small slit extending down to the knees to facilitate walking in the hilly areas.The tradition of using puttees in the Miao has been maintained. Locals wrap their legs with cotton tape, two meters long and eight centimeters wide, and tie these with red strips that are one meter long and have red terries at the end.

海南苗族妇女的头饰也很有特色。她们平时戴两种头巾帽：一种是黑布尖顶帽，这是苗族妇女盛装时喜爱戴的一种帽，在帽底下垫一小块绣有约30厘米见方花纹的方形垫头，垫头一角垂于额前，然后在外面再将一块较长而大，制作别致的深蓝色绣上花边的尖顶头巾套上去，在头上形成尖顶状，帽子后垂下一根红带长及腿部，头巾连头部遮盖垂直到肩间。另一种是小花帽，与黑布尖顶帽大小差不多，中间绣有花纹，做工精美，戴帽时把头巾反包在头上，平时妇女一般在农闲、休息时喜爱戴这种头巾帽。

The Miao women have two kinds of headgear. At the grand events the Miao women cover their heads with square embroidered kerchiefs about 30 centimeters long each side, and one corner of the kerchief droops down over their foreheads. They use a black band to position into the form of a spiked-tipped cap with a red tassel hanging at the back. The other one is the same size as the first one, but its top is flat with embroidery in the middle.

苗族女孩服饰 （图片提供 李运坚）　　苗族妇女服饰（图片提供 李运坚）
The Garment of The Li Girl (Courtesy of Yunjian Li)　The Garment of the Li Woman(Courtesy of Yunjian Li)

6.2.2　苗族染布、蜡染与刺绣 The Miao Ornaments

苗族制作服饰的主要工艺有三种：染布、蜡染与刺绣。其中，用蓝靛染布是一项古老的工艺，大多数苗族妇女会用蓝靛染布技术。首先苗族妇女采集种植于山栏地里的蓝靛草，然后经过加工后提取蓝胶，染布时要把蓝胶和配料按一定的比例配合。用蓝靛染成的布料制成衣服，色彩素雅，不易褪色。

There are three art crafts for making the Miao clothes, respectively dyeing, wax printing and embroidery. It has a very long history to dye their textiles with natural indigo. Firstly, the Miao women collect the grass called "Lan Ding", then process it and extract indigo blue which is mixed with other ingredients to make the pigment. In this way, the cloth dyed this color is not easy to fade with washing.

染蜡是苗族古老悠久的民间传统工艺，是一种历史悠久的传统制蜡方法，也是海南苗族人民最喜爱的饰品之一，寓意苗族妇女对爱情的憧憬和美好生活的向往。苗族妇女的染蜡通常会自养蜂、自取蜡、自点花、自染煮。制作方法有以下步骤，首先将白布平铺于案上，置蜡于小锅中，加热溶解为汁，然后用蜡刀蘸蜡液在白布上画出花纹图案，再把布浸入燃料缸里浸泡，最后捞出晾干，再浸，再晒干，如此三四次后，再用水煮，进行脱蜡、漂洗，白色花纹图案便显现出来（焦勇勤、孙海兰，2008）。蜡染一般在每年八月和十二月农闲季节。苗族蜡染一般用来制作衣、裙、头帕、围腰、床单、被面等，常见图案来源于花、鸟、鱼、虫、山川、河流等表示对大自然和社会环境美的追求。苗族人还喜欢在蜡染过的布料和蜡染布所裁制成的衣裙、头巾、腰布等服饰上进行刺绣，图案多为本地自然风光，山川河流、花草树木等，题材迥异，风格细腻，美不胜收。

Wax printing is an ancient art craft of the Miao. The products made by wax printing are one of women's favorite decorations, which imply their longing for love and better life. It's a complicated procedure to make wax printing. The procedure is as follows: first of all, they draw patterns on the fabric with liquid wax, then dip it into the indigo pigment for several times, at last dry them in the sun, so wax printed cloth is made. In August and December when there is not much work to do in the fields, the Miao women usually do the wax printing. The cloth is made into jackets, skirts, belts, scarves and bedding. The patterns are mainly plants, birds, fish, mountains and rivers which are inspired by daily life and nature. They also like to embroider on the wax printed cloth or clothes and dresses with vivid patterns such as local natural scenery, animals and plants, which are exquisite and magnificent.

海南苗族妇女酷爱刺绣，袖口、衣领、胸襟、裙沿、面巾、头帕等处往往都会刺上精图案。图案多种多样，惟妙惟肖，海南苗族服饰中最常见的花纹图案有花、树木、鸟、鱼、青蛙等。有些还会在织绣品上嵌金丝银箔、羽毛、贝壳、珠帘、铜钱等，更显得光彩夺目。海南苗族服饰具有鲜明的民族特色和乡土气息。

The Miao women like to embroider vivid patterns on their cuffs, collar, upper front of the dress, towel and kerchief, etc. The common patterns are flowers, trees, birds, fish, frogs and others. The embroidered products are inlaid with some gold threads and silver foils, feathers, shells, bead curtain, coins, which make them more dazzling. Therefore, the Hainan Miao costumes are distinctive with national characteristics and local flavor.

苗族刺绣（图片提供 李运坚）
The Embroidery of the Miao People (Courtesy of Yunjian LI)

6.2.3　苗族饰品 The Miao Ornaments

苗族妇女盛装时则会戴耳环、手镯等饰品，特别是银质饰品最受喜爱。海南苗族的银饰品工艺高超，品种繁多，如项圈和手镯就有镂空、圆柱、六方形、菱形等。海南苗族的银饰多数是由本民族的银匠专门制作，富有民族传统特色和风格，图案优美，巧夺天工。

The Miao women usually wear ornaments such as earrings and bracelets, especially silver jewelries. The super workmanship of silver is of great varieties. Necklaces and bracelets are made into different shapes such as hollow, cylinder, hexagon, diamond, etc. Most of the Hainan Miao silver jewelries are manufactured by local skilled silversmith with national tradition style and beautiful patterns.

6.3　回族服饰
Costumes and Ornaments of the Hui People

海南的回族最早可以追溯到唐宋时期，随着海上丝绸之路的兴起，海南成为南海上的重要中转站和避风港，从而海南也成了阿拉伯和波斯商人和水手躲避海盗的港湾，从此以后他们的后代开始定居海南（焦勇勤、孙海兰，2008）。今天的海南回族主要居住在三亚市羊栏区。

Muslims in Hainan can date back to Tang and Song dynasties (AD 618-1279). Hainan became the important transfer stop and port in South Sea for the Muslims with the thriving of the Silk Road on the sea, so some settled down there. Today the majority of the Hui (Muslim) communities are in the Yanglan District of Sanya City.

6.3.1　回族服装 The Hui Garment

总体来说，海南羊栏回族服饰与大陆回族基本上没有太大差异，不喜欢耀眼华贵的服装，特别是回族男子一般不穿艳丽的衣服，不着异冠，主要以黑、蓝、白、绿四色为主，几乎不穿红、黄等颜色的衣服。现在回族男子的服饰基本和当地汉族无异，只是逢礼拜或有重大活动时才着白衣白帽。

In general, there are no big differences in clothing between Yanglan Hui (Muslim) and mainland Muslim. The former don't like glorious and expensive clothes. Especially Hui male usually wear traditional Hui clothes which are black, blue, white or green instead of red or yellow.

羊栏回族妇女的服饰还比较特别，上衣大都为右斜襟大褂，纽扣从颈部沿着上身的右侧开，一般为8颗，以银制作，既显示富贵，有象征吉祥。

Yanglan Hui (Muslims) women's clothes are unique. They usually wear single-colored loose upper garments with the top eight buttons made by silver at the right, which symbolize wealth and good fortune.

6.3.2　回族头饰 The Hui Headgear

头饰是羊栏回族服饰中最具特色的。男子喜欢戴白布制作的圆帽，有六菱形的，也有平顶的。

回族妇女头上常戴"盖头",盖头用不同颜色的棉织品做成,幅面颇宽,自头顶下套,遮住两耳,垂至肩后。

The headdress bears distinctive feature in the Hui ethnic ornaments. Men love wearing white diamond or flat round hat. The Hui women often wear headgears which are made of cotton with different colors. The format of the headgear is quite wide extending to the shoulder and covering ears.

盖头也很讲究,不同年纪的人带不同的颜色的盖头。通常可以分为3种,老年妇女戴黑色,中年妇女戴白色,未婚姑娘则偏爱靓丽的颜色如绿色或彩色。回族妇女的盖头讲究精美,多用质地柔软的丝绸或细棉布制成。回族妇女还喜欢在盖头上嵌金边,绣上风格素雅的花草图案,看上去令人赏心悦目

The Hui women are very particular about their headgears. The female at different ages wear different colors of headgears which can be divided into three kinds. The elder women wear black, middle-aged women like white, and unmarried girls prefer bright colors. The women's kerchiefs are made by soft texture of silk or fine cotton cloth with gold frills. There are beautiful patterns with simple and elegant style on the headgears, which are very enchanting.

披金戴银是女性的最爱,羊栏回族妇女也是如此,此外还喜欢佩戴玉石手镯、金戒指等。他们普遍有扎耳洞、戴耳环的习惯。女孩两耳下端自幼穿孔,幼童、姑娘挂耳环,已婚妇女则挂耳坠。有钱人家还戴金胸花、金发卡、金笼子、金手镯等。

The Han women dress up with jewelries, so do the Hui women. In addition to jade bracelets and gold rings, they wear earrings. The little girl must have ear holesand and wear earrings, whereas the married eardrops. And the rich are fond of wearing gold brooch, blond card, gold cage and gold bracelets.

6.4 疍家服饰
Costumes and Ornaments of the Tankas

在海南有一个古老的族群,被称为"水上人""水户"等,他们以波涛为枕、船为家,泊居水面,以捕鱼、摆渡、运输、贩盐为生,这就是海南的疍民。据史记载,随着唐朝"记丁输课"制度的推行,两广疍民大量移入海南水域。主要分布于岛的西北部一带,并有向岛四周扩张趋势。张朔人说,历代大迁移,使得海南的疍民形成了一定的规模。新中国成立以后,疍民的民族成分归同于汉族。主要聚居在海口海甸港、陵水新村港、昌江海尾、临高新盈港、三亚港、榆林红沙、后海、海棠湾(海尾)等地。

There is an ancient ethnic group known as the Tankas in Hainan. They make a living by fishing, ferry, transportation, and selling salt, taking the wave as pillow and boats as their house. According to the historical records, with the system of Ji Ding Shu Ke being carried out in the Tang Dynasty (618-906), the Tankas from Guangdong and Guangxi gradually immigrated into Hainan. They were mainly distributed in the northwest of the island and expanded to other areas.

Zhang Shuoren said that the Tankas moved to Hainan on a large scale. Nowadays, the tankas mainly live in the port of Haidian of Haikou, Xincun harbor of Lingshui, Haiwei in Changjiang, Xinying port of Lingao, port of Sanya etc.

疍民的服饰与汉族基本相同，旧时以唐装为主，现在随时代变迁，疍民的服饰别具风格。原生态的疍家服饰的制作源于蓝天和海洋的图腾，以蓝色为基调。

The Tanka and the Han people's clothes were basically the same in ancient times. As the time goes by, the Tankas' garment has changed, but it has kept the original clothing on the totem of the blue sky and the sea.

无论春夏秋冬，头戴既可遮阳又可挡雨的竹笠。所戴竹笠很讲究，项上直径为10厘米、高8厘米，下半部为直径40厘米、高为4厘米的筒式竹笠、这种竹笠做工考究，纺织精细，外部要刷上一层金黄色的海棠油。这层油金光闪闪，既是竹笠的保护层，又增加了一分光彩。笠带则为疍家姑娘的杰作，以红、橙、黄、白、紫、蓝、黑等胶丝配上闪闪发亮的贝类小珠编织成。带上这精工制作的竹笠和美丽的彩带，在骄阳下，使你感到更舒畅，显得更美丽。

During the whole year, they wear bamboo hats for keeping both sunlight and the rain off, which are very exquisite. The bamboo hat is 10 cm wide, 8 cm high, while lower part is 40 cm wide and 4 cm high. This hat looks exquisite in craftsmanship with a layer of golden color of Begonia oil on the external by part to keep from corrosion. The bamboo hat is regarded as the Tankas' masterpiece, weaved by red, orange, yellow, white, purple and yellow ribbons with glittering beads. Wearing the exquisite bamboo hat with colorful ribbons in the sunlight makes you feel comfortable and pleasing to eyes.

疍家妇女喜爱留长发，姑娘们把头发结成不容易散开的五绞辫，发梢上缀红绒，休闲时就让长辫摇晃垂及腰际。结了婚的妇女把长辫在头顶上盘成髻。作业时，习惯在头上包一块方格花纹的夹层方布，一角突出前额，一角垂于脑后，疍家俗称猪嘴，方巾的左右两角交结于下颊。这种装束打扮利于海上作业和遮蔽风日，也便于步滩涉水和渔业劳作。当时到处有人穿疍家服饰出海打鱼。在那个时候，穿疍家服饰的人在疍民中是极受人尊重的。

Tanka women always wear their hair long. The girls love plaiting their hair in braids which is not easy to loose. Married women wear their long braids in a bun. They are used to putting on a piece of square cloth with patterns, one corner stretching above the forehead, and one corner hanging on the back of the head, the other two corners tying together around the cheeks. It's commonly known as "pig's mouth" among the Tankas. This kind of dress is suitable for people to work at sea against sunlight, and fish in the sea. At that time the people who wear the Tanka's garment are very respectable.

疍民偏爱于玉器，尤其是碧玉和翡翠。玉为温润而有光泽的美石，是洁白美好的象征。而且女子酷爱银器，往往手套银镯、脚套银环、颈套银圈，全身上下，银光闪烁，走起路来，叮当作响，颇具韵致。

Jade, which is featured with fineness and smoothness, is the symbol of purity and beauty. In addition, women are fond of wearing silverware around necks, wrists and ankles. When they are walking, everyone can hear the sound of ding-dong and the women are pleasing to eyes.

06 海南服饰民俗
Hainan Costumes and Ornaments

6.5 海南"岛服"
Hainan Island Shirts

　　来海南旅游，人们必会体验海南热带海洋服饰——海南岛服。在海南，岛服是非常流行的海南旅游衬衫。"岛服"是一种宽松、舒适的花衬衫，衬衫图案取材于海南民众的日常生活，以及自然物产，如椰子树、热带海洋动植物及热带水果等，色彩缤纷，极具浓郁的海南特色。

　　Those who come to Hainan must like to wear Hainan Island shirts, which are popular among tourists and the locals. Hainan Island shirts bear rich Hainan characteristics. Hainan shirt is loose and comfortable with bright colors and distinctive features which are drawn from customs and tropical plants and marine animals such as coconut palms, shells and so on.

　　"岛服"起源于海南旅游企业，最初是为营造独特文化的工作服。后来，海南省旅游局借助"岛服"弘扬海南旅游文化，设计了海南"导游服"。今天，无论是导游还是游客或是官员都很喜欢这种款式简单却又令人非常精神的岛服。

　　The island shirt originated from the Hainan tourism enterprises for the purpose of creating a unique culture for workers. Later, the Hainan Provincial Tourism Bureau designed the Hainan guide shirt in order to carry on the Hainan tourism culture. Nowadays, whether you are a guide or a tourist or an official, it's popular to wear island shirts.

　　海南岛服样式简洁、质朴，上衣为短袖衫，下裳是宽松七分裤，通常以鲜红、明黄、宝蓝、翠绿、橘红为主色，然后以雪白色为配色，色彩绚丽热情，图案争奇斗艳。岛服用料考究，主要用纯棉进口丝光布所制，其主要的特点：手感柔软、透气、吸汗、折皱性好等；款式也很多，有短裤、中裤、男上衣、女上衣、九分裤、七分裤、男长裤、男短裤等。

海南岛服（朱兵艳 摄）
Hainan Island Shirts
(Courtesy of Bingyan Zhu)

　　The style of Hainan Island shirt is concise and simple with a short-sleeved shirt and loose cropped pants with main colors, such as bright red, yellow, blue, green, and orange, supplemented by white. The materials of Island shirts are mainly imported mercerized cotton cloth which is soft, breathable, sweat absorbent and so on. There are many kinds of styles, such as short pants, pants, coat for men, blouses, men's trousers, shorts and so on.

　　今天，海南岛服成为海南旅游的标志性服饰，倍受游客的欢迎与喜爱。远道而来的游客，脱下西装、旗袍，换上海南岛服，让他们倍感轻松与惬意。因此，无论是在沙滩还是在街道和小巷，处处可见游客身着岛服的身影，成了海南的另一道风景。这也让岛服处处张扬着的休闲、自由、洒脱、纯净、舒适与健康，与这里的蓝天、碧海、阳光、森林浑然一体。无论男女老少，穿上它，不但毫无造作之感，反而令人倍觉亲切、舒适。岛服是海南的自然风光与人类自身相亲相融的一种外在表现形式。身着布满椰枝、海洋、贝壳、珊瑚图案的服装，徜徉、嬉戏于山水之间，体验和浸染着这块热土的文化精神与情愫，周身荡漾着快乐与生动，心中是对生活的感动、对明天的热爱。

　　Currently, Hainan Island shirts are popular among tourists and have gradually become the symbols of Hainan tourism.It's relaxing and comfortable to wear island shirts instead of suit or Qipao. Therefore, tourists have formed another beautiful scene with island shirt in Hainan whether they are on the beach or in the streets and alleys. Dressed in island shirts covered with patterns of coconut palms, marine produces, tourists hang around the beach and mountains happily and lively.

2009年5月，中共海南省委办公厅、海南省人民政府办公厅根据党中央、国务院有关精神，就精简会议文件、改进会风文风发出专门意见：除重要大会和外事场合以外，出席其他会议可着便装或海南岛服。岛服在海南官方和民间对外交往中，与西服具有同样功能的礼服，它的出现顺应了如今国际礼仪趋于简化和不穿西服、不系领带的外交日益增多的趋势。省外事部门将"岛服"变成省领导会见外宾的礼服。多方面的示范效应，加上宽松的"岛服"适合热带海岛度假休闲，其花样体现出独特地域文化，因此引起较大的市场需求。最终，"岛服"成为海南最热门的旅游纪念品。

In May 2009, according to the conference documents of the Party Central Committee and the State Council, the general office of the CPC Hainan Provincial Committee, Hainan Provincial People's government office streamlined that officers can wear casual clothes or Hainan island shirt. Hainan Island shirt has the same function as the suit during foreign affairs, and it has also become more and more popular with the trend of international etiquette not to wear a suit and tie. Provincial Foreign Affairs Department takes island shirt as an important costume when meeting foreign guests. Since the demonstrative effect is good, coupled with the fact that the island shirt is suitable for tropical island resort, and its patterns reflect the unique regional culture, greater market demand is caused. Thus, the "island shirt" becomes one of the most popular tourist souvenirs in Hainan.

海南岛服是海南文化的一部分。有专家指出，"岛服"不是普通的衣服，要承载起宣传海南丰富的旅游文化内涵和多姿的热带民族风情的任务，还要充分挖掘地方人文风情和文化底蕴。因此，若使岛服更具休闲特色，岛服的制作要在图案、款式、风格、布料等上推陈出新。无论从品牌、款式、还是从质量上开发、推进海南"岛服业"，从而带动旅游纪念品的开发与发展。

The expert points out island shirt should broadcast Hainan unique culture and colorful ethnic customs. At the same time, the designer must take much more cultural factors in their works. Therefore, the Hainan Island shirt should be innovative through renewing the colors, styles so that it becomes more attractive with Hainan leisure features, promoting the development of Hainan souvenirs from the brand, style and the quality.

6.6 海南服饰民俗旅游开发思考
Implications on the Tourism Development of Costumes and Ornaments in Hainan

四面环海，得天独厚的生态环境特色，海南黎族、苗族、岛服等特色风情服饰为其增添一份独特的文化魅力。为吸引更多游客，将黎苗族服饰的特色元素融入旅游产品设计中，加强文化内涵建设，以动画媒介为契机宣传海南黎苗特色服饰民俗文化，推广海南黎苗族服饰民俗。

Besides unique geological location and abundant resources, the costumes of the Li and the

Miao are making Hainan even more charming. In order to attract tourists, some unique characteristics of all the ethnic groups can be designed into tourism products for the purpose of cultural construction. Meanwhile, it can take the media to broadcast the Li brocade, embroidery, and the Miao wax printing.

6.6.1 保留黎锦和黎苗特色服饰元素，与其他产品相结合，设计海南特色旅游产品
To design cultural tourism products by absorbing the main elements and the Li and the Miao costumes

众所周知，黎族服饰一般用麻、棉织成，而黎族传统棉纺织染绣技艺（黎族织锦）被誉为黎族文化的"活化石"，其中双面绣和龙被最为华美，是黎锦中的精品。特别是其丰富的图案和复杂的纺织手法、庞大的工作量，人们很难达到批量化生产，因此无论黎锦或是黎苗服饰价格均比较昂贵。同时，还可以将长幅黎锦缩短、再设计，降低成本，与圆柱型椰棕桶结合，既巧妙的运用当地自然资源，又保证价格适中，并通过黎锦所包含的强调吉祥寓意，带给旅游者独特的文化体验，并能够在些许年后勾起旅游者的美好回忆。

It is well-known that the Li costumes are made from hemp, cotton. The Li brocade is known as the living fossil of the Li ethnic group, of which the double-sided embroidery and the dragon quilt are the most beautiful ones. Due to the abundant patterns, complicated spinning and weaving techniques and huge workload, it is difficult for people to produce more within the specific time. Therefore, we can shorten the long pieces of Li brocade, redesigning and reducing the cost. The innovative brocade is designed with auspicious patterns for tourists, which bring tourists special cultural experiences and make them recall their good memories in future.

政府也非常重视黎苗文化的挖掘与传播。根据其织绣工艺的独特性和民俗风情，政府可以组织服饰、黎族文化等有关方面的专家，提炼黎族服饰文化元素，结合现代服饰的布料和技术，生产出传统与现代相结合的布料，制作出既时尚又具有黎苗元素的特色服饰，款式可以多样化，可供作为旅游纪念品或商品出售。

Meanwhile, the government also attaches great importance to spread the costume cultures of the Li and the Miao nationalities. With exquisite handcraft and national characteristics of the Li and Miao People, some relevant experts are invited to make some researches on them, refining cultural elements, and combine them with modern craft to produce innovative costumes both on fashion or cultural elements. The costumes with diverse styles can be sold as souvenirs or commodities.

2015年8月10日，中国创新创业大赛（海南赛区）暨海南省首届"科创杯"创新创业大赛在海口举行复赛，完美融合黎苗传统文化与时尚元素的"黎之语"项目从129个团队项目中脱颖而出，成功入围决赛（中新网海南，2015）。"黎之语"项目是5个年轻的90后大学生基于各自对黎锦文化的理解设计不同的创意产品，丰富的黎锦文化正为其提供源源不断的素材内容和创作灵感。据介绍，黎之语团队以弘扬海南特色民族文化为核心理念，致力于研发、设计、生产和销售具有海南特色文化的旅游纪念品、艺术品。

On August 10th, 2015, China Innovation and Entrepreneurship Competition (Hainan Division) and the first Innovation Cup Competition was held in Hainan. The project of "Li brocade" was shown by the combination of the Li and Miao traditional cultures with fashion elements, and was selected to the finals. The project "Li Brocade" was completed by five students based on their own understanding of the brocade culture. As it reports that the "Li Brocade" takes Hainan characteristic culture as the core, committed to developing, designing and selling more souvenirs, art-crafts with Hainan unique cultures.

6.6.2 通过各种媒介宣传海南各民族特色服饰，吸引国内外游客体验 To broadcast Hainan Island shirts and other costume cultures of all ethnic groups to attract tourists at home and aboard

新闻媒介是一种很好传播文化的方式。政府可以通过各种传播媒介如报纸、动漫作品、宣传片等推广海南独特的海洋服饰文化和民族风情服饰文化，如色彩绚丽、款式简洁、大方的海南岛服，不同方言地区风格迥异的黎族风情服饰、黎锦和龙被等；代表妇女对爱情的憧憬和对美好生活的向往的苗族蜡染和刺绣，以及海南疍民所戴的首饰与竹笠。

Media can be taken to broadcast costume cultures. The government can broadcast Hainan marine and national customs culture through newspapers, animation works and videos. On one hand, it should take these factors into consideration: the colorful island shirts, the ethnic featured Li brocade, costumes and dragon quilt. On the other hand, it has to highlight its inner cultures of wax printing and embroidery, which shows women's longing for love and better life.

动画媒介无疑是宣传海南服饰文化最重要的途径之一。动画中的人物角色是动画的灵魂，其中主要角色服饰造型的设计也是非常关键和重要的。通过人物的服装造型让人们了解其人物的个性特点，因此对形象的塑造有着直观作用，且能辅助剧情的发展、体现作品想要表达的主题思想和艺术内涵。

Undoubtedly, animation media is one of the most important ways to promote Hainan costume cultures. The characters in animation are the souls of the animation, especially the main character's costumes. People can understand the character's personality by their costumes, which have visual effect to shape the image and aid the plot development, and inner cultures.

今天，在国际动画角色造型亦步亦趋的情况下，了解海南黎苗文化艺术形式对动画角色造型设计有着重要影响，对解决当今海南动画角色造型服饰如何与传统民族文化巧妙融合的问题，以及海南动画角色造型风格的确立具有重要的意义。可见通过动画片，我们不仅可以了解黎族、苗族、回族及疍家人的生活习惯，还可以通过这一方法了解他们的服饰色彩和基本形制，领悟其深层次的文化心理及情感，可见动画片不仅仅是一种娱乐的媒介，更是一种传播民族特色的线索。

Today, it's greatly significant to design animation image in Hainan through understanding the Li and Miao ethnic art cultures, and the integration of Hainan animation characters and traditional national cultures. When watching the cartoons, we understand the Li, Miao, Hui and Dan Min people's living habits, as well as their colors and shapes of the costumes, which can help us to comprehend their deep cultural psychology and emotion. Therefore, cartoon is not only a medium of entertainment, but a great way to broadcast national cultures.

In conclusion, it's very important to design and renew Hainan Island shirt and broadcast Hainan ethnic costume to promote the development of Hainan international tourist destination.

07

海南劳动生产民俗
The Production Customs in Hainan

劳动生产民俗,简单来说是指在各种物质生产活动中所产生并需遵循的民俗。这类民俗来源于人们日常的生产劳动,从多方面地反映着人们的民俗观念,在历史上对保证生产的顺利进行有一定的作用。海南各族人民在长期的生产劳动中,在农业、渔猎、种植业等方面形成了一套相对完整而独具一格的生产民俗,大致可分为:农业民俗、渔业民俗、山林狩猎民俗、采集业民俗、种植业民俗、林业民俗、畜牧业民俗和手工业民俗等。

The production customs simply refer to the customs generated in various material production activities and followed by people. These customs originate from people's daily production, and reflect people's folk concept from many aspects, which have certain effects on ensuring the success of the production in history. In the long period of production, Hainan people of all ethnic groups have formed a set of relatively complete and unique customs, which can be roughly divided into: agriculture customs, fishing customs, hunting customs, gathering customs, cropping customs, forestry customs, animal husbandry customs and handicrafts customs, etc.

7.1 农业民俗
Agriculture Customs

海南岛是中国最大的"热带宝地",已开发利用的土地约315.2万公顷(3.152平方千米),其中可用于农业开发利用的约占90%。海南岛属热带季风气候,长夏无冬,光温充足,雨量充沛,有利于农业的生产发展。因此,从古至今,农业始终是海南的支柱产业,约占28%,万宁、三亚、保亭、陵水和乐东一带被视为最佳的农业气候区。海南的农业生产以种植水稻为主,海南许多地方种植的水稻大都是一年两熟,其中三亚、乐东种植的水稻甚至达到一年三熟。

Hainan Island is the largest "tropical treasured place" in China with the total land area of 3.152 million hectares, 90% of which can be used for the development of agriculture. Hainan is featured with tropical humid climate. Throughout the year, it's warm and has abundant rainfall, which is conducive to the development of agriculture production. Therefore, agriculture has been the pillar industry of Hainan since ancient times, accounting for about 28% of it. The areas of Wanning, Sanya, Baoting, Lingshui and Ledong are regarded as the best agroclimatic regions. The agriculture production in Hainan is mainly rice, with two crops in a year, while in Sanya and Ledong, even with three crops in a year.

海南岛上的黎族和苗族人,他们主要生活在中西部偏远山区和盆地。1949 年前,他们过着迁徙无常的刀耕火种的原始生活,与外界接触较少,生活条件极其艰苦,农业生产力较为低下,农作物种类少、产量低,以种植山栏稻、薯、玉米等作物为主,生产工具也相当简陋、落后。汉族则大多居住在岛上的沿海和平原地区,这些地区交通便利,地势较为平坦,适合农作物的生长,与岛上的少数民族相比,汉族人的农作物种类较为繁多,生产工具较为先进,生产力水平也略高一些。

The Li and the Miao People mainly live in the remote mountain and basin of mid-west of Hainan. Before 1949, they lived a moving and slash-and-burn primitive life, with rare contact with the outside world, extremely hard living conditions and quite low productivity of agriculture. They mainly planted Shanlan Rice, potatoes, corns and other crops with humble and backward production tools. Whereas, the Han People mostly live in the coastal and plain areas of Hainan Island where the transportation is convenient and the terrain is relatively flat, which are suitable for the growth of the crops. Compared with the minorities, the productivity level of the Han People is higher with more varieties of crops and better production tools.

海南的农业现代化进程发展缓慢,20 世纪 90 年代以前,海南各族农民在种植水稻、芝麻和花生等农作物时,劳动工具还非常的落后,基本以牛车、人力打谷机、犁、耙、锄头、铁爪、镰刀等为主。在海南各族农民的农业生产劳动中,牛扮演着极为重要的作用。农民利用它来拉车,装载农作物,犁田耕地。1949 年前,为了让牛的耕作技术更加娴熟,农民在驯教牛之前往往会在自家牛栏中祭拜牛神。后来这种习俗已基本废止。随着社会的快速发展,90 年代后,海南省的农业发展迈进了机械化时代,绝大多数地方都使用了拖拉机、播种机、插秧机和收割机等,节约了大量的劳力和时间,提高了农作物的产量。

The agricultural modernization in Hainan developed slowly. Before the 1990s, the important labor tools were bullock-cart, the thresher with hand-fed, plough, rake, sickle, hoe, iron claw and so on. Hainan farmers used these backward working tools to plant crops such as rice, sesame and peanuts. The cattle, which were used to pull cart, load crops and plough field, played an extremely important role in the agriculture production of Hainan. Before 1949, in order to make the cattle more skilled, farmers tended to offer the sacrifices to the spirit of cattle in their stall before training the cattle. But this custom has been almost abolished later. With the rapid development of society, the agriculture development of Hainan province turned into mechanization era after 1990s. The modern production tools such as tractors, planters, harvesters and reapers are widely used by the local farmers, which can increase the labor productivity.

7.1.1 生产工具 Production Tools

海南汉族的传统生产工具种类较多,有牛车、耙、犁、锄头、镰刀等,有许多至今仍然为农民所常用。其中牛车在人们的日常生活中显得尤为重要,既是不可缺少的生产工具也是非常独特的交

07 海南劳动生产民俗
The Production Customs in Hainan

通工具，用途极为广泛。人们通常选用上等的木材如海棠木来制作牛车，使其更加牢固耐用。人们利用牛车来装载货物，上山拉柴火，出远门走亲戚，上医院看病，等等。而海南的黎族和苗族人民因为还没有掌握铸造技术，所以他们的劳动生产工具大部分都是拜大自然所赐，利用木、竹来制作，有竹耙、木犁、木桶等，还有少量从汉族人那儿得来的钩刀、铲、锹和斧子等其他铁制用具。海南常用的生产工具有以下几种：

The Han People have more traditional production tools, such as bullock-cart, harrow, plough, hoe, sickle, etc., most of which are still used nowadays. The bullock-cart seems to be especially important and versatile in people's daily life, which is not only an indispensable tool of production, but also a very unique traffic tool. People usually choose the best wood like Begonia wood to make bullock-cart more solid and durable. The bullock-cart could be used to load goods and mountain firewood, visit relatives living in another country, see doctors and so on. Since the Li and the Miao minorities didn't master the casting techniques, their labor production tools were mostly made from nature. The tools were made of wood and bamboo, such as bamboo rake, wooden plow and barrel, etc. They also had a small amount of some iron tools from the Han People, such as hook knife, shovel, spade and axe, etc. The most frequently used production tools can be summarized as follows:

犁

Plough

犁由在一根横梁端部的厚重的刃构成，通常系在一组牵引它的牲畜或机动车上，用来破碎土块并耕出槽沟，为播种做好准备。有用于犁地的坡地犁和犁田的水田犁两种，是海南各族农民最常使用的一种传统耕地农具。

Plough is one of the most commonly used traditional farm tools in Hainan, which may be made of wood, iron, or steel frame with an attached blade or stick to cut the earth. Ploughs pulled by working animals such as cattle or by tractors, are normally used for digging and turning over soil, especially before seeds are planted. There are two kinds of ploughs, the hillside (fields) plough and the paddy field plough.

耙

Harrow

耙呈"而"字结构，柄长，装有木、竹或铁制的齿，有用于水田地的铁齿耙和旱地的木齿耙两种，是海南农民常用耙来平地、碎土、归拢或散开谷物、柴草的一种农具。

Harrow is an agricultural implement for breaking up and smoothing out the surface of the soil, and scattering the grain in Hainan. It is made of a long handle and some wooden, bamboo or iron teeth, which looks like the Chinese character "而". The harrow with iron teeth is used in paddy field and the one with wooden teeth is used in dry land.

锄头

Hoe

锄头一种长柄农具，其刀身平薄而横装，可用于刨地、翻土、除草、收获等，比较节省力气，是海南农人重要的农具之一。

Hoe is one of the important farm tools which can save energy for Hainan farmers. It is made of a long handle and a blade, which can be used for digging and turning soil, weeding, harvesting, etc.

镰刀
Sickle
镰刀由刀片和木把构成，木把大约有 40 厘米长，有的刀片上带有小锯齿；有手镰和牛角镰两种，前者用于收割坡地作物如牧草稻麦，后者用于收割深水田的水稻，是海南农村收割庄稼和割草的农具。

Sickle is a farm tool for Hainanese used to harvest crops and cut grasses. It is made of a curved blade and a short handle. There are two kinds of sickles, one is the hand sickle used for harvesting crops on slopes such as forage rice and wheat, and the other one is the horn sickle used for harvesting paddy rice.

打谷机
Thresher
20 世纪 90 年代前，海南农村大都使用人力打谷机来打稻谷，也称为脚踩打谷机，即用生铁铸两个带花孔的圆盘，两圆盘之间穿入木条，每根木条上钉一排折成 U 型的八号铁丝，即滚筒；再装上脚踏板，用传动杆将脚踏板上的动力传给滚筒；单脚踩在脚踏板上面，打谷机开始旋转，把一捆割好的稻子放进滚筒里，稻谷和稻草就分离了。后来随着技术的发展，逐渐被动力脱谷机所取代。

Thresher was a farm tool for Hainanese to separate grains of rice from the plant. It was hand-fed before the 1990s. It was small and was about the size of an upright piano. Later it has been gradually replaced by the petrol or diesel-powered thresher with the development of technology.

牛车（刘士祥 摄于海南省博物馆）
An Oxcart (Courtesy of Shixiang Liu)

生产工具（刘士祥 摄于海南省博物馆）
Production Tools (Courtesy of Shixiang Liu)

7.1.2 生产经验 Production Experience

种水稻
Growing Paddy Rice
海南有着不同于我国内陆地区的农耕民俗。如海南汉族种植水稻时，播种前要将备好的酒肉、饭团摆放在自家房外，用以祭祀秧婆，祈祷秧婆能够驱除害虫和田鼠，保佑秧苗茁壮成长以便有好收成；祭祀后开始浸种育秧，盛种的箩筐里要插上一些野菠萝叶来"驱邪"；插秧要选择良辰吉日，首日开插时让一些插秧能手先下田来"压田"。在晚稻收割时，岛上的农民都会用新米来煮一锅干饭，以示"开镰"，希望来年稻谷有好收成。

07 海南劳动生产民俗
The Production Customs in Hainan

Some of the farming customs in Hainan differ from those in the mainland. For example, before sowing, the Han nationality need to place the prepared food outside of their house to offer sacrifices to "Yang Po" (the God of rice seedlings), who can be considered to kill off pests and voles. Then they begin to soak seedlings and insert some leaves of Pandanus tectorius into the seedlings baskets to ward off the "evil". They plant rice seedlings on a chosen auspicious date. On the first day of planting, some expert cultivator would plant first, called "Ya Tian" which means that planting will run smoothly. After harvesting the rice, the farmers will cook the new rice, called "Kai Lian", wishing that they will have a good harvest in the coming year.

砍山栏
Growing Shanlan Rice

海南黎苗族在解放前大多居住在岛内山区，能开垦耕作的水田极其有限，不能满足他们的日常食用，所以他们普遍烧垦山地来种植山栏稻。日积月累，造就了他们砍山种山栏的经验非常丰富。山栏稻一年一造，"砍山栏"的过程大致如下：

Before 1949, the Li and the Miao minorities mostly lived in the mountains, where the cultivated paddy fields was extremely limited and couldn't meet their needs. Therefore they generally cleared the plants in the field to grow Shanlan Rice. They have accumulated much experience on planting Shanlan Rice over time, with one harvest in a year. The process of growing Shanlan Rice was roughly as follows:

在每年冬末春初即春节前后，各户常派一位有生产经验的男子到山林中择优选地，他们认为种植山栏稻的最佳地上必须生长着茂密的树木，树叶浓绿，杂草较少、泥土肥沃，坡度平缓，上面覆盖着些许枯烂树叶。一旦选定这块地，他们就会砍下芒杆叶，捆绑成束，悬挂在所选地的周围，这种打"草标"的方式表示此地已有主，其他人不得占之。

Around the Spring Festival, a man with production experience was sent to select the best field for growing rice. In their minds, the Shanlan Rice must be grown in the fertile soil with lush trees, less weeds, and gentle slope. Once selecting the land, they would cut down the long grass and bundle them into a beam to hang around the selected land, which means others shouldn't possess it.

2月，全家总动员一起出动开始砍山，即到所选的山地上砍伐树木，清除杂草，他们一边砍一边唱起古朴粗犷的《砍山谣》："嘿～唷，迟备园因抓鱼，迟种田因拾螺，迟砍山栏（园）因情迷。山仙姑娘呀，我恼恨情迷，我的歌声是骂声，我的体毛是藤刺。嘿～唷，飞刀惊天地，大树倒，情丝断，种下山栏丰收米。"（邢植朝、王静，2002）

In February, the family went to the mountain together to cut down trees and removed weeds from the selected ground. They sang the simple and pleasant song "Kan Shan Yao" as they worked.

3月至4月烧山，放火焚烧干枯后的树木杂草，渗入土中的灰烬为最好的肥料。清理残烬后，不用翻土等到大雨浇透后表土疏松时，男子用尖木棍戳穴，女子背着盛种子的竹篓跟着下种封穴。大家你追我赶，一边劳作一边唱着特色动听的《山栏歌》："四月来到雨水下，无牛种田难顶当。五月来到人播种，播得种子出不齐。六月来到欠（意：应）拔草，草青草长心早憔。七月来到禾发青，八月来到稻扬花。九月来到割九粘，十月来到谷晒干。十一月来到把谷春，十二月来到是冬至。"（邢植朝、王静，2002）

In March and April, they burnt dry woods and grasses which they had cut down before, and seeped ashes into the soil as the best fertilizers. After burning off the fields, they didn't turn over the soil until the heavy rain soaked into it. The men poked holes with sharpened stakes and the women with the bamboo baskets put seeds in the holes and covered them. They sang the characteristic and beautiful song "Shanlan Ge" while working.

6月,他们给禾苗除草,此前无需施肥和翻土;至9月成熟,用手逐穗捻摘稻穗的方式来收割。山栏种植期间,为了防止飞鸟野鸡等其他小动物来偷啄谷种,他们会在园地的周围插上削尖的竹签和稻草人。作物成熟时,为了防山猪、野狗等偷食,晚上会有男人到山栏园自家搭建的茅寮里进行守园,他们在守夜时通常会自娱自乐地唱着《守山栏歌》:"林中鸟儿乱吵吵,山头大鹭猛嚷嚷,跳跃的瀑布呀,哼着调子跳崖墙。下了山栏中,野鸡过来吃光光,鸟儿满山乱吵嚷,阿爹摇头没法子想。"(邢植朝、王静,2002)

In June, they would weed once or twice, without any fertilization or turning over the soil. In September, they harvested the rice by hands. During the period of planting, in order to prevent the small animals from pecking seeds, they would take some measures, such as inserting the sharpened bamboo and scarecrow around the ground, or sleeping in the cottage room at night. They usually amused themselves by singing the song "Shou Shanlan Ge":

10月,收割后,农人会挑选最饱满的稻穗来做谷种,不脱粒,放太阳底下晒干,然后用绳子吊在谷仓梁上,以免与其他的品种混一起。这样的"穗选法"在当时不失为一种较为先进科学的选种方式。为了年年都能在肥沃的山地上种山栏和有好的收成,山栏种植一年后就轮换生地,即丢弃今年的山栏种地,第二年下种前另选地点重新坎山烧山种植山栏稻,待过了十几年后,这儿的土壤肥力恢复后再回来耕作。这种选了砍、砍了种、种了弃的"轮荒"生产方式,因为耕作技术落后,产量较低,且严重毁林和破坏山中植被,1949后逐渐被禁止。

In October, farmers would choose the most plump-ear rice as seed-corn after harvest. The spike of rice without threshing should be baked in the sun, and then hung on the barn beam with a rope, lest it was mixed with other varieties of the rice. This kind of "Sui Xuan Fa" was regarded as a more advanced scientific selection mode at that time. In order to plant Shanlan Rice on fertile mountain fields and have a good harvest each year, the farmers would discard the mountain field where they planted rice this year, and choose another new field for the next planting. Ten years later, farmers might return to plant rice because of the restoration of soil. This production mode of choosing, cutting, planting and abandoning, called "Lun Huang", was banned after 1949 gradually because of its backward farming techniques, low yield, serious deforestation and destruction of vegetation in the mountains.

合亩制
He Mu System

随着人口的增长和荒山的减少,大多数的黎苗族同胞从山上搬到平地来居住,分到了田地、稻种和一些先进的铁制生产工具,普遍种起了水稻。黎族地区的水田一般用犁来犁田再插上秧苗,如果田里的水过膝不利于犁田,就会通过赶牛过来踩田的方式来解决。"牛踩田"的方法极为简单和实用,无论是黄牛、水牛或老牛、幼牛,只要能走路的都把它们赶来踩田,直到泥土被踩烂即可,再用耙来耙平就可插秧了。农忙时,如果家中的劳动力不够的话,亲戚和邻里如有空则会自愿过来"帮工",这种互帮互助的劳动模式既解决了劳动力的不足,也抓住了农时不让农活落下。农活干完后，为了表示感谢，主人通常会在家里请"帮工"吃一顿饭(高泽强、文珍，2008)。

With the growth of population and the decrease of barren hills, most of the Li and the Miao People moved from the mountain to the plain. They allotted the fields, got rice seeds and some advanced iron production tools, and began to grow the paddy rice. The Li People used to break fields with a plough before transplanting rice seedlings. If the water in the fields was over the knee which was not conducive to plough, they would drive all the cattle to stamp the field. After the soil was trampled, they broke up and leveled soil with a harrow and began seeding. This simple and practical method was called "Niu Cai Tian". At the harvest time, if the labor force was not enough, relatives and neighbors who were free would voluntarily be "helpers". Helping each other not only solved the problem of labor shortage, but also finished the farm work in time. After the work was finished, the host would invite the helpers to have a meal with them at home to express their gratitude.

1949前，黎族地区的水稻耕作通常采用"合亩制"的生产方式，"合亩"(黎语称"纹茂"，意为"大伙做工")是农业生产的单位，以"亩头为首"，由若干户有血缘关系的"亩众"组合而成。主要生产资料为耕地和牛只，在亩头主持下进行集体劳动，基本上按户平均分配产品(焦勇勤、孙海兰，2008)。执行"合亩制"的地区男女分工不同。一般男不帮女、女不帮男，但无论男女老少，都要参与劳动，如果有偷懒者则会遭到众人耻笑。男子一般负责犁田、耙田、围篱、挑担等重力活，而妇女则负责下种、插秧、除草、割稻等。老人负责看管水田里的水，照顾家中幼儿，驱赶前来偷稻谷的小动物。小孩则在家中做一些力所能及的家务活。后来，合亩制渐渐被废除。

Before 1949, the rice farming in the Li ethnic regions usually adopted the production mode of "He Mu System". "He Mu" (The Li People called it "Wen Mao", meaning "working together") was a unit of agricultural production, including "Mu Tou" (the chief of them) and "Mu Zhong" who were based on the ties of blood. Their main production materials were cultivated land and cattle. People did the collective labor under the leadership of Mu Tou, with the average distribution of products. Their duties were divided according to their sex and they should not help each other. Everyone should participate in the labor, otherwise he would be sneered at. Later, the "He Mu System" has been abolished gradually.

休闲农业
Leisure Agriculture

休闲农业是指利用农业景观资源和农业生产条件，发展观光、休闲、旅游的一种新型农业生产经营形态。同时也是大力开发农业资源潜力，调整农业结构，改善农业环境，增加农民收入的一种新途径（邹统钎，2008）。综合性的休闲农业区可以满足旅客的多种需求，既可以观光、采果、垂钓、体验农作、享受乡土情趣，也可以住宿、度假、游乐等。海南岛上秀丽的自然风光、优美的生态环境以及国际旅游岛的开发建设，为休闲农业的发展提供了有利的条件。

Leisure agriculture is a new mode of agricultural production and operation, which makes use of agricultural landscape resources and production conditions to develop the sightseeing tourism. Furthermore, it is a new approach of developing the agricultural resources potential, adjusting the agricultural structure, improving the agricultural environment and increasing the farmers' income. Comprehensive leisure agriculture can meet various needs of tourists, such as sightseeing, picking fruits, fishing, experiencing farming, accommodation, vacation, recreation, etc. The beautiful natural scenery and ecological environment provide favorable conditions for the development of leisure agriculture during the construction of Hainan International Tourism Destination.

海南休闲农业主要有四种类型。一是生态观光型。如琼海市的"龙寿洋国家农业公园",以多个村庄的田园景观为线,展现了"城在园中、村在景中、人在画中"的美景。二是科技示范型。如万宁"兴隆热带植物园",以植物园收集的活植物来进行科普植物科学知识的教育,增强人们的生态保护意识。三是垂钓餐饮型。如海口"火山泉休闲农庄",是一家集采摘、垂钓、爬山和绿色餐饮为一体的农业休闲观光园区。四是休闲度假型,主要依托河流、湖泊等自然景观,开发具有农林景观和乡村风情特色的休闲度假农庄。如海口"加乐湖休闲农业产业园",以村里70多亩的天然湖加乐湖来大力发展"乡村游"。

There are four types of leisure agriculture in Hainan. The first one is for ecological sightseeing, such as "Longshouyang National Agriculture Park" in Qionghai, which shows the countryside landscape of "the city is in the garden, the village is in the scenery, and people are in the picture". The second one is science-tech demonstration, such as "Xinglong Tropical Botanical Garden" in Wanning, which is an education base of botanical sciences. The third one is for fishing and catering, such as "Huoshangquan Recreation Grange" in Haikou, which includes the projects of vegetables and fruits picking, fishing, mountain climbing and healthy catering. The fourth one is for entertainment, such as "Jiale Lake Leisure Agriculture Park" in Haikou, which develops the rural tourism based on more than 70 acres of natural lake in the village.

种山栏(黄月 摄于海南省博物馆)
Growing Shanlan Rice (Courtesy of Yue Huang)

休闲农业(林斌师 摄)
Leisure Agriculture (Courtesy of Binshi Lin)

7.2 渔业民俗
Fishery Customs

7.2.1 海上作业民俗 Customs of Maritime Operations

海南岛四面环海,有多达12个临近海洋的市县,沿岸有68个天然港湾,其中24个为主要渔

07 海南劳动生产民俗
The Production Customs in Hainan

港。海南的近海和外海渔业资源极其丰富,海产品种类繁多,特别适合海洋捕捞业和养殖业的发展,所以渔业也成为了海南汉族最主要的副业之一。在临海的各个市县,居住在海岸边的汉族渔民,形成了众多规模不一的渔村或渔港,尤其以文昌清澜港、琼海潭门港为典范。渔民们一般都是男性,因为连续数月在海上作业,与风浪搏斗,非常辛苦,所以他们捕鱼满载而归后,通常都会穿着拖鞋到茶馆里喝茶解闷、释放压力、养精蓄锐,等待下次出海,极少有时间和精力去顾及家里的事物。女人因惦记着男人出海的艰辛,所以她们大都包揽了所有的家务活和耕种农田等农活,好让自家男人安心出海。久而久之就给人们留下了"海南男人在茶里,海南女人在地里"的不好印象,因此海南男人被打上懒散的印记,而海南女人则被视为勤劳吃苦的典范。但随着社会的发展,男女平等的观念已经渗透到了海南人的生活当中,如今越来越多的海南男人懂得了和妻子一起共同承担家务,抛弃了原先的"大男人"主义思想。

There are more than 12 coastal cities and counties, and 68 natural harbors including 24 major fishing ports in Hainan. With plentiful fishery resources and different kinds of seafood, Hainan is especially suitable for the development of marine fishing and aquaculture industry, so fishery is one of the most important sidelines of Han Nationality. A great many fishermen of the Han who live near the coast, form a large scale of famous fishing villages or fishing ports such as Qinglan Port in Wenchang and Tanmen Port in Qionghai. The fishermen are normally male and usually spend continuous months in maritime operations, battling with the winds and waves. After hard working, they usually wear slippers to drink tea in the teahouse, relax themselves, store up their energy and wait for the next fishing. Their wives think that their husbands' work is so arduous that they mostly do all housework and farm work. As time passes by, people are deeply impressed by "the male drinking tea in the teahouse while the female working in the field". However, with the development of society, the idea of equality between men and women has gradually penetrated into the mind of Hainanese, so more and more men help their wives with housework.

造船
The Building of Fishing Boats

船在海南人民的生活必不可缺,它不仅是交通工具,同时还是极为重要的生产工具。自古以来,海南的渔船基本都是本土渔民自己打造,造船技艺成为本岛先民娴熟掌握的实用技艺。在海南的临高和儋州等地,有着悠久的造船历史和许多著名的造船作坊。经过长期的探索和实践,海南的工匠们把船造得更为结实、实用和美观;同时为了远航的需要,船也越造越大。虽然时代的发展和科技的进步带来了钢质、玻璃钢质以及各种混合结构渔船,但木船仍是海南渔民们普遍适用的生产工具,手工造船这一古老技艺也仍在代代传承。

Fishing boat is not only the means of transport, but also a very important tool of production in Hainan. Since ancient times, the fishing boats have been basically built by the local fishermen, the skills of building fishing boat have become one of the practical skills that they should master. Some cities like Lingao and Danzhou have a long history of building fishing boats and many famous shipyards. After a long period of exploration and practice, the fishing boats become more practical, beautiful and stronger. In order to meet the needs of the voyage, the fishing boats become larger and larger. With the development of science and technology, many kinds of fishing boats are used for fishing, but wooden boats are still used by Hainan fishermen nowadays. And the ancient art of handmade boats is still passed on from generation to generation.

造船的工序非常繁多，需要认真对待每一道工序，才能够造出安全、耐用的船。第一为选木，一般需要树龄几十年以上的老树，以杉木为主。第二为造船，造船是海南各地渔民的头等大事，有着庄重的仪式。先要请风水先生选择吉日吉时，船东带上丰盛的酒食和鞭炮到作坊，请船匠们立起龙骨。在造船的过程中，孕妇、闲人和月经期的女人不得登船，否则会不吉利。第三为下水，渔船造好之后，要请先生择吉日吉时方可下水。海南的渔船上通常挂满了旗帜，上面写着"华光大帝""神山明王"和"祖师功曹"等大字，据说这些都是海上保护神，保佑渔民海上行船平安归来（林贤东，2005）。

Building fishing boats has may processes, and every step should be taken carefully to ensure safety and durability. The first step is the selection of wood, and usually ten years old trees are appropriate like Chinese fir. The second step is building the boat with a solemn ceremony. The geomancer should select auspicious day and the owner of the boat should visit the shipbuilding workshop with rich food, wine and firecrackers, and ask the boat carpenter to set up the keel. In the process of the building, the idle, the pregnant and menstrual period women may not board on the boat, otherwise it would bring bad luck. The third step is putting the boat into water. After the fishing boat is finished, the geomancer will choose an auspicious day for launching. People hang flags on the fish boats with names of deities on it for they believe the deities will protect them.

捕捞作业

Fishing Operation

渔船被海南渔民视为有灵之物，是他们赖以生存最重要的生产工具，所以逢年过节时，贴对联、放鞭炮、祭神等这些活动，都要在船上隆重地进行。由于环球大气和海水的相互运动，每年3月到8月，在琼岛周围水域内形成几次渔汛高潮，当地渔民称之为"三月春"和"六月春"，意味着渔业大丰收的季节就要来临了。出海后由被视为指挥官的船老大来观察鱼情，他会依据丰富的经验，通过季节、风向及潮流的风向来判断此处是否有鱼群出没，并下令同伴们撒网捕鱼（林贤东，2005）。

The fishing boat is the most important production tool for Hainan fishermen. Some activities are held on boat on every major festival, such as pasting couplets, setting off firecrackers, offering the sacrifice to God, and so on. Due to mutual movement of the global atmosphere and sea water, a few fishing season climaxes would be formed in the waters around Hainan every March to August, and the local fishermen call this "San Yue Chun" and "Liu Yue Chun", which means the coming of harvest season. According to his rich experience, the fishing boat commander will observe the fish movement, determine whether the fish is infested here or not, and order his companions to cast nets for fishing.

渔民捕捞上来的大鱼好鱼大都是出售换钱，而小虾米和小螃蟹则被做成酱，供家庭食用或捕鱼淡季时被拿到市集上换些大米、地瓜等粮食。休渔期间经常织网补网，或到外面打短工来补贴家用。后来随着社会的发展，渔民们除了出海捕鱼外，还学会了网箱养鱼的先进方法。此外，还开发沿海多处滩涂来养殖鱼、虾、蟹，增加了经济收入，也提高了自己的生活水平。

The good and big fish are sold for money, while the small shrimp and crab are used to make sauces for fishermen's daily food or exchanged for the rice and sweet potatoes. During the moratorium, the fishermen often mend their nets or do some casual labor to support their family. Later, with the development of society, the fishermen have learned an advanced method of fish cage culture besides fishing in the sea. In addition, many coastal mudflats are exploited to cultivate fish, shrimp and crab, which improves their standard of living.

疍民

The Tankas

在海南的各大港口如海口海甸港、陵水新村港，有一群生活在水上以打鱼为生的渔民家庭，被称为"疍家人"，清光绪《崖州志》里称为疍民。"疍民，世居大蛋港、保平港、望楼港濒海诸处。男女罕事农桑，惟辑麻为网罟，以鱼为生。子孙世守其业，税办渔课。间亦有置产耕种者。妇女则兼织纺为业。"疍民从唐代开始大批迁入海南，他们历经艰辛，在这片海岛上顽强地生活下来，世代传承，为海岛的建设做出了应有的贡献。目前全岛疍民后裔近10万人。

A group of fishermen live on boats and make a living by fishing in some major ports of Hainan, such as Haidian Port and Xincun Port, known as "the Tankas". They began to move into Hainan and passed on from generation to generation through hardships since the Tang Dynasty (618-907 AD). They made many contributions to the construction of Hainan Island. Nowadays the population of the Tankas in Hainan is nearly 100,000.

中华人民共和国成立前，有些疍民像候鸟一样，一年里会有两三次迁移。春夏之季，许多疍家渔船从万宁陵水一带随南风而来清澜。秋冬时节，疍民又随北风南返万宁陵水，所以他们被称为海上的"吉普赛人"。疍民们没有大船，无法远航，只能在近海捕鱼。退潮时，他们下笼下网，捕些鱼虾。他们有着自身独特的、不同于陆上人的民风民俗。如遇到大风浪时，会向海里撒纸钱，祈求死于海上的祖先们保佑其平安无事等。后来随着社会的发展，疍家人除了出海捕鱼外，也在港口利用网箱来养殖，或参与海上运输的商贸活动；有些疍家妇女离船登岸，挑着海鲜走街串巷从事贩卖；还有少数疍家年轻人已经进入附近的旅游景区工作，或者外出打工，被称为新一代的"陆上疍家人"，渐渐适应了城市的生活。

Before the founding of the PRC, some Tankas would move two or three times in a year like migratory birds, so they are called "sea gypsies". Without big boats, they had to fish inshore instead of long voyage. When the tide was out, they would cast nets to catch some fish and shrimp. They have unique customs different from onshore people. For example, they would throw paper money into the sea to pray for safety when encountering large waves. Later, with the development of society, the Tankas also engage in many jobs to support themselves. Some use reticulated boxes to cultivate fish, while others are involved in business activities of maritime transport. Some Tankas women are engaged in selling seafood, and a few young people work in the nearby tourist areas or other cities. The Tankas have gradually adapted well to life in the city.

近几年来，随着海南国际旅游岛的大力开发，如何保护疍家人的传统文化，使疍民们成为国际旅游岛开发的有利得主，政府采取了许多的措施，如政府和疍家人携手合作，举办疍家文化节，吸引大量的游客前来，从而带动了疍家人的经济发展。

In recent years, the government has taken some measures on how to protect the traditional culture of the Tankas and enable them to become favorable winners of the development of Hainan international tourism destination. For example, the government cooperates with the Tankas to hold Tankas Cultural Festival, which can attract a lot of tourists and promote the economic development of the Tankas.

渔船（林斌师 摄）
Fishing Boats (Courtesy of Binshi Lin)

疍民 （张茂 摄）
The Tankas (Source: http://hnrb.hinews.cn/)

7.2.2 河流捕捞民俗

Customs of Fishing in Rivers

海南岛河流众多，北有南渡江，西有昌化江，东有万泉河，流域面积之和占全岛面积的47%，素称海南岛三大河流。而且海南岛雨量充沛，溪流淙淙，全岛各地有很多的湿地和天然水塘，是鱼虾蟹蛤的丰产地，是天然的捕鱼场所。所以在过去缺衣少穿、物匮粮乏的年代里，捕捞是一种相当重要的谋生手段，海南各族人民经常到河溪里捞鱼摸虾，回家杂烩煮后食用，菜味新鲜，营养丰富，足以养活一家老小。

There are many rivers in Hainan Island, and the watershed area accounts for 47% of the total area of the island. Nandujiang, Wanquanhe and Changhuajiang are said to be the three long rivers in Hainan. With abundant rainfall, natural rivers, wetlands and ponds, Hainan is the high yielding place of fish, shrimp, crab and clams. So fishing was a very important means of livelihood in the past. Hainanese used to catch shrimp and fish in the rivers to support the family.

黎苗族群众有丰富的捕鱼经验，他们仔细观察，掌握了鱼儿水涨鱼上、水退鱼下等活动规律，捕鱼起来得心应手、经常满篓而归。而居住在沿海地区的回族，据历史记载也非常擅长于用地曳网进行浅海捕捞，是他们谋生的主要手段之一。他们捕鱼的工具主要有渔网、鱼笼、鱼钩等，其中最有民族特色的为鱼笼。鱼笼主要用竹子编制而成，为长圆状。鱼笼的前端口张开，端口大；在前端口至腰部收紧，洞口一般小于前端口三分之一左右，并用编如漏斗状的篾条塞到里面，让鱼儿能进不能出；自腰部到长圆状中间处又增大，约为前端口三分之二；到长圆状尾端口最小，仅能伸进大人的拳头，用编好的竹罩扣住；鱼笼篾条之间只有半厘米的宽度，所以小鱼可游出，大鱼则关于笼中了。

Based on their rich fishing experience, the Li and the Miao People master the rules of fishing, so they often return home with the full baskets of fish. According to the historical records, fishing was also one of the main methods of making a living for the Hui nationality, who lived in the coastal areas. Their fishing tools were mainly fish netting, fish cages and fish corral, among which the fish cage is infused with rich nationality characteristic.

黎苗族有多种捕鱼方式，其中具有鲜明民族特色的有以下两种：（1）以矛刺鱼或以箭射捕鱼。清代张庆长在《黎岐纪闻》里就曾纪载："黎岐无不能射者，射必中，中可立死。每于溪边伺鱼之出入，射而取之，以为食。其获较网罟为尤捷云。"（2）毒鱼，将采摘而来的毒藤毒树拍烂或捣烂，放到用泥土围好的水域内，使得经过这片水域的鱼被毒昏，在水面上浮游，即可下水抓鱼了(高

07 海南劳动生产民俗
The Production Customs in Hainan

泽强、文珍，2008）。解放后，随着大量水库的兴建和基础水利设施的不断完善，许多的黎苗族同胞不再满足于到河溪里抓鱼，他们通过挖塘来养殖淡水鱼，走上致富之路。

There are many fishing methods of the Li and the Miao ethnic groups, of which two are with distinctive national characteristics as follows. One is to fish with a spear or an arrow. The other is to poison fish with poisonous trees or rotten. After liberation, with the construction of a great many reservoirs and the continuous improvement of water conservancy, the Li and the Miao People were no longer satisfied with catching fish in the rivers, but they began to lead a well-off life by cultivating freshwater fish.

7.2.3 水产养殖民俗 Customs of Aquaculture

海南省海岸线漫长曲折，滩涂广阔，港湾众多，据统计可供养殖的滩涂面积近3万公顷，适宜港养的港湾30多个。这样优越的地理环境特别适合水产养殖业的发展。海南的水产养殖有海水养殖和淡水养殖两种。水产养殖品不仅满足了岛内人们的需求，还被出口到国内外的许多地方，给他们带来了较大利益的经济创收。

According to the statistics, the cultivated beaches available for aquaculture are nearly 3,0000 hectares, and the harbors suitable for aquaculture are more than 30. This favorable geographical environment is fit for the development of aquaculture. There are two kinds of aquaculture in Hainan, seawater aquaculture and freshwater aquaculture. These aquatic products are not only used to meet the needs of Hainanese, but also have been exported to many places at home and abroad, which bring them great economic income.

河流捕鱼（黄月 摄于海南省博物馆）
Fishing in Rivers (Courtesy of Yue Huang)

射鱼（黄月 摄于海南省博物馆）
Fishing with an Arrow (Courtesy of Yue Huang)

7.3 狩猎民俗
Hunting Customs

7.3.1 黎族 The Li Nationality

黎族主要居住在海南岛的中南部，这里群山耸立，丘陵起伏，树林茂密，野生动物众多，常有野兔、山猪、果子狸、坡鹿、蛇、鼠类、鸟类等出没。黎族男子平时爱好上山安装各种捕猎器具，捕捉鼠类、鸟类、蛇类和野猪，以及五指山草龟、金钱龟等野物。在农闲、节日时，全村集众上山放狗围捕山猪、野鹿等，并把兽肉熏干保存日后食用。人们捕捉来的动物不仅是日常生活中肉食的主要来源，而且还通过出卖猎物、猎物的皮毛或兽骨获得货币来购买其他物品，有的还采取以物换物的方式来获得一些日常生活用品，所以狩猎成了黎苗族在1949年前最主要的副业。

The Li People mainly live in the central and southern areas of Hainan Island, where there are many hills, lush forest and many wild animals such as hares, wild boars, etc. The male of the Li People like installing all kinds of hunting tools in the hills to catch wildlife. In the slack season and some festivals, the people in the village would take dogs to the mountain together and hunt wild boars, wild deer, etc., and then they smoke the meat for daily eating. The captured animals were not only the main source of meat in daily life, but also sold to obtain money or exchanged with other some daily necessities, so hunting became the most important sideline of Li and the Miao Nationalities before 1949.

他们打猎的工具主要有：粉枪、弓箭、弩、尖刀、长矛、铁钩等，还有一些独特实用的用于捕捉小动物的工具如山猪套、捕鼠器、扣蛙罩等。其中最为常用的有弓箭和粉枪。弓箭长1.5米，宽2~3厘米。用富于弹性的树木做成，也有以藤做的。黎族人把弓箭作为武器和生产工具，有着悠久的历史。清人张庆长的《黎岐纪闻》写道："深山多恶兽，能伤人，黎人每出门必带弓箭佩小刀，所以防也。其弓屈木为把，剖藤为弦，箭用竹为之，铁镞无羽，弓短而劲，箭利而准。"粉枪是黎族狩猎时最有杀伤力的武器，大大提高了捕捉猎物的效率，清代时由汉区传入。这是一种古老原始的前装式枪，火药收藏在水牛角里，铜火帽则藏在特制的小骨管里。据清代光绪《崖州志·黎防一·黎情》卷十三记载："向时兵器，专尚弓矢，今已久废。改用火枪，家置一杆，有力者或备数杆。每以数牛易一枪，或药一桶。多从岭门、薄沙及海口流入。"（高泽强、文珍，2008）

The tools used for hunting mainly include: powder guns, bows and arrows, crossbows, sharp knives, spears, pikes, hooks and so on. There are also some unique and practical tools for trapping small animals. Among them bows and arrows and powder guns are frequently used. The bow is made of elastic trees, rattan or bamboo. According to the records, the Li People had a long history of taking arrows as weapons and tools for production. Powder gun is the most lethal weapon in Li's hunting, which greatly improves the efficiency of capturing preys, and was introduced into Han areas in the Qing Dynasty (1644-1911 AD).

经过长期的狩猎活动，黎族男子不断地摸索和总结成败经验，形成了一套具有民族特色的科学的狩猎方式。这些狩猎方式大致有以下几种：放狗、装圈、挖陷阱、挂枪、安网、人群合围、巡山、巢猎。

After a long period of hunting, the male of Li People have constantly summed up the experience and formed a set of scientific way of hunting with national characteristics. There are some methods of hunting: unleashing dogs, installing the loops, digging traps, etc.

打猎的形式有个体和集体打猎两种，其中黎族男子最为偏爱的是集体狩猎，即围猎。围猎是黎苗族的一种传统狩猎习俗，至今仍被沿袭下来。进山围猎前，先选出村里最出色的经验丰富的猎手作为猎头，由猎头先念"盘古咒"，祈求山神相助顺利打到猎物，所得的猎物一般是见者有份。

There are two forms of hunting, individual hunting and collective hunting. The male of Li People prefer collective hunting to individual hunting. Hunting is a traditional custom of the Li and the Miao nationalities, and has been remaining till now. Before hunting, the experienced hunters are elected as a headhunter to read "Pan Gu Zhou" for the purpose of hunting successfully. Generally, anyone who sees the prey will get a portion of it.

7.3.2 苗族 The Miao Nationality

苗族的狩猎之风特别盛行。他们的狩猎工具、狩猎方式和猎物分配规则与黎族类似，但也有些不同之处，如：苗族猎手出猎时会随身携带"山猪药"，他们认为这种植物能引诱出山猪等猎物的灵魂，从而能顺利打到猎物；通常在箭头上抹上一种树上所产生"见血封喉"的毒液，当猎物中箭时毒液通过伤口的血管流入心脏，很快致死；制作独特的捕捉工具来捉获小动物，例如罩网和夹子；用粘胶来捕捉小型鸟类，这种粘胶由天然植物提炼而成，涂在长满野果的树枝上，粘住前来啄食野果的小鸟。

Hunting is particularly prevalent among the Miao People. Their tools, methods and distribution rules of hunting are mostly similar with that of the Li People, but there are still some differences. First, the hunters of the Miao nationality bring "Shan Zhu Yao" (named "Ardisia Gigantifolia Stapf", one of the Chinese herbal medicines) with them when hunting. They think it can lure the prey and help them capture the prey easily. Second, the Miao People smear a poison called "Antiaris toxicaria Lesch" on the arrow, which will flow to the heart through the blood vessels of a wound and make the prey die quickly. Third, the Miao People make many unique capture tools, such as the cover nets and clips which are used to capture small birds and beasts. Fourth, they capture small birds with a sticky adhesive which is extracted from natural plants and smeared on branches.

改革开放以来，随着人口的增多，大量的山林被砍伐，动物被屠杀。为了保护生态环境，国家实行封山育林政策，禁止捕杀野生动物，提倡饲养家禽，所以黎苗族的狩猎活动也渐渐消亡了，只是成了一些重大节日时象征性的活动。

After China's reform and opening up, a large number of trees have been cut down and the animals were slaughtered. Chinese government began to close hillside to facilitate afforestation, prohibit killing wild animals and encourage the poultry in order to protect the ecological environment, so the hunting of the Li and the Miao People has gradually disappeared, just acts as a symbolic activity held in some important festivals.

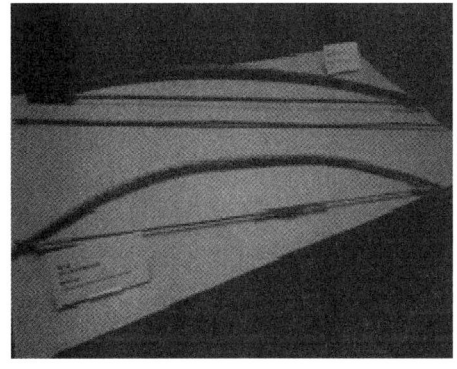

弓箭 （黄月 摄于海南省博物馆）
Bow and Arrow (Courtesy of Yue Huang)

狩猎（王燕 摄于海南省博物馆）
Hunting (Courtesy of Yan Wang)

7.4 采集业民俗
Gathering Customs

海南黎苗族居住的山区，1950年前被开发利用的较少，几乎保持原始的生态环境。漫山遍野布满了热带雨林植物，有多种多样的野果、野菜、天然药材和土特产，如野菠萝、木耳、益智、山桂皮、野生稻、灵芝等。这样的自然条件，为黎苗族群众的采集活动提供了优越的物质基础。因此，采野菜、挖山药、摘野果、捡蘑菇等这些采集活动成为他们重要的家庭副业之一。

The mountain areas were less utilized before liberation, which were in almost the original state. The hills were covered with many kinds of rainforest plants, fruits, vegetables, natural herbs and local products such as Pandanus tectorius, Auricularia auricula, Alpinia oxyphylla, Ganoderma lucidum, etc. These natural conditions provide materials for the gathering of the Li and the Miao's. Gathering, such as mining potherb, digging yam, picking wild fruits and picking up mushrooms, has become one of the important household sidelines in their life.

黎苗族的采集活动有两种形式。一种是目的性较强的专门采集活动，可以获得大量的物品。即在农闲季节，他们会三五成群或单人进行，到达山林中事先商量好的目的地，采集必要的生活食用品或可用于交易的物品，如野果、木耳、竹笋等。另一种是在日常生活中进行的随手采集，即随时随地将自己随手可得的野果、野菜采摘回来补贴家用。据在海南黎族地区传教的外国传教士的游记里记载说：小孩上山放牛时，随身携带弯刀，背着竹篓，见着可食用的野菜野果就顺手采集装到竹篓里；大人出外做工时，腰上挂一个竹篓，拿着弯刀，方便采集可以食用的野生植物，小女孩走在山间田野的小路上，如看见可喂猪的植物或人可食用的野菜野果时也会采摘放在竹篓里。

There are two forms of gathering in the Li and the Miao nationalities. One is the special gathering with strong purpose, which generally obtains a large number of items. In the slack season, they gather the necessary food or items for trading by working in small groups or by themselves. The other is a random gathering in daily life. According to the travel records, the Li and the Miao People, no matter old or young, male or female, always carry machete and bamboo baskets to gather the wild plants and fruits wherever they go.

1949年以前，采集活动对于黎苗族来说，作用很多。采摘得来的野菜、野果较好地给他们补充了营养，解决了吃的问题；采集的木棉和树皮用来织布裁衣，解决了当地群众穿的问题；从山上砍伐或拾捡回来的木材和茅草用来盖间房屋，解决了住的难题。还有采摘回来的益智、山桂皮等药材，被用来交换物品或出卖，解决了经济收入来源的问题。但是改革开放后，为了响应政府封山育林和保护珍贵野生动植物的号召，采集活动日渐减少，黎苗族的生产活动转向了种植业和养殖业等其他方面。

Gathering had a great effect on the Li and the Miao People's life before 1949. The gathering of wild vegetables and fruits, kapok and bark, woods and thatches, and some natural herbs respectively solved the problem of eating, wearing and living. But after China's reform and opening up, the gathering activities have been decreased in response to the government's call to close off hillsides to facilitate afforestation and protect rare wildlife. The production activities of the Li and the Miao nationalities transferred to other aspects like planting and aquaculture.

采集野菜（黄月 摄于海南省博物馆）
Gathering (Courtesy of Yue Huang)

腰篓（刘士祥 摄于海南省博物馆）
Waist Baskets (Courtesy of Shixiang Liu)

7.5 种植业民俗
Planting Customs

7.5.1 传统农作物 Traditional Crops

解放前，海南汉族的种植业以水稻为主，有粳稻和糯稻两种，前者用来日常煮饭，后者有粘性，可用来酿米酒或做糕点。其次为薯类，可食用或用来酿番薯酒。此外，他们种有黑豆、扁豆、毛豆、饭豆等豆类作物，有冬瓜、丝瓜、葫芦瓜、萝卜、生菜、韭菜等瓜菜类作物，有花生油、山柚油、芝麻油等油料作物，还有其他的经济作物如棉花、桑、玉米等。总的来说，这些作物产量较低，主要是供自家食用。

Before liberation, rice planting was the first important farming for the Han nationality. There were two kinds of rice, japonica rice and glutinous rice. The former was used for daily cooking. The latter was sticky and could be used for brewing rice wine or making cakes. Potato was the second important one, which could be edible or used for making sweet potatoes wine. The other important farming were beans crops, vegetables crops, oil crops and other economic crops, such as lentils, melons, peanuts, cotton, corns, etc. In general, these crops had low yield and could only meet the needs of the family.

海南黎苗族以种植山栏稻为主，兼种水稻、番薯和玉米等农作物。在种植玉米时，由于山岭地坡度较高，他们通常采用的是戳穴点种的方法。他们先提前选定平整好种植地，在凿穴点种时一般是两人配合，一人先在前面挖穴，一人跟在后边点种埋土，或一人边凿穴边点种边盖土。为了农作物有好的收成，免受猴子、山猪、山鼠等野兽的破坏，黎苗族人通常利用扎草人或晚上带狗到田间看守等方法来对付兽灾。

The Li and the Miao nationalities mainly plant Shanlan Rice, as well as paddy rice, sweet potatoes, corns and other crops. They usually adopt the method of "Poke holes and dibble in the seeds" to plant corns because of the steep slope. They clear the ground, and then poke holes and dibble in the seeds. In order to have a good harvest, the scarecrow was made or the dog was taken to the field to cope with a plague of beasts.

7.5.2 热带经济作物 Tropical Cash Crops

1949 年后，随着交通条件的改善，很多黎苗族人迁移到山下平地定居，与汉族人一样，开始了热带经济作物的种植，如冬季瓜菜、热带水果和热带作物等。这些经济作物销往国内外的许多大中城市，获得了重大的经济效益，给海南热带农业带来了新的发展机遇，提高了农民的生活水平。

With the improvement of transportation, a large number of Li and Miao People have moved to the plain at the foot of the mountain after 1949. They began to plant the tropical economic crops, such as winter vegetables, tropical fruits and tropical crops. The tropical economic crops would be sold in many large and medium-sized cities at home and abroad, which obtains the great economic benefit and brings the new development opportunity for Hainan tropical agriculture.

冬季瓜菜

Winter Vegetables

我国大部分地区冬季蔬菜严重短缺。而海南纬度全国最低，四季如春，水稻一年可三熟，瓜菜四季都可生长；自然环境优越，瓜菜口感佳。这些为海南冬季瓜菜产业创造了广阔的发展空间。经过多年发展，海南冬季瓜菜已颇具规模，形成了三大菜区，如琼南菜区、琼北菜区、琼冬菜区。

In most areas of China, the phenomenon of seasonal imbalance in supply and demand on vegetables is serious, whereas Hainan is featured with the minimum latitude of the national bloom throughout the year. Rice can be harvested three times a year, and vegetables can be grown in four seasons. With the favorable environment, the vegetables grow nicely and taste delicious. These conditions create a broad development space for winter vegetables in Hainan. After many years of development, there are three big growing areas of winter vegetables in Hainan: the southern areas, the northern areas and the eastern areas.

热带水果

Tropical Fruits

海南被视作中国美丽的后花园。岛上常年生长着多种多样的热带水果，有部分是外地游客极少吃过的，如菠萝蜜、酸豆等。这些热带水果每年都有一定数量远销国内外，尤以荔枝、芒果、菠萝和反季节西瓜著名，成为了海南农民的重要收入来源，对于海南的发展有着重要的影响。热带水果的保鲜期短，容易变质腐坏，为了充分发挥海南热带水果的使用价值，使其在市场流通的时间增长，价值提高，保证农户的利益，海南政府通过招商的形式建立了一些具有实力和规模的果蔬加工厂如海南椰树集团等。这些果蔬加工厂将热带鲜果制成干品，不添加任何化工原料，味道纯正，老少皆宜，是时尚的休闲食品，深受广大游客的喜欢。

Hainan is regarded as China's beautiful garden, with a wide variety of tropical fruits all the year round. There are some exotic fruits which tourists have never seen or eaten before, such as jackfruit, tamarindus, etc. Some of these tropical fruits are sold both at home and abroad, especially litchi, mango, pineapple and off-season watermelon, which become the important income source and have a great influence on the development of Hainan. Tropical fruits have a short fresh-keeping period and are easily spoiled. In order to give full play to the value of tropical fruits, Hainan government has invested on the building of some fruit and vegetable processing factories. Without adding any chemical raw materials, these factories process tropical fruits into dry goods, which become the favorite and fashionable leisure food for the vast number of tourists.

现今，随着生活水平的提高，人们对热带特色水果药用价值和营养价值认知力不断提高，对纯天然的以水果为原料的保健食品的需求越来越高。而海南岛上的许多热带特色水果具有较高的生物活性，能够预防和治疗多种疾病。

Nowadays, with the improvement of living standards, people's demand for healthy food which has pure natural fruit as raw material is becoming higher and higher. Many tropical fruits in Hainan Island have high bioactivity, which can prevent and cure various diseases.

热带作物

Tropical Crops

海南岛属于热带季风气候，降水丰沛，雨热同期，这就为热带作物的生产提供了适宜条件。由于热带作物经济价值高，海南岛在近些年大力发展热带作物的种植，是中国最大的热带作物生产基地。橡胶、椰子、腰果、胡椒、咖啡等热带作物种植面积42.4万公顷，其中椰子、槟榔、橡胶等作物的产量占全国总产量的80%左右。

Hainan Island belongs to the tropical monsoon climate with abundant rainfall, which provides suitable conditions for the production of tropical crops. In recent years, Hainan has vigorously developed the planting of tropical crops because of the high economic value, and become the largest production base of tropical crops in China. The planting areas of rubber, coconut, cashew nut, pepper, coffee and other tropical crops are nearly 42, 4000 hectares, among which the yields of coconut, areca-nut and rubber account for about 80% of the country.

传统的农作物（林斌师 摄）
Traditional Crops (Courtesy of Binshi Lin)

热带经济作物（陈经优 摄）
Tropical Cash Crops (Courtesy of Jingyou Chen)

7.6 林业民俗
Forestry Customs

海南岛森林广阔，植被生长快、植物繁多，是我国热带雨林、季雨林的原产地。从古至今，海南就非常重视防护林、经济林、天然林、竹林等生态林的种植和养护。截止 2013 年，全省森林覆盖率达 61.9%，处于全国领先水平，故有"森林之岛"的美称。森林主要分布于五指山、霸王岭、尖峰岭、吊罗山、黎母山等 5 大林区。岛上有许多珍稀树木，如坡垒、花梨、野荔枝、粗榧等。这些树木材质坚韧、色泽鲜艳、经久不腐、永不变形，是建筑桥梁、船舶、工艺品和高级家具的极佳材料。长期以来，海南各族人民就有植树造林的习惯和良好的民间生态文化，他们崇尚人与自然和谐相处，各村庄的前后一般都有风水林的种植，形成了独特的林业民俗。

Hainan is the origin of tropical and seasonal rain forest in China, with the fast growth of vegetation and numerous varieties of plants. Historically, Hainan has attached great importance to the planting and maintenance of ecological forest like shelter forest, economic forest, natural forest, and bamboo forest. By the end of 2013, the forest coverage rate of Hainan has reached to 61.9%, called the "Forest Island". The forest is mainly distributed in the five big forest regions like Wuzhishan, Bawangling, Jianfengling, Diaoluoshan and Limushan. There are some precious tropical trees in Hainan such as Hopea, Scebte-drose wood, Wild Litchi, Cephalotaxus sinensis, etc. These trees characterized with tough materials and bright color, no decay and deformation, are viewed as the best materials for the construction of bridges, ships, crafts and advanced furniture. Hainanese have the habit of planting Fung Shui trees around the village and advocate harmonious coexistence of mankind with nature, which forms a unique custom of forestry over the years.

7.6.1 按需择树 Planting Trees on Demand

海南各族人民的植树造林历史由来已久，早在清道光的《琼州府志》卷五木类篇中就有记载："榕树，南海多植之，叶大如麻，实如冬青……其荫十亩，故人以为息焉。"又载："苏木，即苏枋，树类槐花，黑子，南人以染绛。凡州县艺植者，十年后始堪用。"由此可见，海南人民种树会根据他们的实际需要来选树种，为了乘凉而种榕树，为染绛而种苏木，为护村舍而栽刺竹，为食用油而种油茶树，为果品和获得经济收入而种荔枝、椰子、菠萝蜜、黄皮等，为取得木材而种桉树、海棠，等等。说到植树，那就不得不说说海南岛上椰子树的种植。椰子树在海南随处可见，是海南人民最喜爱种植的树种之一。海南人民特别崇敬椰树，认为椰子是有灵性和有眼的，它不会砸好人，如果有人走到椰子树下，被椰子砸中，那个人就是坏人。过去，文昌农村的男女订婚、结婚时普遍有互赠椰子苗的习俗，希望夫妻俩似椰影双双，偕老百年，繁子育孙。而在琼海的农村，村民在种植椰子树时会选择吉日吉时，一般选初一或十五种下，象征着"吉利"（海南史志网，2013）。

Hainanese have a long history of afforestation and usually plant trees on demands, such as banyan for cool, caesalpinia sappan for dyed crimson, bamboo for protection of the cottage, camellia oleifera for edible oil, fruit trees for the economic income, eucalyptus and crab apple trees for wood. The coconut palm, one of the most popular trees in Hainan, is seen everywhere. Hainan people reverence coconut palms so much for they think that coconut is spiritual and prophetic and never hits a good man. In the past, Wenchangnese had the custom of exchanging coconut seedlings in their engagement and wedding, wishing the couple a long life together and with many children. While Qionghainese would select auspicious days to plant a coconut tree, generally on the first day or the fifteenth day of every month.

7.6.2 山林权属 The Ownership of Mountain Forest

1949 年以前，海南黎族地区的山林一般归村峒所有，各峒的山林一般以自然的山岭、河流为界，且需经过全峒的亩头、村头、峒首等人共同商定为主。峒界定好后，必须要告知各村民，避免他们过界进行开山种植、伐木、狩猎和采集等活动。如有越界行为发生，一般要给对方峒首赔偿耕牛或酒。如想到别峒的山林里狩猎，要先征得其峒首及村头的同意，并给予一定的租金或礼物来表示敬意，否则会被视为侵犯引起一系列的冲突和斗争。在部分的黎族山区，大多数的山林都是被"奥雅"所占有（黎家人把受人尊重的头人、峒首和德高望重的老者称为"奥雅"），这些人也被称为"山主"。这些山主要是所占的山林过多的话，一般都会将部分的山林出租来换取礼物和谷物（海南史志网，2014）。

Before 1949, the mountains and forests of the Li and Miao nationalities were generally owned by tribes. The forest of each tribe was bounded to the natural mountains and rivers and agreed by the leaders. After that, the tribesmen would be informed not to cross the border to plant crops, cut woods, hunt animals or gather vegetables. If anyone had a cross-border behavior, he should give the leader of the tribe a cattle or wine as compensation. If people wanted to hunt in another tribe, they should gain the approval of the leader of the tribe, otherwise it would be regarded as violations which might cause a series of conflicts and struggles. But in some areas of the Li nationality, most of the forests were possessed by "Ao Ya" (the Li People often name the respected man or the head of the tribe as "Ao Ya"). If "Ao Ya" occupied too many forests, they would rent out some of the forests to exchange for gifts and grains.

海南苗族的生存也特别依赖山林，但大多数的山林都被掌握在山主手中。他们要想利用山地种植山栏或租山使用时一般要向山主批租。苗族百姓在租用的山林里抓获的猎物或采集到的土特产必须要卖给山主或山主指定的商人，否则会被强行没收（焦勇勤、孙海兰，2008）。1949 年以后，国家逐渐实行了稳定山权林权的许多政策，大多数的山林归集体所有，只有少数零星的树木仍属个人所有，还通过封山育林等多种有力的措施来保护森林，维护生态平衡。

The Miao ethnic group was particularly dependent on the mountains and forests, but most of which were in the hands of the leaders of mountains. If they wanted to plant Shanlan Rice or did something in these areas, they needed to rent the mountains from the leaders. If people captured some animals or gathered some local products, they must sell them to the leaders or the designated businessmen, otherwise the products would be confiscated. After 1949, our country has gradually implemented many policies on the stability of the rights of mountain and forest. Most of the forests belong to the community, only a few of them for the individuals. In addition, our country has adopted many effective measures to protect forests and maintain the ecological balance such as closing hillsides to facilitate afforestation.

7.6.3 伐木方式 Methods of Cutting Woods

海南的秋季雨量少，气候干燥，是砍伐树木的最佳时间。砍伐树木时，要注意挑选地势平坦、没有障碍物的地方作为树木倒下的方向。树木砍伐后，伐木者一般通过"牛拖"或"流木"的形式来搬运。牛拖就是先用两根一丈多长、结实的木条做车辕，并在前端用山藤将一支弯曲的木栓紧，后端辕木上再横架两条横木。运方木时，把大的一头栓在上面，用水牛就可以拉下山。牛拖特别适用于山间搬运树木，因为不用劈开山路，较好地保护了山林的生态环境，是海南居民从深山里搬运方木板时的最佳方式。而"流木"的方式则是借助了水流的作用，把木材用山藤捆绑在一起，等到河水高涨时放入河中，借助流水把木材运到目的地，这样就大大地节省了搬运的劳力（邢植朝、王静，2002）。

In Hainan, autumn is the best time to cut wood because of the small amount of rainfall and dry climate. When cutting wood, the woodcutters should choose a flat ground which has no obstacles as the place of the falling trees. After cutting, the woodcutters use the methods of "Niu Tuo" and "Liu Mu" to transport wood. The method of "Niu Tuo" is viewed as a best way for Hainan residents to carry the square wood from mountain because it can protect the ecological environment of forest. While the method of "Liu Mu", ties the woods with rattan and transports them to the destination with the aid of flow of water, greatly saving the labor force.

海南乡村（林斌师 摄）
Hainan Villages (Courtesy of Binshi Lin)

椰林（王虹 摄）
Coconut Palms (Courtesy of Hong Wang)

7.7 畜牧业民俗
Animal Husbandry Customs

海南岛日光充足，有益于杀死空气中的大量病菌，特别适合牧草和热带作物的生长；且全岛四面环海，有利于控制疫病的爆发和阻止疾病的传播，这些对于畜牧业的发展是非常重要的。

The strong sunlight in Hainan is beneficial to kill a large number of bacteria in the air, and especially suitable for the growth of pasture and tropical crops. Surrounded by the sea, Hainan is conductive to control the outbreak of disease and prevent it from spreading. All these conditions are very important for the development of animal husbandry.

7.7.1 传统畜牧业 Traditional Animal Husbandry

07 海南劳动生产民俗
The Production Customs in Hainan

海南各族人自古就有饲养家禽家畜的习惯，但在1949年之前的家庭养殖业并不发达，没有发展到脱离农业和家庭而形成独立的副业。他们通常采用"放养"的饲养方式，人畜混居。

People of all ethnic groups in Hainan have had the habit of breeding poultry or pets since ancient times. But before 1949, the family breeding was not developed into an independent sideline which got rid of agriculture and family. People usually adopted the way of "free-range" to feed the animals, and mixed-living with them.

牛在劳动生产和日常生活中占据着非常重要的地位，所以养牛是海南各族人民最大的副业。养牛多为放养，基本没有圈养。养牛有集体放牧（海南的西部城市如东方常用的养牛方式）和自家野牧（黎苗族人常用的养牛方式）两种形式。集体放牧是指同一生产队饲养牛的各户人家，为了节约时间生产和牛的安全，根据各家所饲养牛的数量，轮流把生产队的牛统一赶到山坡上放牧，时间为早上八九点到下午四五点，俗称"放牛"。家里饲养的牛越多，"放牛"的天数越多。黎苗族养牛通常采用自家野牧的形式，即在牛身上做好标记，早晨把牛牵到山上任其四处觅草，无需看守，需用或傍晚时把牛寻回即可。据说傍晚时分，只要定时在牛栏里撒上一些粗盐，牛群就会按时回到牛栏里。在农忙时节，由于劳动量大牛的体力消耗多，主人会给牛喂一些有营养的饲料，如番薯、米饭等。

The cattle play an important role in production and daily life, so raising cattle is one of the largest sidelines in Hainan. The cattle are mostly free-range. There are two forms of cattle grazing like community grazing and family grazing. Community grazing refers to the form that the families which belong to the same production team graze the cattle together. This form is very popular in the western areas of Hainan such as Dongfang city. In order to save time for production and keep the cattle safe, they will take turns to graze the cattle on hillside. They graze the cattle from eight or nine a.m. to four or five p.m., commonly known as "herding cattle". The Li and the Miao minorities usually take the form of family grazing. The cattle is marked and taken to the mountain to eat grass by themselves. It is said that in the evening, the cattle will be back on time if the master sprinkles some salt in the barn regularly. During busy farming seasons, the owner will feed cattle with some nutritious food because of the large amount of labor.

对于早期的海南居民来说，养猪也是一个很重要的副业，除了满足自家肉类的供给外，还可以出售以增加经济收入的来源，购买一些较大的家庭用具或用来支付孩子们的学费，作用很大。早期的海南人采用的是一种"猪无圈"的养猪方式，饲养的猪白天随意走动在自家门前屋后，有时还会到隔壁家"串串门"，天黑了就回到主人的屋外随处歇息。猪的主食一般为番薯、木薯、仙人掌、酒糟或长在村子周围的一些野菜野草，有路旁的、田间的、河里的，等等。黎族人饲养的猪一般个头不大，嘴尖牙利，被戏称为"五脚猪"或"老鼠猪"，平时很少给这些猪喂养主食，重要是靠自身到野外刨食。所以这种猪的肉特别有嚼劲，吃起来味道很鲜美。

For the early Hainanese, raising pigs was also a very important sideline, which not only met the supply of their meat, but also could be sold to increase their income. They adopted a way of "cage-less" to raise pigs. Pigs walked freely around their house, sometimes walked to the next door, and came back to the owner's house when it was getting dark. The staple food of pigs was sweet potatoes, cassavas, cactus, distiller's grains and some plants in the fields, roadsides or rivers. The pigs raised by the Li People are smaller, with sharp-tongued and pointed teeth, dubbed the "the pigs with five feet" (This kind of pigs always root about for food when they walk, so the mouth is considered as the fifth leg of the pig.). These types of pigs rarely eat main food at shelter, and mostly root about in the mud for their food. Therefore, the meat of these pigs is especially chewy and delicious.

此外,他们还会饲养羊、狗、鸡、兔,以及鸭、鹅、鸽等家禽,在重大节日时宰杀来祭拜神灵祖先,供全家人食用。他们在饲养牲畜的过程中有一定的讲究。如在选猪苗时,会观察它是否"破相",即耳后是否有白毛,尾巴是否翘卷,是否缺趾等。他们认为"破相"猪饲养不利,难以长大。卖猪出门时,女主人会从猪身上拔下一撮毛压在猪的食槽下,希望下次能养出更多更大的猪。

In addition, they also feed sheep, dogs, chickens, ducks, geese, rabbits, pigeons and other poultry. In some major festivals, the owner will slaughter the poultry to offer sacrifices to the ancestors and Gods. They pay attention to the process of raising domestic animals. When choosing a piglet, they will observe whether it is disfigured or not. The pigs with white ear, curling tail or lack of toes are considered to be raised up difficultly. When selling a pig, the hostess will pull a pinch of hair from the pig and put it under the pig trough, wishing more pigs could be raised up next time.

7.7.2 现代畜牧业 Modern Animal Husbandry

改革开放以来,随着人民生活水平的提高,对动物性蛋白的需求量也在不断的增加。海南省建设"无疫区"具有得天独厚的条件:海南岛四面环海,易感动物不能从大陆和毗邻区域任何地方自然进出;海南岛光热资源极为丰富,有利于预防、控制和扑灭口蹄疫等疫病;海南是全国最大经济特区,拥有立法优势。所以从1999年起,海南政府和人民脚踏实地地进行"无疫区"的建设,经过多年的不懈努力,"无疫区"的建设成效显著,为海南畜牧业的快速发展撑起巨大保护伞。

Since China's reform and opening up, the demand for animal protein has increased with the improvement of people's living standard. Hainan has many good natural conditions for the construction of "no epidemic area". For example, the infected animals can not be easily carried to Hainan from the mainland or any other neighboring areas. The rich resources of sunlight and heat are advantageous to the prevention, control and extermination of foot-and-mouth disease. As the largest Economic Special Zones in China, Hainan has the legislative authority. Therefore, Hainan government and people have strived to the construction of "no epidemic area" since 1999. After years of unremitting efforts, the construction of "no epidemic area" has achieved many remarkable results, which give support to the rapid development of animal husbandry in Hainan.

海南生态条件优越,畜牧业历史悠久,岛内分布着丰富多彩、种质特异的畜禽遗传资源,有五指山猪、屯昌猪、临高猪、海南黄牛、兴隆水牛、海南黑山羊(东山羊)、文昌鸡、加积鸭等。这些畜禽具有耐粗饲、抗病力强、适应性广、肉质鲜美细嫩、生长性能优等特点。

Hainan has a long history of the animal husbandry, with rich and special genetic resources of animals, such as Wuzhishan pig, Hainan black goat (sheep), Wenchang chicken, Jiaji duck, etc. These poultry are featured with crude feed tolerance, high disease resistance and adaptability, delicious and tender meat, and excellent growth performances, etc.

放牛（王霞 摄）　　　　　　　　　五脚猪（陈志强 摄）
Herding Cattle(Courtesy of Xia Wang)　Pigs with Five Feet(Source:http://www.hq.xinhuanet.com/)

7.8 手工业民俗
Handicraft Customs

手工业，是指使用简单的工具和设备，以手工操作为主的工业形式。生活在海南岛上的黎、苗、汉等各民族的手工业历史悠久，种类繁多，包括纺织、编织、雕刻和制陶等方面。手工艺制作主要在农闲时间进行，规模较小，大都是为了满足家庭生活的需要，属于家庭手工业。这些手工业品制作工序复杂，工艺精美，特色鲜明，是海南各族成千上万劳动人民勤劳和智慧的结晶（海南日报，2004）。

Handicraft is an industrial form of manual operation by using simple tools and equipments. Hainan has a long history in handicraft, which has wide varieties of weaving, sculpture, and pottery, etc. As a cottage industry, handicraft is mainly done in slack season and satisfies the family's need. Handicraft, with the complex making procedures, exquisite workmanship and distinctive features, is the crystallization of diligence and wisdom of Hainanese.

木器
Wooden Articles

海南岛森林茂密，为木器的制作提供了最充足的材料。许多的黎苗族男子使用凿、刀、锯等工具来制作简单粗糙的木器用具，如木椅、木桶、木犁等。在海南黎族的木器制作中，最有特色的为独木器具如独木舟的制作，用天然的木料刳空制成。它是海南黎族数千年传统文化的见证，是实用性和艺术性的完美结合体，体现了人与自然和谐相处的生态观。

Hainan Island is covered with virgin forest, which provides sufficient timber for the wooden articles. The male from the Li and the Miao nationalities can make some wooden articles such as wooden chairs, wooden barrels and wooden plows. The canoe is one of the most distinctive wooden articles in the Li nationality, which is made of a hollowed log. It is a witness of the traditional culture of the Li nationality and a perfect combination of practicality and artistry, which reflects their ecological concept of harmony between man and nature.

竹器
Bamboo Articles

黎苗族居住的地方长满了竹子，竹子资源特别丰富。他们利用竹子作为原材料，制作了很多种类不一的竹器工具，常见的有竹筐、竹席、竹笠、竹筷等。竹编技术大都是祖传下来，虽然比较粗糙，但家庭使用价值颇高。此外，他们也会做一些精美细致的竹器如妇女的腰篓和竹笠等。这些竹器图案精美、色彩鲜艳，具有鲜明的民族特色，艺术价值很高。随着现代文明的发展，许多竹器用具已经被先进的现代生活用具所代替，竹编手工艺逐渐没落。

A vast amount of bamboos stand straight on the mountains where the Li and the Miao People live, so the materials of bamboo are quite abundant for them. Bamboos can be used to make baskets, mats, hats and chopsticks, etc. The technique of bamboo weaving comes down from the ancestors, with rough technique but high value. In addition, bamboos can be used to make some exquisite and meticulous bamboo articles such as waist basket used by the women. These bamboo articles are featured with the beautiful pattern, bright color, distinctive nationality characteristics and high artistic value. Many bamboo articles have been replaced by advanced utensils with the development of modern civilization, and the bamboo weaving has become a dying trade.

藤器
Rattan Articles

黎苗族地区的山林中盛产各种藤类，黎苗族群众善于就地取材，自古以来就会采割野生藤竹编制箩筐、畚箕、斗笠等生产工具和生活用品，既实用轻巧、又具有美感。近年来，由于藤制品的日益走俏，已经开始人工栽种藤类植物。黎苗族用坚韧、光滑的藤皮编制的工艺品不但美观大方，而且结实耐用，颇为有名。早在唐代，海南的藤器就被用作呈献朝廷的贡品。

There are many kinds of rattan in the living areas of the Li and the Miao nationalities. Since ancient times, they have cut wild rattans and bamboos to weave some production tools and daily necessities, such as baskets, dustpans and hats. All these handicrafts are practical, light and beautiful. In recent years, they have begun to plant rattan because of the best-selling of rattan articles. The handicrafts made of tough and glossy rattan are not only beautiful but also durable. The rattan articles from Hainan were also used as tributes to the imperial court in the early Tang Dynasty (618-907 AD).

骨器
Bone Objects

海南岛黎族自古以来就有制作骨器的悠久文化，至今仍然保留着较为古老的制骨工艺。他们充分利用狩猎或家畜宰杀后留下来的骨骼来刻制成生活用品和艺术品。黎族的骨器制作过程有洗刷去油脂、截料、修整成型、磨制、钻孔雕刻、装饰着色等六道工艺。即选取脱脂干净的兽骨、牛骨或牛角为材料，根据规格、尺寸切成相应形状，打磨光滑。用刻刀把各种花纹、图案，精雕细刻在器物上。刻好后涂上一层乌烟，渗入刻痕中，再抹上熔化蜂蜡做封闭，刻纹中的乌烟黑迹便清晰地显现出来，黑白相间。

The Li nationality has a long culture of making bone objects since the ancient time. They make full use of the bones of prey or domestic animals to make bone objects. The process of making bone objects includes cutting, trimming, grinding, carving, decorating and coloring, etc.

07 海南劳动生产民俗

The Production Customs in Hainan

独木舟（刘士祥 摄于海南省博物馆）
A Canoe (Courtesy of Shixiang Liu)

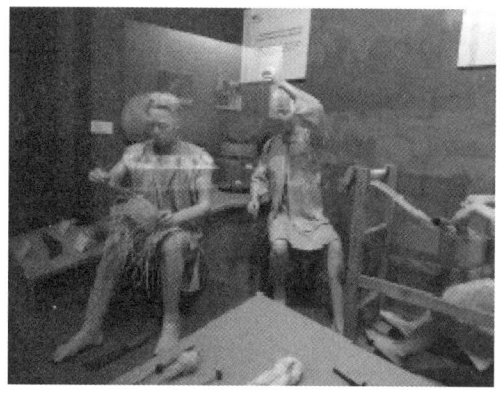

竹编（刘士祥 摄于海南省博物馆）
Bamboo Weaving (Courtesy of Shixiang Liu)

165

08

海南信仰崇拜民俗
Belief and Worship

信仰是指对某人或某种主张、主义、宗教极度相信和尊敬，并视其为自己行动的榜样或指南。崇拜指尊敬钦佩。信仰崇拜最早源自于生产力低下、认知能力有限的人类对大自然的敬畏。随着生产力的发展和认知能力的增强及两者发展的相对局限性，人类在认识自然、认知社会的过程中逐渐形成适应于自身生活环境和生存状态的成体系的世界观与人生观即信仰；或者朴素的对某个或某些人物或神灵的敬畏即崇拜。信仰的对象比较系统、全面，通常是制度化的宗教。宗教有完整的教义，指引、决定信徒的观念、生活方式和行为准则，比如佛教、道教、基督教等。崇拜的对象止于原始的宗教意识即我们常说的原始宗教，未成体系，对信众的生活方式和行为有一定的影响，主要有祖先崇拜、自然崇拜、图腾崇拜等。

Belief refers to a person's absolute trust in and respect for a god, a person or a certain doctrine of a religion by taking it as an example to or guidance for his actions. Worship is the practice of showing respect for one or some of the characters or gods by rituals including chanting prayers, offering sacrifices, dancing, etc. Belief and worship are originated from owe in which people held nature because of low productivity and human's limited cognitive ability. With the development of productivity and human's cognitive ability, and the relative limitation of such development, people have gradually got to know the nature and themselves to a certain extent, and adapted to the living environment and conditions at that time, during which simple respect and reverence for one or some of the characters or gods people have held are worship, while some respect and reverence have been developed into sets of principles or opinions, called doctrines that guide people in their daily life, which make belief. Take it much further, belief is about religions and ideologies which are sets of world view, lifestyle and behaviors that guide believers like Buddhism, Christianity, Marxism and so on, while worship is just about primitive religions, which are not so comprehensive yet with a certain impact on people's way of life and behavior such as ancestor worship, nature worship, totem worship and so on.

海南民间信仰崇拜有敬祖先、敬自然、重和谐的特点。海南民间信仰主要有佛教、道教、基督教、天主教和伊斯兰教等，与他处无异。海南民间各类崇拜则主要有祖先崇拜、自然崇拜、图腾崇拜、俗神崇拜以及一些民间方术，极具本土特色（俗神崇拜在前文已有介绍，此章不再详述）。

There are three features of Hainan folklore of belief and worship: holding ancestors and nature in awe and gratitude and emphasizing harmony between nature and human. Belief in Hainan mainly contains Christianity, Islam, Buddhism, Taoism and the Roman Catholic Church, while worship is basically embodied in ancestor worship, nature worship, tattoo worship, folk gods worship and Fang Shu, which is full of local characters (folk gods worship has been discussed in previous chapters and won't be covered here.).

中华人民共和国成立初期,很多民间信仰崇拜被摒弃。改革开放以后尤其是 2001 年建设国际旅游岛的战略提出后,政府对民间民俗的重视与挖掘让民间信仰崇拜的民俗以本土特色文化的形式重获生命力。

In the early period after the founding of the PRC, much worship was abandoned. After the reform and opening up, especially since 2001 when the plan of constructing Hainan International Tourist Destination was approved, the local government has paid attention to and has explored folk custom, which has revitalized folk worship as an important role of local culture.

8.1 宗教
Religions

据前琼海嘉积教堂周泽龙长老提供的美国基督教长老会在琼工作年鉴记载,基督教于清光绪七年 (1881 年) 正式传入海南,美籍丹麦牧师冶基善在琼山县府城文庄路的吴氏宗祠内,设立临时传教场所,定名为中华基督教琼海区会,隶属美国基督教长老会。随后设立医院、学校并深入黎苗地区。现信众较多。

Christianity was introduced into Hainan officially by an American Danish pastor – Carl C. Jeremiassen (1847-1901) in 1881 during Qing Dynasty. He established a temporary church named Chinese Christian Missionary, Qionghai District, in Wu Temple Wenzhuang Rd. Fucheng Qiongshan County authorized by American Presbyterian. He and subsequent pastors established a hospital and school, explored and preached in the Li and the Miao habitations such as Qiongzhong and Wuzhishan.

海南回族的祖先据说是 700 年前从越南的占城过来的渔民(邢植朝、王静,2004),主要聚居在三亚市羊栏区的回辉、回新两个大村。他们信奉伊斯兰教,严守《古兰经》的规范。

700 years ago, with some fishermen emigrating from Champa of Vietnam, **Islam** was introduced into Hainan. They were the ancient of the Hui who've mainly settled in Huihui Village and Huixin Village Yanglan District Sanya. They believe in Islam and abide by the Koran.

佛教在唐宋时期盛行,三亚南山海岸的南山寺不仅是佛教圣地,更是旅游胜地。

Buddhism was prevalent in the Tang and Song Dynasties (618-1279). The Nanshan Temple in Sanya city is not only a Buddhist holy land, but also an important tourist attraction.

道教于宋代传入海南(公元 960—1279),由于道教"道法自然",追求"天人合一"的教义与黎族敬畏自然、万物有灵的民间崇拜非常相似,道教传入黎区后,被广为接受。现定安县文笔峰盘古文化旅游区较完整的展现了道教文化,亦是旅游胜地。

Taoism was introduced into Hainan in the Song Dynasty (960-1279 AD). It was accepted widely in the Li habitations because many of its doctrines are similar to the primitive religion of the Li People, such as the theory that "man is an integral part of nature" which emphasizes living in harmony with nature. The Taoist Temples in the Wenbi Ridge in Ding'an Hainan is a right place to learn about Taoism.

天主教于明代崇祯三年（1630年）传入海南，由葡萄牙耶稣会派神甫在琼山府传教。

During the Ming Dynasty the Roman Catholic Church was introduced into Hainan in 1630. The first priest assigned by Jesuits from Portugal began to preach in Qiongshan Hainan.

8.2 祖先崇拜
Ancestor Worship

祖先崇拜也叫鬼魂崇拜，崇拜的对象是祖先，是与宗族结合的一种原始宗教形式。

Ancestor worship, also called ancestor's ghost worship, is a kind of primitive belief combined with patrilineal clanship.

8.2.1 汉族祖先崇拜 Ancestor Worship of the Han People

海南汉族家族观念十分浓厚，祖先崇拜的表现也十分突出，视祖先灵魂为家族、家庭的保护神。每家正厅都有公阁，安放着历代祖先神位，以供祖先灵魂栖居。每逢春年、清明、家族大事，都要祭拜祖先。人们认为，祠堂和祖先坟地的风水决定着家族的血脉延续和兴旺。对修建祠堂、修缮祖坟和续修族谱非常重视。

The Han think the ancestors as family gods who protect the family and highlight the worship service. All ancestors' tablets are put in the shrine where ancestors' spirits are dwelling. Ancestors are offered sacrifices to on occasions of Spring Festival, Qingming Festival and some other important family events. Many of the Han people have deemed that Feng Shui of ancestral hall and ancestral graves determines the family's future, so taken the construction of the shrine, repairing graves and continuation of genealogy very seriously.

8.2.2 黎族祖先崇拜 Ancestor Worship of the Li People

黎族崇拜自然、认为"万物有灵"，把作祟的精灵都称为"鬼"。黎族认为祖先鬼是魔力无边的鬼魂，能保佑子孙，人间的好坏是祖先鬼预先安排的，它支配着人们的旦夕祸福。

Sharing some supernatural ideas, myths and legends, the Li People worshiped nature and ghosts, holding "animism", believing that anything has spirit or soul just as human. They intend to hold that ancestral ghosts have boundless magic power and dominate the offspring's fate.

黎族每个家族都有自己的祖先鬼。黎族社会各村落的祖先鬼，主要是指正常死亡的父系血缘男性以及嫁出去后直系血亲妇女的鬼魂。这些祖先鬼中，最有魔力的是始祖，而后依次是二世、三世祖等。如果家人去世，要祭祀祖先鬼，以求祖先鬼早些接纳新鬼。

Each clan of the Li People shares same clan ancestral ghosts and each village has their own sept ancestral ghosts. They are mainly patrilineal male and married female ancestors who didn't die in their boots. Among these ancestral ghosts, primogenitor(s) is (are) the most powerful one(s). If one of the family died, the others used to pray to ancestral ghosts to accept the new earlier by offering sacrifices.

8.2.3 苗族祖先崇拜 Ancestor Worship of the Miao People

苗族的祖先崇拜主要是对盘皇（盘王）、祖先鬼、社主大皇等的崇拜。盘皇是最大的祖先公神，主管人间幸福。每家都设灵台供奉，每逢二月初二、六月初六都做粽粑祭祀。五指山市南圣镇牙南村委会的什拱村每年在二月初二开始筹备六月初六跳的盘皇舞以祭祀开天地的祖先盘古（陈耿、尹秋燕，2007）。在靠近汉族的地区，每逢清明和家族大事，苗族也举行祭祖活动。

The Miao ethnic group mainly worships Pan Wong (Pan Gu King), ancestral ghosts, and so on. Pan Wong is the greatest super human, supernatural, and immortal ancestral god in charge of human's desire and pursuit. Every family pays homage to Pan Wong by setting a shrine for him. Glutinous rice cakes are made and offered to worship Pan Wong on lunar Feb. 2nd and June 6th every year. In Shigong in Yanan Village Committee, Nansheng Town, Wuzhishan City, Dance for Pan Wong-the god who separates heaven from earth-has begun to be prepared since lunar Feb 2nd and is performed on lunar June 6th. In some areas near the Han residence, the Miao also offers sacrifices to their ancestral ghosts on occasions of Qingming Festival and some other important family events.

8.3 自然崇拜 Nature Worship

自然崇拜，顾名思义，是指人类对赖以生存的大自然以及自然现象的崇拜，广泛蕴含于各种宗教、神论和仪式当中。主要包括天上诸神鬼崇拜、地上诸神鬼崇拜和动植物崇拜。

Nature worship is any of a variety of religious, spiritual and devotional practices that focus on the worship of natural phenomena which are attributed to the continuation of the life process (Shailer Mathews, Gerald Birney Smith, 2010). Nature deities mainly derive from the natural phenomena, the earth and creatures.

8.3.1 天崇拜 Spirits in Charge of Weather

黎族地区以农业为主，大多春旱夏涝，人们靠天吃饭，所以敬畏云、雾、雷、风、雨等天体现象。

With mostly spring drought and summer floods in the Li areas, the Li People used to rely on the weather. They used to think that cloud, fog, thunder, wind, rain and any other natural phenomena have a kind of immortal "spirit".

黎族先民会"祭天"以求上天保佑平安、丰收。东方美孚方言黎族每年农历正月初五祭天。久旱无雨也祭天。这种祭天全村人都要到参加，规模大，时间长，祭品为牛。在奥雅家设一面大鼓，全村的铜锣都集中，人们边敲锣打鼓，道公边随着节奏念咒语、跳舞。

Li ancestors "worshiped heaven" in order to get blessed with peace and harvest. Meifu Li used to worship heaven on lunar Jan 5ths and when it was severely droughty. The ceremony that every villager must attend would be big and last long. A big drum was set up in Ao Ya's (also called Lao Ren or Gui Gong, they are messengers who can communicate with ancestors in the underworld or Yinjian) house and all gongs were gathered.

8.3.2　日月崇拜 Sun Worship and Moon Worship

太阳与月亮日夜交替，人们赖此繁衍生息。海南汉族仍有"救日"的习俗，即在日食过程中敲锣打鼓，以吓退天狗，吐出太阳。

The sun and the moon alternate day and night, which has benefited people. The Han in Hainan had the tradition of "save the sun", which was to scare the heavenly dog to spit the sun by beating drums and gangs during solar eclipse.

海南汉族民间称月亮为"月亮娘娘"，妇女们常中秋拜月，以求青春常驻。人们喜欢用"月"字给女婴命名，寓意像月亮一样柔美，像嫦娥一样美丽。

The Han in Hainan called the moon as "Goddess Moon". Women worshiped the moon for eternal youth. People liked to name girls as Yue (the moon, Chinese: 月), wishing them as beautiful as Fairy Chang E (a fairy who lives on the moon in Chinese mythology) and as tender as moon light.

8.3.3　星辰崇拜 Stars Worship

星辰能给人类指明方向，它的繁多和变幻总让人联想到自身的宿命，由此产生了星辰崇拜。海南民间认为，每颗星都代表一个人，天上出现一颗新星，人间就增添一个人；反之，人间死一个人，天上就会陨落一颗星。如同《三国演义》中诸葛亮禳星的情节，海南一些地方还有禳星增寿的习俗，以此为老人增寿。

The stars are indicating the direction to the human but changeable, which was reminiscent of people's own fates, resulting in the worship of stars. Every star in the sky was said to represent a person on the earth. That there was a new star in the sky meant there was a new-born baby. Conversely, there would be a fallen star when a person died. There is still such custom in Hainan as holding some rituals to make the star gleam brighter to extend the elder's life.

8.3.4　雷崇拜 Thunder Worship

雷崇拜即雷公或雷神崇拜。民间认为雷、雨、电由雷公、雨师、电母管辖。雷电所致的自然灾害让人们惧怕而奉其为雷公。黎族的雷公崇拜主要体现在两个方面：一方面，感激雷公，认为雨水是雷公给的，有雨水庄稼才长得好。另一个方面，惧怕雷公。如果触怒了雷公，山栏稻就会长虫；雷公不下雨，作物就会干枯而死。所以，每逢天旱，黎家人常会敲打蛙锣，杀牛宰猪祭雷公，以求雷公施雨。在祭祀祖先鬼时，也要先念雷公鬼的名号，以便用雷公鬼更大的魔力镇住祖先鬼。

The Thunder Gong is Thor in China. All natural disasters were caused by thunder and lightning, which resulted in thunder worship. That Li feared Thunder Gong was embodied in two aspects. On the one hand, the Li People appreciated what Thunder Gong had done. It was said whether crops grew well or not relied on rainwater which was controlled by Thunder Gong. On the other hand, the Li People were scared of Thunder Gong. If Thunder Gong was angered, he would make Shanlan rice field crawl with parasitic insects. Therefore, when it was drought, the Li would beat frog gongs and offer sacrifices to Thunder Gong, praying for rain. When ancestral ghosts were being worshiped, the title of Thunder Gong must be chanted first so that ancestral ghosts were able to be suppressed by the stronger power of Thunder Gong.

8.3.5 地崇拜 Land Worship

地神崇拜是农业社会的产物，是最普遍的自然崇拜。海南各村都建有土地庙祭祀土地神。城镇的守护神为城隍神。民间认为农历二月初二是土地公诞辰之日，当日，各户要用煮熟的母鸡、猪肉供奉土地，以祈求土地保佑人畜平安、风调雨顺、五谷丰登。城隍神则通常在元宵和中秋祭祀。

Land worship, the product of the agricultural society, is the most common natural worship. Generally, special temples worshipping the Local God of the Land were built in villages. And in towns there was a temple for residents to worship the Town God. On Lunar Feb. 2nd which was said to be the birthday of local god of the land, villagers would sacrifice cooked hens or pork for health, safety, good weather, and good harvest. The Town God used to be worshiped on Lantern Festival and Mid-autumn Festival.

黎族认为农作物的丰收是"地母"的恩赐，故每年重要农时都要祭祀地母（地鬼）。"合亩制"地区祭"地鬼"的仪式比较隆重。如在犁田开始时，亩头夫妇先到河里洗澡更衣，然后回到家里静坐。等夕阳西下，亩头才独自去"犁第一路田"，并反复念："大雨降临如倾盆，点点滴滴落田中。"在播种那天，亩头也要先一个人到秧地做些象征性的播种动作，沿途要小心翼翼，以防鸡、狗乱叫，见熟人也不吭声，怕惊动"地鬼"。稻谷熟时，亩头要先捆一捆稻谷，在中间供上小饭团，以谢地鬼恩赐。妇女到田里捻稻接谷魂时，亩头的妻子要念："谷魂回来，鸡犬避开，安回谷仓。"吃新米也要在亩头家饮酒、唱歌祭祀地母。

The Li believed that crop harvest was the gift from Di Mu or Di Gui (or the Land God or Ghost), so they worshipped Di Mu on occasions of important farming seasons. The sacrificial ceremonies were very solemn in He Mu System (a joint farming family system based on Patrilineal kinship) regions. Before ploughing up the field, for example, the couple of the Mu Tou (the headman of He Mu System) was to have a bath in the river, and sat silently at home till dark, and then the Mu Tou went to do the first plough alone, chanting, "Rain, rain, comes to me, every drop goes to the field." When women picked up scattered corn left in the field and met "grain soul" back home, the wife of the leader should chant, "Back, back, soul of grain, Chicken and dogs go away, come to barn quick and safe…" When eating newly-harvested rice, The Li People would drink and dance at the Mu Tou's house to show their respect and gratitude for Di Gui.

8.3.6 水崇拜 Water Worship

水崇拜源于人们对水的感激和恐惧。海南水资源丰富，水崇拜形式多样且各具地方特色，海神众多。黎族认为旱涝皆因水鬼作祟，要用鸡蛋和猪头祭祀才可免灾。如果有人溺水病了，家人要拿一个鸡蛋，由"鬼公"念咒祭鬼。

Water worship derived from the gratitude and fear for water. With rich water resources, water worship forms were various with local characteristics. There were many local Poseidons. Drought and flood, the Li held, were determined by water ghosts or Shui Gui. To meet their desire, eggs and pig head were to be sacrificed. If a person got sick for being drown, family had to ask Gui Gong to perform a ritual and worship the Shui Gui by incantations and offering an egg; if the person got killed, Gui Gong would see the new ghost off by incantation and offering pig and cattle.

8.3.7 山崇拜 Mountain Worship

山的雄伟神秘、物产丰富孕育了山神崇拜。在长期生活在山区的黎族眼中，山鬼统治自然界，包括山川森林、飞禽走兽。黎族猎人认为，打猎就是对山神的不敬，只有在得到山鬼授意的狩猎首领"俄巴"的同意方可打猎。如果围猎前后有猎人身感不适，会被认为触犯了山鬼，需拜祭山鬼以求谅解，并求保佑下次打到大的猎物，全家平安。拜祭仪式如下：备七碗饭、七块猪肉、七个酒杯、七双筷子，到半山腰找一处平地，摆上供品，点七柱香，对山跪拜，然后把供品向东南西北四个方向抛洒，礼毕。

With mysterious and rich resources, the Li People have worshiped Shan Gui (also called mountain ghost), the ruler of nature, who ruled all mountains and forests, birds and beasts. The Li hunters believed that hunting was to disrespect the god, unless they were able to get consent from the hunting leader called "Erba" who was empowered by the Mount Ghost. If one of the hunters felt sick, he would be recognized to have infringed the Mount Ghost. To get released, the hunter had to display seven bowls of rice, seven pieces of pork, seven cups of spirits, and seven pairs of chopsticks on the ground at the half of the hillside, light seven sticks of incense, face the mountain and kneel, then throw the offerings in four directions of east, south, west and north.

黎族这种山神崇拜扩大移植到了农业种植方面。每年正月在选择山栏地时，头人要到深山密林处举行山鬼祭祀，以求山鬼宽恕。烧山前，要把米撒在砍好的山栏地上祭祀山鬼，并请山鬼保护火力和风向。山栏地四周的稻草人据说是山鬼的化身，可以保护山栏地免受鸟兽破坏。

The Li transferred such worship to agriculture. Every lunar January when Shanlan rice fields were to be chosen, the headman would worship Mount Ghost in the middle of the forest, begging for its forgiveness first. When permitted, the headman was to cast rice in the plant-cutting field to pray for Mount Ghost's blessing, and then set off a fire. The scarecrows around the field were also regarded as incarnations of the Mount Ghost and would protect the mountain field from getting damaged by animals.

8.3.8 石崇拜 Stone Worship

海南民间认为某些有灵性的石头可助信奉者达成夙愿，所以崇拜供奉石头。如琼海博鳌的圣公石、文昌铜鼓岭的风动石、琼中黎苗自治县黎母山的仙女石等，常年受到人们的香火祭拜。

Some people in Hainan worshipped stone, holding that they can help people realize their dreams, such as Shengong Rock in Boao of Qionghai city, Wind-Blown Rock on Copper Drum Ridge in Wenchang, and Fairy Rock in Qiongzhong Li Nationality Autonomous counties, and so forth, which have been worshiped by people in neighborhoods nearby and far off.

黎族认为石头神能促进人的生育，也能保护庄稼免受鸟兽破坏。他们视温润细致的石头为"石精"，置室内可"镇家"，随猎手打猎可保满载而归。五色"石精"也称"牛魂石"，每至牛节，黎家都要请出"牛魂石"，用酒浸泡，互相品尝后，再把酒给牛灌饮，为牛招魂，并祈求牛群满栏，家人平安。有一种如拳大小的石头，水磨饲犬，能使猎狗保持勇猛。还有黎族供奉的"石且"，是对人类繁衍和祖先崇拜的象征，在黎人心中地位甚高。

Stone gods, Li ethnic group believed, were able to promote fertility, but also protect crops from birds and beasts. They worshipped a fine and smooth stone as "stone spirit", which was regarded as a "family protector" when put inside the house or to ensure a fruitful result if carried with the hunter. A so-called "cattle soul stone" has five colors. On the occasions of "Cattle Festival", the Li People would welcome reverently the stone and soak it in liquor, drink the liquor, and then feed cattle with it, praying for cattle full bar, family safe. A fist-sized stone used to be ground with water to feed haunts, which was thought to make them stronger and braver. There is also a very important god for the Li, a male-genital-organ-shaped stone called Shiqie, which is a symbol of human's reproduction and ancestors.

8.3.9 火崇拜 Fire Worship

火在黎族古代社会中占有极重要的地位，它能焚烧大片山栏地，烧毁森林和村庄，也能炒菜煮饭，驱赶野兽，因此人们对火由敬畏发展到崇拜。几乎每个黎村都供奉"灶鬼"。每年除夕祀黎在祭祖先鬼时也要祭灶鬼。另外，任何跨过、敲击或乱动用三块石头砌成的"品"字形的炉灶的行为，都被认为是对灶鬼的冒犯，将会受到灶鬼的惩罚。

Fire played a most important role in ancient Li society, because it was able not only to burn forest or villages down, but also to cook and drive beasts away. Generally, there was a tablet for stove ghost in every Li village. Every Lunar New Year eve Qi Li used to worship ancestral ghosts as well as stove ghost. In addition, the acts of walking over, knocking at or moving the triangle stove made of three stones were considered as offence, which would bring about severe punishments.

8.3.10 动物崇拜 Animal Worship

自然界的动物身上具有一些人类无法企及的特点，使得他们可以在恶劣的自然环境中得以生存。出于对这些动物身上表现出来的非凡能力的崇拜，在遭遇无法避免的自然界的灾祸时，海南民间就把希望寄托在这些动物身上，以寻求自我保护。

Many physical features some animals have allow them to survive in the harsh natural environment. People wished they could have owned some of these physical features to protect themselves when some unavoidable natural disasters happened, which resulted in animal worship.

狗

Dogs

狗嗅觉敏锐，与人亲近。民间认为，若狗有反常之举，如狂吠不止、低声呜咽、暴躁不安或咬着主人衣服不放等，都是在暗示主人有不详之事发生。黎族认为黑狗的血可以禳灾驱鬼。举行驱鬼仪式时，黎族要斩杀一只黑狗，取黑狗的血圈住鬼经常出没的地方，这样鬼就被圈在里面，失去了作祟的能力。由于易存活的特性，"阿猫""阿狗"通常被人们用来作为孩子的小名。

Dogs have keen sense of smell and are the closest friends of human beings. Folk have held that a dog has some abnormal behaviors, such as barking, sobbing or biting the owner of the clothes, suggested that something bad would happen to his owner. Dogs played an important role in exorcising evil spirits. The Li believed that black dog blood was able to avert disaster and exorcise ghosts. On the exorcism ceremony, Li used to kill a black dog, and cast its blood to circle around the haunted place, so that the haunting ghost would be trapped inside the circle and lose its power. "Ah Gou" (dog) as well as "Ah Mao" (cat) were always used to name children as infant names because they are easy to feed.

猫头鹰和乌鸦
Owls and Crows

猫头鹰因嗅腐尸而动，乌鸦因通体漆黑如着孝服而均被视为不详。因此，猫头鹰或乌鸦入室或入村，人们必全力驱赶，不让它停宿，以免带来晦气。黎族称猫头鹰为"鬼鸟"，认为猫头鹰乱叫就是鬼进来作祟，这时男子要持粉枪朝屋外鸣放，以镇鬼降妖。第二天，全村要在村口设蘸，摆上祭品，请道公作法驱鬼，保佑全村老少平安。

The emergence of owls was seen as a bad omen because they would take actions when they smell dead bodies. Crows were considered ominous due to its dark feather from head to foot, which was just like mourning garments. If there was an owl or crow flying in a village or even in a house, villagers dead drove it away so as not to encounter rough going. The Li People called owl "evil spirit bird" and thought it suggested an evil spirit coming and haunting when an owl was hooting. In that case men had to shoot towards the outside into the sky to frighten and subdue the ghosts and bogies. The next day, Tao Gong would practice exorcism, praying that everyone could be safe and healthy.

变色龙和四脚蛇
Chameleon and Lizard

变色龙和四脚蛇模样古怪，叫声奇特，喜欢在阴暗潮湿的地方爬行。琼南有些汉族认为它们为不祥之物，见到了会给人带来厄运，甚至会让人死亡；若无法回避，要朝它们吐口水予以禳解。

Chameleon and lizard look weird, sound strange, and they like crawling in the dark, damp places, which made them considered ominous things. If people saw them, they had to spit toward them to relieve misfortune.

8.3.11 植物崇拜 Flora Worship

榕树
Banyan

在海南民众心中，榕树是神树、佛树、福树、寿树，榕树根深叶茂，果实繁多，具有非凡的生命力，象征着易养易活、子孙繁盛，是荫庇子孙的神灵。如果树灵附到婴儿身上，能佑他无病无灾，茁壮成长，同时也能庇佑整个家族香火不断，人丁兴旺。

With thick leaves and deep root, banyan is holy tree and the symbol of vitality and reproduction. At the same time it is a materialized ancestral spirit to bless and protect the descendants. Once the spirit attached to a baby, the baby and his family would get blessed.

加茂树
Jiamaoshu

加茂树就是"见血封喉"树,亦称箭毒木、大药树,它的白浆有剧毒。黎人过去打猎或械斗,曾涂此白浆于箭头。海南黎族认为,暴风雨来临的时候,加茂树会变成鬼,出来害人,要用很多铁钉、马钉,把树魂钉在树里,让鬼不能出来害人。它还是风水树。澄迈一带认为理想的村庄布局就是"前榕后茂",象征"常年繁荣茂盛"。

Jiamaoshu (in Hainan dialect) is antiaris toxicaria. People refer to antiaris as the "Poison Arrow Tree" (Chinese: 箭毒木; pinyin: Jiàndú Mù) because its latex was poisonous and smeared on arrowheads in ancient times by the Li People in hunting and warfare. People thought antiaris spirit always came out to haunt in a storm. Therefore, they nailed many nails or staples into the stem to trap the spirit inside. Hainan Folk have also regarded it as one of Feng Shui trees. People in Chengmai have considered the ideal village layout is "Rong-front-Mao-behind" referring to "lush perennially" and implying "florishing forever".

萝卜
Little Radish

乐东黎族自治县黄流镇和三亚崖城地区的汉族喜欢叫小孩"拉巴仔"(萝卜头),希望孩子像萝卜一样长得又快又高,没有病痛。

Many of the Han People who have lived in Huangliu Town of Ledong Li Autonomous County and Yachen District of Sanya city like to call children as "La Ba Zai" (Hainan dialect, meaning little radish), wishing children could grow fast and tall like radishes without suffering from diseases or clamity.

8.4 图腾崇拜
Totem Worship

图腾崇拜是一种最原始的宗教形式。"图腾"一词来源于印第安语"totem",意思为"它的亲属""它的标记"。在原始信仰中,人们认为本氏族人都源于某种特定的物种、与某种动物或植物具有亲缘关系,或者被守护,这种动、植物便成了这个民族最古老的祖先或保护者,即图腾。

Totem worship is one of the most primitive forms of religion. The word "totem" comes from Indian, meaning "of its relatives", "its mark". People deemed that their own clan or nation was derived from a particular species, had genetic relationship with it, or was guarded by it, which is totem.

8.4.1 龙图腾 Dragon Totem

龙一直被认为是汉族的图腾,其实不尽然。海南黎族某些部落也奉龙为图腾。龙在海南黎语中称为"党",非常美丽,生活于深潭之中。在黎族姓氏、刺绣等方面都可以看到它的痕迹。黎人认为,只要有党就有水,有水庄稼就有好收成。东方市哈方言地区黎族就有意为"龙的孩子"的姓氏。

白沙县黎族妇女的衣服上的刺绣也有抽象的龙纹图案。

Dragon has been considered a totem of the Han nationality, which in fact is not the whole story. The dragon, called "Dang" in Li dialect in Hainan, which is a very beautiful animal and usually hides in the deep lake, is also the totem of some tribes of the Li. It is said that there is water where there is "Dang", which brings about a good harvest. We can trace from the family names and embroidery. There is still a clan who have lived in Ha Dialect region in Dongfang city, whose surname means "the children of dragons". In Baisha county, Li women's clothes are embroidered with abstract dragon pattern.

8.4.2 蛙图腾 Frog Totem

海南师范大学美术学院副教授王沫认为原始社会黎族把蛙当作自己的祖先或保护神来顶礼膜拜，蛙是整个民族的共同标志和象征（王沫，2011）。海南黎族各方言区都有蛙纹身、蛙织锦、蛙锣。黎族妇女常见纹身图式中的青蛙纹是原始母系氏族社会阶段崇拜观念的产物，青蛙是当时盛行的女性生殖器（子宫）崇拜的象征物，具有多子多福的象征意义（刘咸，1983）。而黎锦纹样中的绝大多数"人纹"实则"蛙人纹"，是人与青蛙的结合体（祁庆富、马晓京，2005）。

Wang Mo, a professor of the Arts Department of Hainan Normal University, argued that Ancient Li worshiped Frogs as their ancestors or patrons, which were shared by the whole nation as its symbol or mark. We could trace it from frog tattoos, frog patterns in embroidery and frog gongs. Frogs that are fertile and signify good harvest were the symbols for female genital phase (womb), and the frog tattoo patterns were produced from the prevailing worship for female genital phase (womb) in primitive matriarchal society. Most of the human patterns on embroidery were actually "frog-human" patterns, which combined human with frog, symbolizing reproduction of the nation.

8.4.3 蛇图腾 Snake Totem

海南黎族的蛇图腾崇拜，在创世神话、文身图案、禁忌等方面都有着充分的体现。黎族各支系的创世神话分别有《黎母山传说》《勾花的传说》《蛇郎》《蛇女婿》《五妹与蚺蛇》等，这些神话都认为，黎族始祖来源于蛇。中华人民共和国成立前，美孚方言的黎族妇女在脸部、手背和腿上都纹了复线添点状纹样即蚺蛇图案，因此其他黎族都称美孚方言的黎族为"蚺蛇美孚"（中国民族宗教网，2013）。乐东黎族自治县志仲乡董姓的黎族也把蚺蛇认为是他们的祖先，族人一律不得吃蚺蛇(詹贤武，2008)。

Snake is one of the main totems of the Li, which is embodied in many Genesis myths, tattoo patterns and taboos. Before the founding of the PRC, Meifu Li women tattooed anaconda pattern in the face, back of hands and legs, so other Li peoples called them "Anaconda Meifu". In Zhizhong Township Ledong Li Autonomous County, a Li clan, whose surname is "Dong", worshiped anaconda as their ancestor. Everybody of this clan wasn't allowed to eat anaconda snake.

8.4.4 鸟图腾 Bird Totem

海南岛的汉族祖先由于悬居大陆之外，把每年秋季都从故土飞来的燕子视为"公鸟"，认为它就像"公祖"一样显灵，无论破屋豪宅，照样衔泥筑巢，探望保佑子孙。人们认为"燕子入屋，全家有福"，像善待"祖公"一样善待燕子。人们相信"公鸟"不入恶人屋，如果燕子未能如期而至，大家便觉得这户人家一定做过什么不良的事情。若燕子在非正常迁徙的季节突然离开，这将是对主人的警告，表明将有灾难降临。传统的海南民居在屋檐下用上好的木料制作的两个突出的木墩，就是专门为燕子垒巢设计的。

The ancestors of Han, who lived off their hometown, called swallows as "Ancestor Bird", because they fly back to nest under the eave, feed and take care of their chicks every year, no matter the house was a villa, or a hut, which was just like the ancestors who came back to see and bless their offsprings. There is a saying, "Swallows come into your house, and happiness would come around". And "Ancestor Bird" wouldn't enter any wicked man's. If swallows didn't come as usual, the family would reflect what they had done. If swallows suddenly left in the wrong season, it would be a warning that there would be a disaster. There were two girders made of good wood stretching out of the wall designed for swallows to nest under the eave.

黎族崇拜的鸟图腾主要有甘工鸟和约加西拉鸟。甘工鸟崇拜来自一个爱情故事。海南保亭七仙岭下，聪明美丽的黎家姑娘阿甘和勤劳勇敢的黎家青年猎手拜和真心相爱。凶狠的峒主却想强抢阿甘做儿媳，阿甘坚决不从，把身上所带的银首饰捣制成一对翅膀，变成一只鸟儿，找到自己心爱的人，与他比翼双飞。自此甘工鸟为黎族排忧解难，被视为黎族的保护神。

Gangong bird and Yuejiaxila bird are two of Li's totems. Gangong totem originated from a love story. At the foot of Qixianling Ridge of Baoting in Hainan, a smart and beautiful Li girl named Ah Gan fell in love with an industrious and brave Li boy named Bai He. But the cruel chieftain managed to force her to be his daughter-in-law. Ah Gan refused firmly and made a pair of wings of her silver jewelries and turned into a Gangong bird, flying away to find her lover. Thus Gangong birds became patron birds to solve problems for the Li.

8.4.5 狗图腾 Dog Totem

海南有些汉族地区把狗也视为图腾。在海口市羊山一带以及雷州半岛的当地人把狗的石雕立在门口，称为"石狗公"，是镇宅辟邪、保佑一家老小平安的保护神。黎族进山做事或围猎都需要狗的帮助和保护，把狗作为崇拜的图腾。过去黎族不吃狗，也不许在家煮食，否则被视为玷污祖宗的灵魂。

Some septs of Han areas in Hainan worshipped dog totem. In Yangshan region Haikou city and the Leizhou Peninsula Guangdong province, the locals carved stone into the shape of dog and stood it in front of their houses. They called the stone dog as "Stone Dog Gong" and considered it as a saint patron who can prevent anything unclean especially evil spirits from getting in, and bless the whole family. The Li People who went into the hill to hunt or do some other things needed dogs' company, and therefore they worshipped dogs as a totem. In the past, Li didn't eat dogs, nor cooked it at home. Otherwise, it would be considered as humiliating the ancestors of the soul.

8.4.6 猫图腾 Cat Totem

猫赶老鼠、保谷仓、护衣物、助黎家，也是黎家的保护神。黎族崇拜猫的地区主要是五指山市的毛道乡。乡民们称公猫为祖父，母猫为祖母，把猫视为自己的祖先。猫死后，他们要像对待祖先一样举行葬礼。由两个十二三岁的男童用竹竿把猫抬到村外的猫山或椰子树下选地下葬。埋葬完毕，回家后不能马上吃饭、喝酒，要先单独吃点酸菜，然后才能上座同他人共餐，以示对猫的哀悼。

Cats protect barn, food, and clothing from biting by catching mice, which made them another saint patron. The Li People who lived in Maodao Township Wuzhishan city regarded cats as their ancestors, calling tomcats grandfathers, female cats grandmothers. If a cat died, it would have a funeral. Two boys aging twelve or thirteen would carry the cat with bamboo poles out of the village and bury it at the foot of Cat Mountain or a coconut palm. After the burial, they had to eat some sour preserved vegetables alone before sharing meals with others, to show the mourning.

8.4.7　葫芦图腾 Gourd Totem

在黎族人民心中，葫芦是人类的祖先和保护神。几乎每个黎族地区都流传关于葫芦的神话故事，如《人类的起源》《洪水传说》《姓氏来源的传说》《葫芦瓜》等。有的讲述了人类始祖诞于葫芦的故事，有的则把葫芦描绘成了黎族的诺亚方舟，使人类得以延续。

Gourd is one totem of the Li nationality's, which was their ancestor and saint patron. The mythologies differ from place to place. Some has it that the first human being was born out of a gourd, some describes gourd as a Li's Noah's Ark.

8.4.8　竹图腾 Bamboo Totem

在三亚的田独、鹿回头、乐东的尖峰、东方的中沙等地"符"姓的黎族以竹子为姓氏，也就是氏族的符号。"符"姓，黎语中叫"色顺"，即"竹的孩子"或"竹子丛下"的意思。竹子是他们共同崇拜的原始祖先。以前，凡是"色顺"同姓氏族都聚居在一起，大家杀牛宰猪，祭祀祖先。

In some areas including Tiandu and Luhuitou in Sanya, Jianfeng Ridge in Ledong and Zhongsha in Dongfang some Li's surnames are "符"(fú), which is the symbol of the clan. Fu, pronounced as "Seshun" in Li dialect, means "children of bamboo" or "at the foot of bamboo bush". Previously, all "Seshun" clan people lived together and worshiped their ancestor by offering cattle and pigs on the occasions of great events or festivals.

8.5　民间方术 Folk Fang Shu

海南民间方术起源于本土原始宗教的巫术，同时又受到汉族道教的极大影响，混杂而独具特色。海南民间方术主要体现在各族巫师根据征兆来占卜、驱邪、祈福。

Folk Fang Shu in Hainnan originated from local primitive witchcraft and got influenced by Taoism, which made it complex but of local characters. Hainan Fang Shu is mainly embodied in divination, exorcism, and praying for safety and wealth according to omens by necromancers.

8.5.1 征兆 Omen

先民根据某些反常的自然现象，以及幻象来预知未来将会发生的事情和祸福。这些异变和幻象即征兆或预兆，黎人认为是"祖先鬼"回家报信来了。预兆分吉、凶两种。汉族"左眼跳财右眼跳灾""开门见喜""乌鸦叫，有灾到"这些常见征兆与大陆无异。由于生活环境相近，黎苗的征兆也有许多相似之处。以下是一些常见的黎族征兆：

Ancestors predicted what would happen according to some abnormal natural phenomena or phantom, which were known as omens. There were auspicious and ominous signs. "Left eyelid twitching predicts good luck, right disaster." "Open your door and see magpies, there will be something nice." "A crow cowing, ghosts coming" and alike are common omens among Han. Some of Miao's omens are similar to Li's, sharing similar living environment. Some common omens of the Li are as follow:

黎族男子外出途中，遇见任何蛇类蜕壳（换下来的外皮），预示碰上了好运气，要及时脱下身上的外衣扔掉，寓意你脱我亦脱，你长我亦长。遇见蛇吞蛇，在已方这边的蛇吞了对面的蛇，是吉兆，如果对面那边的蛇吞了这边（近自己一方）的蛇，是凶兆，必须斩死双蛇，并请"鬼公"来辟邪。

That a Li man met any kind of snake's molts was said to indicate he run into good luck, and he should promptly take off his coat and throw it away, signifying that you (the snake) take off your molt and grow, and I take off my coat and grow. It was auspicious to meet a snake closer to you swallowing another snake, conversely, it was ominous. You had to cut the heads of the two snakes, and invite Gui Gong to ward off evil spirit.

天刚黑时，有雄鸡啼叫，必发生火灾；晚上 10-11 时雄鸡啼叫，预报有人要来盗窃；晚上 12-1 时雄鸡啼叫，预兆家里或族里有人要死，应及时请"鬼公"来降神消灾。

When a rooster crowed at dusk, a fire was sure to occur; that it crowed at 10-11 o'clock at night forecasted that someone would come to steal; at 12-1, one person of the family or clan would die, clansmen should ask Gui Gong to ward off evil spirit at once.

梦见自己全身生疥疮，会拾获钱银；梦见自己啼哭，必有喜事临门；梦见有人送手镯自己，将会生个儿子。梦见自家房屋倒塌，全家人会生病而死；梦见大水淹房屋，将有人生病；梦见蛇缠身，早上会被蛇咬伤；梦见挖红薯或织鱼网，家中必有人会死（詹贤武，2008）。

You would pick up money if you dreamed that you have a scabies whole body. Something good would happen to you if you dreamed that you were crying. You would have a son if you dreamed that you were send a bracelet. If a person dreamed that his own houses collapse, the whole family would get sick and die; that houses was flooded, some people would get sick; that a snake twined his body, he would be bitten by a snake the next morning; that he dug sweet potatoes or weaves nets, someone would die at home.

禳解凶兆
Warding off ominous signs

一般的凶兆，可以通过唾口水来辟邪消灾。比如遇无名死尸、老鼠、猫头鹰等，要尽量不看，并连唾三次口水，据说可以化解晦气。有时做了不想的梦，或听到别人讲了对自己不吉利的话，也可用此法消灾。此禳解之法因操作简单在民间广为流传。

Some common ominous signs can be warded off by spitting saliva, which was widely adopted in folk for its easiness and convenience. If you meet with nameless corpse, mice, or owls, try not to look at it, and spit saliva three times. And it also worked when you dreamed of bad things or heard something ominous to you.

如果人们不知征兆凶吉，往往要先通过道公、娘母占卜、查鬼、解兆，再通过作法、祭祀进行禳解。

If people didn't know whether it was an auspicious omen or not, you needed Tao Gong or Niang Mu to interpret it first by divining and telling that it was which ghost who was haunting, and then warded off the misfortunes by special incantations or rituals.

8.5.2 巫师 Necromancers

海南懂得民间方术的宗教职业者有道公、娘母、老人、梦公、梦母等，一般都不是专职的，不脱离日常生产生活。

In Hainan folk, religious Necromancers are mainly Tao Gong, Niang Mu, Ao Ya, Meng Gong, Meng Mu, etc. Generally they are not full-time ones.

道公，海南话称"三叔公"，是法力最强的方士。主要从事查病治病、查鬼祭鬼驱鬼、作斋（丧事中雇请僧道念经诵咒以超度亡灵的迷信活动）等法事活动。海南民间除了三亚回族没有道公外，汉族、黎族、苗族地区均有道公活动。中华人民共和国成立前，有些汉族道士被请到黎族地区查病治病，黎族中便有一些人师承汉族道士，在本族做起道公。黎族道公多为世袭，子承父业。继承者要有一定的文化，能讲海南汉族方言。

Tao Gong, namely Taoist priest or San Shu Gong, engaged in such psychic activities as disease ascertainment, medical treatment, ghost ascertainment and exorcism, Zou Zhai (a ritual to release spirit of the dead from purgatory by incantations at funeral) and others. His mana was said to be the most powerful. Except in Sanya Muslin areas, Tao Gongs were popular. Before the founding of the PRC, some Han Tao Gongs were invited to treat diseases in Li areas, when some Li people began to study necromancy from them and started the career in Li areas. Li Tao Gong was mostly hereditary and literate, and spoke Hainan Han dialect.

娘母是黎族地区的巫医，主要通过做法事查病治病。作法事的时候，不论男女都要穿女装，戴花巾。

Niang Mu, Shaman in Li areas, mainly treated diseases. When practicing rituals, either male or female had to wear lady's vestment and a flower towel as well.

老人，黎族也称"鬼老人"或"鬼公"，主要职责是在举行葬礼时用黎语诵念祖先鬼的名字，以及祖先迁徙的地名，博闻强记，深谙世事，在黎族格外受尊敬。

Ao Ya, also called Gui Gong or Lao Ren by the Li people, had a so good memory as to recite all the names of ancestors and places the clan had lived at in Li dialect at funeral. The Li respected Ao Ya very much.

梦公和梦母是汉族民间招魂问卜的巫师，往往通过某种仪式让神鬼附身，与人交流。当人们无力于人事的时候，往往会通过他们求神问卦，然后依求得之法行事，解忧化煞。有时遇喜事亦可求吉日良辰。

Meng Gong and Meng Mu were a kind of necromancers who were able to summon the spirit of the deceased or a god to attach to their body and communicate with people. When people needed help, they would appeal to spirits or gods through them by casting lots, then do what they were told to. Sometimes people asked for an auspicious time to hold a wedding or warm a house.

8.5.3 方术 Folk Fang Shu

方术即巫术。海南民间方术主要有招魂、叫魂、驱鬼、雷神判和鬼神判。

Hainan folk Fang Shu, namely necromancy or witchcraft, includes sending ghosts, evocation, exorcism, Thunder God's sentence and spirits' sentence and divination.

黎族人认为亡者的"鬼魂"不会自己找到祖宗灵魂们的居所，它们会总在生前住过的房子周围游荡，家人要请鬼公作斋**招魂**，将亡灵引送到祖宗灵魂们的聚居地，并让祖宗鬼接纳其为家人，让它不要打扰活着的家人的生活。

The Li People thought that the spirit of the dead couldn't find the way to its ancestors' spirits' dwelling and was always wandering around home. The family tended to ask Ao Ya to **send the spirit** to the dwelling, and plead with ancestral ghosts to accept the new spirit as family.

叫魂与招魂不同，是海南汉族民间为活人招魂的一种原始巫术。若家人特别是小孩突然病倒或晕倒，醒后一直魂不守舍，食不甘味，要请道公设醮作法，高喊病人灵魂归来。琼北一带的汉族多采用"抽井魂"的叫魂法：拿一碗米饭、一个鸡蛋、一面镜子、一把木尺、一把剪刀、一套衣服到村中的井边摆上，再燃上香火，唱念祭词，祭祀井魂公；然后为小孩叫魂：细数孩子可能吓掉魂魄的种种不快经历，以"自此不怕不痛，胆壮气勇，日玩如龙，夜睡如猪，见饭知香，见糖知甜，平安到老，一生太平"结束；对井神公再行拜祭，烧过"金银元宝"；最后让小孩再换上井边的衣服，吃点祭祀的米饭，礼毕。

Different from sending ghosts, **evocation** was a primitive witchcraft Hainan Han folk practiced to call back the living persons' souls. If the family especially children suddenly fell ill or fainted, and entered into a trance state and had no appetite for food, family tended to ask Tao Gong to practice the ritual of evocation. The Han in Northern Hainan usually practiced the evocation ritual named "pump well's soul" like this: I. have a bowl of rice, an egg, a mirror, a wooden ruler, a pair of scissors, a set of clothes displayed at the wellhead, burn incense, offering sacrifices and the articles of the child to the well soul; II. chant all the unpleasant experiences that might have scared the child, and call out the child's name time and time again, then end with "no fear, no pain from now on, may you be brave as a bear when in trouble, be vigorous as a dragon when playing, be sound as a stone when sleeping, be as greedy as a pig when eating, be safe and healthy till the end of your life"; III. worship the well soul again, burning "gold and silver ingots"; IV. change the kid's clothes with the ones on the wellhead, made the kid eat a little rice of that bowl, and then go home.

驱鬼则是驱逐恶鬼。黎族民间的驱鬼活动主要是为黎家驱除灾病的。

Exorcism is a psychic activity for the Li People to expel evil spirits to keep family safe and healthy.

09 海南海洋民俗
Marine Customs in Hainan

海南的祖先自古就是我国开发南海诸岛和"海上丝绸之路"航行的主力军，都是从事远海作业和远洋航行的好手，在漫长海洋作业历史长河中，他们创造了许多丰富多彩的蓝色海洋文化瑰宝。

Hainanese ancestors, who were good at sailing, were the main forces to exploit maritime silk route of ancient South China. During the long history, they have created abundant marine cultures.

基于海南岛得天独厚的自然条件，丰富多彩的海洋文化资源，它既有中国海洋文化共有的特点，也有海南特定区域的文化气息。总之，海南海洋民俗文化是海南文化甚至是中国海洋文化的重要组成部分，是海南海洋文化中不可或缺的一环，它反映着海南人民对南海的认识历程，折射出人民的生产、生活、信仰等。海南人民开发、利用南海的历史就是创造海南海洋文化的历史。在这个历史过程中所形成的海洋民俗文化，如海洋人生礼仪、海洋建筑文化、海洋饮食文化、海洋服饰文化（详见第六章）、海洋节庆、海洋信仰等包含了丰富的历史信息。基于海洋民俗现状，我们应该正确地去研究它、保护它，为人们更好地了解海南的历史提供经验基础，同时为海南的国际旅游岛建设提供了良好的借鉴经验。

Based on the unique geological location, Hainan has sufficient oceanic resources which bear the common characteristics with the marine cultures in China. In a word, marine customs are the major and indispensable components of Chinese marine cultures which reflect the process of creating life, production and belief for Hainanese. The history people in Hainan exploit and develop the South China Sea is also the history of cultures, during which Hainan-styled marine customs and cultures come into being, including life rites customs, food and beverage customs, costumes and ornaments customs (the contents are introduced in Chapter Six), marine festivals and beliefs. In view of the current conditions, it's of great value to research and protect marine cultures, which are not only conductive to understanding the history of Hainan, but also providing good experiences for people in the process of developing Hainan International Tourist Destination.

9.1 海洋人生礼仪
Marine Customs in Life

海洋人生礼仪民俗是指生活在沿海的居民（主要指疍民）在人生中所经历几个重要阶段，主要包括诞生礼仪、成年礼仪、祝寿礼、婚姻礼仪和丧葬仪式（详见第二章）。除了婚姻礼仪之外，其他习俗都大同小异，因此这节着重介绍疍家人婚俗和文昌东郊沿海一带的婚俗。

Customs in Marine life refer to different rites and ceremonies that people who live along the seaside go through in different periods including birth rite, coming-of-age ceremony, marriage customs, longevity celebration and funeral (the contents are introduced in the Chapter Two). In addition to marriage customs, fewer differences occur in the other customs. Thus, this section mainly introduces Tankas' marriage customs and the people who live along Dongjiao Coconut groves.

首先介绍"疍家人"，即"海上人家"的婚姻习俗。中华人民共和国成立前，疍家人的婚姻也是媒人说亲，父母包办婚姻。举行婚礼前，将船刷干净，涂上新漆，贴上结婚对联。婚日，新郎用十口八口大鼓，鼓得震耳欲聋坐船来接新娘。各兄弟姐妹们聚拢在一起，摆酒宴宾，举行较隆重的结婚仪式。进洞房前，新郎新娘唱四句民歌进行对歌。结婚第二日起，每天大清早新郎用船把新娘的三姑六婆接来款待，晚上再送回去（云林，2011）。

First, the marriage customs of the Tankas, also known as the people living in boats, is introduced. Before the founding of the People's Republic People of China, the Tankas' marriage was arranged by their parents. People had to clean and paint their boats, pasting antithetical couplets before the wedding ceremony. On the wedding day, the bridegroom welcomed the bride by boating while beating drums, with a banquet held to treat friends and relatives. The bride and groom would sing songs in antiphonal style before the bridal chamber. From the next day after the wedding ceremony, the bridegroom invited the bride' relatives, treated them, and sent them back in the afternoon.

1949 年后疍家人已搬上陆地定居，男女多通过自由恋爱而结婚，与其他汉族通婚。双方父母同意男女双方的婚事后，男方父母要聘请媒人，于大年初二带上槟榔到女方家提亲。如果女方家不反对这门婚事，媒人带着女方的生辰八字带回男方家，男方家再请算命先生看两人的生辰八字是否生合命。一旦合婚，男方家即要择良辰吉日，再派媒人到女方家"压命"，经得同意择日举行婚礼。

疍家婚俗：摇船迎新人（符王润 摄）
Welcoming the Bride by the Sampan
(Source: http://hnrb.hinews.cn/html/2014-10/27/content_27_1.htm)

Most of the Tankas moved to the land, and it was free for young people to choose their lovers from the other ethnic groups after founding the P. R.C. in 1949, such as Han. With being agreed by both parents, the males' parents would invite a matchmaker to make a proposal to the females' home on the second day of the first lunar month. If the both families' parents agreed on this matter, the matchmaker would take the females' Ba Zi (Eight characters used in fortune telling). Suppose the fortune teller told them their Ba Zi was supplement to each other, the males' family would choose an auspicious day to held the wedding ceremony.

结婚前天，按照疍家的风俗，男方要给女方行聘礼。根据男方家庭情况，聘礼一般为服装10套、金戒指2只、金耳坠1对、银项链1条、银头钗2支、玉手镯1对，以及数百元现金。为了表示对女方家的尊重，聘礼要用彩船并请鼓乐手一路敲锣打鼓、热热闹闹送到女方家。结婚前的夜晚，疍家有女儿"哭嫁"，即"啼夜"的习俗。疍家姑娘"啼夜"哭得越悲切，越能表示出对父母养育之恩和对娘家的眷恋（云林，2011）。"啼夜"时要用疍家人特有的"咸水调"边哭边唱。若双亲尚且健在，要用哭唱的方式感念生育之恩。

The day before the ceremony, the male would give the gifts, including ten suits, two gold rings, one pair of earrings, two silver hairpins, a jade bracelet, and some cash to the female based on the male's family economic condition when they were engaged.

第二天，疍家男方过门迎亲。媒人和男方嫂嫂、姐姐和4位女傧乘坐一只披红的小舢板，在乐队敲打声中摇到女方家迎亲。新娘头戴凤冠，身穿自己制作的五色衣裙，戴一副墨色眼镜。再由女方家的6名女傧相陪同，坐上男方家的小舢板。这时的新郎则早已等候在自家的船头。接亲的小舢板回来，他便走上前去将新娘搀扶上船。新娘接过来后，要举行拜堂仪式。

On the wedding day, the welcome ceremony was held. Four women, the matchmaker, the bride's sisters and elder sister-in-law took a sampan to welcome the bride with drums beating during the process. The bride wore jewelries, sun glasses, and a beautiful dress made by herself, accompanied by six women, and went to the bridegroom's home by sampan. When the sampan came back, the bridegroom took the bride off the boat. Then formal wedding ceremony would be held in a traditional way.

文昌东郊沿海一带半渔半农地区，订婚、结婚时还有互赠椰子习俗。在订婚时，男方会送女方两颗椰子苗，称为"订婚椰"。结婚时，女方带着椰子苗到男方家"安家落户"。婚后，新婚夫妇一起种两颗椰子树，并默默祈祷，希望夫妻能像这两颗椰子树，椰影双双、白头偕老、永不分离。但是，现在赠送"订婚椰"的习俗已逐渐消失，实行自由婚姻。但种椰子树这种习俗仍保留至今。

There is still a custom going like this in the coastal areas of Wenchang that the male and female send coconuts to each other. When they are engaged, the male would send two small coconut palms to the female, which was called "sending coconuts as engagement". After they got married, the new couple would plant the two small coconut palms together, praying to live together to an old age like the two coconut trees. Nowadays, the custom of "sending coconut palms as engagement" gradually doesn't exist because of the policy of free marriage. But the custom of planting coconut palms is still prevalent.

9.2 海洋建筑民俗
Marine-styled Residence

海南的居民最早大多数是由广东、福建等地区迁移过来的，因而海南民居建筑也体现出深厚的闽南建筑风格。后来，大量来自中原地区的驻军带来了中原文化，使得海南北部地区民居也融入了一些中原建筑特色。到了近代，由于各种原因大量海南人为了生计纷纷前往东南亚地区去谋生，同时带回了一些南洋的建筑文化，海南的民居也有了一些欧洲民居风格，同不仅影响了海南传统民居形式，同时也带来了新的民居格式——海口骑楼（详见第四章）。"水上人家，疍民居住风俗"是疍家人在延续传统水居船屋，结合新时期生产和生活需要建造的，也是现代疍家人为了适应水上养殖、捕鱼和居住为一体的民居样式。

Most of the earliest residents in Hainan migrated from Guangdong, Fujian, etc., for which the style of buildings closely resembles the those in Southern Fujian province. Afterwards, the stationed troops from Central Plains brought their cultures, and the northern and southern residents built houses with the style of Central Plains added. In modern times, in order to make a living, lots of Hainanese went to the areas of Southeast Asian countries and brought a new style named Haikou Qi Lou (Arcade, discussed in Chapter Four). Tankas' boat-house or "Living in the boat", which now is built into pontoon rows of the fisher house, serves as the typical style of the Tankas' dwellings based on the needs of times and production.

9.2.1 疍民"水上人家"居住风俗 Tankas "Living in the Boat"

"水上人家"居民是我国东南沿海地区的一种常住居民，疍民生活的区域分布很广，主要居住地区在福建、广东和海南等沿海地区和岛屿。按南海传统的生活习俗，平时南海渔民出海捕鱼作业，出于安全考虑女人是不能一起出海的，捕鱼的船上只允许男人住。但生活在海南三亚的渔民中，却生活着这样一群妇女，她们带着孩子住在船上跟着自己的丈夫一起出海捕鱼作业。这就是海南著名的"水上人家"的生活写照。据史记载，由于疍民们的生活环境具有特殊性，疍民的居住状况非常简陋，又由于热带风暴的侵害，建筑风格上要求牢固。因此也形成了他们独特的居住方式，他们没有固定的居留住所，平时经常四处漂泊，四海为家，以辽阔的大海为家（戴胜德，2013）。

Tankas' boat-house is a building style for the residents along the coast of Southeast in China. The Tankas mainly live in Fujian, Guangdong and Hainan province. As usual, when the fishers went for deep sea operation, the women were not allowed to accompany her husband considering safety in their traditional customs. However, a crowd of women following their husbands with their children went fishing in Sanyan Hainan, which is their true-to-life portrayal. According to the history, The Kanka's living condition was simple due to their special living environment. Sometimes suffering from tropical storms, so they haven't permanent dwelling places, making their homes wherever they go.

9.2.2 船型屋 Boat-shaped House

在旧时的福建、山东、广东等各沿海地区，都曾有以船为屋的建筑风格。但是，真正集船只与房屋结合且延续至今的是海南文昌、海口、陵水、三亚等地的水上人家。今天，我们已很难在海南的海滨见到船型屋，而在海南深山中的黎寨中我们可以找到原生态的船型屋。那是一座座默默无言的船型屋，看着这一座座船型屋令人想起海上的船型屋，这继承了海岛上的海洋文化。黎族的船型屋与海洋文化息息相关。（详见第四章）

There were some boat-shaped building styles in the coastal areas such as Fujian, Shandong and Guangdong. But the real combination of boat with house was in Wenchang, Haikou, Lingshui and Sanya, which has lasted till now. Nowadays, it's difficult to see the boat-shaped house along the seashore, whereas the traditional boat-shaped houses can be found in the remote mountains in the Li ethnic group. At the sight of the boat-shaped houses in the Li nationality, we can't help recalling the boat-shaped house along the seaside. Above all, it approves that the boat-shaped houses are closely related to the marine cultures.

9.3 海洋饮食
Marine-styled Food and Beverage

　　自古以来人类就有"民以食为天"的说法。人们常说："靠山吃山，靠海吃海。"沿海居民的食物中大多数就地取材以海洋食物为主，从大海中捕捉贝类食物来充当食物。现在我国沿海地区发现大量遗存的贝丘遗址，这些贝丘遗址以前都是我们的先民们把吃剩下来贝壳抛弃在居住地附近，长年累月堆积而成的。随着社会生产力的不断提高，航海事业也随之不断发展，捕鱼工具不断完善，先民们逐渐开始以海洋捕鱼为生，过着以海为家的海洋生活。

　　在长期的海洋生活过程中，南海渔民的吃、穿、行无不表现出特定的海上渔家风俗习惯，就是一切都在围绕着"海洋""海岛""海味"来展开，而且深刻体现出海洋文化独特的魅力和特定的海洋生活特征。

From time immemorial, a famous saying goes like this, people regard food as their prime want. It is also said that those living on a mountain live off the mountain while those living near the water live off the water. Therefore, the people living along the coast live off the ocean, such as some shellfish. Some shell mounds, which were thrown by people and piled for a long time after eating, were found in coastal areas in China. With the development of social production and navigation, the fishermen's tools were improved, and their ancestors gradually took fishing to make a living. The fishermen in the South China Sea formed some typical customs in eating, wearing, and working at sea, some of which would be introduced in the following.

9.3.1　南海渔民的海鲜食俗 Fishermen' Food Custom in the South China Sea

　　古往今来，沿海渔民的生活始终都紧紧与"鱼"联系在一起。在日常生活上渔民在吃鱼、吃海鲜中所体现的习俗，真可谓是五花八门、形式不一、风格各异。而且，现在有不少鱼和海鲜的独特吃法，就是由以前的饮食习惯传承下来的。当时生活在海边的渔民食鱼时候，最喜欢的做法还是烩，不仅在制作时更加精细，而且添加有关的佐料，使制作出来的味道更加香脆可口，让人在享受时能够回味无穷。马鲛鱼一直是疍家人的传统美食，疍家人沿袭着古老的海洋味道，没有煎炒烹炸的繁琐工艺，保留原汁原味。疍家人用马鲛鱼做的手打鱼丸，2009年被选入"三亚十大名菜"之一的疍家咸鱼煲，让人垂涎欲滴。节日期间，疍家人一起做一些特色小吃，如糯米团子、海鲜烧烤、月子姜等。猪脚姜是疍家人的招牌传统菜肴之一，是疍家女人在坐月子期间必吃的美食之一。

Fishermen's life along the coast is closely related to fish throughout the ages. That the ways to eat fish and seafood are various leads to special customs of fish eating. Among traditional ways to eat fish, braising is their favorite, which has still been remained till now. The

Spanish mackerel has been a traditional dish for the Tankas. And the ancient method of cooking without frying has been inherited, which keeps the original tastes and prolonged aftertaste in the mouth. The Spanish mackerel balls and the salted fish pot made by Tankas, being listed one of top ten famous dishes in Sanya, would make people watering. The Tankas made some specialties together, such as glutinous rice balls, roasted seafood, etc. Pettitoes with ginger is one of traditional specialties for the Tankas, which is an indispensable dish for women who enter a period of confinement after giving birth to a child.

鱼羹，是渔家人海鲜饮食中一大特色风味食品。鱼、蟹之肉，都可以作为主料来制做鱼羹，如黄鱼羹、鲳鱼羹、鲈鱼羹和蟹肉羹等都是有名的菜肴。因此从古至今，在南海生活的渔姑、渔嫂总是喜欢把做鱼羹和织渔网一样作为自己必须要掌握的管家手艺。鱼羹已经成为渔民的美味佳肴。无论逢年过节还是婚嫁喜宴，酒席上都要摆上一道精制的鱼羹。另外鱼粥、鱼饭，也是南海渔民的海鲜风味美食。制作鱼粥和鱼饭，一般要选取新鲜带鱼作为制作材料。每逢头水带鱼上市或到冬至节时，南海一带的渔家人，总是喜欢做出满满一锅带鱼粥或带鱼饭，让自己家人尽情品尝享受。

Custard of fish or crab, a jelly-like food, is one of specialty for the people living along the coast. The meat of fish and crab can be taken as the main material to make jelly-like food. Fisherwomen, therefore, have regarded making custard of fish and weaving fishing nets as skills from time immemorial. Nowadays, custard of fish has been a delicious dish, which serves as a necessary dish during festivals or weddings. In addition, fish porridge and fish rice are also special. When making fish porridge and fish rice, fresh fish would be taken as materials. Once the winter comes, the fishermen in the South China Sea often make a full pot of fish porridge or rice to entertain their family members.

9.3.2 南海渔民的饮酒习俗 Fishermen's Customs of Beverage in the South China Sea

疍民在新船造好后，举行祭海神、祭船官菩萨仪式，尽情喝着祈求吉祥、平安的喜庆酒，表示即将使用新船挑战大海，谋求生活，求得平安。每年休渔期结束后第一天出海，渔家人总要聚集在渔港滩头，举行隆重的祭海神仪式，用烤猪、水果、糕点、酒等祭品供奉海神，仪式结束，祭品倒入海中，与海神分享丰收，祈求海神的保佑出海平安、大获丰收。祭海神的仪式结束、捕鱼平安归来，疍民也会饮酒。海马、海参、海蛇、海虾等海珍配以酒水，即为海珍酒，有祛风除湿、壮腰补肾、强身健体等功效。

When the new boat was built by Tankas, they used to drink wine and offer sacrifices to the sea, praying for safety and good luck. After a long break, when the fishermen went to the sea the first time, they always gathered to hold a grand celebration of the sea with roast pigs, fruits, cakes and wine at the fishing harbor. After the ceremony finished, the sacrificial offerings were thrown into the sea to share with the Sea God praying for safety and good harvest. When the fishermen went fishing and returned safely, they usually drank a kind of wine, which combined hippocampus, trepang, snake and shrimp with wine together, with the functions of eliminating wind and dampness, invigorating kidney, keeping fit and so on.

9.4 海洋节庆
Marine Festivals and Holidays

海南海洋文化传统浓厚，海洋节庆民俗别具一格，已成为海洋民俗旅游不可或缺的重要组成部分。

Hainan is blessed with traditional marine cultures and particular marine festivals, which have become an indispensable part of the maritime tourism.

9.4.1 元宵节"鲤鱼灯游村" Parade with Carp-shaped Lanterns during the Lantern Festival

元宵之夜，琼海沿海渔乡"鲤鱼灯闹春"是展现海洋文化的一道风景线，其历史渊源可追溯到明朝，历经600余年至今仍常盛不衰（甘先琼，1995）。《琼海县志》第三章"民间文艺"的第一节"灯彩"记载："民间流行的灯彩有两类：一是配有锣鼓、演员，载歌载舞的灯彩，如鲤鱼灯……潭门镇的鲤鱼灯等，甚享盛名。""表演者手持鱼珠、蛟龙、鲤鱼，由7～9人组成。一人操举鱼珠，戏逗蛟鱼游动，其式样有鲤鱼结珠、吐珠、穿梭和戏水等。每逢春节、元宵期间，鲤鱼灯常到农民、渔民家拜年，主人摆设香茶，热情迎接。表演结束前，鱼灯对正堂香案行一鞠躬，并呼'恭喜发财'。后由主人赠送红封，以示'还福'。"

During the Lantern Festival, the custom of Carp-shaped Lantern reveling in the spring in coastal villages of Qionghai is featured with marine culture, which can date back to the Ming Dynasty (1368-1644). It was recorded in *Qionghai County Annals* that carp-shaped lanterns in Tanmen used to be well-known. People held the carp-shaped lanterns and sent greetings to fishermen or peasants during the Spring Festival and the Lantern Festival. They would be received warmly, treated with tea, and handed a red envelope containing money for their best wishes.

沿海地区，鱼代表着财富，鲤与利谐音，寓意大吉大利、财运亨通；灯与丁谐音，寓意人丁兴旺。当鲤鱼灯队开始游进某座村庄时，"咚咚锵、咚咚锵……"的锣鼓声便开始响起，按惯例首先要到村公庙拜祀村公神明。鲤鱼灯队在村公庙前祭拜村公神明，庙祝给过红包，然后燃放鞭炮。在村公庙表演结束，庙祝便带鲤鱼灯队挨家挨户拜年祝福。"鲤鱼灯闹春"庆祝过去一年的丰收，展望来年的美好，增添了春节的喜庆气氛。

Fish represents wealth and fortune in the coastal areas. The character "鲤" (lǐ, carp) is homophonic with "利" (lì, profit, gain or good luck), and "灯" (dēng, lantern or lamp) is homophonic with "丁" (ding, member of family, a flourishing population). When the carp-shaped lantern team paraded through a certain village, they would pay respect to gods in the village temple, with the sound of drums and gongs heard here and there. The red envelopes with money would be handed to them, and the firecrackers would be set off. After the carp-shaped lantern show, Miaozhu (person in charge of incense and religious serve in a temple) would lead them to the village and send greetings from door to door. The custom of Carp-shaped Lantern reveling in the spring is to celebrate the harvest in the previous year and look forward to prosperity and good luck in the following year, which adds the festivity of the occasions.

9.4.2 "二月二"三亚龙抬头节 Sanya Dragon's Head-raising Festival on 2nd Day of 2nd Lunar Month

海南民间保留淳朴的崇龙习俗。农历二月二日,海南各地民众尤其是渔民,都会自发到龙神庙或水畔焚香上供祭祀龙神,开展祭海活动,祈愿来年风调雨顺,五谷丰登。是日,海口举行盛大祭海仪式。为了深入挖掘中国传统民俗信仰,展现海南崇龙文化,着力推进海南旅游文化建设,首届三亚龙抬头节于2005年举行。2016年农历二月二日,第十二届中国三亚龙抬头节在三亚大小洞天旅游区隆重举行。南海龙王别院祭祀广场正对海面上约300只渔船自发组织参加龙抬头祭龙仪式,船上挂龙旗、放鞭炮,集体祭祀南海龙王,传承并发扬南海祭海、祭龙的民间习俗,表达中华儿女对风调雨顺的祈愿和捍卫南海主权的决心。龙抬头节期间,游客可尽情享受龙抬头节特色美食、海南民俗表演,塑造更多独具三亚魅力的民俗活动,进一步塑造三亚龙抬头节的品牌形象。

Hainan retains the customs of dragon worship. On the 2nd day of the 2nd lunar month, people in Hainan, fishermen in particular, will go to temples or river banks to offer sacrifices in the hope of a bumper grain harvest in the following year. In order to probe into dragon worship and other Chinese traditional folk beliefs, the 1st Sanya Dragon's Head-raising Festival was held in 2005 to highlight typical tourism cultures in Hainan province. The 12th Dragon's Head-raising Festival was staged on the same day in 2016, with 300 boats or ships participating in passing on the traditional custom of offering sacrifices to the Dragon King in the South China Sea. Tourists could enjoy the local dishes and distinctive folk performances during the festival, which was good for shaping the brand image of Sanya Dragon's Head-raising Festival.

9.4.3 "洗龙水"的端午节 Xi Long Shui during the Dragon Boat Festival

海南端午节约始于宋代,有"洗龙水"、包粽子、洗艾水、赛龙舟等传统习俗,其中"洗龙水"颇具特色。海南民众坚信,经过"洗龙水"会沾染龙神的吉利,身体更加健康(详见第三章)。

The Dragon Boat Festival in Hainan may date back to Song Dynasties (960-1279), with the customs of Xi Long Shui (swimming or bathing in dragon water), bathing with mugwort, making Zong Zi (pyramid-shaped dumplings made of glutinous rice wrapped in bamboo or reed leaves), and participating in the Dragon Boat Race, with the first one filled with typical features. The local people near the sea in Hainan will flock to the beach to swim, and they firmly believe that the water on that day is associated with good health and the dragon which is the emblem of good fortune in Chinese culture.

9.4.4 七月半"鬼节" The Ghost Day on 15th Day of 7th Lunar Month

农历七月十五日,道教称中元节,佛教称为盂兰节,俗称"鬼节"。海南称七月十五日为"七月半",也叫"鬼节"。海南不同区域习俗不一样,从农历七月九日至十五日都有人过节,烧五色纸和放孔明灯,除祭祖先(做公婆)、七方老爷和土地公(琼海人称为"割红",必须先在称之为香火室的自家主屋"割红"后"做公婆")之外,有些万泉河沿岸民众还有"送水灯"习俗,祭上、中、下多河侯王,沿海群众还要祭海神、"放海灯"。

The 15th day of the 7th lunar month is known as Zhong Yuan Festival by Taoists, the Obon

Festival by Buddhists, and the Ghost Day by common people. Customs during the festival vary from town to town, including burning five-colored papers, launching Kongming Lanterns, offering sacrifices to the gods or goddesses first and their own ancestors followed, and putting the lanterns on the river or the sea in honor of the deceased King and God of the Sea.

9.4.5 海南潭门南海传统文化节 The South China Sea Traditional Cultural Festival in Tanmen Hainan

海南潭门渔民是世界历史上唯一连续开发南海的特有群体。自宋代开始，潭门渔民自编自用《更路簿》扬帆起航到过西沙、中沙、南沙辛勤耕耘南海"祖宗海"。潭门渔民自古以来就有开捕祭海的民俗。为了展现原汁原味的潭门渔民传统民俗、传承南海航道更路簿等非物质文化遗产、全力打造特色旅游经济文化、宣传潭门渔民勇闯南海的创业精神和维护祖国主权和领土完整的爱国主义精神，自 2010 年首次举办至 2015 年 10 月，海南琼海潭门镇已成功举办六届南海传统文化节。海南琼海南海传统文化节期间，潭门举办传统民间祭出海仪式、渔民传统生产技能比赛、舞龙舞狮表演等，颇具地方特色。2015 年潭门镇第六届南海传统文化节于 8 月 1 日上午举行，举行了祭龙王、海神娘娘、祭船，送渔灯等活动，独特的祭海民俗历史悠久，文化内涵丰富。

Tanmen fishermen, the only special group of people in the world history, are dedicated to developing the South China Sea. Since the Song Dynasties (960-1279), Tanmen fishermen have been hunting fish in Xisha, Zhongsha, and Nansha islands of the South China Sea with the help of self-compiled navigation manual named Geng Lu Bu (Ancient Hainanese Navigation Manual in the South China Sea). Tanmen fishing port was recognized as one of the top projects by national Department of Agriculture in 2004, and a nation-wide civilized fishing port in 2010. The custom of offering sacrifices to the sea commenced from time immemorial as long as they started fishing. The 1st South China Sea Traditional Cultural Festival was held in 2010 with many activities, such as lion dance, tug-of-war, fishing net knitting, conch blowing, etc. The sixth Festival was held on the morning of August 1st 2015, and the 1st Beachcombing Festival was held on the afternoon of the same day, with time-honored sacrifice-offering ritual most impressive among many activities.

9.4.6 海南潭门赶海文化节 Beachcombing Festival in Tanmen

根据潮涨潮落的规律，赶在潮落的时机，到海岸的滩涂和礁石上打捞或采集海产品，即为赶海。

Going to the beach to collect seafood on the coastal shoals and reefs when the tide ebbs is named Beachcombing.

潭门位于南海之滨，海岸线绵延 8 公里，从海岸线伸至海里 2 公里纵深为礁盘地质结构，构架起近 20 平方公里开阔而平缓的浅滩。受益于天梯引力和特殊地理位置，潭门形成了独特的潮汐规律，成为世界少有的优质赶海场所。潭门潮汐为典型的全日潮，农历每月初一、十五之后的两三天内，各有一次大潮，潮水涨得最高退的最低。初八、廿三之后两三天内，各有一次小潮，涨退幅度不大，当地人称之为"思潮"。农历九月至次年三月，每月初一、十五日及前后三天，涨潮的高潮期均在上午，当地人称之为"冬潮"。每年农历四月至八月，每月初一、十五日及前后三天，退潮最低的时间均在白天午后，当地人称之为"夏潮"。当地渔民在高潮期可围网"打八袋""钢铁压网""潜水探宝",低潮期可徒步"涉水刮裸""赤脚拾贝"。此时,阳光没有那么热毒,潮水退的低,有些地方甚至裸露海底,捡螺拾贝最惬意。

Located in Qionghai city, Tanmen's coastline stretches for 8 kilometers, and 2 kilometers from the coastline to the sea is reef geological structure, which forms a shallow area of nearly 20 square kilometers. Thanks to the gravity and special geographical position, Tanmen is bestowed with a unique tide, which makes it one of the top beachcombing beaches. There is a syzygial tide on the second or the third day of every lunar month, and the other is on the sixteenth or seventeenth day of every lunar month, when the ebb tide is most suitable for beachcombing. Local fishermen take various strategies to collect seafood when the tide ebbs. During the above mentioned short specific period from the fourth to the eighth lunar month, people can enjoy beachcombing while bathing in the sun.

2015年海南潭门首届赶海节于8月1日下午在琼海市潭门镇隆重开幕,活动包含赶海寻宝大赛、渔港之夜沙滩音乐会、赶海随手拍大赛、潭门海鲜盛宴、"一带一路"文化展等,当天约吸引全国各地8万名群众。该节日持续两天,共吸引11万人次。2016年,潭门赶海节升级为赶海季,从7月到8月,开展三大主题活动:赶海季启动仪式、海洋宝贝养成计划、潭门赶海节,游客可欣赏传统民间祭海仪式、潭门渔港之夜音乐晚会、赶海寻宝大赛等活动。

The first grand opening ceremony of Tanmen Beachcombing Festival was held on the afternoon of August 1st in 2015. The activities include the treasure hunting, beach concert, Beachcombing photos contest, seafood feast, culture exhibition of the Belt and Road Initiative-related countries or regions. The festival lasts two days, attracting approximately 110,000 people across the country. The second festival in 2016 was upgraded to beachcombing season from July to August with commencing ceremony, baby cultivation plan, and beachcombing festival held, During the Beachcombing Festival, visitors can take part in activities, such as the traditional Sacrifices-offering Ceremony to the sea, live concert on the beach, Treasure Hunting Contest, etc.

9.4.7 三亚国际海洋文化节 Sanya Marine Cultural Festival

三亚结合浓郁的渔乡风情和滨海旅游特色,打造出缤纷的三亚(国际)海洋文化节。首届三亚(国际)海洋文化节于2010年12月成功举办,内容包括海洋文化、海洋经济、美丽经济等三大板块,举办海洋文化论坛、诗书画作品展、海洋产品博览、国际游艇展、海洋旅游推介、"海上丝绸之路"国际小姐形象大赛、文艺晚会等活动,海洋文化品味深厚。

Integrating distinctive features of fishing villages with coastal tourism, the first Sanya Marine Cultural Festival was staged in December 2010, including marine culture forum, exhibition of poetry, calligraphy and painting, marine products Expo, international yacht exhibition, marine tourism promotion, the Maritime Silk Road International Miss competition, entertainment show, and other activities.

9.4.8 三亚疍家文化节 The Tanka's Cultural Festival

疍家人被称为"疍民",即水上居民,以海为田、以鱼为活的海上游牧民族。"疍民"起源可以追溯到7000年前的河姆渡时期。发源于海洋的疍家文化是三亚的根文化,经过数千年的传承和发展，已经形成了特色民俗风情和文化内涵。为了更好地传承疍家文化艺术精髓，打造三亚本土海洋特色文化品牌形象，2014年6月，为期5天的"中国·三亚首届疍家文化节"在三亚大东海广场正式开幕，通过举办疍家文化讲坛、疍家美食、疍家图片展示、主题晚会等系列活动，沿袭着古老的祭海习俗，上高香、敬五谷五果与三牲，唱咸水歌、跳祭舞、舞龙灯鱼灯，让普通民众和游客能进一步了解这个特殊的"水上人家"族群，了解三亚神秘的疍家文化。伴随海南省非物质文化遗产项目"疍歌"代表性传承人——梁云志演唱的悠扬咸水歌曲调，2015年11月24日，来自陵水、昌江、海口等地的疍家渔民代表一同参加在三亚技师学院体育馆举办的中国·三亚第二届疍家文化节开幕仪式。为期两天的文化节将举办"开幕式暨咸水歌大赛、醉美疍家百图摄影展、最美渔家女织渔网大赛和闭幕式暨颁奖晚会"等四大特色主题活动。

The Tankas or boat people, who have traditionally lived on junks in coastal parts of Guangdong, Guangxi, Fujian, Hainan, Zhejiang, Hong Kong, and Macau, are an ethnic subgroup. Tankas' origins could be traced back to the native ethnic minorities in southern China 7000 years ago. In order to preserve native traditions of the Tankas, the first Tankas' Cultural Festival was celebrated in Dadonghai Square of Sanya by holding Tankas' culture forum, cuisine show, Tankas' picture exhibition, theme parties, and other activities, followed by the traditional customs of offering sacrifices to the sea, burning the incense, singing Xianshui folk songs, etc. to unveil the mystery of the Tankas in Sanya. November 24th 2015 witnessed the opening ceremony of the second Tankas' Cultural Festival in Sanya Technician College of Hainan by singing a Xianshui folk song first, with the Tankas from Lingshui, Changjiang, Haikou, etc. participating in four activities, namely Xianshui folk songs contest, Tankas photography exhibition, women's net-weaving competition, and award party.

9.4.9 琼州妈祖文化节（天后圣母节、妈祖信俗）Qiongzhou Matsu Cultural Festival (Matsu' Day, Matsu Belief and Customs)

为了弘扬民族文化，传播妈祖精神，首届琼州妈祖文化节于2013年4月在海口市比干妈祖文化园隆重举行。妈祖文化起源于宋代，明朝妈祖文化逐渐走向世界，是传承了上千年的民俗文化之一。2006年5月，妈祖祭典被列入第一批国家级非物质文化遗产名录；2009年9月，妈祖信俗在联合国申报人类非物质文化遗产代表作名录获得成功，成为中国首个世界级文化遗产的信俗类非物质文化遗产项目。琼州妈祖文化随闽人渡琼传入海南，至今已有700多年的历史。妈祖在海南信众较多，民俗文化活动丰富。

The first Qiongzhou Matsu Cultural Festival was held in Bigan and Matsu Cultural Garden in Haikou to promote Matsu culture. Matsu cultures and customs may date back to Song Dynasties (960-1368), and scattered all over the world, which made it pass on from one generation to another for thousand years. Mastu Memorial Ceremony was listed in the national intangible cultural heritage by the State Council in May 2006. The Matsu Belief and Customs, as the first worldwide belief-and-custom intangible cultural heritage, was officially included in the intangible cultural heritage by UNESCO in 2009. Matsu culture and custom were introduced to Hainan by the immigrants from Fujian province 700 years ago. With a great many people believing in Matsu home and abroad, plenty of activities are held during the grand festival every year.

9.4.10 文昌南洋文化节 Nanyang Cultural Festival in Wenchang

文昌是海南的重点侨乡，120多万文昌籍海外华侨华人遍布世界50多个国家和地区。为了加强与海内外乡亲沟通交流合作、畅叙乡情、传承并弘扬华侨文化，自2012年举办首届文昌南洋文化节，已成功举办五届。2016年文昌第五届南洋文化节，共有来自19个国家和地区200多人参加，参与的国家（地区）、社团数量和参与人数均屡创历史新高，举办文艺晚会、美食展销会、海内外乡亲座谈会、书画展、羽毛球、乒乓球及门球友谊赛等活动。

Wenchang is a key hometown of overseas Chinese in Hainan, about 1200000 overseas Chinese from Wenchang scattered in more than 50 countries and regions. In order to facilitate the communication, exchanges and cooperation, Nanyang Cultural Festival has been successfully held annually since 2012. More than 200 overseas Chinese from 19 countries or regions participated in the 5th Nanyang Cultural Festival, during which many activities were held, such as entertainment party, cuisine fair, informal discussion, calligraphy and painting exhibition, friendly badminton match, etc.

9.4.11 沙雕节 Sand Sculptures' Festival

2013年1月，由中国舟山国际沙雕协会、海口市艺术家协会主办，滨海·新天地承办的海南省首届沙雕艺术节暨沙雕嘉年华艺术创作大赛在海口西海岸拉开帷幕，邀请了来自全国的16个沙雕代表队参赛，完成"天涯海角""白雪公主""帝国大厦""迪斯尼乐园"等作品佳品，吸引了众多市民和爱好者前往观看。

The first Sand Sculptures' Festival was co-organized by China Zhoushan International Sand Sculpture Association and Haikou Artists Association in Haikou, with 16 teams participating in the contest and some stone sculptures completed, such as Tian Ya Hai Jiao, Snow White, Empire State Building, Disneyland, etc.

限于篇幅，其他海洋性节日，如世界海洋日、航海日、风筝节、渔灯节、休渔放生节、渔船生日、海南潭门海鲜美食文化周等，不再赘述。

Due to the limited space, other marine festivals, such as the World Ocean Day, Maritime Day, Kite Festival, Fishing Lantern Festival, Fishing Moratorium and Free Captive Festival, Fishing Boats' Birthday, Hainan Tanmen Seafood Cultural Festival, will not be described in this section.

9.5 海洋神灵崇拜
Marine Worship

据史载，早在夏商周时期，帝王就对大海祭礼。海南海神崇拜较为普遍，涉海神话传说在海南民间广为流传，这些已深深植根于海南民间的传统习俗。

It is recorded that the emperor offered sacrifices to the sea since the period of Xia, Shang and Zhou Dynasties (2070 BC-221 BC). Worship for Gods or Goddesses of the Sea is common, and marine-related tales are also quite popular with the folk, which have been deeply rooted in

Hainan folk customs and traditions.

9.5.1 妈祖 Matsu (Ma Zu)

妈祖是海南民间崇敬的神祇，民众妈祖信仰历史悠久。相传妈祖为福建莆田林姓人家女儿，生于宋太祖建隆元年（960年），从小吃斋茹素，后来羽化升天，经常在海上抢险救难，被皇帝敕封为"天后""圣母"。据记载，宋元时期"天后娘娘"落籍海南。不完全统计，海南各时期共修建妈祖庙达 100 处之多。海口中山路天后宫，保存完整、年代久远，已有 700 多年历史。临高调楼镇的妈祖庙，临海而建，为海南最高大的妈祖庙，已有 300 多年的历史。妈祖信仰已深深融入海南沿海民众，尤其是渔民的血液（司徒尚纪，2009）。每逢农历三月廿三妈祖诞辰日、九月九日妈祖升天日，祭典仪式都较为隆重。

Matsu has been respected and worshiped for a long time by the folk people. It is said that she was born in 960 in Putian of Fujian province with surname Lin. She was a vegetarian, and went to the heaven after passing away. She often rescued the people in the sea, and was conferred on the Queen of the Heaven by the emperor. It is reported that Matsu was introduced into Hainan between Song and Yuan Dynasties (960-1368). Incomplete statistics indicate that more than 100 temples have been built in Hainan, with the one on Zhongshan Road retained for over 700 years. The Matsu Temple in Diaolou town of Lin'gao county is the largest one with a history of more than 300 years. Matsu Belief is deeply implanted in the people's minds along the coastal areas, with the fishermen in particular. The sacrifices offering ceremony will be held on the 23rd day of the 3rd lunar month and the 9th day of the 9th lunar month.

9.5.2 108 兄弟公 108 Bothers

海南"108 兄弟公"为本岛土生土长的海神。据传，清朝咸丰年间，"108 兄弟"于农历 9 月 15 日不幸遇难者，他们的英魂变成了海神，扶弱救危，显圣海上，被封为"昭应英烈 108 忠魂"。后来，人们在文昌的铺前和清澜港建庙祭祀称"昭应庙""孤魂庙"或"兄弟公庙"。如今，海南人到达过的几乎所有地方，都为"兄弟公"单独建庙或在其他寺庙中拜祭他们。潭门人每年正月十五、五月初五和七月十五要祭拜三次"兄弟公"，祈求保佑出海的人平安归来。

108 Bothers are the regional marine gods for Hainanese. It was said the 108 Bothers died on the 15th day of 9th lunar month during the reign the Emperor Xianfeng (1851-1861) in Qing Dynasty (1636-1912), and turned to sea gods to protect and rescue the people who were in trouble, so they were conferred on 108 heroes. 108 Brothers Temples with various names were built in Puqian port and Qinglan port of Wenchang. Nowadays, 108 Brothers' Temples have been built wherever Hainanese go, and they are offered sacrificed even they are placed in other temples. The people in Tanmen will pay respect to 108 Bothers on the 15th day of the 1st lunar month, the 5th day of the 5th lunar month, and 15th day of the 7th lunar month respectively to pray for fishermen's safe return.

9.5.3 水尾圣娘 Goddess Shuiwei

水尾圣娘，源于海南文昌清澜港，全称"南天闪电感应火雷水尾圣娘"，亦称南天夫人，被奉为海南人的乡土神，被渔民视为守护神。作为一种海神信仰，信徒主要分布在海南文昌、海口、琼海，以及文莱、柬埔寨、泰国等琼籍华人聚居区。相传，文昌清澜所东岸（今东郊镇）北港村潘氏族人潘敏理所修建的"圣娘庙"位于"水尾"（海水之终点），故此庙取名"水尾圣娘庙"。海南当地人一般亲切称水尾圣娘为"婆祖"或"祖婆"，而海外文昌人称其为"南海第一灵神"。海南民间把农历10月15日定为水尾圣娘诞辰纪念日。自农历10月15日至17日为水尾圣娘庙会日，信徒们烧香祈祷，祈求万事顺心如意。

Goddess Shuiwei was considered as one of the Gods of the Sea by Hainanese in Wenchang, Haikou, Qionghai of Hainan province, and the some regions in Brunei, Kampuchea, Thailand, etc. It is said that the Holy Mother's Temple (Goddess Shuiwei Temple) was built by Pan Minli in Beigang village of Dongjiao town in Wenchang city. Due to the fact that the temple is built at the end of the sea, it is called Holy Mother's Temple (Goddess Shuiwei Temple). The people in Wenchang commonly call the Goddess Shuiwei Po Zu (the beloved mother), and the 15th day of the 10th lunar month is set as her birthday. The period from the 15th to 17th day of the 10th lunar lunar is Goddess Shuiwei Temple Fair, with various folk activities held to pray for good luck.

9.5.4　泰华三仙 Immortals Taihua

泰华仙妃，原名陈玉英，她和两位弟弟被称作"泰华三仙"，是护佑渔民和航海商船的海神。为表彰仙妃，弘德扬善，琼州知府曾奏请元文宗下旨封泰华仙妃为泰华灵感仙妃，清朝再受荣封。据《泰华堂碑文》记载，道教信众为感恩泰华三仙显灵救世，由王德吉带头捐款并于1890年建造泰华堂，供当地居民前往敬拜。每年农历6月12日，泰华仙妃纪念日那天，海口一些群众演戏、焚香、跪拜仙妃婆祖。

Tai Hua Xian Fei (Fairy Maiden Tai Hua) who was originally named Chen Yuying, and her two younger brothers were called Immortals Taihua to protect fishermen and merchant in the sea. In order to praise Fairy Maiden Tai Hua for her charitable deeds, the magistrate of Qiongzhou Prefecture presented a memorial to the Emperor Yuan Wenzong (1304-1332) in Yaun Dynasty (1271-1368) to issue an imperial edict in hope of conferring Telepathic Fairy Maiden Tai Hua upon her. It is recorded in the inscription on the tablet of Tai Hua Memorial Hall, Wang Deji took the initiative in denoting money and built the temple in 1890 in honor of her. On the 12th day of the 6th lunar month, some people in Haikou would put on performances, burn incenses, and kowtow to Fairy Maiden Tai Hua.

9.5.5　三江晶信夫人 Madame Jingxin of the Three Rivers

三江晶信夫人是海南琼海地区信奉的海神。传说，南海龙王的爱妾万泉妃子经不住博鳌美景的诱惑，偷偷带着龙滚、九曲两位太子前往博鳌港嬉戏龙珠。南海龙王得知后龙颜大怒，脱下玉带掷向博鳌，玉带顿时化作沙滩，挡住了归路。归期过后，玉带变成了玉带滩，龙身化作三条河流，龙珠变成三座岛屿。后人以万泉、龙滚、九曲命名三条河流，并在东屿岛修建三江庙，世代供奉造福一方的万泉妃子和两位太子。据《正德琼台志》记载，三江庙"在县（乐会）东十里博鳌浦，宋天圣元年，乡人建祀三江晶信夫人，七月二日持牲致祭。"

Madame Jingxin of the Three Rivers(namely Wanquan River, Jiuqu River and Longgun River), who is deemed a local marine goddess, has been widely worshiped in Qionghai. According to the folk tale, one of the Dragon King's concubines named Wanquan in the

Southern China Sea couldn't help going to enjoy the picturesque landscape in Bo'ao, she went there with two princes named Longgun and Jiuqu, and played with a pearl in Bo'ao port. The Dragon King became furious when knowing everything, and cast his jade belt to Bo'ao, which immediately turned into a shoal blocking their way back. And the jade belt turned into Jade Belt Beach, the King's concubine Wanquan and princes becoming three rivers named Wanquan River, Jiuqu River and Longgun River. Local people built Sanjiang Temple to worship them. It is recorded in *Qingtai Annals* compiled during the reign of the Emperor Wuzong (1506-1521) in Ming Dynasty (1368-1644) that Sanjiang Temple was completed in 1023 in Bo'ao. And people used to offer sacrifices to her on the 2nd day of the 7th lunar month.

9.5.6 峻灵公 Jun Ling Gong (the God of Rock)

峻灵公为海南西部地区渔民信奉的神灵，主要集中在海南临高、儋州、昌江、东方、乐东一带，是海南民众信奉的乡土海神之一。因供奉峻灵公的庙宇坐落在昌江黎族自治县昌化岭下昌城村西，民间亦称其为"昌化公""神山明王"。峻灵公不是人化的神灵，而是因为岭有灵气而得名。据记载，大陈山（今昌化岭）上有一巨石，似人直立，曾被封为镇海广德王。北宋元丰五年（1082）改封峻灵王，建峻灵王庙。渔民出海捕鱼，若看见昌化岭乌云突起，他们就认为是昌化公显灵，告诫渔民风暴即将来临，应立即返港。一些市县还将峻灵公请到当地供奉，如东方港门的"港门老爷"，信徒包括渔民、农民、商贾等。

Jun Ling Gong is one of the marine gods worshiped by the people in the western coastal areas, such as Lin'gao, Danzhou, Changjiang, Dongfang, Ledong, etc. Due to the location of Jun Ling Gong's Temple in Changhua, Jun Ling Gong is also named Chuanghua Gong. As a matter of fact, Jun Ling Gong is well-known for the telepathy of Changhualing Ridge. It was recorded that in the Ridge stood a huge rock which looked like a giant seen from afar. The rock was conferred the Mercy King of the Sea, and Jun Ling Gong in 1082 with a temple built in Northern Song Dynasty (960-1127). They would return to the harbor immediately whenever the fishermen went fishing with the dark clouds over the Changhualing Ridge, because they would think Jun Ling Gong was to foretell that the storm or hurricane was approaching. Some people in other counties have invited Jun Ling Gong to their hometown for worship by fishermen, peasants and merchants, such as the Lord Gangmen in Dongfang city.

9.5.7 南海龙王 The Dragon King of the South China Sea

华夏儿女被认为是龙的传人，在南海受到渔民普遍认可的是南海龙王。三亚大小洞天风景区南海龙王别院，安放有高1.9米、重1吨的南海龙王铜像。由于海南四面环海，出海捕鱼风险较大，人们将祝祷寄托在南海龙王身上，希望可以风调雨顺、救灾救难、保佑平安，也将龙王崇拜具象化、生活化。因此，海南很多沿海村镇都建有龙王庙，更延续和传承了千年祭海、"二月二龙抬头"南海龙王祭典、五月端午节"洗龙水"等传统习俗。

Chinese people are believed to be the Dragon's descendants, and the Dragon King of the South China Sea is accepted widely by fishermen in the southern part of China. A 190-centimeter-high bronze statue of he Dragon King of the South China Sea, which weighs 2000 kilograms, is placed in Sanya Dongtian Park. Hainan is surrounded by sea, and it is of high risk to go fishing in the vast South China Sea. Fishermen and other people alike pray for favorable weather, instant rescue, blessing and safety while fishing or farming with the help of the Dragon King of the South China Sea. Many Dragon King's temples, therefore, have been built in coastal villages or towns, for which the traditional customs of offering sacrifices to the sea, Sacrifice-offering ceremony to the Dragon King on the 2nd day of the 2nd lunar month, Xi Long Shui (swim or bathe in dragon water), etc. have been passed on for hundreds of years.

9.5.8 观音 Bodhisattva

海南民间供奉观音的寺庙不计其数。众多菩萨中，观世音菩萨最为民间熟知，是慈悲和智慧的化身。1993 年中国国务院宗教局和海南省人民政府批准，在三亚南山寺寺前的海中塑高达 108 米的海上观音圣像，一体化三尊，历时 6 载修建。2005 年 4 月 24 日（农历 3 月 16 日）举行盛大开光仪式。如今，前往南山文化旅游区祭拜观世音菩萨的省内外游客络绎不绝。

Bodhisattva is worshiped in numerous temples by people in Hainan. Guanyin Bodhisattva (Mercy Goddess or Goddess of Mercy, avalokiteśvara), who serves as the embodiment of mercy and wisdom, is most well-known among the common people. With the approval of the State Bureau of Religious Affairs of the People's Republic of China and People's Government of Hainan province in 1993, it took 6 years to build 108-meter-high Guanyin Statue on the South China Sea, with the left hand holding sutra in the front side, prayer beads in the right side, and lotus flower in the left side. The grand consecration ritual was held on April 24th, 2005. Nowadays, travelers home and abroad stream to the three-sided Guanyin Bodhisattva on the South China Sea.

9.5.9 船神 God(dess) of Fishing Boats

船神又称船菩萨或船关老爷。很多渔船造好，后舱都设有神龛，祭神仪式后，船神入位，成为保护神。神龛门额挂红绸或黄缎制成的幔帘，横额书写或彩线绣"船官菩萨"四字，条幅上写"顺风得利"等吉祥语。船菩萨旁边站有"顺风耳""千里眼"两位神仙，蕴含"眼观六路，耳听八方，知风识鱼，确保丰收"之意。

A shrine to the God(dess) of Fishing Boats will be set in the rear cabin of the newly-built fishing boat after sacrifices-offering ritual, which would protect the boats and the fishermen from their viewpoints. A heavy red or yellow silk curtain will be hung on the upper part of the lintel of the shrine, with auspicious signs, such as Chinese phrase "船官菩萨" (Bodhisattva in charge of the vessel) or "顺风得利" (handsome catch of fish without trouble). The two immortals named Shun Feng Er (Clairaudience, supernatural being who can hear long-distance voices in traditional Chinese novels) and Qian Li Yan (Clairvoyant) stand by the Bodhisattva to ensure the fishermen can catch plenty of fish with no trouble.

9.5.10 其他 Others

除以上海神信仰，有些海南渔民也信奉木头公、西楚霸王、飓风神、护国圣娘、鲁班师傅至巧大神、忠显灵应大侯王、司禄梓潼帝君、御天显应法师、座道灵公天英上帅、青帝铁笔辛天君、五灵五显火光大帝、赵马将军、儋州"姐妹岩"、儋州"将军印"、某些海洋生物、临海山石或山洞等。限于篇幅，不再赘述。

In addition to the above-mentioned marine god worship, some Hainan fishermen also believe in Mu Tou Gong (or Ben Tou Gong in local dialect, a man named Bai Pixian in Zheng He's Voyages from 1405-1431), the Conqueror Xiang Yu (232 BC-202 BC), the God of Hurricane, etc. Due to the limited space, they would not be discussed here in detail.

2015年4月23日，海南省道教协会在定安文笔峰成功举办"恢复南海诸岛民间庙宇及其民俗文化活动"学术研讨会，研讨如何传承和保护中国沿海人民海洋信仰的文脉。南海诸岛庙宇有娘娘庙（妈祖庙）、108兄弟公庙、观音堂、土地庙、大王庙、石庙、公庙、孤魂庙等。南海岛礁庙宇是重要的文化标志，也是渔民在岛上活动的核心场所之一。恢复南海诸岛的庙宇设施，对传承中国固有的南海祭典文化、满足中国南海渔民的日常信仰需求、维护中国海疆领土完整和民俗文化主权等，影响深远。

The symposium *Restoring the Temples and Folk Cultural Activities on the islands of South China Sea* was held on April 23, 2015 in Wenbifeng Resort of Ding'an county by Hainan Taoist Association to discuss how to inherit and preserve the people's marine worship in coastal areas. There are many temples for Matsu, 108 Brothers, Bodhisattva, etc. on the islands of South China Sea, which serve as important cultural signs and key worship plots on the islands. Therefore, restoring the temples on the islands of the South China Sea is of great significance to pass on the inherent sacrifices-offering ceremony to the Sea, meet the needs of the fishermen in the waters, and maintain the territorial integrity and folk cultural sovereignty.

9.6 海洋文学艺术
Marine Folk Literature and Arts

海洋孕育了生命，也为文学艺术的创作提供了无数的素材。海南人们在耕海过程中，充分发现南海，利用海洋，创造了璀璨的海洋文学艺术。

The vast sea has given birth to life in various forms, and also provided a myriad of materials to create literature and arts. In the process of exploring the South China Sea, Hainanese have been trying their best to discover the South China Sea in an all-round way and making the best use of it, which has yielded scores of literature and arts.

9.6.1 航海天书——《南海更路簿》An Arcane Voyage Book: Geng Lu Bu (Geng Lu Jing, Ancient Hainanese Navigation Manual in the South China Sea)

在海南潭门等地渔民开发南海、经营南海的过程中，最杰出的成果之一即为《南海更路经》，又有《南海水路经》《南海定时经针位》《西南沙更簿》《顺风得利》《注明东、北海更路簿》《去西、南沙的水路簿》等名称这是海南为国家做的历史性贡献，使"南海是中国的"在法理和事实上有了历史明证。《南海更路径》分两类：手抄本形式，流传至今，俗称《南海更路簿》；口头传承，俗称"更路传"。2008年6月，潭门、文昌等地自编自用的《南海更路经》经国务院批准列入第一批国家级非物质文化遗产名录。据考证，《南海更路簿》最迟形成于明代，是我国海南渔民在西沙、南沙等南海海域的航海手册，内容包括航海路线、观天知识、气象和水文知识以及航海线路图等，是古代海南人发现和开发南海诸岛的真实记录。《南海更路簿》中的"更"是一个兼具时间和空间的词，"路"是指帆船在大海中的航路，"簿"则是世世代代相传的手抄本子（许俊，2016）。

While developing and managing the South China Sea, fishermen from Tanmen of Qionghai city and Wenchang city in Hainan completed one of the most outstanding masterpieces named Geng Lu Jing (Ancient Hainanese Navigation Manual in the South China Sea), with other various names, which is of historical importance to prove the vast area in the South China Sea belongs to China based on facts and acts of the fishermen from Hainan. Geng Lu Jing, which is classified into two written and oral types, with the former one commonly known as Geng Lu Bu and preserved till now. Geng Lu Jing was listed in national intangible cultural heritage in June 2008. It is recorded Geng Lu Bu came into being before Ming Dynasty (1368-1644). Geng Lu Bu, which served as a navigation manual in the South China Sea for then fishermen from Hainan, recorded the chart, the climate, meteorological and hydrological knowledge in the South China Sea. In fact, *Geng* is term for both time and space in Chinese, *Lu* for the route in the Sea, and *Bu* for a hand copied book passed on from generation to another.

2015年8月，海南大学周伟民、唐玲玲教授撰写的《南海天书——海南渔民"更路簿"文化诠释》出版发行，该书是首部全面介绍"更路簿"的权威著作。2016年7月10日，《南海更路簿——中国人经略祖宗海的历史见证》图书发行仪式在海南省琼海市潭门镇草塘村举行。由海南省委宣传部指导、海南广播电视总台、三沙卫视制作的电视专题片《我们的更路簿——三沙属于中国的历史证据》于2016年7月11日晚23点27分在央视一套播出，通过采访老船长、更路簿传承者、海疆研究问题专家、外交研究员等全面诠释海南渔民凭借更路簿延续千年的耕海民俗与文化。

The monograph An Arcane Book about the South China Sea: *Cultural Interpretation of the South China Sea Voyage Book formed by fishermen in Hainan* province co-authored by professor Zhou Weimin and Tang Lingling of Hainan university was published in August 2015. The release ceremony of the book *Geng Lu Bu in the South China Sea: Historical Records to Manage our Chinese Ancestor's Sea* was staged on July 10th 2016 in Caotang Village of Tanmen town of Qionghai city. Guided by Publicity Department of the Hainan provincial Party Committee, a television documentary *Our Geng Lu Bu: Historical proof of Chinese Ownership of Sansha Waters* co-produced by Hainan Broadcasting Group and Sansha Satellite TV was broadcast in CCTV-1 on July 11th 2016.

9.6.2 海洋传说 Legend and Myth

椰子

Coconut

关于椰子的传说版本较多，此处仅介绍与海洋相关的其中一个版本。传说，很久很久以前，海南岛遭遇严重干旱，每天都有很多人因为干渴失去生命。危急关头，一位姑娘挺身而出，独自到海边夜以继日挖掘，可一点淡水也没有找到，即使筋疲力尽但她也没有放弃。姑娘的善举打动了妈祖。妈祖给她一颗火红的果子，让她吞下去，姑娘顿时变成了美丽的孔雀，但却像有团火在焚烧她的五脏六腑。于是，孔雀使劲往地下钻，终于，她碰到了甘甜的泉水，痛快地喝了起来。但想到正在遭受干渴折磨的父老乡亲，她使劲地吸水，但水太多了，她的头埋在沙子里再也拔不出来了。后来，孔雀的头和嘴变成了树根，身体变成了树干，尾巴变成了树叶，结出了很多沉甸甸的果实。乡亲们摘下果子，尽情引用甘甜的汁水，终于得救了。那位勇敢的姑娘永远地化作了树，因为她的名字叫椰子，为了纪念，人们便称这种树为椰子树，果实为椰子。无论海南暴风强度、海水咸度多大，英雄化身的椰子依然挺拔。如今，海南椰林遍地，延续着那位姑娘的善良和勇敢。至今，海南很多市县依然保留结婚、生子时栽种椰子的习俗。

  There are many legends about the coconut, and one of them associated with the ocean is introduced as follows. Once upon a time, Hainan Island suffered from a severe drought, and a lot of people died of thirst every day. A girl took the initiative in digging a well for fresh water by the seaside day after day, but in vain. She didn't give up no matter how exhausted she was, which moved Matsu deeply. And Matsu presented her with a fiery fruit, and asked her to swallow it. Suddenly, the girl turned into a beautiful peacock, but the fiery fruit seemed to be burning in her stomach. The peacock drilled into the ground on and on, sweet fresh water spurted out, and she helped herself to water. She wanted to drink as much water as possible when taking thirsty people into account. She drank so much water that she couldn't pulled her head out of the sand. And her head and mouth turned into the root, body to trunk, and tail to leaves, which resulted in a high yield of coconuts. The people plucked coconuts for water, and they were saved. The girl became a tree, which was named coconut palm in honor of her due to the fact that her name was Coconut. Coconut palms still grow by the seaside to continue the girls' bravery. The custom of planting coconut palms has been remained till now when marrying somebody or giving birth to babies.

博鳌

Bo'ao

  传说，南海龙王敖钦的女儿"小龙女"艰难诞下一子，名"鳌"，长相奇异：龙头、龟背、麒麟尾。龙王见女儿生此怪物，勃然大怒，一气抽出腰间玉带抛向凡间便形成海河最窄交界的"玉带滩"，阻隔"鳌"母子欲归南海之路。小龙女苦苦哀求，望龙王认"鳌"，三秋未果，心力交瘁，最终化作"龙潭岭"。"鳌"凶性大发，兴风作浪，祸及百姓。观音闻讯，脚踏莲花赶至南海，将"鳌"降服，点化"鳌"成"鳌龙"，留下原身化作"东屿岛"，卸下莲花宝座，即为现在的"莲花礁"。终于，惊涛骇浪化为龙滚河，聚百川千水为万泉河，合纵溢横流为九曲江，三江鳌头会合，直泻南海。观音乘"鳌"而去，留下这片美丽而神奇的宝地——博鳌。如今，博鳌小镇已成为亚洲博鳌论坛永久会址。正如唐代怀仁和尚云："伏鳌者圣，得鳌者贤"，博鳌论坛正扮演越来越重要的角色，向世界发出最强音。

  According to the legend, the South China Sea Dragon King Ao Qin's daughter gave birth to a son after going through difficulties, and named Ao (a kind of huge turtle in legend) with a strange look: dragon's head, turtle's neck, and kylin's tail. The Dragon King burst into fury at the sight of Ao and cast the jade belt into the shoal to keep them from returning to the South China Sea. The Dragon King's daughter pleaded with the King to take Ao as one of the family members, but in vain. She turned into Longtanling Ridge, which made Ao angry. And he did damage to many people. Guanyin Bodhisattva (Mercy Goddess or Goddess of Mercy, avalokiteśvara) heard the news, rushed to the South China Sea to make Ao gave in, and turned him into a dragon. Ao's original body changed into Dongyu Island. At length, turbulent river returned to normal, which was named Longgun River. Together with Wanquan River and Jiuqu River, the three rivers meet at the head of the Ao and flow to the South China Sea. Guanyin flew away by Ao, with the beautiful land remained. Nowadays, the Bo'ao town has been the permanent site of Bo'ao Forum for Asia (abbreviate for BFA), which has been playing an increasingly important role in the world.

哩哩美

Maiden named Lilimei

哩哩美又称哩哩妹起源于临高新盈等地的南海民谣,在海洋生活与生产中以口头传唱而孵化出的优美动听的渔歌。其于 2008 年被列入海南省第二批非物质文化遗产名录。渔歌哩哩美的传说都与爱情有关。据《临高民间故事荟萃》之《哩哩妹与乃马哩》描述:南宋绍兴年间(1131—1162年),新盈港有一位漂亮阿妹,歌声极美,人们称她为哩哩妹。她貌美无比,吸引无数渔家小伙,也招来邻港渔霸垂涎,并扬言要在八月十五中秋节娶她为妾。一个名叫乃马哩的小伙子一直暗恋哩哩妹,他机智勇敢,带领渔民战胜渔霸,最终与哩哩妹喜结良缘。婚礼当天,众人纵情高歌,并把哩哩妹和乃马哩作为衬词加入歌曲,渔歌"哩哩美"由此诞生。另一个传说也是凄美哀婉的生离死别故事。中国水利水电出版社出版的《民歌故事集》中写道,很久以前临高角居住着一位美丽的仙女,她与雷州半岛一位英俊青年相爱,但两人被琼州海峡分隔难以相见。二人痛下决心修筑堤堰,他们的真心感动海龟和海鸟,都参与帮忙,但要合拢时被巡海的夜叉发现,引来风暴吹跨堤堰,不愿分离的男女青年变身灯楼角和临高角,两人用渔歌哩哩美隔海传情。如今,渔歌哩哩美传唱南海,在广东、广西、海南等沿海港口,都能听到哩哩美动人的旋律。

Originating in the folk song in Xinying town of Lin'gao city, the fishing styled songs Li Li Mei in Lin'gao style, which was created based on the marine life and production, was listed in Hainan intangible cultural heritage. The folk song is closely related to love stories. According to the Lin'gao Folktales, a beautiful girl named Lilimei lived in Xinying town during the Shaoxing period (1131-1162) of the Southern Song Dynasty (1127-1279), and she was good at singing songs. She was so pretty that many young fishermen chased her, including some gangsters, one of whom asserted to marry her as a concubine on August 15. A young man named Naimali had a crush on her secretly. He was brave to lead the fishermen to defeat the gangster, and eventually married Li Li Mei. During their wedding, people were indulged in singing folk songs, with their names added into the song, which made the song Lilimei come into being. The other one in Folk Song Stories published by *China Water and Power Press* goes like this: a beautiful fairy lived in Lin'gao Cape, who fell in love with a young man in Leizhou Peninsula, but separated by the Qiongzhou Strait. They were determined to build a dike, and their sincerity moved the turtles and seabirds who helped them build the dike. Unfortunately, the dike was destroyed when being discovered by patrol Yakşa. And the young man and woman became Denglou Cape in Xuwen county of Zhanjiang city and Lin'gao Cape, who conveyed their tender feeling by singing folk songs Li Li Mei. Nowadays, the folk song is still sung by people in coastal areas, including Guangdong province, Guangxi province, Hainan province, etc.

限于篇幅,南海鲛人、天涯海角、鹿回头、大力神、网神海瑞、北斗七星兄弟、儋州海头"二月二"等传说,不再赘述。

Due to the limited space, other legends, such as the mermaid in the South China Sea, Tian

Ya Hai Jiao, Lu Hui Tou, etc., will not be discussed.

9.6.3 海洋谚语 Proverbs

在耕海历程中，海南渔民总结了很多涉海谚语，如"春前有雨春后干，春后有雨打台风"；"三月东风晒死草，四月东风拖船走"；"六月东风拖船走，八月东风收米斗"；"走平地，防摔跤；顺水船，防暗礁"；"嘱子嘱孙，勿忘三月春"；"三月三，海舷尽人脚"；"春钓边，秋钓滩，夏季钓中间"；"七月初七夜，捉鱼无处晾"；"抢过大船头，三年不用愁"；"无风起长浪，必有强风刮"；"龟背潮，是雨兆"；"鱼虾返水面，大雨将没田"；"九月九，台风卷船走"；"潮水哈哈响，要有大风降"……这些谚语用词朴实易懂，句式工整对称，读起来朗朗上口；通过白描、夸张、拟人、比喻等修辞手法，将科学性与实用性融于一体，言简意赅，把海洋生活的哲理表达得淋漓尽致。

In the process of exploring the South China Sea, many marine related proverbs have been created by the fishermen in Hainan: Where there is rain before the beginning of the spring there will be drought during the spring; Where there is rain after the spring there will be typhoon; East wind in the third lunar month makes the grass die, and east wind in the fourth lunar month makes the boat go; East wind in the sixth lunar month makes the boat go, and that in the eighth lunar month brings plenty of rice; The third lunar month does count; Fortune knocks while fishing on the bank in the spring, on the low-lying land in the autumn, and the middle in the summer; Fortune comes at the night of 7th day of the 7th lunar month; Who drives faster yields more while fishing; Billows without wind brings typhoon; Turtle's wet back is the sign of rain; When fish and shrimp swim in the surface, the heavy rain will come; Typhoon in the 9th day of the 9th lunar month makes the boat go; Strong wind comes with the loud sound of tide, etc. All the above-mentioned sayings with exaggeration, personification, metaphor, etc. depict the marine life vividly.

限于篇幅，海洋诗词歌赋、涉海雕刻、涉海舞蹈、涉海影视、涉海命名、涉海禁忌等不再赘述。

Due to the limited space, marine related poems, sculptures, dances, videos, naming, taboos, etc. are not to be discussed in this section.

10

海南民间艺术民俗
Hainan Folk Arts and Customs

民间艺术是劳动人民直接创造的或劳动群众中广泛流传的艺术,包括音乐、舞蹈、造型艺术、工艺美术等。它从不同层面集中地反映了当地各族人民在音乐、舞蹈及工艺美术方面的民俗历史风貌。在近半个世纪的生产生活中,海南人民创造了多彩、辉煌的民间艺术,处处彰显着颇具海南特色的民俗风情。

Folk arts are the kind of arts that were either created by the working class or the arts that were already widespread among the people. They reflect the historic customs of the local people and encompass items such as music, dance, visual arts, handicrafts and others. Not only do these definitions apply to Hainan, in fact, in addition to it, people of Hainan have created very colorful and exceptional folk arts with great characteristics of their own. This has been more profound, particularly during the past fifty years.

10.1 海南民间工艺美术
Hainan Folk Arts and Crafts

10.1.1 海南民间雕刻 Hainan Folk Carvings

雕刻,是指用各种可塑材料(如石膏、树脂、粘土等)或可雕、可刻的硬质材料(如木材、石头、金属、玉块、玛瑙等),创造出具有一定空间感的艺术形象,以反映社会生活、表达艺术家的审美感受、审美情感的艺术。海南因其独特的地域特点,民间雕刻的选材极具地方特色。这里将主要介绍贝雕、椰雕、牛角雕、根雕及海南黄花梨工艺品。

Actually, a wide range of materials can be used for carving. However, they are generally either plastic materials such as plaster, resin and clay which can easily be formed into objects or hard materials such as wood, stone, metals and jade which require more efforts to turn them. Skillful hands of the artists and craftsmen create pieces of arts that not only express their thoughts and emotions, but at the same time reflect people's social life and their views. Because of the unique geographic characteristics of Hainan, the materials used for carving are various, special and have great local distinctiveness of their own. However, here in this chapter our attention is mainly focused on the carving of shell, coconut, animal horn, tree roots, and Hainan Huang Hua Li rosewood.

贝雕

Shell Carving

艺人们根据原贝的形状、色泽与纹理，经过剪取、车磨、抛光、堆砌、粘贴等工序，将其精心雕琢成平贴、半浮雕、镶嵌、立体等多种形式和规格的工艺品的工艺（黄学魁，2008）。

Through clipping, grinding, polishing, stuffing, gluing and some other techniques, and based on the shape, color and texture of shells, craftsmen meticulously carved them into flat stick, half-relief, mosaic and three-dimensional forms.

海南贝雕在明代时就已达到了很高的艺术水平，后逐渐与椰雕结合在一起，是俗称"螺钿"镶嵌工艺的一种，多出现在山水、花鸟、人物等传统题材中。至20世纪五六十年代，海南贝雕特别吸收了牙雕、玉雕、木雕和国画的精髓。题材更侧重于表现海南地域特色的黎苗风情，并逐渐脱离椰雕，以独特面示人。如今的海南贝雕业已具备了国画的神韵、刺绣的空灵、玉雕的质感、珍珠的光泽，着实令人赞叹！

Hainan shell carving had reached to its artistic height during the Ming Dynasty (1368 AD – 1644 AD). However, at some stage later with the development of new techniques it was amalgamated with coconut carvings. Today, it is commonly known as "Luo Dian", which is a mosaic form. This method of fabrication is often used in presenting traditional subjects like people, landscapes, flowers, birds and the like. During the fifties and sixties of the twentieth century, Hainan shell carving was gradually appreciated to deserve the level and qualities of ivory carving, jade carving, wood carving and traditional Chinese painting. Its subject matters became more varied and more of Hainan' Li and Miao customs and traditions were incorporated into them. Later on, shell carvings detached itself from coconut carving and developed its own unique styles and characteristics. Hainan shell carving products subtly blend the charm of traditional Chinese painting, delicate embroidery, jade textures and the luster of the pearl.

此外，海南丰富的贝壳资源成就了品类繁多的贝雕作品，如酒具、摆件、挂件、项链、胸饰等，其精美华贵程度不亚于玉石。因此，贝雕也已成为海南旅游市场上最受游客青睐的民间工艺品之一。而这其中备受瞩目的莫过于砗磲工艺品了。

Hainan is rich in shell resources and has a wide variety of items such as wine cups, ornaments, pendants and necklaces carved out of shell, with an exquisite luxury rivaling jade. Currently, shell carving is one of the most sought after folk crafts on Hainan's tourism market, with Tridacna (Giant Clams) artworks topping the list.

砗磲是海洋中最大的双壳贝类，素有"贝王"之称，最大体长可达1.8米，重达500公斤以上。其外壳巨大，壳质厚重，壳面粗糙，略呈三角形，多呈黄褐色或灰色；内壳则洁白光滑，白皙如玉，是不可多得的贝雕原料。此外，砗磲、珍珠、珊瑚以及琥珀被誉为西方四大有机宝石，与金银、琉璃、玛瑙、珊瑚、琥珀和珍珠并称为"佛家七宝"，且佛家认为他能够驱邪避凶，因此人们常将砗磲置于佛堂神桌之上或供奉于家中作为镇宅之宝。

Giant Clam which is dubbed as "King of the Shells", is the largest bivalve mollusk. The larger ones can measure up to 1.8 meters long and weigh more than 500 kilograms. Their outer walls which are triangular shape are quite large, heavy, rough and mostly brown or gray in color.

However, the inner surfaces are white and smooth, resembling the white jade, and a perfect material for shell carving. Tridacna, pearl, coral and amber are known as the four organic gems in the West; while gold, silver, glass, agate, coral, amber and pearl are known as the "The Seven Treasures of Buddhism in the East." Buddhists believe that the giant clams can drive the evil spirit away. Hence, they often keep the artworks made of it somewhere in the house or place them on the table of the family shrine at home to protect the whole family.

在我国，砗磲主要分布在台湾、海南、西沙群岛及南海诸岛。目前，海南省琼海市潭门镇是砗磲原料和砗磲工艺品的重要集散地,其砗磲工艺品加工产业也已初具规模。小镇上的工艺品店从十几家快速发展到现在的 300 多家。值得一提的是 2014 年 2 月 23 日，在琼海潭门旅游工艺品展销会暨精品拍卖会上，一件起拍价 59.8 万元的砗磲艺术品"锦绣前程"被竞拍者以 70 万元的高价拍得（南海网，2014）。

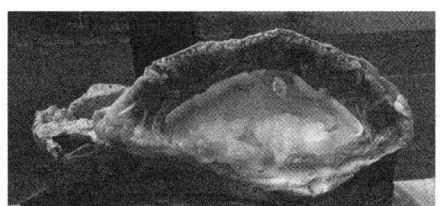

砗磲艺术品"锦绣前程"（黄丹 摄）
Tridacna Artwork "Promising Future"
(Source: http://www.hinews.cn/news/system/2014/02/23/016477385.shtml)

In China, tridacnas are mainly located around Taiwan, Hainan and island of the South China Sea such as Paracel Islands. At present, Tanmen County of Qionghai City in Hainan Province is known to be the hub for raw tridacna materials and its arts and craft works. Furthermore, giant clam processing industry has also begun to flourish there. Craft shops have rapidly increased in number, reaching to over 300 of them in town. It is worth to mention that during Tanmen Tourism Crafts Fair Auction on 23 February 2014, a tridacna Artwork called "Promising Future" with a starting bid of RMB 598,000.00 was sold for RMB 700,000.00 on the fall of the hammer.

另外一种备受人们喜爱的工艺品则是玳瑁。因其背部有 13 片鳞甲，所以也叫"十三鳞"。玳瑁栖于温、热带海岸，在中国分布于福建、台湾、海南岛和西沙群岛等地。其角质板可制成手镯、戒指、镜框及其他工艺品。但过度捕捞已致使玳瑁濒临绝迹。我们常说"没有买卖就没有杀害"，因此我们更加希望人们能够抑制购买欲望，进而保护这一物种。

Another kind of much-loved folk arts and crafts are those made from the Sea Turtle shell. Sea Turtles have generally 13 segments on their back shell, hence the origin of the term "Shi San Lin" in Chinese. Here in China, sea turtles can be found in the warm coastal waters of Fujian and Taiwan, and the tropical waters of Hainan and Paracel Islands. Sea Turtle's shell can be made into bracelets, rings, picture frames and the like. However, because of excessive harvesting they have become one of the endangered species and nowadays they can rarely be seen in Chinese coastal waters. Hence, no demand for their shells and trading of their shell products will hopefully results in no killing and saving them.

近些年来，海南贝雕名胜鼓噪，在博鳌亚洲论坛年会上频频亮相，并在全国各地的工艺博览会上多次获奖。仅在"2014 老庙·九天名玉第六届上海玉龙奖珠宝玉器评选活动"上，海南砗磲贝雕首次亮相就一举夺得了最佳工艺奖、银奖、铜奖三个奖项（南海网，2014）。

In recent years, Hainan shell carvings have regularly been displayed during the Boao Forum for Asia Annual Conference. They have also won numerous awards in craft fairs throughout the country. During the "2014 Laomiao · Jiutian" or "The Sixth Shanghai Yulong Jewelry and Jade Contest" in 2014, Hainan tridacna shell carving made its debut and won the "Best Technique" award, one artwork won the Silver Medal and the other one won the Bronze Medal.

 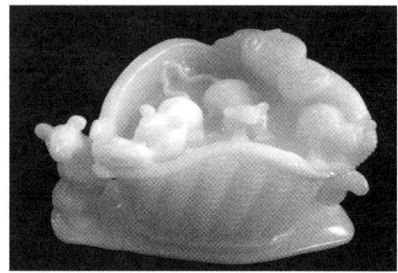

"虎溪三笑"（海南贝壳行业协会 供图）　　"五鼠运财"（海南贝壳行业协会 供图）
"Hu Xi San Xiao" and "Five Mice Delivering Fortune"
(The picture is contributed by Hainan Shell Industry Association)

2012 年 5 月，海南贝雕被列入第四批海南省非物质文化遗产代表性项目和扩展项目名录。

In May 2012, Hainan shell carving was registered and included in the fourth intangible cultural heritage list of representative projects and expansion projects of Hainan Province.

椰雕
Coconut Carving

椰雕工艺分为三类：一是椰壳雕，二是椰棕雕，三是椰木雕。椰壳雕是一种根据椰子壳天然形态，将椰壳和贝壳镶嵌结合，拼接成工艺品的工艺。产品有椰碗、茶叶盒、牙签筒、烟灰缸、花瓶、二胡、拼贴工艺画等。椰棕雕则是采用切、割、烫等方法加工工艺品的工艺。产品有椰猴、椰猪、椰妹等各种人物或动物造型。而椰木雕在海南主要是用于加工房梁。

Coconut carving can be divided into three main categories, namely: coconut shell carving, coconut coir pasting and coconut timber carving. In the first category, sea shells are spliced with coconut shell to create the desired works. A variety of coconut shell carvings such as bowls, tea boxes, toothpick holders, ashtrays, vases and even Erhu (a traditional Chinese musical instrument) can be found in the market. In coconut coir pasting, depending upon the natural texture of coconut, through cutting, burning and other means, dolls, animal and other figures could be made. As for the coconut timber carving, this has mainly been used for processing beams in the construction of houses.

海南椰雕历史悠久，最早可追溯到中唐宣宗元年（公元 810 年）。到宋朝时，工艺精致的椰碗、椰杯、椰壶更是备受上层社会的喜爱。明、清两代时，椰雕则常作为珍品进贡朝廷，享有"天南贡品"的美誉（中新网海南频道，2014）。

Hainan coconut carving enjoys a long history. It can be dated back to the first year of Emperor Tang Xuanzong (810 AD) in Tang Dynasty (618 AD—907 AD). During the Song Dynasty (960 AD—

1279 AD), elegant coconut bowls, cups and pots have been widely used at the banquets of intellectuals. In Ming (1368 AD—1644 AD) and Qing (1644 AD—1911 AD) dynasties, exquisite items carved out of coconut were often presented by the officials as a token of their respect towards the Imperial Court, hence it became to be known as "Tribute from the Southernmost".

制作椰雕工艺品要经过选料、造模、雕刻、嵌镶、刨光、修饰等几道工序。产品种类繁多，既有颇具欣赏性的摆件、吊件，又有兼具艺术性、实用性的生活用品。

Coconut carving consists of the following procedures: selecting the materials, modeling, carving, embedding, polishing and modifying. One may found amazing ornamental works and fine practical household items in the market.

而现代椰雕的代表作应属1999年澳门回归时海南向澳门特区赠送的纪念品，由海口市椰雕工艺厂创作的《椰树传说》和《天涯欢歌》两件椰雕嵌贝花瓶了。这对花瓶瓶体与镂空荷花底座高1.999米，最大直径为0.8米，每只重80公斤。瓶身上的每株椰树都结有9个椰果，衬以9片树叶，寓意1999年澳门回归祖国。花瓶由5200个精挑细选、色泽相同的椰子壳加工成的12400片弧度一致、一寸见方的小片拼接而成。并在瓶体表面嵌入了由280公斤夜光螺加工而成的人物、椰树等图案。在32000朵桂花、6万粒沙子的衬托下，椰树雄伟挺拔，人物栩栩如生。花瓶由30名工匠耗时10个月才完成，堪称海南椰雕史上的奇迹（南海网，2009）。

A masterpiece of the modern coconut carving is two shell-inlayed coconut vases created by Haikou Coconut Carving Craft Factory, named "The Legend of Coconut Trees" and "The Song of Joy at the Edge of the Sky". They are the gifts of Hainan people to Macau Special Administrative Region when Macau was handed over to China in December 20, 1999. Each vase is 1.999 meters tall, weighs 80 Kilogram and has the largest diameter of 0.8 meters. The shell-inlayed coconut trees on the vase have nine coconuts and nine leaves each, representing Macau's return in 1999. A total of 12,400 coconut flakes were used in the construction of vases. They were carefully selected from 5,200 coconut shells of the same color and were processed into uniform size and matched throughout the production process. Furthermore, a total of 280 kilograms of bright and reflective snail shells were used to inlay the Chinese characters and other patterns on the vase. The coconut trees look tall and straight, and the characters look vivid against the backdrop of 32,000 osmanthus flowers and 60,000 grains of sand. The vase was created by 30 skilled craftsmen in 10 months, which is indeed unprecedented in the annals of Hainan's coconut carving.

1999年赠送澳门特别行政区的嵌贝椰雕花瓶（吴中葆 摄）
Shell inlayed coconut vases granted to the Macau Special Administrative Region in 1999 (Courtesy of Zhongbao Wu)

牛角雕

Ox Horn Carving

海南牛角雕主要以水牛角和黄牛角为原料。艺人们深谙公、母牛以及老角、幼角在色泽上的细微差别。根据其天然形态进行合理想象，并通过不同的雕刻力度、刻线的长短，及漂染时间等进行创作。牛角在民间历来被认为有辟邪镇灾的作用，把它摆在厅堂显眼的位置，既能辟邪镇宅，又极具观赏价值。另外，牛角本身是一种珍贵的中药材，具有清热解毒，降血压，去风湿，治淋通石的药用功效。经常使用牛角梳梳头，能有效地减少和消除脱发、断发和头皮屑。

Buffalo and ox horns are the main raw materials used in Hainan ox horn carving. By the shade of horns, craftsmen can tell if one comes from a male or female animal, as well as an old or a young one. They create their works based on the natural forms of horns, with different intensity, length of the engraved lines, and the dyeing time. The horns are believed to repel the evil spirits and misfortunes. They are generally placed in a prominent location in the hallway not only to ward off bad luck, but for the decorative purposes too. In addition to above, the horn by itself is believed to be a valued traditional Chinese medicine, used for detoxification, lowering blood pressure, relieving rheumatism, and treating strangury. It is also believed if hair is frequently brushed with a comb made from ox horn, this may reduce and eliminate hair loss and treat damaged hair and dandruff.

根雕

Root Carving

选材一般要求木质坚韧、耐燥耐温的树根。这里主要介绍一下东方神木"海沉木"。"海沉木"特指海南古沉木。古沉木则是对久埋于地下或江河湖泊中未腐朽、可以为器的多种珍贵古木的总称。经大自然千万年磨蚀造化，古沉木兼备木之古雅与石之神韵，其质地坚实厚重，色彩乌黑华贵，不仅耐潮、耐虫、耐腐，有些还有香味，可谓百害不侵，万年不腐。

The basic criteria for root carving are to select strong, dry, and temperature-resistant roots as the raw materials. Here in this section, we focus our attention on "Hai Chen Mu" or the "Mysterious Oriental Tree" in English. Actually, "Hai Chen Mu" is a terminology used to specify Hainan's "ancient deadwood". Strictly speaking, "ancient deadwood" is a generic term that is used for a range of precious woods that have either been long buried underground or submerged in the rivers, and yet have not rotten at all. Despite going through thousands of years of natural changes, the ancient deadwood with its romantic charm, solid texture and luxurious black color, remains to be exquisitely appealing. Not only is it resistant to moisture insects and decay for a very long period of time, it is also fragrant.

海沉木一直被视为名贵木材，稀有之物，是尊贵及地位的象征。我国素有"纵有珠宝一箱，不如乌木一方"的民谚。历代以来，特别是明清时期，古沉木常常是各代帝王建筑宫殿和制作棺木的首选之材（新华网海南频道，2013）。因其数量稀少，不可再生，又极具观赏和收藏价值，其经济附加值也相应地水涨船高起来。

"Hai Chen Mu" has always been regarded as a valuable rare timber and a symbol of honor and social status. As the Chinese proverb says, "A box of jewelry is not as valuable as a square of ebony". In Chinese history, especially during the Ming (1368 AD—1644 AD) and Qing (1644 AD—1911 AD) Dynasties, ancient deadwood was the emperors' preferred construction material for building palaces, as well as coffins. Due to the limited supply of this non-renewable wood, as well as its ornamental and collecting values, it is now getting to become more pricey.

根雕讲究"三分人工，七分天成"。合理而慎重地取舍，也就是说除了对局部作少量的修饰和必要的雕琢外，重点都放在合理地运用木材的自然形态上，如枝、须、洞、节、疤、纹理、色泽等，使自然美的"奇"与人工美的"巧"，自然地结合起来，实现作品的艺术美。

It is believed that root carving is essentially "thirty percent craft, and seventy percent nature".That is to say except reasonable and cautious trade-off and a small amount of necessary modifications, the craftsman should try to make full use of the roots' natural formation, such as its branches, fibril, holes, sections, scars, texture, color, etc. So as to realize the "fancy" of natural beauty and the "skill" of artificial beauty spontaneously.

海沉木"洞中弥勒佛"造像（陈水雄 摄）
Hai Chen Mu Statue "Maitreya Buddha in the Cave" (Courtesy of Shuixiong Chen)
这是海口一家木雕工作室首席雕刻师，国评工艺美术师曹小武的一件海沉木雕刻作品。
This sculpture is created by Cao Xiaowu from Fuzhou, Jiangxi province. He is a national industrial artist and the chief engraver in a wood carving studio in Haikou, Hainan province.

海南黄花梨木工艺品
Hainan Huang Hua Li Rosewood Crafts

海南黄花梨又称海南黄檀木、降香黄檀，原产于中国海南岛吊罗山、尖峰岭等海拔100米左右、阳光充足的平原和丘陵地区。因其成材缓慢、木质坚实、花纹漂亮，始终位列五大名木之一，目前为国家一级保护植物（白羽，2014）。据《中国树木志》记载，野生海南黄花梨主要集中在海南岛东方、万宁、陵水、五指山等市。其中尤以东方市俄贤岭、昌江王下地区的海南黄花梨最为珍贵。

Hainan Huang Hua Li rosewood is also known as Hainan fragrant rosewood or Dalbergia odorifera fragrant rosewood. Originally native to the plains and hills of Diao Luo Shan Mountain and Jian Feng Ling Ridge in Hainan Island, Huang Hua Li rosewood usually grows in locations with sufficient sunshine and at an altitude of about 100 meters. Because of its long growing period, solid textures of its timber with distinctive ornamental patterns, it has always ranked as one of the top five famous trees in China. Hainan Huang Hua Li rosewood is currently amongst one of the state-level protected trees and plants. According to *"Flora of China"*, wild Hainan

Huang Hua Li rosewood mainly grows in Dongfang, Wanning, Lingshui and Wuzhishan City of Hainan. However, rosewoods from Er Xian Ling Ridge of Dongfang city and Wangxia region of Changjiang are more pricey.

近 10 年来，随着中国仿古家具的兴起，古典家具作为家居陈设已成为一种风尚。海南黄花梨家具肌理花纹如行云流水，不用上漆，只需稍稍打磨上蜡，就已是艳压群芳。且黄花梨木有一定的药用价值，《本草纲目》中记载：海南黄花梨有舒筋活血、降血压、降血脂的作用。因此，黄花梨家具、摆件及手串都颇得人们喜爱。

With the rise of popularity and interest in Chinese antique furniture since the past 10 years, home furnishing with rosewood has become fashionable. Taking into account the natural and smooth texture and patterns of Hainan Huang Hua Li rosewood, furniture made from it even with minimal polishing and waxing look quite elegant. Furthermore, Hainan Huang Hua Li rosewood has also medicinal usage. It is mentioned in the "*Compendium of Materia Medica*" that Hainan Hua Li rosewood may be used as a muscle relaxant, may stimulate blood circulation, reduce blood pressure and cholesterol. Hence, the reasons for the popularity of furniture, ornaments and bracelets made from it.

10.1.2 编扎 Weaving

藤编
Cane Weaving

藤编作品主要包括三个流程：原藤处理、编织和打磨上漆。第一步：将原藤做防霉防虫处理后分类、晒干；第二步：开藤，剥开藤皮、藤蕊后造架、编织（有些产品不需造架）；第三步：把产品进行二次防霉防虫处理后晒干，最后打磨上漆。

海南黎族藤编工艺最具代表性的要数夹葵叶三层防水盛衣藤篓了。它采用细藤篾编织内胆及外形，中间夹一层葵叶，鼓腹带盖，具有防水、防潮的功能和作用（黄学魁，2008）。黎族人家家里的衣物、被褥等均用这种藤篓来盛放，相当于现在的衣柜。

Generally, there are three steps involved in the making of a cane product, namely: processing the raw material, weaving, polishing and lacquering. To begin with, the raw canes need to be classified and dried-up first, then mold and insect-proofed. In the second stage, before building the frame and starting to weave, canes have to be peeled off, cracked open and their cores removed. However, some products do not need to have a frame. As the final steps, when weaving is done the product needs to be mold and insect-proofed again, then dried up, polished and lacquered.

The three-layer waterproof clothes basket is the most descriptive cane product of the Li nationality in Hainan. Its inner and outer layers are weaved with thin rattan strips; while the middle layer is stuffed with livistona chinensis leaves. This basket which is protruded at the middle portion and covered with a lid, is water and moisture proof. Li people store their quilts and clothes in these cane baskets, as they prefer them over the wardrobes.

竹编
Bamboo Weaving

竹编是黎族民间最普遍，也是最流行的一种编扎工艺。这主要得益于竹材容易获取和加工。竹编的器物种类繁多，包括竹箩、竹筐、竹篮、捕鱼笼、谷仓等。在干栏船形楼居茅屋的搭建过程中也用到了竹编工艺，主要是构架作用。

Owing to the abundance of raw material and ease of processing, bamboo weaving is the most common, widespread and preferred method of the Li ethnic group. An assortment of items such as bamboo baskets and fish barrels are weaved with bamboo strips. Bamboo weaving is also used in construction of cymbiform pile dwellings, where different kinds of bamboo poles are tied together by cane strips to build the structural frame.

彩扎

Colourful Tie-works

彩扎工艺系扎骨和剪纸相结合的一种工艺。黎族民间彩扎经过几百年的经营改造，已颇具特色。其主要服务对象是丧葬活动。亲朋们会为亡灵准备各种彩扎工艺品，包括彩扎牛、彩扎马、花灯和走马灯等。

Colourful tie-works is the combination of tying and paper-cutting. After hundreds of years of learning, practice and progress the Li people's colorful tie-works has developed its own distinctive characteristics. These are mainly used for funeral ceremony where the relatives of the dead prepare an assortment of colorful tie-works, including cow, horse, lanterns and revolving scenic lanterns.

彩扎工艺用料讲究，工序多，工艺复杂。其中最具代表性的作品要数走马灯了。黎族的走马灯与汉族走马灯外形相似，灯身均为六棱柱形，灯内共计三层。外层为灯笼骨架，第二层为立轴，内层为旋转叶轮，每层都糊有纸剪的门、窗等做装饰。叶轮下边，立轴底部近旁，装有一个油灯架。点灯时，产生的燃气上腾，推动叶轮旋转，立轴中部沿水平方向悬挂数根发丝，每根发丝都系着一件纸剪的人、马、鱼等，旋转时会映出舂米、筛米、搏斗、劳作、游鱼等生产生活画面（黄学魁，2008）。

Colorful tie-works has complex standards and procedures to follow. Revolving scenic lantern is the most representative work among all. The Li lantern is similar to the Han version in shape, with a hexagonal prism outline and three layers inside. Outer layer is the skeleton of the lantern; while the middle one is a vertical shaft; and the inner one is its rotating impeller. Each layer is decorated with paper-cut doors, windows and the likes. A small oil lamp is placed beneath the impeller, near the bottom of the vertical shaft. The heat generated by the lamp forces the impeller into rotation. Several hair strands are horizontally placed on the middle part of the vertical shaft with paper-cut images such as people, horses, and fish tied to each strand. This produces realistic scenes resembling thrashing rice, farm works and fishing.

10.1.3 海南苗族发绣 Hainan Miao People's Hair Embroidery

海南苗族发绣最初以五指山苗族少女的头发代线绣制。传统的发绣只采用自然色的头发来绣制，色彩比较单调，作品显示出的只是白描的效果。如今，苗妹们已经学会利用染色的头发来表现多彩的画面和物体的明暗了，漂染的发色多达近千种，创作的绣品种类也更加丰富。

Hainan Miao People's hair embroidery primarily uses natural hair strands of Miao girls from Wuzhi Shan Mountain. Traditionally, the Miao people only use the natural hair in the needle works; hence they only have a single color to demonstrate the effect of their sketches. However, Miao girls have already mastered to dye hair in numerous different colors, helping them utilize those hairs strands to present the light and shade and enable them create rich variety of works.

苗族发绣的制作过程十分严谨,从搜集头发到筛发、选发、分档、分色、软化、退脂等,都有一套完整的科学处理程序。处理后的头发不霉、不烂、不蛀、不褪色。根据制作过程可分为:传统型和现代型。传统型即是先将缎子在绣架上绷紧,然后勾上铅笔底稿,再开始绣制,完稿后,将裁好的三夹板粘在作品的反面,再下绷装裱;而现代型,则像绷油画布一样,在内框上绷好布帛,再在绣架上夹紧即可创作,一般先由专业人员勾上铅笔稿或彩色稿,完成后装上画框即可,此类型对画面的构成、组合更为有利。

Miao hair embroidery works follows a very meticulous and strict procedure, from collecting hair to sieving, selecting, categorizing its quality, color separation, softening, fat reduction, processing, etc. This whole set of these procedures make sure that hair is immune to decay and fading. Essentially, there are two methods of production for hair embroidery works: the traditional and the modern ones. In the traditional method, satin is first stretched on the embroidery frame and sketches of the subject matter are then drawn on it with pencil, before starting the needlework. After finishing the embroidery, glue is applied to its back and it is mounted on plywood. However, in the modern style, cloth is stretched on the frame and like a painting canvas it is stapled to it. Embroiders will then sketch it with pencil or colored-pen. The finished work will then mounted, which makes this method more advantageous in terms of the picture's composition and layout.

在 2009 年第七届中国(海口)国际旅游商品交易会上出现的海南五指山苗族发绣作品《清明上河图》长 9.68 米,宽 0.32 米,至少用了 20 个苗族少女的秀发。十几个绣娘花了一年时间才完成了这幅被誉为"天下一绝"的发绣艺术品(中国新闻网,2010)。

In 2009, a 9.68 meters long and 0.32 meters wide Miao hair embroidery work called "Riverside Scene at Qingming Festival", was exhibited during the Seventh China (Haikou) International Tourism Trade Fair in Wuzhi Mountain, Hainan. It used hair strands from at least 20 Miao girls and took several professional hair-embroiders for a year to complete this artwork, which was then commended as "the world-class art".

苗族发绣代表作《清明上河图》局部(苏建强 摄)
A masterpiece of the Miao People's hair embroidery artwork
"Riverside Scene at Qingming Festival" (Courtesy of Jianqiang Su)

目前，苗族发绣工艺品已远销到东南亚一带，受到了更多人的青睐和喜爱。

So far, Miao hair embroidery handicraft has been sold to Southeast Asia, favored and loved by more people.

10.1.4　剪纸 Paper-cut

黎族剪纸
The Li People's Paper-cut

黎族剪纸主要流行于乐东黎族自治县。乐东剪纸以单色剪纸为主，结合了北派的粗犷和南派的清秀。其构图自由新颖，形象生动，多以乡村风土人情、生活起居、生产劳动为主要题材，具有浓厚的生活气息。

The Li People's paper-cut is mainly found and practiced in Ledong Li Autonomous County. Ledong paper-cut is essentially about monochrome paper-cut, combining the straightforward style of the north and the fresh and soft style of the south. Its design is freestyle, creative and vivid. The themes are generally derived from the local customs and daily life, which demonstrates a strong sense of living.

苗族剪纸
The Miao People's Paper-cut

苗族剪纸有时剪，有时刻，一次可刻多层。无论剪或刻，都要先把图案在表层纸上画好。所用的纸，旧时用当地手工作坊生产的白皮纸、黄草纸，有些地区使用苗家自制的丝绵纸。白皮纸薄且韧，经得起搓揉。丝绵纸是蚕在木板上吐丝结成的薄皮，既挺括又柔和，是最佳选择。20世纪60年代后，苗族妇女多采用28克以下的书写纸，颜色也有了更多选择。多层纸叠合剪刻时，苗族妇女们习惯用白皮纸捻或缝衣线将纸穿钉成本，一幅图案视大小固定数个点，以保证剪刻中各层不错移。白皮纸捻如小铁钉，长约2厘米，一头粗，一头尖，剪刻完撕揭时不用去掉纸捻，从纸捻尖揭起，要几张，揭几张，剩下的不会松散，便于保存（黄学魁，2008）。

Generally, small scissors or knives are employed to produce the Miao People's Paper-cuts. The paper used cannot be too thick, otherwise knives are needed to carve through multiple layers at a time. Whether cutting or carving the paper, patterns are drawn on the first layer of the paper, as a guide. Normally, papers used for these works are either the traditional white paper, or straw paper produced by the local manual paper mills, or Miao's homemade silk paper. White paper is thin and tough, and can hold its shape well even when rubbed. Papers made from silk are smooth and have soft texture, which make them the material of choice. After the 1960s, Miao women began to use color papers weighing less than 28 grams. When cutting through multilayer of papers, Miao women fix and hold them together with a white paper string or thread. Then fix a number of points based on the size of the picture, in order to make sure that each layer stays still during the cutting process. Actually, the white paper string looks like a small nail which is about 2cm long, with a large head and a sharp tip. After fixing it, they leave the string there. They remove the paper-cut from the sharp side of the string without making the rest loose and easy to keep.

10.1.5　海南蝶翅画 Hainan Butterfly Wings Painting

海南蝶翅画以蝴蝶翅膀为主要材料，经科学方法回软、展翅、防蛀、防腐、干燥及后期制作等 30 余道手工工序，利用其独特的花纹，采用特殊工艺拼贴，使之成为具有油画、国画、水粉画效果的工艺画。海南制作的蝶翅画以国内罕见的蝴蝶品种如透翅宽带凤蝶、箭纹丽蛱蝶、啄蝶、紫光蝶等为材料手工制作，有较高的观赏价值和收藏价值。

Butterfly wings are the core material for producing these paintings. Before a painting is finally produced and rolled out, butterfly wings must go through over 30 different processes such as softening, stretching, moth-proofing, anticorrosion, drying and some other post-production procedures. Based on the unique patterns on the butterfly wings, artists use special techniques to patch the wings together. This is amazingly remarkable as it combines luster of oil painting, the beauty of traditional Chinese painting all in one. Hainan butterfly wing painting uses rare butterfly species such as pecking, arrow patterns, purple light, and broadband swallowtail butterfly with transparent wings, are used as the raw materials for Hainan butterfly wings painting. These handmade works have high ornamental value as well as collection worth.

10.2　民间戏曲音乐 Folk Operas and Music

10.2.1　琼剧 Hainan Opera

琼剧出自海南琼州（今琼山县），是海南的主要地方剧种，至今已有 360 多年的历史。琼剧源自江西弋阳腔诸剧，它在海南流行的杂剧基础上，吸收闽南戏、徽戏、昆腔、潮州正音戏、白字戏（潮剧）、广东梆黄和海南民歌、歌舞八音、傀儡戏、道坛乐曲等民间戏曲的精华，后逐渐形成了一个弋阳腔支戏的地方剧种（邢纪元，2008；焦勇勤、孙海兰，2008；赵康太，2008）。

Hainan opera is hailed from Hainan Qiongzhou (the present QiongShan County), hence the origin of its name. It is an acclaimed local opera, born from YiYang Melodies of Jiangxi, with a history of over 360 years. Based on the popular operas in Hainan, it absorbed the essence of Minnan Opera, Hui Opera, and melodies for Kunqu Opera, Chaozhou Opera, Baizi Opera, Guangdong Banghuang, Hainan folk songs, Ba Yin (8 musical instruments in Hainan style), puppet play, and Taoist temple music. Thus, it gradually developed into a local opera of YiYang melodies.

琼剧的行党角色最初仅生、旦、净、丑四大行当，到清代同治至光绪年间发展为生、旦、净、末、丑、杂六大行当。各行当各有各的表演艺术和脸谱、唱腔。例如小生大都手执白纸小扇，以示文雅、倜傥。花生只在鼻梁处涂小块白粉，扇子往往插于颈间，脚尖经常前后左右伸缩，以表轻浮放荡。生、末登帐、升堂，往往踢开袍角，叠上碎步。武戏的武功属男派，使用铁、铜武器，还掺有杂技、魔术的表演（焦勇勤、孙海兰，2008；赵康太，2008）。

At the beginning, Hainan Opera only had four major roles, namely, Sheng (male roles), Dan (female roles), Jing (painted roles) and Chou (clowns). It was not until emperor Tongzhi's to

Guangxu's reign in the Qing Dynasty that the roles developed into six major roles, with Mo (senior male roles) and Za (acrobats) added. Each role has its traditional performing arts, different makeup and singing methods. For example, male roles in the Qingwen opera usually hold a white small paper fan to show their elegance and charm. Huasheng roles show their frivolous characteristic with a small piece of white powder at the bridge of the nose, a fan in the collar, and frequent steps. Sheng and Mo roles usually kick the robe with frequent steps when they appear on the stage. The martial arts of male roles required the performance using iron and copper weapons, also mixed with acrobatics and magic shows.

其传统剧目丰富多样，大致可分为三种：文戏、武戏、文明戏。其中文戏又称唱曲戏，以唱功为主，共800多出；武戏又称科白戏，以做工、武打为主，共400多出；文明戏，又称时装旗袍戏，共130多出（焦勇勤、孙海兰，2008）。1949年后经过整理、改编、创作和移植其他剧种的古装、现代剧目，总数已达1500多出。其中《红叶题诗》《张文秀》《搜书院》《狗衔金钗》《红色娘子军》等已成为传统经典剧目。

Hainan opera has a rich variety of traditional shows, which can be roughly divided into three categories: singing opera, fighting opera, and modern opera. The singing opera focuses on singing methods, and it has a total of more than 800 plays; fighting opera is also known as Bai play, which is based on martial arts with a total of more than 400 plays; modern opera is also known as the cheongsam fashion play, with a total of more than 130 plays. Through sorting, adaptation, creation, and combining other types of plays after 1949, Hainan Opera has reached more than 1500 plays, among which "Poems on Red Leaf", "Wenxiu Zhang", "Searching the Institute", "A Dog and a Gold Hair Pin" and "The Red Detachment of Women" have become the traditional classic plays.

其剧情多以历史和民间故事为题材。借脸谱唱腔及动作来表达剧中人物的身份和故事内容，尤为注重生、旦的剧情与剧路。一般程序为先苦后甘，善有善报，恶有恶报，有情人终成眷属，大团圆的结局。

Its plots are mainly extracted from history and folk tales. The characters and plots are carried out by facial makeups, singing melodies and movements. Sheng and Dan's story generally follows the line from bitterness to sweetness, with the good well rewarded and the evil punished. Finally, they all reach to a happy ending and deserve the happy marriage.

琼剧与粤剧、潮剧、汉剧并称为"岭南四大剧种"，是海南广大群众和琼籍华人、华侨、华裔喜闻乐见的艺术形式。此外，广东的雷州半岛，及东南亚地区的新加坡、马来西亚、印尼、泰国、越南、柬埔寨等国热爱琼剧的人也很多。琼剧又有"南海红珊瑚"的美誉。

Hainan Opera, Cantonese Opera, Chao Opera, and Han Opera are known as "Lingnan Four Operas"(Lingnan mainly refers to Guangdong and Hainan Province). Hainan Opera is very popular among Hainan people and overseas Chinese who were born in Hainan. It is also popular in Leizhou Peninsula of Guangdong, and in other countries in Southeast Asia, such as Singapore, Malaysia, Indonesia, Thailand, Vietnam, and Cambodia. It is honored as "the red coral in the south China sea".

10.2.2　临高人偶戏与临剧 Lingao Man-and-puppet Show and Lin Opera

临高人偶戏是人偶同台演出的木偶戏。一般的木偶戏演出时，舞台四周围着布，观众只看到木偶，看不到演员。而临高人偶剧则采用大舞台，不设布幛，演员手持木偶化装登台，人偶合扮同一角色，并根据剧情交叉表演，即"人偶同演"。表演时演员不仅操纵木偶，还声情并茂的念唱对答，以自己的喜怒哀乐等来弥补木偶的不足。临高人偶戏使用临高土语演唱，重比兴对偶，主要唱腔有"啊罗哈"和"朗叹"两种，伴奏以双唢呐为主（符耀彩，2008）。

Lingao Man-and-puppet Show is a performance art with puppeteers and puppets performing on the same stage. Usually, puppeteers are backstage operating puppets to perform for the audience. The audience cannot see the puppeteers as the puppeteer area is enclosed by curtains. However, Lingao puppet play is performed on a big stage without curtains. You can see both the puppeteers and the puppets. The puppeteer and the puppet perform the same role, and take turns to act according to the plot, in other words the Lingao puppetry is "simultaneous performance of the actor and the puppet". During the performance, the puppeteers not only operate the puppets, but also have lines that supplement the puppets' lack of emotional displays. The play lays great emphasis on antithesis and is performed in the Lingao dialect. Its two major melodies are "A Luo Ha" and "Lang Tan" (both are based on folk songs), and is accompanied by double zurna horn.

临高人偶戏所用的木偶，一般一套有20多个，分有生、旦、净、丑、末等角色。在木偶脸谱的制作上，正生和正旦都塑得十分俊俏美丽，丑角都雕刻得非常丑恶，胖的肥头肥脑、瘦的皮包骨头，对比十分鲜明。原来的木偶，只有拳头般大小，造型也不大讲究，1979年以后，民间艺人对木偶进行了改进，制作了造型美观、眼睛能灵活转动、嘴巴能开合的大木偶。

每逢喜庆或传统节日，大都演出木偶戏。这种习俗主要流传于海南岛西北部的临高、儋州、澄迈地区。

Usually a set of more than 20 puppets are used in a play, each playing different stereotypical roles of Sheng, Dan, Jing, Chou, Mo, etc (the "common male", "common female", "outstanding male", "comedic relief", and "elderly male"). The leading male and female puppets wear beautiful makeup, while the comedic relief puppets are often made up to present a sharp contrast to the leads, with ugly designs such as extreme obesity or skinniness. The original puppets were only as big as a fist, without much attention being paid to the shape. After 1979, folk artists improved the puppets, making them bigger, more attractive and even added details such as flexible eyes and mouth.

The puppet shows became a tradition, celebrating happy events and festivals. This tradition has spread mainly in the northwestern regions of Hainan, such as Lingao, Danzhou, and Chengmai.

临剧土调"啊罗哈"临剧是临高人偶戏的一个变种。20世纪20年代后，临高艺人开始尝试放下木偶，只用临高方言演唱，后逐渐演变为今天富有地方特色的临剧。临剧唱腔主要是民歌土调，如"啊罗哈""朗叹""哩哩美""小放牛"等（焦勇勤、孙海兰，2008），是由民歌和民间音乐整理创作而成。

Local Melody "A Luo Ha" of Lin Opera is a variant of Lingao puppetry. After the 1920s, artists began putting the puppets aside, and sing and perform in the Lingao dialect. This gradually evolved into the Lin Opera. The melodies of Lin Opera are mainly synthetized from folk songs and folk music such as "A Luo Ha", "Lang Tan", "Li Li Mei", "Little Cowherd", etc.

10.2.3 儋州调声 Danzhou Diao Sheng (Folk Song Sung in Antiphonal Style in Danzhou Dialect)

儋州调声出现于西汉时期，现在仅流传于海南省儋州一地，是独具地域特色的汉族民间歌曲。调声用儋州方言演唱，节奏明快，旋律优美，感情热烈，可歌可舞，被誉为"南国艺苑奇葩"（石应宽，2006）。

Danzhou Diao Sheng is a remarkable folk music tradition of the Han people. It originated in the Western Han Dynasty (202 BC-9 AD), and now only exists in Danzhou, Hainan. The voicing is done in the Danzhou dialect, with a sprightly rhythm, beautiful melody, and strong emotions. People can sing and dance along with the voicing, and the music tradition is honored as the "Miraculous Art of the South".

儋州调声主要是男女青年在逢年过节或农闲时，在乡镇集市或山坡野地，互相以歌抒情的对歌比赛活动。对歌时男队和女队面对面站成 2 队，列距 3 米左右。对歌前每队队员互相勾住尾指，由"歌头"起调、领唱、指挥和选择歌词。男队先唱，女队答唱。唱完第一段后，唱一两句曲调代替乐器过门，接着唱第二段。队形随时变化，时而半圆，时而一字摆开。歌手手拉手，两脚有节奏地前后左右摆动。对歌不受时间限制，以"唱倒"对方为止。对歌比赛时，各队都有统一的服饰，连草帽、眼镜、鞋子、手表都相同。每年的"中秋歌会"尤其热闹，参加者往往成千上万。2006 年 5 月 20 日，儋州调声经国务院批准背列入第一批国家级非物质文化遗产名录（羊中兴，2008；杨兹举、罗海燕、李柏青，2008）。

Danzhou Diao Sheng itself is mainly performed as an antiphonal singing competition between young men and women during the holidays or in their spare time on town fairs or on hillsides. Men and women stand in two rows of about three meters apart, facing each other while holding one another by the little finger. The starters choose the voicing and lyrics. Men would sing first, and the women would follow. After each song section, the singers would hum some melody to serve as the transition, then the singing is passed on to the next member. During the competition the team formation may change arbitrarily. Singers would swing back and forth along with the rhythm. There is no time limit, and the competition ends when one side concedes defeat. In the competition, singers on each team would usually wear the same clothes, same hat, glasses, shoes, and even watches. The annual "Mid-Autumn Singing Gala" is especially well-attended, with tens of thousands of participants.

On May 20th 2006, the Danzhou Diao Sheng was listed among the first set of State-level intangible cultural heritage arts, announced by the State Council.

10.2.4 公仔戏 Gong Zai Xi (Puppet Show)

公仔戏又称木偶戏、傀儡戏，是海南的地方表演艺术，流行于琼北一带。公仔戏的偶像现今有 20 多种。其公仔（木偶）头部由木头雕刻而成，长约 30 厘米，肩膀由藤竹编织而成，下半身用袍裙遮掩，再以靴或鞋代脚，偶身插入木棍或藤条，藏于体内与头相连，以方便操纵。木偶整体宽约 30 厘米、高 100 厘米。后木偶有所改进，头部增为 40 厘米，眼睛能转动，舌头可伸缩（焦勇勤、孙海兰，2008）。

Gong Zai Xi is known in the vernacular as the "puppet show". It is a local performing art in

Hainan, and enjoys popularity in the northern part of the province. There are now about 20 types of puppets used in this art. The head of the puppet is carved wood, about 30cm long. The puppet's shoulders are woven from bamboo and rattan. The lower body is covered by the puppet gown, and shoes are placed to indicate feet. The puppet hands are made of wood as well, and the body is connected through wooden sticks or canes hidden in the body, making it convenient to operate. The puppet measures about 30cm in width, and about 100cm in length. Later, models of puppets have larger heads measuring 40cm, and improved and flexible eyes and tongue.

操纵木偶的艺人叫"驶公"。可以表演作揖、跺脚、拂袖、跑马、射击、晃牛耳、打虎架、滚翻、跳跃、舞步、眼睛转动、胡须拂动、嘴张合、舌伸缩等20多种动作。这些艺人个个都是全才，一人可以同时驾驭几个公仔，男女角色间不同唱调能够自由转换。其表演风格多变，惟妙惟肖。

The puppeteer is called "Shi Gong", and is capable of making the puppet perform more than 20 different movements, such as swinging hands, bowing, stamping, swinging sleeve, running, shooting, moving ears, tiger fighting, rolling, leaping, dancing, blowing beard, and individual eyes, mouth and tongue movement. The puppeteers are very versatile and can operate several puppets at once, and can even switch singing styles from male roles to female roles freely, making the show remarkably funny and vivid.

10.3 民间舞蹈
Folk Dance

10.3.1 黎族舞蹈 Dances of the Li Nationality

总体而言，黎族民间舞蹈按其来源基本分为三类：第一类是祭祀类舞蹈，即宗教仪式舞蹈，如《敬祖舞》《年舞》《招福舞》《跳鬼舞》《跳娘舞》等，相对黎族其他的舞蹈而言，这类舞蹈节奏较慢。第二类是生产舞蹈，为劳动助乐性舞蹈，以黎族姑娘的《舂米舞》最具代表性。第三类是生活舞蹈，如《打柴舞》《咚铃伽舞》《椰壳舞》等（焦勇勤、孙海兰，2008；马晓莉，2009）。

In general, Li folk dances can be divided into three categories, based on their origin. The first is ritualistic, for worshipping ancestors, such as the "Ancestor Worship Dance", "Spring Festival Dance", "Fortune Calling Dance", "Ghost Hunting Dance", "Bowl-Tapping Dance", etc. This type of dance is relatively slower when compared with other Li dances. The second type is associated with production, and is mainly danced during work, such as the "Thrashing Rice Dance" of Li girls. The third kind reflects life, such as the "Firewood Dance", "Dong Ling Ka Dance", "Coconut Dance", etc.

敬祖舞
Ancestor Worship Dance

敬祖舞一般在每年秋收后表演，全寨男女老少全部出动围观。舞者一次十人或三十人不等，男女各半。舞者的服饰和道具各有讲究，巫师（黎族称"三伯公"）身穿汉族丝绸长袍；其余男士头扎红布，上插雉鸡毛以示威武；女的身着鲜艳的民族服装；每个人手上都拿着一支从椰子树或槟榔树上取下的嫩叶叶尾，以象征生命与丰收。起舞时先由巫师出场，他口念族谱，请历代祖先神灵到场。念罢做几步向前进的动作，随后蹲下取出自种的烟丝，这时另一舞者登场将烟点燃，随后二人来到场地边沿，后又向着相反的方向跳过去，以示迎来了祖先神灵。舞者们通过舞蹈感谢祖先在过去一年对族人的庇佑并祈求来年获得大丰收。原来的两行队就改成三行，女的单行，男的分两行，他们踏着锣鼓声的节奏，时而做向祖先神灵敬献的动作，时而又做敬酒动作，舞蹈进行半个小时左右（焦勇勤、孙海兰，2008）。整个舞蹈的配乐在一面鹿皮鼓和七面铜鼓的打击伴奏下完成。

Ancestor worship dance occurs on an auspicious day after the autumn harvest. Men, women, the old, and the young gather to watch the dance. The troupe may range from 10 to 30 people, half men and half women. Dancer's costumes and props are unique: wizards (also known as "the third uncle" within the Li people) wear the Han silk robe; men generally would wear red bandannas on their heads, adorned with rooster feathers to demonstrate power; women would wear colorful tribal costumes. Everyone would hold a budding branch from a coconut tree or a betel nut tree, as a symbol for life and good harvest. The wizard begins by reading a genealogy to welcome ancestral spirits. After the reading, he would step forward, squat down and hold out some self-produced tobacco, while another dancer come forward to light it up. Together, they dance forward and back, indicating that the ancestors have come. By dancing they want to show respect to the ancestors to garner their blessings for the people, and praying for peace and a good harvest in the coming year. Then, the original two lines of dancers change into three lines, one line for women, and two for men. Following the rhythm of the drums, they sometimes show respect to ancestral spirits and sometimes perform a toast. The dance continues for half an hour. The entire dance is accompanied by a deerskin drum and seven bronze drums.

年舞
Spring Festival Dance

又称"平安舞"，流行于五指山地区。舞蹈开始时，舞者身体正直，慢步前进，双手在腰的两侧前后摆动，到第三步时，双脚并立，双膝向左右两侧时曲时直，反复循环。每逢正月初二，黎寨里的男女穿好传统服饰，在老辈人主持的新春仪式上杀猪、摆祭祀品，敲着独木皮鼓和铜锣，跳起年舞，以祈求来年人畜平安，幸福美满。

Spring festival dance is also called the "safekeeping" dance, and it is famous in the Wuzhi mountain area. Dancers begin by keeping their body straight and balanced, walking forward slowly, with both hands swaying back and forth near the waist. On the third step, they close their feet and keep bending their knees to the left and right sides. Every second day of the month, the Li men and women sacrifice pigs to celebrate the New Year on a ceremony hosted by the elders. They wear traditional costumes, play the drum and dance to pray for a peaceful and happy year ahead.

招福舞
Fortune Calling Dance

又称"招魂舞"。农历三月间的"牛日"和晚稻插秧时农历七月间的"牛日"都会跳招福舞，前者为牛举行招魂仪式，后者为禾苗举行招魂仪式。

The fortune calling dance is also known as the "spirit calling dance". The dance is performed on the "cow day" of the third and the seventh month according to the lunar calendar. The former is the evocation ceremony for the cow, while the latter is for the rice.

招魂仪式一般在亩头家举行。亩头夫妇身着传统服饰，面向亩众（陈立浩、陈兰、陈小蓓，2008），先用"招福酒"进行祭拜，而后喝下"招福酒"开始跳舞。只见亩头妻子高举"招福酒"酒碗，亩头拿着蘸有"招福酒"的红藤叶，在热烈的锣声中从屋内到门口来回舞动，同时挥动红藤叶向亩众挥洒"招福酒"。随后，亩众们也加入舞蹈，男的身穿各种长袍，挥舞着衣袖从屋内至门口来回舞动，女的则手捧酒碗，边跳边向男的敬"招福酒"。舞者前进一步，后退一步，嘴里念念有词，以示招魂入屋。招魂仪式一般会持续一整晚（焦勇勤、孙海兰，2008）。

The evocation ceremony is usually held in Mutou's house, the leader of the Li patriarchal society which used to exist in the 1950s. The Mutou couple, wearing traditional clothes and facing everybody, hold the "blessing wine" to worship. Then they drink the wine and begin to dance. At first, the wife holds the wine bowl above her head, while the husband holds some Sargent glory vine leaves that are dipped in the wine. Accompanied by passionate gongs, they dance back and forth, from the room to the gate of their yard, with the Mutou waving the leaves to sprinkle wine on everybody. Then, men dressed in robes join in, and dance back and forth, from the room to the gate yard, and women would dance and make toasts to the men. Dancers take a step forward and then a step back, murmuring as if inviting the spirits into the house. The evocation ceremony usually lasts a whole night.

跳鬼舞
Ghost Hunting Dance

又称"捉鬼舞"。舞者分别为"道公"和"娘母"。他们左手持一把铁剑，右手拿一把尖刀或红藤叶，在紧锣密鼓声中起舞，表演捉鬼、赶鬼和招魂动作。

The ghost hunting dance is also known as the "ghost catching dance". Dancers are called "Dao Gong" and "Niang Mu" respectively. They hold an iron sword in the left hand, and a knife or some Sargent glory vine leaves in the right. They perform ghost hunting, ghost chasing and evocation movements accompanied by gongs.

跳娘舞
Bowl-Tapping Dance

亦称"打碗舞"，在保亭黎族苗族自治县一带较为流行。舞者清一色女子，排成纵队，用两种形式的舞蹈动作进行，一是每人手捧花草，边唱边舞；另一种是每人头顶顶个小白酒碗，右手拿一根筷子，边唱边跳，边敲打头上的碗。

The bowl-tapping dance is popular in the Baoting autonomous county of Li and Miao tribes. All the dancers are women. They stand in two rows and perform the dance in two ways. One is dancing and singing while holding flowers and plants. Another is dancing and singing while tapping the wine bowl on their heads with a chopstick in their right hand.

舂米舞
Thrashing Rice Dance

源于黎族妇女的舂米劳动。现在，舂米舞已由原来的四个人跳发展到了六人跳。该舞以杵和臼为道具，通过杵臼的击打、杵和杵的击打，发出铿锵有力的节奏，并通过模拟舂米的劳动过程来表演舞蹈动作（黎族百科，2012）。舞蹈节奏轻快，极具喜感。

The thrashing rice dance grew from rice thrashing. Originally it was performed by four women dancers, but now often six dancers. Wooden pestles and mortars are necessary stage props. Forceful rhythms are made by the mortar and pestle, as well as pestle and pestle. The dance moves simulate the rice thrashing work and gives the audience a joyful feeling.

春米舞
Thrashing Rice Dance (Source: http://lizu.baike.com/article-295536.html)

打柴舞
Firewood Dance

打柴舞源于古崖州（今三亚市），一般在新谷登场那天或元宵节举行。

舞蹈用的"柴"通常是精心挑选的红铃木，也可用大竹竿。舞前，人们在晒谷场上平行放置两根相距约 2.5 米，长约 4 米的"柴"作垫架；垫架上横放 10 根约 3 米长的"柴"作跳竿。舞者分为"打柴"和"跳柴"两组。舞时，垫架两边各蹲或跪 5 个人，每人双手握住"柴"的末端，按一定的节拍将手中"柴"和地上的"柴"相互叩击，发出清脆的乐声；"跳柴"的人四人一组，踩着节奏，在"柴"空隙中穿梭，同时跳出各种舞姿。"打柴人"变换着坐、蹲、站 3 种打法，敲击的节奏由慢到快，复杂的图形增加跳跃的难度，逐渐把"打柴"推向高潮。舞蹈时，通常用二胡、竹笛、小唢呐、小鼓、铃等乐器伴奏（焦勇勤、孙海兰，2008）。

"打柴舞"经过艺术加工，现在已经成为黎族舞蹈中最有代表性的舞蹈。

Firewood dance is originated from Guyazhou (Sanya), which is held on lantern festival or for the new harvest.

The firewood is usually selected from red trees and bamboos. Before the dance, people put two wood sticks which are about 4 meters long on the field in parallel as a mat, with the distance of 2.5m. Ten three-meter-long firewood sticks are placed on the mat as the jump stick. Dancers are divided into "firewood tapping" and "firewood jumping" groups. Five people are on each side of the pat holding the end of the "firewood". They tap the wood on the ground according to a certain rhythm to make clear sounds. Firewood jumping dancers are in groups of four, dancing in the gaps between the firewood on the rhythm with beautiful gestures. "Firewood tapping" person changes from sitting, squatting, to standing, and they move faster and faster. Complex graphics increase the difficulty of the jumping, which pushes the dancing gradually to a climax. During the dance, erhu, bamboo flute, small zurna, small drum and bell are usually used for accompaniment.

Firewood dance has now become one of the most representative dances of the Li people.

竹竿舞
Bamboo Rod Dance

竹竿舞又称"打竹舞",与打柴舞十分相似,区别仅仅是活动器材不同,一个是"柴",一个是"竹"。20世纪80年代竹竿舞被列为海南民间艺术舞蹈,现在每逢年节,尤其是农历"三月三",黎族人民都会组织跳竹竿舞庆祝。

The bamboo rod dance is also called the "bamboo tapping dance", and is very similar to the firewood tapping dance. The difference lies in the equipment. The latter uses "wood", while the former uses "bamboo". The bamboo dance was listed as a Hainan folk art in the 1980s. Nowadays, the Li people would organize a bamboo pole dance to celebrate every festival, especially the Hainan San Yue San Festival (held on the 3rd day of the 3rd lunar month).

咚铃伽舞
Dong Ling Ka Dance

咚铃伽是黎语音译过来的,指的是簸箕、钱铃和尖刀这三种生活用具,也是表演该舞的三件道具。舞蹈中,舞者身穿传统服饰,头缠红巾,两人一对,一人手执30厘米长的双刀,另一个手拿70厘米长的钱铃棍子,各占一方,随着有节奏的音乐互相格斗。执刀者绕着钱铃,刺向对方,持铃者挡驾搏击(黎族百科,2012)。整个表演动作粗犷有力、豪放自由,彰显着黎族猎手高强的武艺。

The Dong Ling Ka dance is named after the three daily tools used in this dance, namely the dustpan, coin bell, and knife, as they are pronounced in the Li language. The two male dancers are dressed in traditional costumes, with red scarves around their heads. The pair of dancers, one holding a 30 cm long knife and another holding a 70 cm long coin bell stick, would fight each other along with the music. The one with knife attacks the other dancer, who uses the coin bell stick to protect himself. The whole performance is powerful and unrestricted, revealing the martial skills of Li hunters.

打柴舞 (陈文 摄)
Firewood Dance(Source: http://www.hainan.gov.cn/hn/zjhn/dfts/whjq/jjfy/201206/t20120611_701813.html)

咚铃伽舞
Dong Ling Ka Dance
(Source: http://lizu.baike.com/article-239201.html)

椰壳舞
Coconut Shell Dance

流行于三亚、陵水一带,是一种富于椰岛情调的黎族儿童舞蹈。不限人数,取材方便。舞蹈器具是将若干个椰壳对半锯开,钻孔后用椰叶系牢。舞者双脚趾夹着椰叶,脚踩半边椰壳,手拿半边椰壳，然后按一致的节奏拍打，同时自由变换各种队形。敲击椰壳发出清脆的声音，充满黎家乡村气息，极富儿童情趣。

The coconut shell dance is popular in Sanya and Lingshui area, and it is a Li children's dance full of the fun of coconuts. There is no limit to the number of dancers, and the dance prop is easily accessible. People cut the coconut in half and drill the shells to tie them up with leaves. Dancers step on one half of the shell with their toes clipping on the leaf. They hold the other half of the shell and strike them in the same place. While dancing, dancers may change their positions freely. The clear sound of the shell gives a strong sense of the Li village atmosphere, and is also very fun for children.

10.3.2　苗族舞蹈 Dances of the Miao Nationality

苗族舞蹈大都与宗教仪式有着密切关系，代表性的有《作斋舞》《招龙舞》《三元舞》《跳月舞》。

The Miao nation's dances are often closely related to religious rituals, and some representative dances include the "Monk Dance", "Dragon Dance", "San Yuan Dance", and "Moon Dance".

作斋舞

Monk Dance

舞者仅为男性，即"道公"。跳舞时道公不穿法袍，人数因作斋大小而不等。通常大斋跳舞的道公可多至十三人，小斋四人。舞步主要分两种：一种是原地踏步，手持神位、祭品或法剑等物，双膝微微弯曲，上身稍前倾，若干舞步后，向左右各转一圈，全身左右反复摇摆，另有一人在旁敲锣打鼓合拍。第二种是原地踏步，不断重复蹲立动作，手持锣、鼓等乐器，边跳边敲，若干步后即向左或右转身一周，动作较快，无专人伴奏（焦勇勤、孙海兰，2008）。

The monk dance is limited to males, dancers are called "Dao Gong". They do not wear special costumes and the number of dancers depends on the scale of the event. There can be as many as 13 people in a large event, while a small event may have only 4 dancers. There are two forms of dancing: one is having people step in place, holding sacrificial goods and props, and bending their knees with the body leaning forward slightly. After a few steps, they turn a circle to the left and to the right, swing their bodies left and right to the accompaniment of gongs and drums. Another form is having people step in place, and squatting and standing repeatedly. They strike gongs and drums while dancing, and turn in circles to the left and right after every few steps. They move swiftly without dedicated musicians.

招龙舞

Dragon Dance

苗族视龙为祖先，祭拜完毕后，由文、武大道公手持代表龙的长木剑，头戴龙帽，身穿绣有龙图案的长袍，带着小道公表演祭拜祖先招龙的各种动作（焦勇勤、孙海兰，2008；黄友贤、黄仁昌，2008）。招龙舞主要在每年元宵节、中元节和中秋节时进行。

The Miao people regard the Asian dragon as an ancestor. After sacrificing and the worshipping the dragon, civil and martial "Dao Gong" would hold wooden swords representing the dragon. The Dao Gong would wear robes with dragon patterns, and a dragon-head like hat, leading younger Dao Gongs to perform the actions of sacrifice and worship. The Dragon dance is performed every Lantern Festival, Ghost Festival and the Mid-Autumn Festival.

三元舞
San Yuan Dance

用于祭祀盘古开天地和怀念苗族人民的祖先。舞者人数不限，道具仅是一块苗族特有的长方形布巾，布巾扎成短小的棒形，双手捧于胸前。舞蹈的动作都不大，音乐节奏简单，在苗族地区广为流传。

The San Yuan dance (The Heaven, the Earth and the Ancestors Worshipping Dance) is danced to worship the deity Pan Gu who separated heaven and earth and to remember the Miao people's ancestors. There is no limit to the number of dancers. The only prop is a piece of Miao rectangular cloth, folded into a short bar, which is held in front of people's chests. The dance movement is not violent, and the music is simple. It is widespread in the Miao area.

跳月舞
Moon Dance

苗族于每年立秋这天举行盛大的"赶秋"庆典时跳的一种传统舞蹈。每到这天晚上，苗族青年们都要载歌载舞，在歌舞中寻找自己的意中人，据说在这天相爱的人，他们的爱情就会像天上的月亮那样纯洁而永久。

The moon dance is a traditional dance that the Miao people would perform on the autumn greeting ceremony signifying the beginning of autumn. In that particular evening, Young Miao people would sing and dance, and search for mates through the event. It is said that the couple who fall in love on that day will possess a pure and perpetual relationship like the moon in the sky.

10.4　民间乐器
Folk Musical Instruments

10.4.1　海南特色乐器 Hainan Styled Musical Instruments

八音
Ba Yin (8 musical instruments in Hainan style)

据记载，唐代时海南就有了八音性质的器乐活动，在宋元时期已开始流行，到了近代，"八音"已发展成为海南的主流民间音乐，广范应用于节日喜庆、婚丧礼仪、开张剪彩、宗教祭奠等民间活动。

Historical records show that the rudimentary Ba Yin started to take shape in Hainan as early as the Tang Dynasty (618 AD-907 AD) and later became popular in the Song (960 AD-1279 AD) and Yuan (1271 AD-1368 AD) dynasties. In modern times, the Ba Yin is so welcomed that it is widely played on occasions such as festivals, marriages, funerals, opening ceremonies, religious events, and other civil activities.

八音因使用八种乐器演奏而得名，既包括乐器，也包括乐曲和乐队。这八种乐器分别是弦、琴、笛（唢呐）、管、箫、鼓、锣、钹。其中，前五件称为"文牌"，后三件称为"武牌"。"文牌"

乐器以弦、笛为主奏，弦排在首位，为掌调乐器，故称"调弦"。近年来"文牌"乐器一般由单人操作，该人被称为"首手"。"武牌"乐器以鼓为主奏，且鼓经常起着指挥乐队演奏时的起板、煞板，掌握节奏强弱快慢的作用，由此打鼓的人被称为"掌板"（焦勇勤、孙海兰，2008）。

Ba Yin is named after eight different musical instruments. Apart from musical instruments, the term Ba Yin can also include music composition and the band itself. The eight instruments are strings, violin, flute (zurna), tubes, pipes, drums, gongs, and cymbals. Among them, the first five instruments are called "Wen style", and the last three are "Wu style". "Wen style" side of the band is led by strings and flutes, with strings controlling the tunes. Therefore the strings are called "tuning". Nowadays, the "Wen" instruments are often played by one person, called "Shou Shou(the leading player)". The "Wu" instruments are led by the drum, which also controls the rhythm, the speed, and the strength of the music. Thus drummers are called "Zhang Ban (the controller)".

八音按演奏形式大体可分为清音、锣鼓清音、大吹打和戏鼓等四种。

Ba Yin can be divided into clear sounds, drum sounds, great percussion and drum play in accordance with the form of the performance.

清音是采用"文牌"弦、管等除笛之外的乐器，演奏曲调轻快、流畅的乐曲。

The clear sounds use "Wen style" instruments such as pipe, but not the flute. The clear sounds are characterized by light, fluid, and lively music.

锣鼓清音，分为两种：一种是以小唢呐为主奏乐器，配合小件打击乐大花鼓、深边鼓、大钹，用以表现声势浩大、喜庆热烈的场面。因这种演奏形式多用草子锣和草子镲，也称"草子清音"；另一种是以大唢呐为主奏乐器，用以演奏宏伟雄壮的乐曲（焦勇勤、孙海兰，2008）。

Drum sounds are divided into two: one is led by the small zurna, accompanied by big flower drum, deep side drum, and cymbals, to play delightful music signifying warm welcome. Due to the frequent use of grass seed gongs and grass seed cymbals, this type of performance is also called "grass character sounds". The second style is mainly led by the big zurna to play grand and splendid tunes.

大吹打，以双笛吹奏，配合大件打击乐（大花鼓、工字鼓、大钹等），用以演奏气势磅礴的乐曲，渲染热闹而盛大的场面。

Great percussion is a performance led by double flutes and accompanied by big percussion instruments (like big flower drum, H-shaped drums, cymbals, etc.). Its music is characterized by grandiosity, and is often used to render grand scenes.

戏鼓是一种采用地方戏曲主要板腔连奏而成的"连套曲"。以笛的吹奏代替琼剧演员的演唱，辅以其它乐器伴奏的一种演奏形式。

Drum play is a "divertimento", combining main tunes of local operas. The singing in Hainan Opera is replaced by the flute, and accompanied by other musical instruments.

除了上述四种演奏形式外，还有一种叫"清唱"，这种演奏形式必须有"八音"乐音并配备演唱人员，少则一二人，多则三四人。演唱人员要求熟悉多个琼剧曲目，能够胜任各行当的戏，甚至一人可担任全剧所有角色。

Beyond the above four forms, there is another form called "clear singing", a performance involving actors singing along with Ba Yin instruments. The number of actors may range from one to four. They have to be familiar with the lines and be good at performing different roles. Sometimes, one skilled actor may play all the roles.

现在，随着社会的急速发展，这项古老的艺术的传承与发展正面临着前所未有的困难。

But with the rapid development of society, the art is now having great difficulty in finding inheritors.

10.4.2 海南黎族乐器 The Hainan Li People's Musical Instruments

黎族的乐器种类繁多且别具特色，共有 40 多种。传统乐器主要有：峒鼓、叮咚琴、口弓、鼻箫、唎咧、哔哒、拜、灼吧等八大件（石应宽，2006；高泽强、文珍，2008）。可分为吹奏乐器和打击乐器两大类。

There are more than 40 kinds of musical instruments belonging to the Li nationality, and some are quite unique. The eight most representative instruments are the dong drum, dingdong musical instrument, harmonica, nose flute, Li Lie (mouth flute), Bi Da (panpipe), Bai (a kind of bamboo zurna) and Zhuo Ba (a wind instrument). They can be divided into two main categories, namely wind and percussion.

峒鼓

Dong Drum

因昔日这种鼓由峒头掌管，故称"峒鼓"。峒鼓外部呈圆柱形，鼓面通常绘有人物、鸟兽或花草树木等各种图案。旧时黎族头人以击峒鼓为号，动员众人抵抗外敌或举行宗教仪式。今天峒鼓主要作为大型打击乐器，在庆贺丰收、乔迁新居或举行宗教仪式时演奏。

Dong drum is named after "Dong Tou", the chief of the tribe. It is cylindrical, with paintings of birds, animals, flowers, trees, and people, etc. on its surface. They were struck as the signal to assemble people against invaders, or on religious occasions. Today, it is usually played in celebrations, moving into a new house, or in religious rituals.

叮咚琴

Dingdong Musical Instrument

是黎族民间古老的单人敲击木质乐器，构造十分简单。丁冬琴最初的主要部分是一根横木，两端分别用绳子拴住，悬挂在木架子上；取两根木质坚硬的小木棍作敲击器。后来发展为两根横木为主。每根长 2~2.4 米，直径 0.1~0.3 米，一根是"丁"音，另一根是"冬"音。敲打演奏时，用藤条将"丁"棍吊在上面，"冬"棍吊在下面，两根棍子相距 0.15 米左右。现在，为演奏出更多的音阶，丁冬改由用两根或两根以上的横木制作。两根横木的丁冬，可以敲击出 4 个音阶，上为 1、5，下为 3、6；用两根以上横木制成的丁冬，可以演奏出 7 个音阶。音调的高低通过移动吊挂木头的绳索的位置调节（焦勇勤、孙海兰，2008）。

The Dingdong musical instrument is an ancient wooden striking instrument of the Li people. Its structure is quite simple. It is mostly a ledger, with two sides dangling on the shelf, held by strings. Two tough wooden sticks were used to strike it. Later, the instrument developed to consist of two ledgers, with a length of 2 to 2.4 meters, and a diameter of 0.1 to 0.3 meter each. One ledger played "ding" sounds and for the other "dong" sounds. The two ledgers are of different heights, with the distance of approximately 0.15 meters apart. Today, people may use more ledgers to play more musical scales. Two ledgers can play four scales, with the upper one playing the first and the fifth, and the lower for the third and the sixth scale. An instrument made with more than two ledgers can generate seven scales. People change the tones by moving the strings attached to the ledgers.

口弓

Harmonica of the Li People

长 12 厘米，宽 1.5～2 厘米，头大尾尖呈扁梯形。主要由竹片和铜片制成，中间放 4 厘米长的活片针（焦勇勤、孙海兰，2008）。吹奏时左手将口弓放在嘴唇前，用右手拇指摆动弓头，利用吐气、吸气的技巧，即可奏出"1、2、3、4、5"五个音阶，音色粗犷悠扬。黎族青年男子常吹口弓向女方表达爱慕之情。

The harmonica of the Li People is made of bamboo chips and copper sheets. It is 12cm long, 1.5 to 2cm wide, in the shape of a flat trapezoid, with one side big and another side sharp. A needle of 4cm long is placed in the middle. Performers hold the harmonica by the lips with their left hand, and pluck another side with the right thumb. Performers can play the tones from the first to the fifth by controlling breath and airflow. The timber of harmonica is rough but melodious. The Li young men often play it for girls to show their affections.

鼻箫

Nose Flute

是黎家独有的一种管乐器。因用鼻孔吹奏而得名，至今已有 1000 多年的历史。鼻箫选用一根无节的"粗皮竹"或"山竹"细管制成。一般管长 60～70 厘米，管径约 1.6 厘米，两端保留着原始竹节，共 4 个孔，一个吹气孔，三个音位孔。吹奏时，箫管由左鼻孔向右鼻孔横斜，箫头贴紧右鼻孔，由左鼻孔吹气。可奏出 5、6、1、2、3、5（焦勇勤、孙海兰，2008）。其音色清幽低沉。

The nose flute is a special wind instrument of the Li people. It is named because it is played with the nose, and the nose flute is more than 1000 years old. It is made from a bamboo tube without joints, usually 60 to 70cm long, with a diameter of 1.6 cm. The bamboo joints are on the two ends. The flute has four holes, one blow hole and three phoneme holes. The flute inclines from the left nostril to the right, and the head of the flute leans on the right nostril, while the left nostril blows air. It can play 5, 6, 1, 2, 3, and 5, with 5 for both bass and treble. The tone is low and quiet.

鼻箫
Nose Flute (Source: http://image.so.com/)

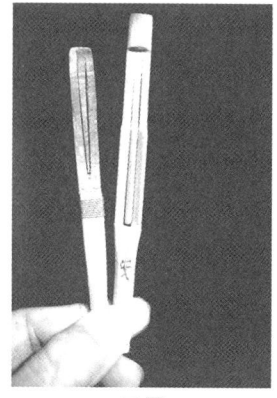

口弓
Harmonica of the Li People (Source: http://lizu.baike.com/article-872605.html)

227

唎咧
Li Lie

唎咧又称"口箫",是黎族民间特有的一种传统乐器。以山竹尾竿为原料,按 3 厘米一节、小管套大管节节相套的方式,制作出头小尾大、长 24 厘米、八节左右的乐器。吹奏时,音色响亮、粗犷有力,是黎族青年男子最喜欢吹奏的一种乐器。

Li Lie is also known as the "mouth flute", and it is a traditional folk instrument of the Li people. It is made from the bottom part of the bamboo, with each section being 3cm long. Eight sections are inserted into one another, making an instrument with a total length of 24cm. Its tone is loud and powerful, making it a favorite instrument of the Li young men.

哔哒
Bi Da (Panpipe)

哔哒又叫"黎族排箫",由两支管身长短和粗细完全相同的筚达并排绑扎而成,两管孔距和簧片的位置均相同。演奏时,口含两管簧片,手指同时按两管音孔。其音色奔放,又因两管的音高稍有差异,使其音响效果颇富山野气息。

The panpipe is also called "double pipe of the Li people". It is made of two identical pipes bound together. People put the reed of the pipes in their mouths and press on the holes of both pipes. Its tone is loud and bright, and the different tones of the two pipes grant its music a vivid countryside flavor.

拜
Bai

拜相当于一种竹唢呐。拜由六、七节长短、粗细不同的竹管由小到大、由细到粗依次套接而成。管首置有荔枝叶或椰子叶卷制的簧哨;管尾喇叭口多由当地所产的一种麻卷制而成,有时也用树叶或硬纸卷制。常见的拜,通高约 32 厘米左右。

The Bai is a kind of bamboo zurna, with six or seven sections arranged in order. At the head is a reed made of litchi leaf or coconut tree leaf. The horn shaped bottom side is usually made of local linen, but people may also use leaves or hard paper. The instrument usually is 32 cm in length.

演奏时,其姿势和方法均与唢呐相似。不同的是就音质而言,拜的发音清亮、柔和,音色则悠扬而甜美。演奏时采用循环呼吸法(黎族民间换气法),声音连续可长达两个小时之久。

The Bai is played in a similar way to that of the zurna. However, its tune is different. The Bai has a clear, soft, gentle, and sweet tune. People use the circulating breathing method (which is a Li folk method) to make the instrument play a continuous sound which may last for almost two hours long.

灼吧
Zhuo Ba

灼吧是黎族独有的吹奏乐器。一支细长的竹管横插入略粗的竹管中,呈"7"字形,进气孔细且带拐弯,这就是灼吧了。其音色优美,耐人回味。

The Zhuo Ba is a unique wind instrument of the Li people. A thin and long bamboo inserts into a bigger bamboo, making an instrument shaped like an Arabic numeral "7". The air intake hole is small and curved. It's sound is melodious and moving.

10.5 民间绘画
Folk Painting

10.5.1 黎族民间绘画 Folk Painting of the Li People

文身刻画
Tattooing

文身刻画是黎族女性结束少女生活、步入成年必须完成的一个程序，至今已有 3000 多年的历史。文身的图形、普制、施术年龄等都有严格规定。黎族有五个方言，各个方言妇女文身按照祖先遗传的图案，互不相同。3000 多年来黎族文身的方式和图案基本没有变化。比如美孚方言妇女以几何方形纹、泉源纹或谷粒纹组成的图案文身，而润方言妇女则以树叶纹或方块形图案文身。青蛙是黎族最崇拜的动物之一，因此，黎族文身常以青蛙作为主要图案。黎族少女长到 12 岁左右起文身，必须按照祖先遗留下来的特殊标志接受文身，黎族人称为"开面"。所刺部位也有一定次序：脸、背、胸前、腿、手（黄学魁，2008；焦勇勤、孙海兰，2008）。从脸到脚的文身过程都是分别进行的，有的长达几年时间分段进行施文，这样做可以缓解疼痛。

Tattooing is a necessary step for young girls in the Li tribe to become adults, and this custom has more than 3000 years of history. There are strict rules for tattoo graphics, with tribe graphics and age for different tattoos, etc. The Li has five dialects and the tattoo of each dialectical area is different according to their ancestral genetic pattern, unchanged for more than 3000 years. For example, women in the Meifu dialect have geometrical square, spring or grain patterns, while Run dialect women may paint leaf or diamond shaped tattoos. The frog is one of the most worshipped animals for the Li people. As a result, Li tattoos often use frogs as a main pattern. Li girls would start tattooing at age 12, in accordance with a special pattern left by ancestors, called the "open face". The tattoo location also has a certain order: from the face, back, chest, legs, to hands. The procedures are carried out in order, sometimes lasting several years to ease the pain.

有关黎族妇女文身的缘由有多种说法。一说为黎族祖先因崇拜蛙、蛇图腾而在自己身上绘制相似的图案，后来也成为身份等级尊贵的象征；一说是文身作为黎族人生前氏系区分和死后认祖归宗的民族标志。总体来看，这些说法共同反映了黎族的宗教信仰和社会组织形式，也体现了深沉的审美观念，被人誉为"刻在人体上的敦煌壁画"。然而，随着现代生活方式和审美观念的深入影响，从 20 世纪 60 年代开始，黎族妇女文身的古老习俗也渐渐消失了（黄学魁，2008）。

There are many proposed rationale for these tattoos. One is that Li ancestors worshipped frogs and snakes and viewed them as symbol distinguishing higher social status; another is that the tattoo is used to distinguish their tribal origins. Overall, these rationales reflect the religious beliefs and social organizations of the Li nation, and also reflect their aesthetic ideals. These tattoos are often known as "Dunhuang frescoes inscribed on the human body". However, since the 1960s, the custom of tattooing has gradually disappeared under the influence of modern lifestyles and aesthetic concepts.

10.5.2 苗族民间绘画 Folk Drawings of the Miao People

海南苗族的民间绘画多为宗教画像，多绘于清代晚期。彩绘基本上是由一个母本复制，一传十，十传百，进而覆盖苗族的相关地区。绘制者都是当地的道公或其徒弟（黄学魁，2008）。

Hainan Miao folk paintings in the late Qing dynasty were mainly religious portraits. Color paintings were basically copied from one original version, passed on among the Miao from one to a hundred, and eventually covered all areas associated with the Miao people. The painters are often local monks or disciples.

因为道公又分为文道公和武道公，与各文武鬼神相对应。他们分工不同，文道公主管绘制、传承文官画像，武道公则掌管武官画像的绘制和传承。因此有文派画像和武派画像。文派画像由"三清图"和"右圣左师图"组成，共五幅，前者三幅，后者两幅。"三清图"中的三清即"玉清""太清""上清"，图高110厘米，宽40厘米。每幅图内容均分为上界、阳界和阴界三部分。"右圣左师图"高68厘米，宽42厘米，内容为"圣""师"骑猛兽行法（黄学魁，2008）。

Monks are divided into civil and martial monks corresponding to religious spirits, and thus have different roles. Civil and martial monks are responsible for the creation and keeping of the portraits for civil and martial celestial officials respectively. Therefore, there are civil and martial styles of portraits. Civil portraits consist of "three Qing figures" and two "right saint left teacher figures", totaling five portraits. The "Three Qing figures" include "yu qing", "tai qing", and "shang qing", each 110 cm high and 40 cm wide. Each figure is divided into the upper region, Yang region, and the Yin region. "Right saint left teacher figures" are 68 cm high and 42 cm wide. They typically depict the saint and the teacher riding beasts and exercising their powers.

武派画像一般长122厘米，宽22厘米。所画的内容为掌管上界、法律、天文、地理、生产、生活的官员的画像，每像配一坐骑（黄学魁，2008）。

Martial portrayals are usually about 122 cm long and 22 cm wide. They may include portrayals of officers managing the heaven, law, astronomy, geography, production, and life, and each figure sits on a beast.

11

海南竞技民俗
Hainan Sports Customs

竞技民俗是一种集体力、技巧、技能为内容的娱乐性竞赛活动。它是一种以竞技消遣为目的文化样式，主要通过竞技达到娱乐、和谐的境地，从而使人们幸福安康、健康有序。海南的民间体育竞技活动主要源于日常生产实践活动，具有浓厚的生活气息，富有浓郁的地方色彩和民族特色。

Sports customs are competitive folk sports refer to recreational activities, combined with physical strength and skills. People take athletic activity as a way of pastime. Hainan sports activities are originated from daily production with pronounced local color and national characteristics.

海南竞技活动丰富多彩，很多项目是逢年过节不可缺少的活动。在海南的汉族常见的比赛项目有篮球、排球、台球、拔河、象棋等，其中排球是海南人民的最爱，文昌是我国著名的"排球之乡"。此外，汉族民间还有许多富有地方特色的游艺，如削甘蔗、赛牛等，以及一些儿童游戏竞赛游戏，如跳绳、打柴、射玻璃球、转车轮等。

Hainan competitive folk sports are rich in farm and variety, some of which are indispensable during holidays or festivals. Basketball, volleyball, table tennis, tug of war and playing chess are common sports activities, of which volleyball is people's favorite sport in Hainan. And Wenchang is well-known as a hometown in China. In addition, there are some recreational activities with local characteristics, such as Peeling Sugar Canes, Bullfighting. Some activities, such as Rope Skipping, Threshing Woods, Flipping Glass Beads and Turning the Wheels, are very popular among children.

黎族、苗族、回族各县群众性的体育活动日益活跃，并踊跃开展形式多样的民间体育竞赛活动。每逢"三月三"、黎苗族节、国庆节、五一节、春节、元旦等节日，竞赛活动更加丰富多彩。据统计，海南黎族传统体育项目约有 47 项，竞赛项目除了有爬竿过树、赶狗归坡、串藤圈等传统竞技项目外，还有后来兴起的粉枪射击、摔跤、弩箭打猎、射鱼、跳竹竿、拉乌龟等竞技项目。黎族的传统民间体育活动，在一定程度上反映了黎族人民的生产生活方式及民风民俗。

The county and part of the township, such as in the Li, the Miao and the Hui minorities actively carry out warious forms of sports which have been increasingly with people. Some traditional sports and recreational activities are more colorful than before such as, on every March the 3rd, the Li and Miao Festival and Spring Festival. The traditional sports of the Li ethnic group are composed of 47 projects such as Climbing the Tree, Gan Gou Gui Po (similar to hockey ball), String of Rattan Ring. Traditional athletic events, and the subsequent activities, which are the Powder Gun Shooting, Wrestling, Crossbow, Hunting, Shooting Fish, Bamboo Rod Dance and La Wugui (tug-of-war) etc. The Li sports activities, to some extent, show the people's way of production and customs.

海南苗族竞技活动极具民族特色,如八人秋、搓麻线、顶棍、斗牛竞赛、割橡胶比赛等竞技活动。海南回族的民间竞技活动也具有强烈的民族特性,如传统的体育项目荡秋千、点烟竞赛、盲人背哑巴、三脚竞走、斗牛等传统民间竞技。

There are also a lot of traditional sport activities in the Miao ethnic group such as Eight People Swing in the Autumn, Rubbing the Rope (made of fiber plants like hemp with the hands), Ding Gun (two people hold the same stick and push each other), Bullfighting and Rubber Tapping, which reflect unique national characteristics of the Miao nationality. Furthermore, the traditional sport activities are featured with national characteristics in the Hui ethnic group, such as Swing, Lighting Cigarettes, San Jiao Jing Sai (the race of tying two people's feet) and Bull Fighting.

竞技项目是人们在物质条件具备之后的一种放松身心的健康活动,不仅有利于身心健康,还能增加人与人之间情感的沟通。

Sports activities are aimed for relaxation and health mentally and physically, but facilitate the interpersonal communication between people.

11.1 海南黎族传统竞技项目
Traditional Sports Activities of the Li People

根据文献统计,海南黎族传统体育项目约有47项,根据其特点与功能大致可分为娱乐竞赛、力量竞技、射击、击打、田径及其他、游戏等6大类(见表11.1)。其中跳竹竿、赶狗归坡、射箭、射弩、粉枪射击、打秋千、拉乌龟等传统竞技项目尤其受大家的欢迎。

It's recorded that the traditional sport activities of the Li nationality are about 47 projects, which can be divided into 6 major categories including entertainment, strength, shooting, hitting, athletic and games (Table 1). According to the characteristics and functions, the Bamboo Rod Dance, Gan Gou Gui Po, Shooting, Crossbow, Powder Gun Shooting, Swing, La Wugui (tug of war), etc. are extremely popular with people.

表 11.1　海南黎族群众参与民族传统竞技活动项目表
Traditional Sports Activities of the Li People

类　型 Types of Competition	项　目 Projects
娱乐竞赛 Entertainment	跳竹竿（Bamboo Rod Dance）、荡秋千（Swing）、攀藤摘花（Picking Flowers by Vine）、串藤圈（Picking Flowers by Vine）、打陀螺（Whipping-top）
力量竞技型 Strength	摔跤（Wresting）、顶棍（Carry the Stick against each other）、拔河和拉乌龟（Tug-of-war）
射击类 Shooting	射箭（Archery）、射弩（Crossbow）、弹弓（Catapult）、粉枪射击（Powder Gun Shooting）
击打类 Hitting	打狗归坡 Driving the Ball（similar to hockey ball）、打木（柴）节（Threshing Woods）
田径类及其他 Athletics and others	竞走（Heel and Toe Walking Race）、爬竿过树（Climbing the Tree）、赛牛（Bull Fighting）
游戏类 Games	守营（Stand Guard at the Camp）、背人碰撞（Carry People to Bump each other）、水中格斗（Fighting in the Water）、抛石子（Throwing Stones）

跳竹竿
Bamboo Rod Dance

海南黎苗族传统竞技活动之一。跳竹竿前，人们通常会用平行的方木头作垫架，上面横放若干根长竹竿。持竿者坐或蹲着相对双手各执一条竹竿末端。在有节奏、有规律的碰击声中，跳舞者在竹竿分和的空隙敏捷的跳跃，并作出各种优美的动作。如今，竹竿舞"在形式和功能上经历了多次与现代文化元素的互动、融合，发生了巨大的变化。"竹竿舞"已演变为集歌、舞、体为一体的体育娱乐项目，具有了更强的观赏性、竞技性、惊险性、新奇性和娱乐性，并已走出黎族地区，不仅活跃在黎族传统节日"三月三"、春节、元宵节节庆活动中，也已成为当地学校学生和社区居民的健身活动项目，深受大众喜爱。该项目运动量适度，气氛热烈，既能使人们感受到快乐、调节情绪，又能锻炼大家的灵活，协调和加强身体机能（海南——南中国海的天堂岛，2005）。

The bamboo rod dance is one of the traditional sports in the Li and Miao ethnic groups. Usually, the dancers leap on the top of two square timbers over which two parallel bamboo poles are quickly tapped together and pulled apart. In order not to have their feet caught, the dancers must hop up and down quickly. The tapping of the bamboo poles against the wood makes a rhythmical sound. The dancers leap through the bamboos, and make graceful poses. Nowadays, the bamboo rod dance has greatly been changed with the combination of modern cultures whatever in forms and functions, which has become a recreational activity. Therefore, bamboo rod dance is held during holidays or festivals, such as March the 3rd, Spring Festival, La-tern's Day, and it becomes a body-building activity for students and residents, which makes people feel happy and healthy.

赶狗归坡
Gan Gou Gui Po (similar to hockey ball)

一项类似曲棍球的民间体育娱乐活动项目，流行于三亚鹿回头一带的黎族村寨。由于居住在山区里，较偏远，交通闭塞，古代黎族人很少与外界往来，生活比较单调。为满足人们的娱乐生活需求，黎族许多自娱自乐的体育活动便产生了继而慢慢地发展起来了。黎族赶狗归坡运动是黎族人民在田里收割完稻子，为了健身娱乐，就用椰子的树叶编织成球的形状作为双方击打的物体。但是，由于稻根和泥巴的阻挡，球很难在稻田里快速的滚动，于是人们就想到砍下"L"形状的树枝用来打球，球在田里的速度就变得非常快了。后来，人们不仅在收割后的稻田里开展这项运动，还在其他空旷的场地里进行此项运动比赛。比赛时，场地大小因地制宜，人数不限，分成两队，两队人数相等，比赛由双方商定，比赛宣布开始后，双方用"L"形状的球棒互相竞逐击打球，传接球，凡把球赶到对方底线球门的便得一分，在规定时间内得分最多的球队为获胜队。比赛结束后，负方队员被罚四肢着地模仿狗爬行走，胜方则骑在负方背上吆喝退场，故名"赶狗归坡"。

Gan Gou Gui Po (similar to hockey ball) is popular among the Li People in the Lu Huitou village of Sanya. In ancient times, the Li People lived in the remote mountains, rarely contact with outside world. In order to meet their recreational needs, lots of physical activities were produced and gradually developed. Gan Gou Gui Po refers to the game that people play the ball which is made of coconut palms for fitness and entertainment after harvesting in the field. Then, the Li People got the idea of cutting down the "L-shaped" branches to hit the ball, which makes the speed much faster. Later, they play the game not only in the field but also in other open air. Generally speaking, there are two teams with equal numbers, and the length of time is agreed upon by both teams. When the competition begins, both teams take the "L-shaped" branches to hit the ball against each other. The team who score higher within the specified time is the winner. After that, the members of the defeated team should imitate walking like a dog, with the winners leave the field by riding on their backs, which is the origin of "Gan Gou Gui Po".

赶狗归坡（朱兵艳 摄于海南省博物馆）
Gan Gou Gui Po (Courtesy of Bingyan Zhu)

游客体验射弩 （朱兵艳 摄）
Tourist Experiencing Crossbow (Courtesy of Bingyan Zhu)

射弩场（朱兵艳 摄）
Crossbow (Courtesy of Bingyan Zhu)

射箭、射弩
Archery or Crossbow

射箭比赛是黎族一项古老的体育活动，这与古代狩猎、放牧的生活方式有关。古时候黎族人民为了生存的需要，常用木、竹等制成的弓箭来防身自卫和进行狩猎。弓箭和弩是黎族先民护身狩猎的重要工具。弩的制法和造型都与弓相似。比赛时以击鼓为号，将牛（猪）腿或羊悬于树上为靶，射手们在 50 米外的地方站立，持弓拉弦瞄准射击，在规定箭数内，射中靶心多者为胜，优胜者取走牛腿与同村参赛者分享。射技高超的青年射手常常成为黎族姑娘"比赛竞婚"的对象。每逢"三月三"传统佳节，都要举行射箭、射弩活动，以从其中挑选神箭手。如今射箭比赛与现代射箭运动进行了多次融合、接轨，逐步由村寨进入了学校，当地业余体校还专设射箭班，为了保留射箭、射弩这一民族特色（海南省志·民俗志，2006）。

Archery or crossbow is also a traditional sport of the Li People. This activity can be traced back to ancient hunting. In the primitive society, the bow and crossbow were made by woods or bamboos for the purpose of defending themselves. The way to make bow and crossbow was similar, and both of them were the important hunting tools for the Li People. When the competition started, the competitors standing 50 meters away shot the cow or pigs which were hung on the tree. The winner who shooting arrows could take the best part of the cow or pigs sharing with other contestants. The best shooter often became the Mr. Right who was hunted for the Li girls. Nowadays, the competition is held on the 3rd day of the 3rd lunar month to choose the best ones in village or school. And even some schools have remained crossbow classes with national characteristics.

粉枪射击
Powder Gun Shooting

粉枪射击又称土枪射击，是黎族传统的体育活动。在抗日战争时期，粉枪是黎族人民对敌斗争的主要战斗武器。随着社会的发展，虽然狩猎的生活方式与战争的内容已逐渐淡化，但黎族粉枪射击活动仍然是黎族群众最喜爱的活动之一。每逢"三月三"传统佳节，黎族村寨都要进行粉枪射击比赛，参加这项活动的主要以青年男性为主。男子扛着粉枪，成群结队，在空旷的场上排成一字队形，先对天空鸣枪，然后轮流瞄准靶子射击，打中者给予奖赏。然后大家饮酒对歌，欢度民族的传统节日。有的地方在村头以贴红纸为目标，在距离几十米处站立比赛枪法，射手们举枪转体180°急射，俗称"打红"，含有驱逐邪气，象征迎吉祥的意思。粉枪射击也是男女青年相互接近的好机会，女青年可乘此机会挑选自己满意的枪法好的意中人。

Powder gun shooting, well-known as shotguns shooting, is one of traditional sports of the Li nationality. During the period of war of resistance against Japanese aggression, the powder gun was the main weapons against the enemy. With the development of society, the Li powder gun hunting has gradually faded, but shooting is still one of the favorite activities for the Li People. The powder gun shooting competition is held in the Li village during the 3rd day of the 3rd lunar month. The participants in the activity are mainly young males. They carry the guns in droves and row in the open field, give a shot into the air first, and shoot targets in turns. The one who hits the shot will be rewarded with celebrations followed. The red papers are stuck to some places as the goals at a distance of tens of meters, and the competitors swivel 180º degrees to shoot, which is commonly known as "shooting at the red" to drive away evils and welcome to auspicious things. This activity is a good opportunity for the young men and women to communicate with each other. Young women can take this chance to choose their Mr. Rights.

打秋千
Swing

打秋千是黎族群众最喜爱，开展得较广泛的活动项目之一，参加者主要是青少年。男女青少年放牧或到看管山栏稻时都可以打秋千玩乐。秋千的制作方法很简单，把麻绳绑在结实粗大的芒果树枝干，这种方法能保证麻绳和枝干以及整个秋千架子的结实和坚固，确保安全。荡秋千时，有单人和双人，也可以男女搭配。青年们相互比赛看谁荡得高，时间长。秋千此起彼伏，喧闹嬉戏，充满着黎族人民勇敢、豪放、乐观向上的民族精神。

Swing is the one of the favorite activities for the Li People, which reflects the Li People are brave, bold with optimistic spirit. Most of participants are mainly young people, and they play it for fun. When the teenagers put out to pasture or attend to the Shanlan rice, they often swing for entertainment. The method of making the swing is to tie the ropes on the strong branches of the mango trees to make sure of their safety. Singles and doubles would be frequently adopted while playing on the swing. The one who swings higher and longer is the winner.the 3rd day of the 3rd lunar month the 3rd day of the 3rd lunar month

拉乌龟
La Wu Gui (similar to Tug-of-war)

拉乌龟活动，是黎族青年男子在农闲季节或喜庆节日举行的一类体育项目。是黎族民间传统体育活动之一，是民间模仿乌龟行走方式而创造出的一项趣味性很浓的体育竞技项目。这一比赛项目类似于拔河。通常两人一组，一人扮"乌龟"，另一人扮拉"乌龟"的人。比赛时，代表乌龟的人做乌龟状，在界线的一端，双手双膝着地，头向外；拉乌龟的人站在界线的另一端，双手拉着绳子或布带的另一头。双方之间有三条平行线，在比赛还没开始时，裁判会把这个"中分结"控制在居中的一条直线上，比赛哨声一响，就立即松手，"乌龟"竭尽全力往前爬，拉者拼命向后拽，最先把对方拉过规定的界线者为胜。拉乌龟活动对于锻炼人腰腹力、培养人的拉力技巧有一定益处。

La Wu Gui (similar to tug-of-war) is one of the traditional sports for the Li nationality. It originated from imitating the way of turtle walking, which is similar to the tug of war. In general, there are two groups of people, one of whom acts as a "turtle" and the other one pulls the "turtle" on the other side. The referee puts the "knot" in the middle of a straight line before the game starts. When the whistle sounds, the one who acts as the "turtle" makes every effort to go up. Meanwhile, the other one also pulls desperately. At last, the one who is pulled out the provisional line fails.

拉乌龟 （刘士祥 摄）
La Wu Gui (tug-of war) (Courtesy of Shixiang Liu)

11.2 苗族传统竞技项目
Traditional Sports Activities of the Miao People

由于苗族人民长期与黎族混居与交往，他们也吸收了很多黎族民间竞技娱乐项目，具有明显的民族文化融合特性。苗族也有八人秋、斗牛、顶棍、割橡胶等很多民族传统项目。

Due to frequent communication between the Li and the Miao People in the long-term, the Miao People also absorb the strong points of the national folk sports and entertainment from the Li People such as Swing, La Wu Gui. In addition, there are other traditional activities in the Miao ethnic group including Swinging for Eight People, Bull Fighting, Ding Gun (push the stick against each other), Rubber Tapping and so on.

八人秋
Eight People Swing

八人秋即八人秋千，是苗族的一项传统民间体育项目，是苗族每年立秋这天称作"赶秋节"必不可少的比赛活动。顾名思义，八人秋即秋千架上有八个人。在八人秋架上，分别坐着四男四女，架下站着两位老人——秋公和秋婆，先由秋公、秋婆念几句诗，再唱"开秋歌"，然后由秋公秋婆转动秋千，这就是"开秋"。当快速旋转的秋千停下来以后，谁停在最上面的两个人对歌，直到大家满意为止。

Eight people swing is one of traditional folk sports in the Miao ethnic group. It is an indispensable competition at the beginning of autumn (13th seasonal division point) which is called "Gan Qiu Day". As the name suggests, eight people swing includes eight people, four males and four females sitting on the swing, and the elder man and woman standing under the swing. Before the competition begins, the elder woman reads a few verses and sings a song about autumn and they begin to play, which is called "Kaiqiu" (swing begins). When the fast rotating swing stops, the two people who stop above sing in antiphonal style until the others are satisfied with their songs.

斗牛竞赛
Bull Fighting

海南苗族一项民间娱乐活动。每年定期举行以展示敬牛、爱牛、崇拜牛的民族特征。斗牛比赛那天，人山人海，男女老少纷纷前往观赛。赛场中央的栏杆中有几十头群众自家养的公牛。斗架之前，牛的主人要请牛喝糯米酒，使公牛更凶狠。开始斗牛时，把两头牛的牛眼用树叶掩盖，牵到场地中后再揭开，两牛照面后怒目相视。主持斗牛的人一声令下，互相进攻，对撞牛角，进行决斗。经过激烈的角逐，几个回合可见分晓。获胜的公牛身披红绸，角装银饰，张开大嘴，吼叫了几声。人们会把红绸布挂在牛犄角上，以示奖励。回家后还摆庆功酒，喜庆斗牛胜利，奖励养牛有功的人。海南苗族斗牛不仅是一种娱乐活动，还是养牛技术的比赛，从而可促进养牛活动。

Bull fighting is one of folk entertainment activities of the Miao People. It is held annually to show their national characteristics of respect, love and worship for bulls. On that day, a sea of people flock to watch the competition. Before the competition begins, the bull owners feed bull with rice wine to make them more vicious. When the bull fighting begins, both the two bulls' eyes are covered with leaves (bull is a kind of buffalo in Hainan). After leading the bulls to the arena and taking the leaves away, the two bulls glared at each other. With the order given, the bulls begin to attack each other. After a few rounds, some bulls fail or even die on the spot. The last one left is the winner. The winner bull wears a red silk with silver horn, opening mouth wide and roaring a few times. The red silk cloth is hung on the bull's horn as a reward. What's more, the celebration will be held for victory, rewarding the owner who raises the bull. The bull fighting is not only a kind of entertainment, but also the competition of feeding quality bulls.

顶棍
Ding Gun (push the stick against each other)

顶棍是传统的力量型竞技项目，比赛时两名身强力壮的小伙子各执一根长3米的木棍的一端相互对推，谁先将对方推出划定的圆圈谁为胜。哨声一响，两边的大力士齐发力，双手紧握木棍奋力向前推，两边互不相让，观众也被这充满激情的比赛所带动，加油助威声一浪高过一浪。

Ding Gun (push the stick against each other) is a traditional athletic activity of strength. Two strong middle-aged men hold each side of the 3 meters long stick and then push against each other. The one who is first pushed out the circle loses the competition. When hearing the sound of the whistle, two strong men hold the stick tightly and fiercely push against each other, the excited audience cheering again and again.

顶棍比赛（李运坚 提供）
The Competition of Ding Gun (Courtesy of Yunjian Li)

割橡胶
Rubber Tapping

由每个村选拨几个割橡胶能手，参加比赛。评委一宣布开始，在 10 分钟内用时最短且割最快，又伤不到树的选手获胜。比赛现场，气氛紧张又激烈，参赛选手动作敏捷又熟练。通过割胶比赛，为村民搭建割胶技能交流平台有利于增加村民之间的情感，同时也促进并提高村民割胶技能。

Rubber tapping is one of competitive activities in the Miao ethnic group. Those, who are good at tapping rubber are selected by each village, take part in the competition. Once the judge announces the beginning of the competition, those who tap the rubber faster without hurting the trees within 10 minutes are winners. Under the intense competition, the contestants are agile to finish the task. The competition builds a platform for communication on tapping skills for sharing tapping skills.

割橡胶比赛（李运坚 提供）
The Race of Rubber Tapping (Courtesy of Yunjian Li)

11.3 回族传统竞技项目
Traditional Sports Activities of the Hui People

受日常生产生活条件及环境的影响，海南回族的民间文体娱乐活动有着很强的地域和民族特色。他们勤劳、勇敢，在劳动实践中发挥自己的智慧，创造富有本民族特色的传统体育活动，其内容精彩纷呈，场面十分壮观，活动引人入胜。

Influenced by the living environment, the sports activities of the Hui ethnic group in Hainan are featured with strong regional and national characteristics. The activities are fascinating, and the scene is spectacular, which originate from their daily work, courage and wisdom.

荡秋千

Swing

荡秋千是具有回族民族特色的一项传统体育项目。其活动的内容和对象与黎苗族荡秋千不甚相同。回族荡秋千的主要对象是青少年女子。几位少女坐在秋千板上，上悬一条粗绳，另用两条稍小的绳子拴住粗绳，再由两位少女拉曳，使秋千前前后后有节奏地摆动，十分有趣。

Swing is one of the traditional sports in the Hui ethnic group. Compared to the Li and the Miao minorities, the contents and contestants of the activities vary a bit. The main contestants are teenage girls who sit on the swing, with two girls dragging the rope and making it swing back and forth rhythmically.

点烟竞赛

Competition of Lighting Cigarettes

点烟竞赛是一项以锻炼灵活敏捷为主要内容的赛跑活动。在距起跑前面 10 米的地方竖两个木桩，在二根木桩上用绳系上众多已燃的香头。参者两手反扣。口衔未燃香烟，点着烟后，跑回原地，以先达终点者为优胜。

The competition of lighting cigarettes is an activity to test contestants' agility. At a distance of 10 meters from the starting point, two wooden stakes are erected 10 meters away and tied with burned incense. Participants put their hands back with unlit cigarettes in their mouths, and quickly run to where he or she stood after lightening the cigarettes, with the first one running back being the winner.

找物竞技

Competition of Hunting for Goods

找物竞技是一项比较简单却又妙趣横生的竞技活动。比赛规则是：裁判在许多条子签上写上所需要找之物置于箱子里。参赛者从箱子抽一签，遵循"按图索骥"的办法，如抽条写的是"小孩"，就找小孩抱上，写的是小凳，就找小凳拿起，然后按规定跑回原地，以准确、最快者为优胜。趣味盎然。

The competition of hunting for goods is relatively easy but interesting. The rules can be summered as follows: the referee puts the lots with some words written on them into the box. Contestants draw lots from the box by following up a clue. If someone draws a lot and gets the note "the kid" or "chair", he or she should pick up a child or a chair as soon as possible, and then run back to the starting point with the fastest one being the winner.

三脚赛跑

San Jiao Sai Pao (a Walking Activity with Two People)

三脚赛跑是一项由双人配合的竞走活动，以两人为一组。各组把不同的两人的左右腿绑在一块，手搭着手，肩并着肩，各组以领先者为胜。比赛中，若摔倒了，再爬起来继续竞走，到达终点照样获胜。这个项目虽然难度大，要富有韧性而机动灵活才能取胜。因为情趣性浓郁，往往惹得观众捧腹大笑，气氛非常热烈（海南史志网，2014）。

San Jiao Sai Pao (a walking activity for two people) is extremely popular among people.

Usually, there are two people in a group, and one of them ties his or her left leg with the other one's right leg, hand in hand, shoulder to shoulder, and walk to the finish line together. The team who goes ahead is the winner. This project requires the team members flexible and elastic physical conditions. During the competition, their performance makes them burst into laughter.

女子穿针引线竞赛
Competition of Needlework for the Hui Women

海南回族民族传统竞技项目之一。这是一个团体项目，比速度与默契的娱乐活动。比赛方式，由若干组进行比赛，每组两人，一人拿针，一人拿线，两人距离不远。比赛时，拿线者向拿针者投奔，穿针引线后，拿针者回原地，快者为优胜。穿引时，另一只手不能帮忙，只能用原来拿针或线的手，否则犯规者算输。

The competition of needlework is one of traditional sports of the Hui nationality, which is a team project for the race of speed and secret agreement. Generally, several groups take part in the competition at a time, each of group is composed of two people, one with a needle and the other one with line. When the competition begins, the one with the line runs toward the one with needle, then finishes needlework quickly and returns to the starting point. The group members who finish the needlework first without breaking the rules are winners.

木球
Cricket

回族同胞十分喜爱的传统体育活动。相传，它是由宁夏回族自治区流行的"打毛球"和"打篮子"发展逐渐改进而成的球类体育运动。这项运动的比赛方法、规则、时间、裁判和场地等都有比较明确的规定。比赛人数共10人，各队分别有5人。在交锋过程中，进一球得一分，进球多者为优胜。

Cricket is a traditional sport activity which is very popular among the Hui people. There was a legend that the cricket originated from "playing the ball or basket", which was loved by the people in the Hui autonomous region. Players score points by hitting with a wooden bat and running between two sets of upright wooden sticks. As usual, there are two teams respectively with five people. The more scores the participants get, the more chances they win the game during the competition.

11.4 汉族儿童竞技游戏
Sports Activities for Children of the Han Nationality

除了汉族、黎族、苗族、回族诸多具有民族特色的竞技游戏外，海南民间还有许多富有地方特色的儿童竞技游戏。儿童在玩耍中开展竞技游戏，如单手脚摔跤、赛牛、打柴、弹玻璃球等项目，具有较强的娱乐性与趣味性。

There are also lots of sport activities for children except for the Han, the Li, the Miao and the Hui ethnic groups, and the children have fun in experiencing these games such as Wrestling, Buffalo Race, Firewood, Flipping Glass Beads, and so on, which are full of entertainments and interests.

单手脚摔跤
Wrestling with Hand and Foot

海南各地农村儿童所喜欢玩耍的游戏比赛。比赛分两队，各队人数相等，可任意组合。参赛者左手抓住自己的右脚趾，或以右手抓住自己的左脚趾，然后一对二、二对一，或几对一单脚蹬跃，撞向对方，被撞倒或手和脚趾脱离者为输，一般以三局定胜负。海南各族都有此游戏，有些地方亦称为"搭脚架"（海南省志·民俗志，2012）。

Wrestling with hand and foot is a popular game among the children in the countryside. Usually, two teams with equal number take part in this activity. During the competition, the contestant seizes his left toe with the right hand, or grasps his right toe with left hand. Then they start wrestling with several people to one or one to one. The one whose hand or foot touches the field fails the game.

赛牛
Buffalo Race

海南各地农村儿童所喜欢玩耍的游戏比赛，此项比赛可锻炼参赛者的胆量、技艺。比赛规则是：在草地或空旷地上划出比赛距离，比赛开始，各自骑在牛背上，两脚夹紧牛背，一手抓住牛绳，一手抓紧牛尾，以防止从牛背上摔下来，用牛棍抽打牛背，让牛在路上奔跑，先到达目的地者为胜。

The buffalo race is one of the favorite games for the children in the countryside. The rules of the game are as follows: when the competition begins, the contestants respectively ride on the buffalo's back running. Who gets the finish line at first is the winner.

打柴
Threshing Wood

海南农村儿童所喜欢玩耍的游戏比赛。比赛时将规定长度的小木棍高高抛起，然后用"柴母"（比赛时用来击打其他木棍的长棍）击打小木棍。若小木棍被击出规定的区域之外，则该木头为击者所得。

Threshing wood is the competition loved by the children in the countryside. When the competition begins, it's required to throw the small sticks highly which are hit by firewood that is a longer stick. If the small sticks are hit out the specific areas, they belong to the one who hits the small sticks with the firewood.

射玻璃球
Game of Flipping Glass Beads

海南农村儿童经常玩耍的游戏比赛。游戏规则为先在地上挖好4个小洞，比赛时，孩子们从规定的地点用手指把玻璃球依次弹进4个小洞，先弹进入第四个洞穴者为胜利者。他们通常使用"石头、剪刀、布"或其他方法决定各人的发球顺序。

The game of flipping glass beads is popular among children in the countryside. The rules are as follows: first, dig four small holes under the ground, then shoot off the glass balls to the four holes respectively in the specific time. The one whose glass ball gets into the fourth hole at first is the winner. Children often use the finger play game to decide who first shoots off the ball.

转车轮
Racing of Turning Wheels

海南农村儿童经常玩耍的游戏比赛。比赛人数为6人以上，必须是双数。比赛前，先找一块砖头放在人群中间，然后划拳，胜方围坐在地上，双脚蹬在砖头上，输方则穿插站在胜方之间。输方拉起胜方的双手围着圆圈转动，速度不断加快，一直到胜方瘫倒在地为止。然后双方交换角色，游戏继续进行。

Racing of turning wheels is an another popular game among children in the countryside.The people who take part in the competition can't be more than six people with even numbers. Before the race begins, a brick is put in the middle of the crowd, and then the finger-guessing game is played. The winners sit around the circle and two feet put on the bricks. The losers hold the winners' hands revolve quicker and quicker till the winner fall down. After that, the two groups exchange position and continue to play the game.

11.5 海南传统竞技项目民俗旅游开发思考
Implication on the Tourism Development of Traditional Sports Activities in Hainan

依托海南自然资源优势形成的高尔夫公开赛、环岛自行车赛、环岛大帆船拉力赛、潜水、沙滩排球等特色赛事和运动项目已成为国际旅游岛最重要的名片和最主要的高端休闲旅游产品。如果文化是国际旅游岛建设的灵魂，竞技体育就是重要支撑。海南作为我国沙滩排球、帆船帆板、举重等运动项目的训练基地，为我国体育事业的发展做出了贡献。在现有的基础上，结合海南独特的地理优势与海南黎苗族特有的传统竞技项目，开发特色民俗旅游资源，吸引更多国内外游客。

The competition of world class Leader-board Golf, Cycling around the Island, Sailing Rally, Diving, Beach Volleyball have become the most important leisure tourism products in building Hainan international tourism destination. If culture is its soul, the competitive sports are one of the important backbones. Hainan has made great contribution to sports as the training base for beach Volleyball, Sailing, Weightlifting, etc. Besides we should develop distinctive folk tourism resources based on sport customs of all ethnic groups for the purpose of attracting more tourists at home and abroad.

11.5.1 "海南"被誉为排球之乡，发展排球，尤其是沙滩排球海南国际旅游岛建设进程中的重点和突破点 Hainan, well-known as a volleyball hometown, should stress to develop beach volleyball in the process of development of Hainan tourist destination.

目前，海南是我国沙滩排球训练基地。沙滩排球也是集阳光、健康、时尚、休闲、娱乐于一身的运动项目，最符合休闲体育的发展趋势。海口副市长韩美在2010亚洲沙滩排球锦标赛开幕式上表示本次比赛沙滩排球是海口依据自身地域特点、环境气候和城市文化特色，为国际旅游岛度身打造的世界级对外文化体育交流平台。我们将凭借资源优势，力求把（海口）亚洲沙滩排球锦标赛打造成亚洲最有特色、最精彩、最有影响力的沙滩排球赛事。同时，为了吸引游客可以定期举办各种沙滩娱乐性排球比赛项目，游客在比赛的过程中可以相互交流，提升海南旅游魅力。

At present, Hainan is the training base of beach volleyball in China, which is a entertainment sport with sunshine, health, fashion, leisure and entertainment. At the opening ceremony of the beach volleyball in 2010, Haikou vice mayor Mrs. Han held that beach volleyball was a platform of sport exchanges for Hainan international tourist destination. People would strive to build (Haikou) Asian beach volleyball into the most distinctive, exciting and influential beach volleyball tournament in Asia by virtue of its advantages. Meanwhile, in order to attract tourists, Hainan can organize recreational beach volleyball events on a regular basis. Visitors can play beach volleyball for building health. Meanwhile tourism charm of Hainan can also be enhanced.

11.5.2 整合海南黎苗民俗旅游资源和热带海岛休闲旅游资源，挖掘海南国际旅游竞技民俗旅游的亮点 It's necessary to exploit the highlights of sport customs by absorbing strong points of all ethnic groups.

随着全球休闲旅游业的发展，国际旅游岛的建设应该加快发展竞技体育，结合体育运动项目与热带海岛度假休闲旅游资源，着重打造民俗特色旅游项目，如把海南黎苗族射箭、射弩、拉乌龟、顶棍等力量型竞技项目打造成竞技休闲型旅游项目；把跳竹竿、八人秋或打秋千、三脚赛跑、找物竞技等项目打造成娱乐型旅游项目，结合海南黎苗回族传统特色体育项目，挖掘海南国际旅游岛民俗旅游的亮点。

With the rapid development of global leisure tourism, it has to speed up the development of athletic sports and strives to build folk custom tourism projects with national characteristics. For example, the sport projects such as Crossbow, La Wugui, Dinggun of the Li and Miao minorities are built into leisure tourism projects with strength competition. And the entertainment projects such as the Bamboo Rod Dance, Swing for Eight People with ethnic characteristics are built into entertainment tourism projects.

宋静敏教授从黎族传统体育历史、黎族传统体育起源说、黎族传统体育的现状与评价等方面进行了介绍。通过前期调查和历史考证发现，他指出海南黎族曾经有过52项很有特色的民族传统体育项目，但目前仅有4个项目仍在黎族地区流传，8个项目接近失传，40个项目已经失传或几乎失传了。他希望通过对我国黎族传统体育的发掘、整理、教学、传承、开发竞赛模式，为海南省发掘、重现、保留一批原汁原味的黎族传统体育项目。他还提出海南黎族传统的体育项目适合进驻旅游景区，为海南旅游增添民族特色。

Professor Song introduced the history, present situation of the traditional sports of the Li nationality. He pointed out that there were 52 traditional national sports of the Li nationality, but only four projects can be still carried out in the Li region, 8 projects are nearly lost and 40 projects have been lost. He hoped to exploit and develop a number of authentic traditional sports competitions by exploring, organizing the Li sport activities. He also held that the Li traditional sports can add some national characteristics in tourism for Hainan.

因此，我们有责任和义务传承和宣传这些体育竞技项目，同时将它们与海南的旅游资源相结合，形成海南特有的民俗旅游项目，这样我们不仅能保留传统，还能建设具有文化内涵的国际旅游岛。

Therefore, it's our responsibility to maintain and broadcast sport projects. We must take some measures to combine traditional sport activities with tourism. We not only keep the tradition, but an international tourism destination with its inner cultures.

12

海南礼仪禁忌民俗
Taboo Folk Customs

《中国公民出境旅游文明行为指南》中有一条公约"习俗禁忌，切勿冒犯"（胡锐、赵建苹，2012）。这条公约表明了解一个地方当地的习俗、禁忌是去该地旅游的必修课，也是文明安全旅游的前提。禁忌意为在某个文化习俗中"犯忌讳的话或行动"（中国社会科学院语言研究所词典编辑室，2002），这种"话或行动"被认为是对神灵或他人的冒犯和不敬，会给自己或他人招致霉运和灾祸，通常会让人感到尴尬、不安、抵触、甚至愤怒。禁忌一旦被打破，人们通常会采取措施来进行禳解和补救，即被动的事后补救。后来人们为预防这方面的无心过失，会进行积极的事前设防，这些事前设防的"话或行动"便是各色民间习俗的由来，这些内容已在前面章节有了详尽的介绍。本章主要就海南民间"犯忌讳的话或行动"以及其事后禳解进行介绍和探讨。

There is an article of etiquette rule, "Be careful to observe the local customs or taboos. Don't violate or offend against them" in Tourism Etiquette Rules for Chinese Citizens Travelling Abroad, which represents the importance to learn the local customs especially taboos at a new place during a holiday, which is a required course before you set out, also the premise of travel. Taboo refers to "the words and the acts" that people find offensive or embarrassing, some of which even bring oneself or others bad luck and disasters in a certain culture. Once a taboo was broken, people tended to take measures to remedy the bad situation or ward off the misfortune, namely passive remedy. But people have learned to take measures to avoid the misfortune caused by such unintentional negligence in advance, namely active precautions, which have resulted in a great variety of folk customs of celebrating festivals and great events, which we have described in detail in the previous chapters. This chapter focuses on "the words and the acts" and the remedies.

禁忌最早源自原始人类对大自然的敬畏。台湾学者林明峪认为"禁忌早在人类使用手势或口语以前就已普遍存在"（林明峪，1981）。由于生产力低下，原始人缺乏足够的认知能力认识自然、改造自然，在天灾人祸面前只能被动地认为反常的自然现象源自自身偶然性的举止不当，试图通过规范自身的行为避免再次触怒神灵，这些"举止不当"便是最初的禁忌。

Taboos originated from the earliest awe in which prehistoric men were of nature. Lin Mingyu holds that "taboos had been prevalent among human beings before prehistoric men communicated by using gestures or colloquial way." Due to low productivity, primitive men lacked enough cognitive abilities to know about the nature. When confronting a natural disaster they had no choice but to ascribe it to their own casual "inappropriate behaviors" and try to regulate their own behaviors to avoid offending the spirits again. And the "inappropriate behaviors" were thought to be the initial taboos.

禁忌是一种大众心理现象的反映。弗洛伊德认为它有两层含义：一是"崇高的""神圣的"；二是"神秘的""危险的""禁止的""不洁的"（弗洛伊德，2005）。禁忌是人类最古老的无形的法律，它通过心理上的认同来对人们的外在行为进行约束，从而维系个人与集体的平衡，保护整个族群的生存与发展。

Taboo is a reflection of the mass psychological phenomena. Fraud believes "The meaning of 'taboo', as we see it, diverges in two contrary directions. To us it means, on the one hand, 'sacred', 'consecrated' and on the other 'uncanny', 'dangerous', 'forbidden', 'unclean'."(Sigmund Freud, 2001) Taboos are the oldest invisible laws of humanity in a sense, and they have had people's external behavior constrained by psychological identity, and thus maintained the balance between individual and collectivity, and protected the survival and development of the entire population.

民间禁忌形成于特定的人文地理环境，因时因地各异。海南是移民地区，海南民间禁忌习俗同其他习俗一样主要受中原民俗文化的影响，经过对宗土传统文化的坚守与传承以及因时因地的发展，形成了自身独特的本土禁忌。比如海南至今盛行的宗祠祭祀禁忌文化就源自远离故土的游子对宗土文化的坚守和强烈认同，与内地的宗祠文化相比，有过之而无不及。海南外来移民和当地各族先民有着多样各异的禁忌习俗，在长期的生产生活中经过交流与融合，也形成了很多各族共有的民间禁忌。比如海南黎家砍山栏不能在虫日、猴日、火日、狗日进行，是黎族独有的历法和禁忌，而对榕树的敬畏和避讳与其他民族却无二致。

Folk Taboos have formed in a specific geographic environment and varied from place to place from time to time. Majority of Hainanese are immigrants. Inheriting from the Central Plains of traditional culture as well as converging with the local customs, the taboo folklore in Hainan, like other folklores, has become different. Take taboos about ancestral worship rituals for example, they have prevailed in Hainan, which derived from the strong sense of identity in their native land and culture the immigrants have persisted in holding, while those in most parts of mainland have decayed. Meanwhile, Hainan local ancestors of all ethnic groups and immigrants who had different taboos have formed something in common after long-term communicating and converging in production and daily life. For example, the Li People still have the taboo on clearing the field for Shanlan rice on insect days, monkey days, fire days, and dog days, which is unique, while the taboos about banyan worship are almost the same as those of other peoples.

由于禁忌民俗涉及人们生活的方方面面，内容比较庞杂，我们将选取其中比较有代表性的内容与大家探讨。

Due to the complexity and wide range, we have to focus on some of them to discuss.

12.1 海南人生礼仪禁忌
Taboos and Rites

海南人在生老病死等各种人生历程中都有着不同于其他地方的禁忌。怀孕、黎族女子文身和葬礼方面的禁忌很有代表性。

The taboos on words and acts during giving birth, getting married, being illness, funeral and other life events of Hainan people are of unique local features. We'll discuss taboos about getting pregnant, Li girls' tattoo and funeral.

12.1.1 怀孕 Getting Pregnant

民间认为，一个人的德行会影响开枝散叶，故有"男人修身好过海，女人修身好生崽"的说法。久不生育的，可以通过抱养别人的小孩、在家供奉送子观音、祭拜榕树来求子。

Folk believed that a person's moral influenced his or her reproduction, just as a saying goes, "Only when a man is good, can he have a good harvest. Only when a woman is kind, can she give birth to a baby." Adopting a child, invoking the Goddess of Mercy, or worshipping the spirit of banyan are alternatives to solve the problem of having no baby for a long time.

一旦怀孕，除不能参加葬礼、不能挪床、禁食兔肉等常见禁忌外，还有些特有的禁忌：

Besides taboos on attending funeral, moving beds, eating rabbit meat alike, once a woman gets pregnant, there are still some different taboos in Hainan:

禁 忌	后 果
（汉）用木炭在墙壁和屋顶画圈	胎儿脸上带黑疤
（黎、苗）孕妇烧火时，将柴枝尾部先放入灶	分娩时胎儿倒置而生
（苗）在孕妇住的房子内或周围打桩、围篱笆	孕妇手脚和腰背疼痛，触犯胎儿，造成难产
（汉）食屈头鸡（没有孵化出来的小鸡）	孕妇难产
（汉）食用黑芝麻、黑豆之类食物	婴儿皮肤黑
（黎）食用蛇肉、猴子肉	生怪胎
（汉）食用螃蟹	婴儿像螃蟹一样拧捻别人

Taboos against	Consequences that may happen
(Han) Drawing circles on the walls or roof with charcoal	black birth mark on the face of the foetus
(the pregnant of Li, Miao) putting the tail of the faggot into the stoves first when attending the kitchen fire	that the fetus would get inverted when being delivered
(Miao) doing piling in or around the house, like building fence where the pregnant women living	that the pregnant's hands, feet and back hurt, or dystocia because of the foetus' being disturbed
(Han) eating unhatched chicken	dystocia
(Han) eating black food including black sesame, black beans	a black-skinned foetus
(Li) eating snake or money meat	that the baby would be a freak
(Han) eating crab	that the baby would pinch others like a crab

乐东黎族自治县哈方言区的黎族妇女则没有什么肉类禁忌，她们对家禽家畜，飞禽走兽都可以食用。

There are no taboos on eating meat for Ha Li women during their pregnancy in Ledong Li Autonomous County.

12.1.2 黎族女子文身 Li girls' Tattoo

在黎族的习俗中，姑娘若无文身就被视为貌不出众，嫁不出去，没有地位，终身受歧视，死后将不被祖先承认，成为孤魂野鬼（纪俊超，2008）。文身不能在家中或公共场合进行，必须在"隆闺"里。要将树叶挂在门口，以示禁止入内。伤口痊愈期间，不许外出、洗身或同外人讲话，否则文身可能会失败。文身的图式是遵循祖训而世代传下来的，若擅自修改，就是对祖先的大不敬（詹贤武，2008）。

If a girl didn't tattoo, according to Li's tradition, she would be considered to be unremarkable and difficult to get married in her whole life and would not be admitted to the family by her ancestors and become wild ghosts after death. Tattoo was not to be held at home or in public but in the girl's "Long Gui", when some green branches had to be hung at the door, indicating "No entering". After that, the girl was not allowed to go out, have a bath, or speak to outsiders during the process of wound healing, otherwise tattoos might fail. Tattoo patterns have been passed down from generation to generation, and forbidden to be changed out of reverence for ancestors.

12.1.3 丧葬 Funeral

海南岛各处汉族丧葬禁忌大体相同，也会因地而异。海南汉族认为必须在自家供奉祖先牌位的"正厅"里去世，死后鬼魂才能认祖归宗，接受子孙祭拜。如果不在"正厅"逝世，必须请道公做道场"招魂"，引领鬼魂找到归宗的路。在琼海，在外意外死亡的要在村外搭棚停放遗体，从棚里出殡，不能进村，否则鬼魂会留在村里，扰人安宁。

Han Funeral taboos are somewhat the same in Hainan. Many Han people have believed that they must die in the "main hall" of their own house, and thus their spirits would find the way to the ancestors' spirits' dwelling. In Qionghai, people who died in their boots were to be carried to cemetery directly from the shed set up temporarily out of the village instead of from home. Otherwise their evil ghosts would haunt in the village.

报丧时不能进他人宅院，以免他人沾染晦气。避用忌讳语。若有子女在外，要等到子女回来见死者最后一面方可入殓。

Don't enter others' house or courtyard when giving an obituary notice so as not to bring bad luck to them, or say "He (or she) died". If the child of the deceased works out, it's a must to wait until the child gets back before encoffining him or her.

在海口、文昌，葬礼只有家里人才参加，而在东方，村邻亲朋都要过来追悼；忌与死者犯冲的人出现在葬礼上；忌擅自改变墓地地点；忌棺材半路停歇；返回时，送葬者不可回头看墓穴，否则亡灵将附着其身而随其返家。在琼海，参加过丧事的人得了红包必须在回家前把它花掉；在琼山、海口等地，回家后必须洗头、喝茶。

In Wenchang and Haikou, only family can attend funeral, while all the villagers, relatives and friends can come to the memorial in Dongfang. It was forbidden to attend the funeral for the persons whose Chinese Zodiac don't get well along with the deceased's. To change the tomb location determined by Mr. Feng Shui at random, or pause the coffin halfway would disturb the dead and bring bad luck to the living. On the way home, mourners were forbidden to look back. Otherwise they would be attached to by the new ghost and bring it back. In Qionghai, mourners have to use up the gift money received from the bereaved before going home, and the ones have to wash their hair and drink tea when back home in Qiongshan and Haikou.

黄流地区服丧期间首虞（头七）之内戴孝者不得洗头、洗澡、穿鞋，不得回房睡，吃饭不能坐，不能拜访他人。一年内禁止娱乐和庆祝活动，比如贴春联、吃汤圆、包粽子、起屋造房或出嫁迎娶，也不能参加别家的嫁娶、满月、开张等吉事。

During the first seven mourning days in Huangliu the bereaved ought not to wash their hair, have a bath, wear shoes, etc., neither ought they to attend or hold any recreational activities or such auspicious things worth celebrating as holding a wedding within a year.

黎族认为，人死就像太阳下山，必须下午出殡。在过去合亩制地区，全村或全峒的人都要来吊唁，三天不吃主粮，不做重工（《黎族简史》编写组，2009）。下葬时用过的锄头、铁锹回家后不能马上洗，要等孝期满后拿到河里或溪边洗净(王学萍，2004)。

The Li believed that people die like the sunset, so the remains had to be buried in the afternoon. All people of the village or tribe were to mourn the dead with no staple food, no hard working for 3 or more days in previous He Mu system regions.

苗族死者入殓时钉棺材不能用铁钉，只能用木钉或竹钉，因为铁钉被认为会钉住死者的鬼魂。苗族会把死者用过的生活器皿埋在墓前，以供死者在阴间继续使用。若碗是完好无损的，要把碗沿敲破一点，以示死者生前用过，禁止任何人捡回再用。

The Miao has to nail the coffin with wooden or bamboo nails instead of iron nails which were said to nail the spirit of the deceased. Miao people thought the daily utensils the deceased used had to be buried as well in front of the tomb for their daily life underneath afterwards.

三亚回族称死亡为"归真"。丧葬从速，早亡午葬，夜死晨埋，不超过一天。送葬时不得燃放鞭炮，不得丢纸钱，不得哭丧。

Sanya Hui regards death as to "Return to the Real World". The remains of the decease should be encoffined and buried within one day. At funeral there are taboos on setting off firecrackers, casting Joss paper or wailing.

12.2 海南岁时节日禁忌
Taboos about Festivals

岁时节日是集中体现乡风民俗、最具代表性的文化现象，有关岁时节日禁忌亦是如此。海南有许多极具地域特色岁时节日禁忌。

Festivals are the most representative cultural phenomena that embody local folklore, so are festival taboos. There are many taboos about festivals of local characteristics.

12.2.1 春节 Spring Festival

春节作为中国最重要的节日，有着最为繁琐的禁忌。民间认为春节前的打扫预示着辞旧迎新，但春节期间就另当别论了。海南黎族要到初五才能把节间宰杀禽畜留下的毛和垃圾倒进箩筐，再用竹条扎架，放上稻草人作"神架"，然后由两人抬着箩筐和"神架"，点燃香烛，全家老少陪同走出家门，以示"旧魂"已随神出村，新的一年将人畜平安。

Taboos about Spring Festival are sure to be the most cumbersome. Cleaning before the Spring Festival predicates that the past would pass away like rubbish, and everything new is waiting for us. Hainan Li had a similar taboo with Han on collecting rubbish including cattle hair and bird feathers before the fifth of the first lunar month, on which people would put the garbage into the bamboo basket, and put a scarecrow onto a rack made of bamboo strips, namely "Shen Jia", and then carried the basket and "Shen Jia" to the entrance of the village, signifying the "old ghosts" have gone out of the village with the "Shen" (god), and the livestock and the whole family would be healthy and safe.

忌用往年留下的春联；妇女撰写春联被认为是家中人丁不旺的征兆；忌评论贴好的春联。黄流、琼海等地，有丧事的家中一年内不得张贴春联，或被视为不孝。鞭炮要一次点响，忌中断，忌沉闷短促，否则就不吉利。拜年需先燃放鞭炮方可进门。

Couplets written last year or even earlier can't be put up; it was a taboo for women to write couplet; once couplets have been posted, no more comments were needed. In Huangliu and Qionghai, the family in which there was a funeral within one year can't put up couplets. Firecrackers must burn out once set off. A person must set off firecrackers first, and then enter the owners' when paying a New Year call.

大年初一没有祭祀祖神前，家人禁食荤腥。在海口，初一要吃斋，不能杀生，以图吉利。海南苗族认为初一至十五，米缸不能空，否则是断炊之兆，故此间忌舂米，必须年前就把粮食备足。

A family mustn't eat meat before ancestor-worshipping ritual. In Haikou, people used to only eat vegetables all day, praying for good luck. Miao people hold that the grain vat can't be empty from the first to the fifteenth in the first lunar month, or they would run out of grain some day.

过去除夕之夜，家中处处要掌灯，忌中途熄灭。澄迈黎族的禳解办法是：元宵节这天，趁本村抬神偶巡村时，请道公到家中唱跳，以解除厄兆。大部分地区初一不拜年，初二开始拜年。但乐东黄流地区，除夕夜十二点上香后，村里亲戚间就可以相互拜年，讨要红包了。

On New Year Eve, all lights had to be on without a break. If a light turned out, a solution among Li people in Chengmai was that the family asked Dao Gong to practice exorcism in their house to break the ominous sign on the Lantern Festival. People ought not to pay New Year calls each other on the first day of the first lunar month in most parts of Hainan Island. But in Huangliu Ledong, people can do it since the incense is lighted at midnight on New Year Eve.

12.2.2 清明节 Tomb-Sweeping Day

海南的宗祠文化盛行，华侨、外地游子春节不一定回家祭祖，清明节必定回家扫墓，否则会被视为不孝。故民间有"亲不亲，坟上认"的说法。上坟祭祀祖先的祭品，一般不能拿回家，如要食用也只能在坟前，寓意和祖先一起吃饭。

With the ancestral worship culture being prevalent, overseas or domestic Hainanese who work in other places must come back and attend the ancestor worship on Tomb-Sweeping Day. Otherwise, they would not be regarded as filial offspring who remember the root. The sacrifices offered at the grave mustn't be taken back and eaten at home, instead, they could be shared at cemetery.

12.2.3 汉族禾仙节 Han's Hexian Festival

汉族禾仙节，也叫吃新节。琼海等地在吃"祭禾仙"饭时，全家要穿戴整齐，禁止赤膊、穿短裤，民间认为这样会冒犯"禾仙娘"而遭到惩罚，收不到下一季的禾种。

On Han's Hexian Festival, also called Newly-Harvested-Grain-Eating Day, the whole family must be dressed neatly and formally in Qionghai. Otherwise, "Goddess Hexian" would punish the offender by not offering seeds for next season.

12.2.4 饲牛节 Cattle Festival

冬至也是万宁一带的"饲牛节"，当日，牛不耕田，以示对牛的敬意。

People in some parts of Wanning call the Winter Solstice "Cattle Festival", when cattle must rest as a reward for its hard working throughout the year.

12.2.5 黎历禁忌 Li Calendar

黎历主要以十二生肖计日：猪、鼠、牛、虫、兔、龙、蛇、马、羊、猴、鸡、狗，大部分黎历以猪日开始，狗日结束，接着进入下一轮的"十二生肖日"，以此类推循环。黎历禁忌很多。比如，若某个家庭有人在某个生肖日去世，那么以后这个家庭就不宜在这个生肖日进行生产劳动了；牛日牛不耕田，人不下田劳作，否则稻会生虫，忌盖牛舍，否则牛会生虫，忌卖牛，否则以后出生的牛犊会死掉，忌穿牛鼻子，否则牛会瘦弱至死；猪日忌卖猪；鼠日忌建谷仓等（詹贤武，2008）。

Li calendar is mainly to use Li's zodiac to count day: pig, rat, cattle, insect, rabbit, dragon, snake, horse, sheep, monkey, rooster and dog. Most Li calendars start with Pig Day, end with Dog Day, and then go to the next turn. There were many taboos about Li calendar. For example, if someone in a family died on a Dog Day, the whole family couldn't work on Dog Days later on; On Cattle days Li mustn't build cattle stables or make cattle work. Otherwise cattle would suffer from worms or illnesses to die or grain would suffer from insects.

12.2.6 苗族安村节 AnCun Festival of Miao

苗族认为农历六月作祟鬼神最多，故设安村节以驱邪祛病。三日不食油、荤，只食净菜。

The Miao held the sixth lunar month as a period of time when most ghosts were haunting, for which Miao set AnCun Festival to exorcize evil spirits and illnesses. People mustn't eat meat within three days, but vegetables without cooking oil.

12.2.7 苗族禾斋节 Hezhai Festival of Miao

祭品只能祭祀完"禾斋公"后才可以吃，否则会招致"禾斋公"的不满，使庄稼歉收。祭祀的粽子只能给家人食用，不能分给外人，否则就会把全年的好运让别人带走。

On Hezhai Festival of Miao, the sacrifices couldn't be eaten until the worship ritual had been completed, or Hezhai Gong would be angered and make reduction happen. Zongzi used as sacrifices must be shared by family only, or the whole year's good luck would be passed to the outsiders with the Zongzi given away.

12.2.8 回族开斋节 Eid al-Fitr & Eid al-Adha of Hui

海南三亚回族的开斋节是斋月结束时庆祝斋功圆满的节日。斋月期间从每日东方发白前到日落时，凡成年健康穆斯林都要自觉戒饮食和房事等。伊斯兰教历十二月十日为古尔邦节，妇女不得参加游坟。

Hainan Sanya Muslim's Eid al-Fitr is to celebrate the accomplishment of Ramadan, during which Muslims fast and be celibate from sunrise to sunset. The 10th day of the last Islamic lunar calendar is Eid al-Adha Holiday, when women mustn't participate in the rituals of ancestors worship.

12.2.9 军坡节 Junpo Festival

以海口新坡镇为例，当地军坡节是每年农历二月初六至十二，新坡人禁食猪肉、猪油、狗肉，菜场也会禁售，这一禁忌习俗与冼夫人的一个传说有关。相传每次打仗前，冼夫人和士兵都会听师父的训导三天，并戒食猪肉和狗肉，认为这样才容易打胜仗。

Take Xinpo Town for example, people here mustn't eat pork, lard and dog meat, and they can't buy these things in local markets during Junpo Festival. Such custom is from a legend about Madame Xian. Madame Xian and her soldiers would listen to their Shifu for three days before every battle started, and abstain from pork and dog meat. In this way, they thought, it was more likely to win the battle.

12.2.10 三月三 San Yue San Festival

东方、昌江美孚方言地区的黎族青年禁止在"三月三"活动中同村同峒男女相邀，因为同村同峒同宗同血缘的，是严格禁止婚恋的。

On March 3rd Festival, the youth of Meifu Li who are from the same village or tribe mustn't date each other in Dongfang and Changjiang, for they share the same blood.

12.3 海南衣食住行禁忌
Taboos about Food, Clothing, Shelter and Traveling

在日常生活中，由于偶然性事件而形成的习惯性思维或是科学的生活经验总结使人们形成了在衣食住行方面的禁忌。我们将与大家主要探讨海南人的住、行禁忌。

Taboos about food, clothing, shelter and traveling were attributed to the reflexes caused by accidents and the lessons learned from daily life.

12.3.1 居住 About Housing

选址 海南非常注重宅地的坐落朝向，故有"大门朝南，子孙不寒；大门朝北，子孙受罪"之说。"前面临水后靠山"则是最理想的宅基福地：房屋后地势高，不积水，屋前地势低，就有"风水塘"。但要注意"屋前塘大，人寿不长，屋后塘大，少年夭亡"。房屋不能建于两条道路斜交、形似剪刀口的狭窄地段，因为这种宅基地不符合四平八稳的原则，有趋凶之兆。若门前有水，则要注意选择门口的朝向，否则会影响到主人的未来，"秀水朝门，主发横财。水近侧门，主人不安。水直冲门，主人离散"。

Hainan Han pays highly emphasis on the location and orientation of the house. It is the ideal location that the house faces the south and a small pond with the back towards the north and a hill. It is said that a house can't be located at the crossing point of two roads which don't form a right angle, because the foundation can not be a balanced square that signifies smoothness and steadiness, peace and safety in Chinese traditional culture.

主人若一年（过去多为三年）内无服丧之事，可兴建宅屋。汉族民间建宅择日与婚嫁择日相似，不尚三、五、七月，一般选在二、四、六、九、十月，避开雨季。

If there has not been a funeral for one year or even three years in the family, they can build a new house. Han always chooses an auspicious day to start building in February, April, June, September and October, which are lucky months and out of the rain season.

建房 之前，不可先建墙院和外门，因形似"囚"字而主凶相。

Don't build the courtyard wall and its door first, otherwise, people hold, the family will be trapped by the "wall" and can't get outstanding since then.

海南民居禁用苦子木、花梨木当正梁。因为苦子木木质虽好，但意味着主人子孙苦难繁多；花梨木木质优良但由于过于名贵，而且砍伐后根部随即枯死永不再生，被认为不够繁盛，容易断子绝孙。造过墓地的材料不能用来建屋，房子会"不干净"。黎族忌用直径较大的木材建屋，他们认为大木只能用于凿造独木棺材。

Bitter trees and Hainan rosewood are not able to be used as beams because it is thought that in spite of good texture, bitter trees are "bitter", signifying the offspring's sufferings, and rosewoods are too rare, and won't live on if they're cut, which signifies the decay of the later offspring. The house would be "not clean" (haunted by ghost) if its building materials are from those of graves. Li tends to choose thin timbers to build house instead of large timbers whose diameters are long and which generally are used to chisel into canoe coffins, implying death.

升梁 时，忌头尾倒放，忌沾人血，忌女人从梁上跨过，否则主人将会厄运临头。横梁不可压住床位和座位，否则家人就会经常生病。

Beams mustn't be placed up side down or up above the beds or chairs, be stained by human blood, or be stridden over by women, which would lead misfortunes to the family.

乔迁 入宅前要选好黄道吉日方可迁居，否则家中将会人畜不安，诸事不顺。乔迁之日，忌送钟，因与"送终"谐音；不欢迎鳏夫寡妇，否则这户人家会有伤亡。

The house warming day should be auspicious through carefully considering. Don't send a clock as a gift, as its pronunciation in pinyin "sòng zhōng" is the same with that of "nail the coffin" in

Chinese. And widowers or widows aren't welcome, who are considered to bring about bad luck.

布局海南人必须在自家"正屋正厅"里断气。客厅不留后门或在后门前设置玄关,以便聚财纳气。客厅中门不能正对着大树、电线杆和别人家的屋角,否则出入不安。

If there is not a screen in front of the backdoor of the main hall, there can't be a backdoor. The main door of the main hall mustn't face trees, electricity poles or the corner of other's. Otherwise something wrong would happen to the family.

黎族居住的地方一定要"干净",死过人或有不好传说的地方不能建村。

Li's residence has to be "clean". A village can't be located in the place where people died in their boots or bad legends happened.

黎族十二生肖计日法中的"牛日""猪日""鸡日""龙日"是挖柱脚的好日子,尤其是"龙日",但这几个日子不能与主人家的"忌日"相冲。上午是立柱的好时辰。立柱后,要在柱头上插蒌叶和红藤刺叶,并在屋顶中央用竹竿挂起葵叶,表示神鬼勿近,新居安宁。黎族人不在"猴日""虫日""火日"等建房子。新屋建成后,杞黎忌进屋就哭,不吉利。

According Li's calendar, the morning of dragon days are good time to **set up the pillars** as well as cattle days, pig days, chicken days on which no family died. Once the pillars are set up, the owners have to hang betel and leaves of Sargent gloryvine at the upper head of the pillars, and hang Chinese fan palm at the upper end of a bamboo pole inserted into the ground in the middle of the house, driving away all the ghosts and praying for peace and safety of the new house. Li wouldn't build house on monkey, insect and fire days. It was ominous and so forbidden for Qi Li to cry when the new house was completed.

在黎族村寨,家门口的**插青**除了有祈求平安吉祥之意外,不同枝叶标志着不同的禁忌。家门口挂一束翠绿的山藤叶表示主人出门劳作,禁止陌生人进屋;如门口再多挂一束厚皮树叶,表示家中有人生病或分娩,禁止外人进屋。如果村寨前后都挂了一束这样的树叶,那说明这天全村寨的人都去祭神了,不欢迎外村人打扰。

In Li villages there are special pubic signs named Cha Qing, or Branch Taboo Signs marking different taboos and good wishes for peace and harvest as well. A bunch of green vine leaves hanging at the door tells the visitors that the host is not at home, and strangers aren't welcome. Another bunch of thick leaves added shows someone is sick or giving a birth, and outsiders mustn't get in. Such bunches of leaves hanging at both entrances to the village shows that all villagers are attending religious activities, and outsiders are not welcome.

12.3.2 出行 About Transportation

海南民间忌捡路上毛巾。传说很久以前,有个农夫在路上捡了一条毛巾,遇失主折返,并要求还其毛巾和其中银元,双方争执不下,告到官府,糊涂官判农夫有罪。农夫之妻把案子告到知府,知府查明真相才释放农夫。海南民间从此视其为招来横祸的东西,路遇而不拾。

There was a unique taboo on picking up the towel on the road, which originated from a legend. It goes like this: Long ago, a peasant picked up a towel on the road. Soon the owner rushed back and asked him to return the towel and the silver wrapped in it. The peasant got surprised and the two men couldn't reach an agreement, so they appealed to the county magistrate. The silly official couldn't tell the truth, and jailed the peasant. The peasant's wife appealed to the prefect who made the truth clear and released the peasant. Since then Hainan folks have chosen to ignore towels.

因海南经常有强风天气，坐船或飞机最忌听到"一路顺风""一帆风顺"等带"风"字的祝福。

As boats or aircrafts are very sensitive to strong winds, such blessing language as "Bon voyage" or "Everything is going smoothly" mustn't be used, which include the Chinese character "风" when translated into Chinese. And "风" means "wind".

12.4 海南劳动生产禁忌
Taboos about Production

海南传统产业主要有农业、渔业、林业、饲养业、手工业等。过去，纺织、印染、酿酒以及狩猎主要是各族人民自给自足，不参与商品流通，本节将主要介绍农、渔、林、饲养业禁忌。狩猎禁忌将在渔业禁忌介绍。

Hainan traditional industries mainly include agriculture, fishing, forestry, livestock breeding, handicrafts, and so on. In the past, all the nationalities are mainly self-sufficient in textile, printing and dyeing, brewing industry, and hunting which are not normally involved in the circulation of commodities. Taboos about the four main industries will be described here with hunting in the part of fishing.

12.4.1 农业禁忌 About Agriculture

海南农业生产决不能误了农时。"生产经验千万条，不误农时最重要。"

The most important taboos about Hainan agriculture is not to miss the farming season.

海南汉族下种要尽量避开他人，他们认为种芽刚露头，见不得生人，也闻不得生人味。不能在大年初一下种，否则种子不发芽会耽误农事。插秧剩余的秧苗要全部带回家抛到屋顶上，据说这样可以防止水稻生"瓦蛆"。

Hainan Han peasants think sowing seeds should avoid coming across others, because the emerging shoots don't dare to see strangers, nor smell them. Don't sow seeds on the first day of the lunar New Year, otherwise seeds would not germinate and miss the farming season. All the rest seedlings after transplanting should be taken home and thrown on the roof instead of being left in the field, by which, people thought, "tile maggots" could be prevented.

黎苗族农民到深山里选定种植山栏稻的地段后，要用钩刀砍下芒叶，捆绑成束，打上活结，悬挂在选定的地段周围，表示此地已有人选定，任何人不得占有。

After the mountain location for Shanlan rice has been selected, Li and Miao peasants cut leatherleaf by hook, tie them into bundles with slipknot, and hang around the selected area, indicating that this field has been selected, and others mustn't take up.

合亩制地区的黎族山栏稻种植主要有以下禁忌：犁地之前不能让耕牛在田间拉屎，否则会影响当年的收成；举行开犁仪式后，亩头四天内不能睡午觉，不准喝酒，不准唱歌，不准吃肉，不准与女人说话；播种当天，亩头要独自偷偷去秧地象征性地播撒种子，以免惊动地鬼；插秧的第一天，亩头不能在田间睡觉，以免生病，否则预示庄稼经不起风吹雨打；任何人不能讲对稻苗不吉利的话，否则水稻会减产；收割第一天，亩头忌吃青菜、油盐、肉类、不睡午觉，否则田里杂草丛生，禾苗倒伏；当天做完祭地鬼仪式后，亩头要从山上折一支青树叶回来，挂在门口，三天内忌外人入室，否则当年的庄稼必然遭灾。

  In He Mu system regions, taboos about Shanlan rice planting are mainly as follows: that the cattle shit in the field would impair the harvest; after the plowing ceremony, Mu Tou could not take a nap at noon, drink, sing, eat meat, or speak to women for the first four days; on the day to sow seeds, Mu Tou had to go to the field alone secretly so as not to disturb the Land Ghost and sow some seeds symbolically; on the first day to transplant seedlings, Mu Tou was forbidden to sleep in the field so as not to get sick, otherwise crops would not withstand the wind and rain; nobody could say anything inauspicious to the seedlings, which would impact the result; on the first day to get in the rice, Mu Tou couldn't eat vegetables, oil, salt, meat, nor sleep during the day, otherwise the field would grow more weeds, and seedlings would fall off the field; after worshipping the Land Ghost, Mu Tou had to cut a branch of green leaves in the mountain and hang at the door of his house signifying "No entry", or the crop would meet with calamity.

  黎族有"牛日不犁田，鸡日不插秧"的忌讳。黎族在收获庄稼吃第一顿新米饭时，要祭祀祖先鬼，不能邀外人同吃，也不能同吃山猪和牛羊肉，否则是对祖先不敬，家中的东西会被人拿走，来年的庄稼也会遭山猪、牛、羊的报复而被糟蹋。

  The Li People held that "No ploughing on Cattle Days, no transplanting on Chicken Days". When eating the first newly-harvested rice, Li people wouldn't share with others or eat the meat of wild boar, cattle or goats at the same time. Otherwise ancestral ghosts would be violated, and take away the utensils, tools even furniture, and further more, the crops next year would be destroyed by wild boars, cattle and goats.

  苗族平时忌把白藤、白纸条从山栏田或水田横拖跨过，这样预示田里结不出饱满的稻穗。农历七月二十日雷公母要回家，忌开仓取谷，谷物进仓封仓时，忌谈老鼠，以防日后老鼠成群结队来偷吃粮食。

  According to Miao's tradition, white vines or white ribbons mustn't appear in the field, or full ears won't grow; it's forbidden to open the barn to take rice on 20th of the seventh lunar month when the Thunder Mu goes home; and mentioning mice when close the barn will end up with mice's stealing rice in flocks.

12.4.2 渔业禁忌 Fishing

  渔业是人们直接向大自然索要食物的行业，也许正因为这个原因，渔业风险很大，渔船出海有可能满载而归，还有可能船覆人亡，所以禁忌很多。

  Fishing is an industry through which people ask nature directly for food, and perhaps for this reason, fishing is very risky. Fishing vessels may return with a rewarding result, and may end up with a shipwreck. Therefore there have come many taboos.

  一些在其他人看来无碍的语言和动作是严格禁止的。比如，"翻""倒""沉"等话语，挪动或翻动盘中的鱼都预示着翻船。"喝水"要说成"喝茶"，以免有人跌入海中，被水淹死。盐要说

"粉",因为过去渔民出海意外死亡,尸体就是用盐巴腌渍后随船运回的。喝水时不能往杯子里吹气,否则会招来台风。

Some habitual words such as "turn over" "pour off" and "sink" and acts such as moving the dish of fish and turning the fish over in the dish which may be nothing to others, were strictly prohibited among fishermen as ominous signs of shipwreck. Fishermen say "drink tea" instead of "drink water", fearing someone might fall into the sea and get drowned in water, and call "salt" as "powder", because "salt" was used to pickle the remains of fishermen who died in accidents at sea long before. And even to blow into the cup was a cause of a typhoon in their eyes.

过去出海捕鱼,一般禁止女人随同。儋州、临高一代把没有结婚的男人看成是未开身的人,禁止未婚男子出船捕鱼。

Except tankas, fishermen didn't bring women along when fishing at sea. Fishermen in Danzhou and Lingao thought unmarried men as boys, who weren't accepted in a ship.

狩猎也是直接向大自然直接索要食物的一种手段,是海南黎苗族重要的生产方式。黎族忌妇女从打猎武器上跨过、男子抚弄妇女的纺织工具、未过正月初四猎手与妻子同桌吃饭、同房、丈夫三日内,外人12日内进产房,否则打猎无获。自己制作的弓箭只能自己使用,别人用过的弓箭将无法打到猎物。

Hunting is another way to ask nature directly for food for Hainan Li and Miao. Li women mustn't stride over the hunting weapons, hunters are forbidden to touch textile tools, or have dinner or sex with their wives before 4th of the first lunar month, nor enter delivery room of their own wives within 3 days and others' 12. Otherwise they would come back with no harvest. The arrows made by the hunters mustn't lend to others, or they wouldn't hit prey any more.

12.4.3 林业禁忌 Forestry

海南民间一直懂得保护珍稀树种。凡进入封山育林区砍伐林木果树的,要进行惩罚,除树木归公和当众认错外,还要适当罚款,并责令补种树木;驱赶牛群、羊群进入幼林区踩坏树木的,要责令其将牛羊赶出林子,不听劝告者则将牛羊打死。

Hainan folk have known how to protect rare species long time ago. Anyone who enters the forestation areas to log must be punished by fine, and he must replant trees, hand in logged trees and apologize in public as well; anyone who drives herds to trample into the young forest areas must drive the herds out at once, or his herds will be slaughtered.

海南民间忌雨季砍伐树木,认为最佳砍伐时间是秋季,因为此时海南较旱,山路硬实,蚂蟥较少,砍伐、搬运都比较方便,而且此时树木含水量较少,木材不易缩水、变形,也不易生虫腐烂。故有"七柴八竹九山竹"之说。砍伐时猎杀山上动物,会触犯"山水公"而受到惩罚。放排时忌讲"谁在前,谁在后"之类的话,不然放排会不顺利。黎族在砍山栏时,家里的妇女忌织布梳头,据说这样会缠住丈夫的手脚,使他精力分散,导致他从树上掉下,不能顺利完成砍伐。

Hainan folk can't log in rain season. The best season to fell trees is autumn when it is drier, mountain roads are harder with fewer leeches, and trees are dryer too, which are not easy to shrink, deform, grow insects or start rotting. Don't kill animals in the mountains, or the loggers would get punished when logging and rafting. Li women staying at home mustn't weave or comb when their husbands were logging or clearing the Shanlan rice field, or it's said that the men would be trapped by cloth or hair and get distracted, falling off the tree.

12.4.4 饲养业禁忌 Livestock Breeding

民间认为破相的小猪比如耳破（也叫"通风"）、缺趾（也叫三足），难以养大，养者不吉；乐东黄流一带有"猪怕一，狗怕六"的讲法，母猪若一胎一仔，说明猪种不好会让农家白忙半年，要把崽猪扔到荒郊野外以解衰运；母狗一胎六仔又会把家吃穷。黎族认为母狗一胎三仔也不吉利，三是凶兆，除灾要杀掉小狗。

Many peasants think such disfigured pigs as the ones having broken ear or lacking a toe (also called three-legged) were difficult to raise, and would bring about misfortune to the owner. Han in Ledong and Huangliu held that a sow born only one piglet indicated the owner would work a half year in vain, to ward off which, the owner should throw the piglet out in wilderness, while that a bitch born six puppies implied the family would get poor. Li believed that a bitch born three was not auspicious, unless the puppies were killed.

12.5 海南信仰崇拜禁忌
Taboos about Worship

制度化宗教禁忌基本与内地相同。民间崇拜禁忌极具特色，在第八章略有提及。这节我们主要探讨拜祭禁忌。

The taboos of local worship are very unique, a few of which have been mentioned in Chapter VIII. We'll focus on taboos about worship services here.

祭祀是为了得到神灵的保佑，必须虔诚，就不能心不在焉或不按照祭祀规矩进行。民间认为，如违反其中一些禁忌，不仅自己的愿望不能实现，还会遭至神灵的责怪甚至惩罚。

Being distracted, not standing in awe of the gods or spirits, or violating some taboos, folk believe, would bring about bad consequences. Not only their aspirations could not be achieved, but also the gods would blame the offenders and even their family through calamity.

宗祠是安放祖先灵位的地方，平时要保持肃静，不得行不敬之事，如饮酒划拳、争执斗殴、谈情说爱等，违者将按家法惩治。家中公阁不许乱爬乱翻，打扫清理公阁忌用扫帚。

In ancestral temple, where ancestors' spirits dwell, people should keep quiet and not do anything irreverent such as drinking, quarrelling, fighting, dating, etc. It's forbidden to climb or search the shrine for things, or to clean the shrine with broom.

庙宇是敬奉神灵的地方，不能与人畜杂居一处，汉、黎、苗族的土地庙、回族的清真寺一般都建在村落外部，其他供奉山神、海神的庙宇一般都建在山中或海边；衣着不整、穿拖鞋、短裤者禁止入内；庙内不能大声喧哗；不得随地大小便、吐痰；不得行男女交媾之事；不能踩踏门槛。

A temple is a place to worship the gods, where humans and animals can not inhabit and anything that is thought to offend gods isn't allowed to happen. Taboos on making noise, spitting or having sex have worked in the temple since it was built. The gods would not respond to the persons who trod on the threshold of temples.

祭器和祭品不得触碰和损坏；祭祀用酒忌用商店出售的瓶装米酒；有些地方认为，鸭子不能用于祭祀，因为鸭子叫声犹如哑巴，往往引起神灵或祖宗的不悦，有可能让后代子孙生出哑巴来；一般的家族祭祀女性不得参加。有些神灵则只限女性祭拜，比如管生育的床婆神，忌男性参拜。

Generally, sacrificial utensils and offerings were not allowed touching or damaging; the bottled rice wine bought from the shop can't be served as sacrifice; in some areas the duck can not be offered, because ducks' quack sounds like a dumb, which would displease gods or ancestors who might cause the birth of a dumb; women were forbidden to participate in family worship before. There were also some gods that only women could worship, such as the Bed God who is in charge of procreation.

如今，随着人们生产生活方式的转变，许多禁忌早已淡化。一部分禁忌在中老年人当中虽依旧保留，很多时候则只是把它们作为民俗文化遗产重新挖掘或保留下来的。

Today, with people's production and lifestyle changing, many taboos have disappeared. Despite some taboos still remain among the elderly, in most cases they have just been rediscovered and preserved as folk cultural heritage.

参考文献
Bibliography

[1] SHAILER MATHEWS, GERALD BIRNEY SMITH. A Dictionary of Religion and Ethics [M]. New York: The Macmillan Company, 2010.

[2] 白羽. 木中黄金：海南黄花梨收藏与鉴赏[M]. 北京：新世纪出版社，2014.

[3] 陈耿，尹秋艳. 海之南:来欣赏从远古走来的苗家盘皇舞[EB/OL].[2016-06-11]. 南海网，http://www.hinews.cn/news/system/2007/10/15/010157411_01.shtml.

[4] 陈立浩,陈兰,陈小蓓. 从原始时代走向现代文明——黎族"合亩制"地区的变迁历程[M]. 海口：海南出版社，2008.

[5] 党朝峰. 海南 10 类传统民居揭秘[EB/OL].[2016-08-21]. http://www.haikoutour.gov.cn/info/news_view.asp?ArticleID=26376.

[6] 董强. 中国民俗文化丛书——婚嫁卷[M]. 合肥：安徽人民出版社，2013.

[7] 董强.中国民俗文化丛书——丧葬卷[M]. 合肥：安徽人民出版社，2013.

[7] 董武. 海南琼海印尼村借异域风情打造城市特色名片[EB/OL].[2016-08-02].中国侨网，http://www.chinaqw.com/gqqj/2015/05-18/49733.shtml.

[8] 方华文. 中国民间风俗[M]. 北京：五洲传播出版社，2001.

[9] 弗洛伊德. 图腾与禁忌[M]. 文良文化,译. 北京：中央编译出版社，2005.

[10] 符耀彩. 临高人偶戏[M]. 海口：南方出版社/海南出版社，2008.

[11] 高泽强，文珍.海南黎族研究[M]. 海口：海南出版社，2008.

[12] 海南苗族饮食文化[EB/OL].[2016-03-21]. 海南保亭政府网，http://baoting.hainan.gov.cn/lypd/ftrq/201408/t20140828_1364182.html.

[13] 海南省人民政府新闻办公室. 海南——南中国海的天堂岛[M]. 北京：外文出版社，2005.

[14] 海南省地方志办公室. 海南省志·地方志[M]. 海口：南海出版公司，2006.

[15] 海南省地方志办公室. 海南省志·民俗志[M]. 海口：南海出版公司，2012.

[16] 海南地方志书·民俗志[EB/OL]. [2016-03-03].海南史志网，http://www.hnszw.org.cn/dfzs.php?type=3.

[17] 胡锐，赵建苹. 旅游英语翻译实训教程[M]. 北京：机械工业出版社，2012.

[18] 黄丽华. 海南少数民族民俗旅游开发思考[J].琼州学院学报，2013(2).

[19] 黄丽华. 论海南民族民俗文化旅游开发[J]. 琼州学院学报，2014(3).

[20] 黄学魁. 海南民族民间工艺美术[M]. 海口：南方出版社/海南出版社，2008.

[21] 黄友贤，黄仁昌. 海南苗族研究[M]. 海口：南方出版社/海南出版社，2008.

[22] 黄宇，罗艳菊，毕华. 海南黎族民俗旅游开发探析[J].特区经济，2011(2).

[23] 黄闻健. 中国海南菜[M]. 海口：海南出版社，2013.

[24] 高泽强，文珍. 海南黎族研究[M]. 海口：海南出版社，2008.

[25] 洪寿祥，周伟民. 海南地方志丛刊[M]. 海口：海南出版社，2004.

[26] 纪俊超. 英语海南导游[M]. 北京：中国旅游出版社，2009.

[27] 焦勇勤，孙海兰. 海南民俗概说[M]. 海口：海南出版社，2008.

[28] 想了解黎族民间传统舞蹈《咚铃伽》吗？[EB/OL]. [2016-03-03].黎族百科，http://lizu.baike.com/article-239201.html.

[29] 《黎族简史》编写组. 国家民委《民族问题五种丛书》之二《中国少数民族简史丛书》（修订本）：黎族简史[M]. 北京:民族出版社, 2009.

[30] 林明峪. 台湾民间禁忌[M]. 台北：联亚出版社，1981.

[31] 林贤东. 海南岛的海洋民俗文化[J]. 浙江海洋学院学报（人文科学版），2005(1).

[32] 刘士祥，朱兵艳. 海南民俗文化的海洋性特征探讨[J]. 重庆科技学院学报（社会科学版），2016(3).

[33] 楼庆西. 中国传统建筑文化[M]. 北京：中国旅游出版社，2008.

[34] 马晓莉.海南黎族民间舞蹈演变浅析[J].海南广播电视大学学报，2009(4).

[35] 海南砗磲贝雕首次亮相玉龙奖评选斩获最佳工艺奖[EB/OL]. [2016-08-06]. 南海网，http://www.hinews.cn/news/system/2014/05/08/016655484.shtml.

[36] 1999 年，椰树传情庆回归[EB/OL]. [2016-06-05]. 南海网，http://www.hinews.cn/news/system/2009/12/21/0106472.

[37] 宁梦黛.海南黎族的恋爱婚嫁习俗[Z]. http://wenhua.youth.cn/mins/hj/200909/t20090923_1032171.htm

[38] 祁庆富，马晓京. 黎族织锦蛙纹纹样的人类学阐释[J]. 民族艺术，2005(1).

[39] 赛门·卡尔巴赫，鲁道夫·兰诗保尔，蔡弴岚. 海南——热带天堂[M]. 海口：南海出版公司，2007.

[40] 单德启. 中国民居[M]. 北京：五洲传播出版社，2004.

[41] 沈志成，沈艳. 海南文物记[M]. 海口：海南出版社/南方出版社，2008.

[42] 石应宽. 海南儋州调声和黎族民间乐器的传承[J]. 贵州大学学报（艺术版），2006(3).

[43] 孙令正. 海南民俗：乐东黄流镇乡村清明节 传统祭拜习俗[EB/OL]. http://www.hinews.cn/news/system/2012/04/03/014242148.shtml.

[44] 唐胄. 正德琼台志[M]. 海口：海南出版社，2006.

[45] 王贵章. 琼州百庙[M]. 海口：南海出版公司，2011.

[46] 王沫. 浅析海南黎族蛙图腾崇拜的象征意义[J]. 文艺争鸣，2011(6).

[47] 王学萍. 中国黎族[M]. 北京：民族出版社，2004.

[48] 文京，文明英.中国黎族[M]. 宁夏：宁夏人民出版社，

[49] 吴礼冠. 中国古民居[M]. 北京：五洲传播出版社，2007.

[50] 吴忠军. 中外民俗 [M]. 2 版. 大连：东北财经大学出版社，2007.

[51] 夏骏，阴山. 人居中国[M]. 北京：五洲传播出版社，2007.

[52] "海南之 宝"海沉木[EB/OL].[2016-08-05]. 新华网海南频道，http://www.hq.xinhuanet.com/fukan/2013-12/02/c_118375179.htm.

[53] 邢纪元. 海南琼剧史略[M]. 海口：南方出版社/海南出版社，2008.

[54] 邢植朝，王静. 中国民俗大系[M]. 兰州: 甘肃人民出版社，2004.

[55]　阎根齐.海南古代建筑研究[M].海口：海南出版社，2008.

[56]　杨春虹.月月有节庆　周周有活动　节庆旅游成海南旅游新亮点　收入约占海南旅游总收入30％[EB/OL].[2016-05-06].http://hnrb.hinews.cn/html/2012-05/20/content_478737.htm.

[57]　叶朗，朱良知.中国文化读本[M].北京：外语教学于研究出版社，2008.

[58]　云林.文昌海洋文化[M].海口：南方出版社，2011.

[59]　詹贤武.海南民间禁忌文化[M].海口：海南出版社，2008.

[60]　赵德钦.对发展海南民族民俗旅游的认识[J].琼州大学学报（社会科学版），1998(3).

[61]　政协琼海市委员会.琼海居家文化[M].北京：中国文化出版社，2009.

[62]　郑庆杨.海南饮食文化[M].香港：香港天马出版有限公司，2007.

[63]　海南黎族生育习俗[EB/OL].[2016-11-02].中国民俗网，http://www.chinesefolklore.com/News/news_detail.asp?id=2542.

[64]　海南宗教生态现状及其面临的问题和挑战[EB/OL].[2016-06-08].中国民族宗教网，http://www.mzb.com.cn/html/Home/report/407459-2.htm.

[65]　蛇年话蛇：少数民族神秘的的蛇文化[EB/OL].[2016-09-22].中国民族宗教网，http://www.mzb.com.cn/html/Home/report/368350-2.htm.

[66]　中国大百科全书出版社编辑部.中国烹饪百科全书[M].北京:中国大百科全书出版社,1992.

[67]　中国社会科学院语言研究所词典编辑室.汉英双语现代汉语词典[M].北京：外语教学与研究出版社，2002.

[68]　"黎之语"：海南黎苗传统文化的时尚演绎[EB/OL].[2016-09-22].中新网海南，http://www.hi.chinanews.com/hnnew/2015-08-14/393020.html.

[69]　邹统钎，等.乡村旅游：理论·案例[M]．天津：南开大学出版社，2008.

附录 1
海南省级非物质文化遗产代表性名录
Provincial Intangible Cultural Heritage in Hainan

项目类别 Type	中文名称 In Chinese	英文名称 In English
民间文学	琼侨歌谣	Overseas Hainanese ballad
	黎族民间故事	The Li People's folklore
	海螺姑娘传说	Fairy story about conch
	海南谚语（临高渔谚）	Marine proverbs in Hainan
	黎从六之歌	Song about Li Congliu
传统音乐	儋州调声	Diao Sheng (folk song in antiphonal style in Danzhou dialect) during the Autumn Festival in Danzhou city
	崖州民歌	Folk song in Yazhou of Sanya city
	黎族民歌（琼中黎族民歌）	Folk song in the Li People's style
	海南八音器乐	Music by 8 musical instruments in Hainan style
	黎族竹木器乐	Music by bamboo-and-wood musical instruments in the Li People's style
	海南军歌	Army song in Hainan style
	海南斋醮科仪音乐	Taoists' ritual music in Hainan style
	儋州山歌	Danzhou folk song sung in the fields or mountains
	临高渔歌	Fishermen's folk song in Lin'gao
	疍歌	Tankas' song
	黎族赛方言长调	Folk song named Chang Diao by Sai people of the Li nationality
	海南苗族民歌	Folk song in the Miao People's style
传统舞蹈	黎族打柴舞	Firewood dance in the Li People's style
	黎族钱铃双刀舞	Dance with Qianling waddy and two daggers in the Li People's style
	盅盘舞（文昌盅盘舞）	Dance with cups and plates in Wenchang style
	海南苗族招龙舞	Dragon dance in the Miao People's style
	黎族舂米舞	Threshing rice dance in the Li People's style

传统舞蹈	黎族共同舞	Group dance in the Li People's style
	海南苗族盘皇舞	Panhuang dance in the Miao People's style
	黎族面具舞	Mask dance in the Li People's style
	黎族老古舞	Ancestor worship dance in the Li People's style
	海南虎舞	Tiger dance in Hainan style
	海南麒麟舞	Kylin dance in Hainan style
传统戏剧	琼剧	Qiong opera
	临高人偶戏	Puppet show in Lin'gao
	海南公仔戏	Puppet play in Hainan style
	海南斋戏	Opera for sacrifice-offering in Hainan style
传统美术	海南椰雕	Coconut carving in Hainan style
	龙塘雕刻艺术	Longtang carving arts
	传统炭画像工艺	Traditional charcoal drawing or portrait skills
	木雕（花瑰艺术）	Wood carving in Chengmai style
	海南贝雕	Shell carving in Hainan style
传统技艺	黎族传统纺染织绣技艺	Traditional skills in spinning, weaving, dyeing, and embroidering in the Li People's style
	黎族树皮布制作技艺	Bark clothes making skills in the Li People's style
	黎族骨器制作技艺	Bone instrument making skills in the Li People's style
	黎族原始制陶技艺（黎族泥条盘筑制陶技艺，黎族泥片贴筑制陶技艺）	Traditional pottery making skills in the Li People's style (Pottery making by weaving round pieces of clay; Pottery making by combining slices of clay)
	黎族钻木取火技艺	Fire making skills by drilling wood in the Li People's style
	东坡笠制作技艺	Dongpo-styled Bamboo hat making skills
	黎族干栏建筑技艺	Stilt house building skills in the Li People's style
	南海珍珠传统养殖技艺	Pear breeding in the South China Sea
	海盐晒制技艺	Salt making skills by evaporating brine in the sun
	黎族船型屋营造技艺	Boat-shaped house making skills in the Li People's style
	黎族藤竹编技艺	Rattan and bamboo weaving skills in the Li People's style
	黎族独木器具制作技艺	Single-log carving or instrument in the Li People's style
	海南黄花梨家具制作技艺	Hainan Huanghuali rosewood furniture making skills
	后安刀锻造技艺	Hou'an Knife forging skills
	椰胡制作技艺	Coconut-shaped Banhu making skills
	黎锦纺染织绣工具制作技艺	Li brocade's spinning, weaving, dyeing, and embroidering instruments making skills

附录 1　海南省级非物质文化遗产代表性名录

Provincial Intangible Cultural Heritage in Hainan

传统技艺	土法制糖技艺	Sugar making skills with indigenous methods
	文昌鸡养殖与烹调技艺	Wenchang chicken breeding and cooking skills
	海南苗族传统刺绣蜡染技艺	Traditional embroidery wax printing skills in the Miao People's style
	海南粉烹制技艺	Hainan rice noodles producing and cooking skills
	鹿龟酒酿泡技艺	Lugui Wine brewing and steeping skills
	沉香造香技艺	Agalloch eaglewood balm generating skills
传统医药	黎族医药（骨伤疗法，蛇伤疗法）	Traditional medicines in the Li People's style (for bone injuries and snake biting)
民俗	军坡节	Junpo festival (Mrs. Xian belief and customs)
	海南黎族苗族"三月三"节	San Yue San (March 3rd) Festival in the Li and the Miao style
	黎族服饰	Costumes and ornaments in the Li People's style
	府城元宵换花节	Flower exchange festival in Fucheng during the Lantern Festival
	黎族传统婚礼	The Li People's traditional wedding
	黎族渡水腰舟习俗	Huge gourd-supported ferry in the Li People's style
	回族传统婚礼	The Miao People's traditional wedding
	祭祀兄弟公出海仪式	Rites of sacrifices-offering to the 108 Brothers
	天后祀奉	Matsu belief and customs (Matsu worship)
	海南春节习俗（鲤鱼灯闹春，乐城岛闹元宵）	Customs during the Spring Festival in Hainan (Carp-shaped Lanterns reveling in the spring, customs in celebrating the Lantern Festival in Lecheng Island)
其他	南海航道更路经	Ancient Hainanese Navigation Manual in the South China Sea

附录 2
海南省国家级非物质文化遗产项目名录
National Intangible Cultural Heritage in Hainan Province

项目类别 Type	中文名称 In Chinese	英文名称 In English
传统音乐	儋州调声	Diao Sheng (folk song in antiphonal style in Danzhou dialect) during the Autumn Festival in Danzhou city
	崖州民歌	Folk song in Yazhou of Sanya city
	黎族民歌（琼中黎族民歌）	Folk song in the Li People's style
	海南八音器乐	Music by 8 musical instruments in Hainan style
	黎族竹木器乐	Music by bamboo-and-wood musical instruments in the Li People's style
	海南斋醮科仪音乐	Taoists' ritual music in Hainan style
	临高渔歌	Fishermen's folk song in Lin'gao
	海南苗族民歌	Folk song in the Miao People's style
传统舞蹈	黎族打柴舞	Firewood dance in the Li People's style
	黎族老古舞	Ancestor worship dance in the Li People's style
传统戏剧	琼剧	Qiong opera
	临高人偶戏	Puppet show in Lin'gao
	海南公仔戏	Puppet play in Hainan style
	海南斋戏	Opera for sacrifice-offering in Hainan style
传统美术	海南椰雕	Coconut carving in Hainan style
	木雕（花瑰艺术）	Wood carving in Chengmai style
传统技艺	黎族树皮布制作技艺	Bark clothes making skills in the Li People's style
	黎族原始制陶技艺	Traditional pottery making skills in the Li People's style
	黎族泥片制陶技艺	Pottery making by combining slices of clay in the Li People's style
	黎族钻木取火技艺	Fire making skills by drilling wood in the Li People's style
	海盐晒制技艺	Salt making skills by evaporating brine in the sun
	黎族船型屋营造技艺	Boat-shaped house making skills in the Li People's style
民俗	冼夫人信俗（军坡节）	Mrs. Xian belief and customs
	海南黎族苗族"三月三"节	San Yue San (March 3rd) Festival in Li and Miao style
	黎族服饰	Costumes and ornaments in the Li People's style
	天后祀奉	Matsu belief and customs (Matsu worship)
其他	南海航道更路经	Ancient Hainanese Navigation Manual in the South China Sea

附录 3
海南省主要民俗文化旅游景点景区
Customs and Traditions Featured Resorts in Hainan Province

海口/Haikou City：7

西海岸带状公园 Western Coast Park

火山群世界地质公园 Haikou Volcanic Cluster Global Geopark

五公祠 Memorial Temple for the Five Officials

海口骑楼小吃风情街 Haikou Qilou Snack Street

海口白沙门公园 Haikou Baishamen Park

海瑞纪念园 Hai Rui Memorial Park

琼台书院 Qiongtai Academy

三亚/Sanya City：10

亚龙湾国家旅游度假区 Yalong Bay National Holiday Resort

南山文化旅游区 Nanshan Cultural Tourism Zone

大小洞天 Wonders of the Sea and the Mountain

天涯海角 Tian Ya Hai Jiao

蜈支洲岛 Wuzhizhou Island

鹿回头 Luhuitou Park

三亚凤凰岭海誓山盟景区 Sanya Phoenix Ridge Scenic Spot

京润珍珠博物馆 Jingrun (gN) Pearl Museum

三亚宋城旅游区 Sanya Songcheng Resort

古崖州城 Ancient Yazhou Town

陵水/Lingshui County：4

分界洲岛 Demarcation Islet

南湾猴岛 Nanwan Macaque Peninsular

椰田古寨 Ancient Village in Coconut Grove

吊罗山国家森林公园 Diaoluoshan National Forest Park

五指山/Wizhishan City：2

五指山热带雨林风景区　Tropical Rainforest Scenic Spot of Five Finger Mountain

海南民族博物馆　Hainan Museum of Nationalities

保亭/Baoting County：4

呀诺达雨林文化景区　Yanoda Rainforest Cultural Tourism Zone

海南槟榔谷黎苗文化旅游区　Hainan Areca Palm Valley with Li and Miao's Culture

七仙岭温泉度假区　Qixianling Hotspring Resort

仙安石林　Xian'an Stone Forest with Tropical Karst Landscape

其他市县/Others：

文昌/Wenchang City：3

椰子大观园　Wenchang Coconut Park

宋氏祖居　Former Residence of Song Qingling, Song Meiling, Song Ailing, etc.

文庙　Confucius Temple

琼海/Qionghai City：5

万泉河游览区　Wanquan River

博鳌亚洲论坛永久会址　The site of Bo'ao Forum for Asia

琼崖红色娘子军纪念园　Commemorative Garden of the Red Detachment of Women

博鳌东方文化苑　Bo'ao Oriental Culture Garden

蔡家大院　The Cai's Former Residence

万宁/Wanning City：4

兴隆温泉旅游区　Xinglong Hotspring Resort

东山岭　Dongshanling Ridge

兴隆亚洲风情园　Xinglong Garden with Various Asian Styles

日月湾海门游览区　Haimen Scenic Spot in Sun-Moon Bay

定安/Ding'an County：1

文笔峰盘古文化旅游区　Pangu Cultural Resort in Wenbifeng Ridge

儋州/Danzhou City：2

东坡书院　Dongpo Academy

白马井古迹　Ancient Baimajing Scenic Spot

澄迈/Chengmai County：1

海南永庆文化旅游景区　Yongqing Cultural Resort

附录 4
海南民俗节庆简表
Festivals and Holidays in Hainan Province

一月 January

春节 Spring Festival

苗族花山节 Hua Shan Festival in the Miao People

苗族吃斋节 Vegetarian Festival in the Miao People

人胜日 Human Day

元霄节 Lantern Festival

行符日 Xing Fu Day (From the 7th to the 30th day of the 1st lunar month)

海神娘娘生日 Birthday for Goddess of the Sea

公期 Gong Qi (Memorial Day for the Clan Ancestor or the Gods or Spirits)

海口府城换花节 Fucheng Flower Exchange Festival

二月 February

二月二 Er Yue Er Festival (February 2nd Festival on the 2nd day of the 2nd Lunar Month)

三亚龙抬头节 Dragon's Head-raising Festival in Sanya

团结日 Solidarity Day among the Miao People

冼夫人文化节（军坡节、冼夫人信俗）

Mrs. Xian' Cultural Festival (Junpo Festival; Mrs. Xian Belief and Customs

春分 Vernal Equinox

三月 March

苗族吃斋节 Vegetarian Festival in the Miao People

天后圣母节（妈祖文化节、妈祖信俗） Matsu' Day (Matsu Cultural Festival, Matsu Belief and Customs)

圣纪节 Mohammed's Birthday

海南黎族"三月三"

San Yue San Festival in the Li People (Held on the 3rd day of the 3rd Lunar Month)

琼海（会山）苗族传统文化节

The Miao People's Traditional Cultural Festival in Huishan Qionghai

苗族姐妹节 Sisters' Day among the Miao women

文昌南洋文化节 Nanyang Cultural Festival in Wenchang

三亚南山太极文化节 Nanshan Tai Chi Cultural Festival in Sanya

四月 April

寒食节 Hanshi Day (or Cold Food Day)

清明 Tomb-Sweeping Day

禾仙节 He Xian (the God of Rice) Festival

海南乡村旅游文化节 Rural Tourism Cultural Festival

五月 May

端午节 Dragon Boat Festival

城隍公节 Town God's Day

两伏波将军日 General Fu Bo's Day

关圣帝生日 Guan Yu's Birthday

西天公节 Wang Zuo's Commemoration Day

海南乡村旅游文化节 Rural Tourism Cultural Festivals

三亚疍家文化节 Tankas' Cultural Festival in Sanya

六月 June

苗族禾斋节 He Zhai (the God of Rice) Festival in the Miao People

灶公节 Festival for God of Kitchen

安村节 Harmonious Day for the village

临高渔民文化节 Lin'gao Fishermen Cultural Festival

七月 July

乞巧节（七夕节） Qi Qiao Festival or Qi Xi Festival

中国海南保亭七仙温泉嬉水节 Qixian (7th Fairy) Hot Spring Water Splashing Festival

黎族牛节 Cattle's Day in the Li People

吃新节 New Rice-Eating Festival

万宁国际文灯节 Wanning Lanterns Festival

送鬼节 Ghost-Sending Day

三江晶信夫人 Madame Jingxin of the Three Rivers

中元节 Zhong Yuan Festival (Ghost Day)

八月 August

中秋节 Mid-Autumn Festival

儋州中秋调声节 Danzhou Diao Sheng Folk Songs Contest

黎族称中秋节为"八月会"或"调声节"

The Li People called the Mid-Autumn Festival the August Get-together or Diao Sheng Festival (singing songs in antiphonal style in local dialect)

苗族新禾节 New Rice Festival in the Miao People

九月 September

重阳节 Double Ninth Festival

三亚南山健康长寿文化节　Nanshan Longevity Festival in Sanya

黎族禾节　Rice Festival among the Li People

供新节　Gong Xin Festival (Harvest Festival)

古尔邦节　Corban Festival

开斋节　Lesser Bairam (Eid al-Fitr; Festival of the Fast-Breaking)

十月　October

108 兄弟公信俗　108 Bothers Belief and Customs

水尾圣娘庙会日　Goddess Shuiwei Temple Fair

黎族牛节　Cattle's Day in the Li People

海南花梨文化节　Hainan Huang Hua Li Rosewood Cultural Festival

十一月　November

黎族山栏节　Shan Lan Festival in the Li People

海南欢乐节　Hainan Carnival

临高渔歌节　Lin'gao Fishing Songs Festival

三亚西岛海洋节　West Island Marine Festival in Sanya

琼海南海文化节　The South China Sea Cultural Festival in Qionghai

万宁国际冲浪节　Wanning International Surfing Festival

东坡文化节　Su Dongpo Cultural Festival

冬至（冬节、小清明）　Winter Solstice

光棍节　Singles' Day (Double Eleventh Day)

三亚天涯国际婚庆节　Tianya International Wedding Festival in Sanya

十二月　December

祭灶公（送灶公）　Sacrifices-offering to the God of Kitchen

除夕　Chinese Lunar New Year's Eve

附录 5
海南特色乡村田园
Idyllic Villages in Hainan Province

2016 中国美丽休闲乡村（特色民俗村）

2016 Top Leisure Villages in China (with Featured Customs and Traditions)

三亚吉阳区中廖村 Zhong Liao Village in Jiyang District of Sanya City

2016 中国特色小镇

2016 Beautiful Towns with Local Characteristics in China

海口市云龙镇 Yun Long Town in Haikou City

海口市潭门镇 Tan Men Town in Qionghai City

2015 中国最美休闲乡村（特色民居村）

2015 Top Leisure Villages in China (with Featured Residence)

琼海市北仍村 Bei Reng Village in Qionghai City

文昌市葫芦村 Hu Lu Village in Wenchang City

2015 中国最美休闲乡村（特色民俗村）

2015 Top Leisure Villages in China (with Featured Customs and Traditions)

白沙县芭蕉村 Ba Jiao Village in Baisha County

2015 中国最美休闲乡村（现代新村）

2015 Top Leisure Villages in China (with Modern Features)

琼海市鱼良村 Yu Liang Village in Qionghai City

2014 中国美丽田园

2014 Top Leisure Gardens in China

琼海市龙寿洋"稻田景观" Rice Field Landscape in Qionghai City

2014 中国最美休闲乡村（特色民居村）

2014 Top Leisure Villages in China (with Featured Residence)

三亚市槟榔村 Bing Lang Village in Qionghai City

2014 中国最美休闲乡村（现代新村）

2014 Top Leisure Villages in China (with Modern Features)

海口市琼山区田心村 Tian Xin Village in Qiongshan District of Haikou City

2014 中国最美休闲乡村（历史古村）

2014 Top Leisure Villages in China (with Historical Features)

琼中县什寒村 Shi Han Village in Qiongzhong County

2014 海南十大最美乡村
2014 Top Ten Villages in Hainan Province

白沙黎族自治县细水乡老周三村
Lao Zhou San Village in Xishui Town of Baisha Li Autonomous County
琼中黎族苗族自治县红毛镇什寒村
Shi Han Village in Hongmao Town of Qiongzhong Li Autonomous County
乐东黎族自治县佛罗镇丹村
Zhen Dan Village in Foluo Town of Ledong Li Autonomous County
琼海市嘉积镇礼都文明生态村片区　Area around Li Du Village in Jiaji Town of Qionghai City
海口市石山镇美社村　Mei She Village in Shishan Town of Haikou City
定安县岭口镇皇坡村　Huang Po Village in Lingkou Town of Ding'an County
澄迈县金江镇美榔村　Mei Lang Village in Jinglang Town of Chengmai County
儋州市木棠镇铁匠村　Tie Jiang Village in Mutang Town of Danzhoui County
万宁市长丰镇文通村　Jiao Tong Village in Changfeng Town of Wanning County
文昌市东路镇葫芦村　Hu lu Village in Donglu Town of Wenchang County

2014 海南十大最美小镇
2014 Top Ten Towns in Hainan Province

万宁市兴隆华侨旅游经济区
Xing Long Town (with Returned Overseas Chinese) in Wanning City
吊罗山森林旅游风情小镇
Diao Luo Shan Town (a tourist attraction for forest) in Qiongzhong Li Autonomous County
琼海市博鳌镇　Bo'ao Town in Qionghai City
琼海市潭门镇　Tan Men Town in Qionghai City
澄迈县福山咖啡文化风情镇　Fu Shan Town (famous for coffee) in Chengmai County
海口市云龙镇　Yun Long Town in Haikou City
昌江黎族自治县七叉镇　Qi Cha Town in Changjiang Li Autonomous County
白沙黎族自治县邦溪风情小镇　Bang Xi Town in Baisha Li Autonomous County
五指山市水满乡　Shui Man Town in Wuzhishan City
海南省国营八一总场　State-owned Eight One Farm in Danzhou City

附录 6
中国历史纪年简表
Timetable of Chinese History

五帝时代 Period of the Five Legendary Rulers 2600 BC-2070 BC		黄帝 Huangdi	
		颛顼 Zhuanxu	
		帝喾 Diku	
		尧 Yao	
		舜 Shun	
夏 Xia Dynasty		2070 BC -1600 BC	
商 Shang Dynasty		1600 BC - 1046 BC	
西周 Western Zhou Dynasty		1046 BC - 771 BC	
东周 Eastern Zhou Dynasty 770 BC-256 BC	春秋 Spring and Autumn Period	770 BC-476 BC	
	战国 Warring States Period	475 BC-221 BC	
秦 Qin Dynasty		221 BC-206 BC	
汉 Han Dynasty 206 BC-220 AD	西汉 Western Han	206 BC-25 AD	
	东汉 Eastern Han	25-220	
三国 Three Kingdoms 220-280	魏 Wei	220-265	
	蜀汉 Shu Han	221-263	
	吴 Wu	222-280	
晋 Jin Dynasty 265-420	西晋 Western Jin	265-316	
	东晋 Eastern Jin	317-420	
南北朝 Northern and Southern Dynasties 420-589	南朝 Southern Dynasty	宋 Song	420-479
		齐 Qi	479-502
		梁 Liang	502-557
		陈 Chen	557-589

南北朝 Northern and Southern Dynasties 420-589	北朝 Northern Dynasty	北魏 Northern Wei	386-534
		东魏 Eastern Wei	534-550
		北齐 Northern Qi	550-577
		西魏 Western Wei	535-556
		北周 Northern Zhou	557-581
隋 Sui Dynasty			581-618
唐 Tang Dynasty			619-907
五代十国 Five Dynasties and Ten States	五代 Five Dynasties 907-960	后梁 Later Liang	907-923
		后唐 Later Tang	923-936
		后晋 Later Jin	936-946
		后汉 Later Han	947-950
		后周 Later Zhou	951-960
	十国 Ten States 902-979	北汉 Northern Han	951-975
		吴 Wu	902-937
		南唐 Southern Tang	937-975
		吴越 Wuyue	907-978
		闽 Min	909-945
		南汉 Southern Han	917-971
		楚 Chu	927-951
		荆南 Jingnan	924-963
		前蜀 Former Shu	907-925
		后蜀 Latter Shu	934-965
宋 Song Dynasty 960-1279	北宋 Northern Song		960-1127
	南宋 Southern Song		1127-1279
辽 Liao Dynasty			916-1125
金 Jin Dynasty			1115-1234
西夏 Western Xia Dynasty			1038-1227
元 Yuan Dynasty			1279-1368
明 Ming Dynasty			1368-1644
清 Qing Dynasty			1644-1911
中华民国 Republic of China			1912-1949
中华人民共和国 People's Republic of China			1949-

附录 7
二十四节气
The Twenty-Four Seasonal Division Points

季节 Seasons	节气名称、顺序 Order and Name of Seasonal Division Point	节气的公历日期 Date on Gregorian Calender
春季 spring	1. 立春 Beginning of Winter 2. 雨水 Rain Water 3. 惊蛰 Waking of Insects 4. 春风 Vernal Equinox 5. 清明 Qing Ming 6. 谷雨 Grain Rain	4 or 5 February 19 or 2 February 5 or 6 March 20 or 21 March 5 or 6 April 20 or 21 April
夏季 summer	7. 立夏 Beginning of Winter 8. 小满 Grain Budding 9. 芒种 Grain in Ear 10. 夏至 Summer Solstice 11. 小暑 Small Heat 12. 大暑 Great Heat	5 or 6 May 21 or 22 May 6 or 7 June 21 or 22 June 7 or 8 July 23 or 24 July
秋季 autumn	13. 立秋 Beginning of Winter 14. 处暑 Limit of Heat 15. 白露 White Dew 16. 秋分 Autumnal Equinox 17. 寒露 Cold Dew 18. 霜降 Frost's Descent	8 or 7 August 23 or 24 August 8 or 7 September 23 or 24 September 8 or 9 October 24 or 23 October
冬季 winter	19. 立冬 Beginning of Winter 20. 小雪 Slight Snow 21. 大雪 Great Snow 22. 冬至 Winter Solstice 23. 小寒 Slight Cold 24. 大寒 Great Cold	8 or 7 November 22 or 23 November 8 or 7 December 23 or 24 December 8 or 9 January 24 or 23 January

附录 8
天干地支
Heavenly Stems and Earthly Branches

天干 Heavenly Stems		相应元素 Corresponding Elements		相应星宿 Corresponding Stars	
甲	Heavenly Stem One	木	Wood	木星	Jupiter
乙	Heavenly Stem Two				
丙	Heavenly Stem Three	火	Fire	火星	Mars
丁	Heavenly Stem Four				
戊	Heavenly Stem Five	土	Earth	土星	Saturn
己	Heavenly Stem Six				
庚	Heavenly Stem Seven	金	Metal	金星	Venus
辛	Heavenly Stem Eight				
壬	Heavenly Stem Nine	水	Water	水星	Mercury
癸	Heavenly Stem Ten				

地支 Earthly Branch		生肖 Symbolic Animals		相应时间 Corresponding Time
子	Earthly Branch One	鼠	Rat	11:00 p.m.-1:00 a.m.
丑	Earthly Branch Two	牛	Ox	1:00 a.m.-3:00 a.m.
寅	Earthly Branch Three	虎	Tiger	3:00 a.m.-5:00 a.m.
卯	Earthly Branch Four	兔	Rabbit	5:00 a.m.- 7:00.a. m.
辰	Earthly Branch Five	龙	Dragon	7:00 a.m -9:0 a. m.
巳	Earthly Branch Six	蛇	Snake	7:00.a.m -11:0 a. m.
午	Earthly Branch Seven	马	Horse	11:0 a.m-1:00 p.m.
未	Earthly Branch Eight	羊	Goat	1:00 p.m.-3:00 p.m.
申	Earthly Branch Nine	猴	Monkey	3:00 p.m.-5:00 p.m.
酉	Earthly Branch Ten	鸡	Rooster	5:00 p.m.-7:00 p.m.
戌	Earthly Branch Eleven	狗	Dog	7:00 p.m.-9:00 p.m.
亥	Earthly Branch Twelve	猪	Pig	9:00 p.m.-11:00 p.m.